Computer-Aided
Architectural Graphics

Computer-Aided Architectural Graphics

DANIEL L. RYAN

Clemson University
Clemson, South Carolina

MARCEL DEKKER, INC.   New York and Basel

Library of Congress Cataloging in Publication Data

Ryan, Daniel L., [date]
    Computer-aided architectural graphics.

    Includes index.
    1. Architectural practice--Data processing.
2. Architectural design--Data processing. I. Title.
NA1996.5.R9 1983   720'.28'54   83-7433
ISBN 0-8247-1901-8

MARCEL DEKKER, INC.
270 Madison Avenue, New York, New York 10016

Current printing (last digit):
10 9 8 7 6 5 4 3 2 1

PRINTED IN THE UNITED STATES OF AMERICA

Preface

Computer-aided architectural graphics and its impact on building
design and construction is one of the revolutionary concepts
developed during the twentieth century. In the case of direct
application, computer use in architecture has been evolutionary
rather than revolutionary as this book points out in several chapters. The final impact of computer aids in architecture will eventually be felt in the last 20 years of the century. Architecture
directly affects society and the computer is affecting such things
as planning, drafting, bill of materials, and specification writing
presently being done in architect's and engineering offices throughout the United States. Computer-aided graphics plays an important
role in this field, for it is from the computer data base that the
initial information is obtained for the architect and for the even-
tual production of planning sheets, drawings and material specs,
notes, and written specifications.

This book is intended to acquaint the reader with the computer-
aided architectural evolution that has taken place to date. It does
not forecast future events. It is based upon the assumption that
the reader is familiar with architectural office procedures except
those relating to the digital computer. In the case of the computer, no previous experience is assumed. Therefore many examples
deal with rather detailed computer procedures in step-by-step
fashion. To the experienced computer person these are extremely low

technology examples, but to others they are absolutely necessary in understanding even the simplest tasks. The appendix to Chapter 3 is an example of this type of step-by-step computer code for lettering used on drawings. At the same time, many basic architectural design situations are discussed without lengthy explanations of architectural office procedures. This makes it possible to keep the emphasis on computer-aided design graphics.

Methods and procedures for using existing computer-aided architectural graphics are stressed, as is the procedure for developing new problem—solving routines. The discussion centers on the use rather than the creation, however. It is the author's belief that this delimitation is necessary in an introductory level computer book for advanced architectural students or graduate architects in the field who are seeking a "first exposure." In addition, a complete annotated bibliography is contained at the end of this book for those who wish to delve further into the subject. The unique features of this book are:

1. It is a study of computer-aided architectural graphics, not a computer text or architectural handbook.
2. Fundamental concepts of using the computer to do ordinary office tasks are explained in simple step-by-step fashion.
3. The book has a common illustrative pattern for showing architectural displays generated from computer memory.
4. Examples are shown during and after construction for complete understanding of "how-to-do-it."

The author makes no claim to the design originality of the illustrations used throughout the book. Many have been supplied by architects, computer graphics equipment manufacturers, and the author's classroom students. Each illustration is footnoted or identified by a courtesy line. This book draws heavily on the earlier works of others; it is, however, a pioneer effort in the computerization of some isolated manual methods. It is the author's hope that those concerned with automating an architectural office will find this book a source of useful information.

The author deeply appreciated the kindness and generosity of Charles Brack for the many hours of conferences and for supplying considerable information and illustrations on the many practical uses of computer-aided architectural graphics. Most of all, special encouragement was given the author during the writing of this book by his family: Tessa, Timothy, and Connie. The author's indebtedness to an understanding family is hereby reaffirmed.

Daniel L. Ryan

Contents

Contents

Computer-Aided
Architectural Graphics

1 Introduction to Computer-Aided Architectural Graphics

Architectural engineering graphics is a design language that is used to express and convey ideas of shape, size, and construction of items that are of architectural importance. To have optimum value, the format of the architectural drawing must be clear, concise, and subject to one and only one interpretation. To produce computer-aided drawings or use computer programs that conform to accepted standards and practices, professional planners and architects make use of certain types of computer hardware, equipment, materials, and instruments. Since time is costly in any architectural work, an understanding of the tools and techniques available for computer-aided graphics is important, if not critical, to the process of preparing automated architectural drawings. In this chapter the architect is introduced to the different architectural engineering presentations available. It assumes no previous exposure to or familiarization with computer graphics. Therefore, the discussions are very basic and fundamental to remaining chapter explanation.

ARCHITECTURAL ENGINEERING PRESENTATIONS

Much has been written about the computer and its possible role in architectural engineering practice; for the most part these essays have tried to justify or ridicule the computer replacing the human in an age of increasing automation. During the last few years a renewed energetic discussion has grown up around the architect-computer relation. The advent of computer graphics for architects has underscored this relationship. To some this new relationship has meant, "Let the architect do the design or thinking, and the computer will carry out the drafting work," with the tacit assumption that somehow this could be done by some other people not usually specified. This book was written for those other people. This book fills a gap in automating the architectural engineering office. What has been lacking is a technique which can achieve a degree of coupling with a human (architect) and machine (computer).

This coupling must not force the architectural engineer to change thinking habits, language habits, or time response habits. In this chapter, the reader will understand how this coupling is possible by careful study of each of the graphic examples shown. The computer industry has been and is striving to make this coupling by graphic programs which attempt to give a human a language reasonably close to the natural or professional frame of reference--this is a powerful step in the right direction. That same industry has done little to match a human's habits or responses in the time domain. This text will attempt to close this gap. Yet even with an architect's understanding of the design process, some things are known about human-computer time responses.

CAG (Computer-Assisted Graphics)

If one studies our short but dynamic history in the computer graphics industry, it is possible to note a few who have understood the problem of the presentation of graphic data for architectural engineering applications. In the early 1960s, the analog computer group cried loud and long that the architectural engineer at a console, with a real-time response to inquiries, was a vital requirement to effective computing. Somehow the digital half avoided this criticism by changing the subject and talking about accuracy, the general-purpose advantage of digital systems, and prohibitive cost factors of one user tying up one machine.

About 10 years went by before the digital graphic capabilities were recognized as having architectural engineering value. The operator had three techniques available:

1. Read from a CRT (cathode ray tube, a type of display screen) highspeed digital computer
2. Write crudely by pointing with a light pen or other device to cause human input to be accepted without coding in computer-like languages
3. Direct the feedback response for each input action. The architectural engineer saw immediately, in his or her own language on the CRT, the result of the input as a variable on a set of responses already underway. This response was

in 15 seconds or less, and the architect could make
corrections or monitor the results of the inputs immediately.

The three principles of graphic reading, writing and obtaining
responses are the basic ingredients of an architectural engineering
graphics system.

The design and graphics system just described is seldom a
single combination of commands or sequence of operations. More
often questions and answers are necessary. The user makes an
assumption and sees what the result will be. The architect then
tries again and gradually converges in a solution of logical position which seems to match the situation. When the responses seem to
diverge, the architect must change assumptions and try again. This
human design sequence must be preserved in a human-machine relationship. There is only one CRT screen to hold the various tries. A
device for recording CRT images directly on microfilm has speeded up
the preservation of design sequences. The architectural engineer
may view each step of the design process by viewing the microfilm on
a reader at a later date.

The use of these techniques has helped match the computer to
the human. Without this there was little chance the human could
remember the exact thought process at a later date. Now the human
does not have to adapt his or her mental processes to the machine.

Graphic Design Aids

While this was ideally suited to static images or drawings, it was
not suitable for dynamic displays in creative design. Most architectural engineers remember the chapters on creative design of a
building or design sequence that produced motion. The classic
textbooks used equations, vectors, model representation, and any
other technique to display a thought of motion. Now the motion
itself is displayed. Simple techniques exist for placing static
images together in strip fashion called frames. The frames are then
buffered to remove any jerk or jump in the picture. The Saturday
morning cartoons are produced in this manner.

Of course few architectural engineers are interested in making
cartoons. The remainder would like to use the computer in this
dynamic mode in the early formulative stage of design as well as in
the solution stage. The aim of dynamic operations is to relieve the
open-ended nature of building design and the difficult situation of
putting the user in close touch with the computer processing. By
providing an architectural user with a method or language which is
natural to the set of design problems, perhaps the time has come

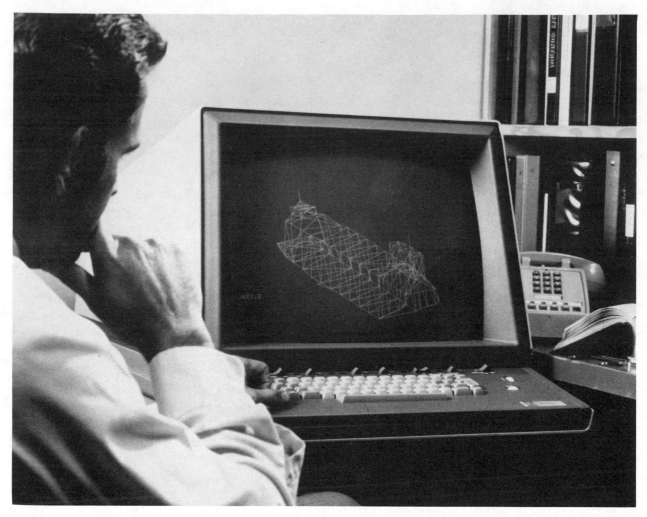

FIGURE 1.1 Architectural engineer at a typical work station
(Courtesy of Tektronix, Inc., Beaverton, Oregon).

where the architectural engineer and digital computer are a high
speed, highly useful combination.   •

The three principles of graphic reading, writing, and obtaining
responses can be implemented by typewriter and a fairly fast computer.   However, the impact of such a human-machine situation is
fairly low.   To appreciate more dramatically how these principles
can have far-reaching effects on our situation, see Figure 1.1, an
operator at a CRT.   The operator has a light pen to use as a writing
tool, a pointing or selecting medium, and a keyboard to insert
alphanumeric information.

By coupling the graphic capability of a human to the speed of a
computer, a whole host of applications can be considered which
heretofore have caused digital computer to fall short.

Structural Studies

The design of buildings is a prime case of an architectural user who often wants to deal with graphics. The problem of using computers in this field has been limited by two basic shortcomings in our computer technology:

1. Graphics (architectural drawings are the worst case) is a language all its own. Translating graphics into a computer language by hand is tedious, error prone, time consuming, and normally more difficult than creating the original drawings.

2. Translation of a concept from the designer's mind into graphics is complex. It is a series of intricate steps which eventually converge as a designer brings many individual and sometimes unrelated ideas into the complete and final design.

The design and development of complex structures require the solution of complex problems. Each of the thousands of parts that go into a nuclear power plant or a steel skyscraper or even a solar collector must be individually designed and tested before it is integrated into a final structure. With design budgets reaching the multimillion, even billion dollar mark, an economic method of pretesting designs is becoming increasingly important. In recent years structural engineers and architects have turned more and more to computer-aided design tools.

Finite Element Modeling. One of the prime computer-aided design tools is called finite element modeling and is used to help in the testing of structural designs as illustrated in Figure 1.2. With a finite element modeling program a structural engineer uses a computer display to test the design for a complex structure without having to build an actual physical model of the structure. Finite element models greatly reduce both the design time and prototype costs. They also provide a means of economically testing many variations of the design in a very short time period. Creating a three-dimensional model of a part for a structure to be tested is the most time-consuming and costly step in this process.

Three-Dimensional Presentation Views. Three-dimensional representation is simple because the graphics are immediately available in mathematical digital form. These data can be displayed in a number of different ways:

1. Pictorial illustrations
2. Single-line drawings
3. Multiline drawings
4. Layout and design drawings
5. Diagrams, charts, and graphs

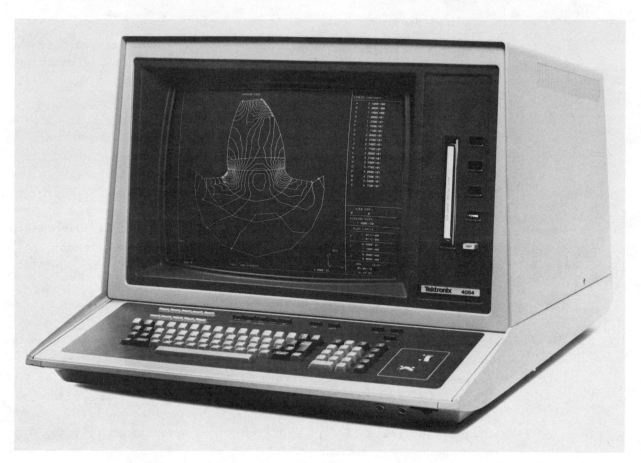

FIGURE 1.2   Use of finite element model to test design (Courtesy of
Tektronix, Inc., Beaverton, Oregon).

Some automated drafting systems are two-dimensional only.   This
limits the production of architectural documents in the following
way: draftspersons prepare original sketches and layouts (not
needed in a 3D format); graphic programmers prepare data for
computer processing and editing, and revisions take place (the
architect or draftsperson must communicate with the graphics
programmer); now the preparation of tapes for the drawings is made.
This text will introduce a method for streamlining 2D systems and
the steps necessary to prepare a 3D system.   A 2D system is fairly
awkward, while the 3D system is easy to operate.

Single-Line Drawings

Based on the assumption that the numerical description of the object
to be detailed has been stored as three-dimensional, the generation

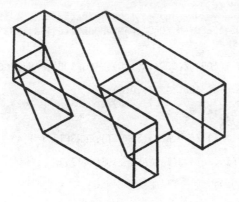

GRAPHIC ENTITIES   WIREFORM

FIGURE 1.3 Description of 3D object as wireform. A wireform is a type of template display where all points in the database are connected by line segments. Wireforms are a mathematical solid representation containing only a visible line, not a plane surface. All wireforms are transparent and when rotated into orthogonal viewing positions, all lines are visible - none appear hidden or dashed.

of single-line drawings is quite simple. First the user describes the object in wireform as illustrated in Figure 1.3. The three-dimensional storage array contained in the display subprogram shown as Figure 1.4 has been set for 400 elements, or up to 400 pen controls may be used to describe the wireform. A wireform is a mathematical form for an object. Objects displayed in this manner do not have solid surfaces; a surface is represented by visible line segments. A line segment is formed by a pen control code which connects two or more of the data points in the computer memory.

Wireforms do not have hidden or invisible line segments. The viewer of such an object feels that he or she can reach through the object. When models of these types of objects are constructed, a person can run a finger through the plane surface. Figure 1.5 is an example of an object displayed in this manner, while Figure 1.6 is the same object displayed in a working view relationship. At this point all lines are represented as object lines, and only in simple cases is this desired. The architectural engineer now points to those lines that should be hidden on the CRT. A list especially designed to handle hidden line representation is used. By touching the listing labeled DASH, the user is sending a command to the computer to recall a subprogram to do the following:

```
//CEERYANA JOB (0913-6-001-AH-4,:02,2),'BOX 17 MARK'
//STEP1 EXEC FTG1CL,PDS='CEERYAN.LOAD',NAME=BOBB,PLOTTER=IBM3277
/*ROUTE PRINT TEXT
//C.SYSIN DD *
      DIMENSION X(100),Y(100),Z(100),R(100),SANG(100),EANG(100)
      CALL PLOTS
      CALL CIRCL(21.,8.,90.,180.,1.,1.,0.0)
      CALL CIRCL(20.,5.,0.0,-90.,1.,1.,0.0)
      CALL CUPID1(63,15.,15.,20.,2)
      CALL PLOT(4.,4.0,-3)
      READ(20,*) (X(I),Y(I),Z(I),R(I),SANG(I),EANG(I),I=1,4)
      DO 999 I=1,4
      CALL ZARC(X(I),Y(I),Z(I),R(I),SANG(I),EANG(I))
999   CONTINUE
      CALL PLOT(0.,0.,999)
      STOP
      END
      SUBROUTINE CUPID1(NPTS,XTRANS,YTRANS,ANG,IPIC)
C NPTS=# OF POINTS, OR MOVES, OR DATA CARDS TO DEFINE 3-D DRAWING.
C XTRANS= DIST FROM LOWER LEFT OF FRONT VIEW TO LOWER LEFT OF SIDE VIEW.
C YTRANS= DIST FROM LOWER LEFT OF FRONT VIEW TO LOWER LEFT OF TOP  VIEW.
C          ISOMETRIC OR PICTORIAL IS DRAW AT (XTRANS,YTRANS).
C ANG= ANGLE THAT ISOMETERIC IS DRAWN AT.
C IPIC= 2 ISOMETERIC IS DRAWN.
C        3 ISOMETERIC IS NOT DRAWN.
C   NOTE: YOU MUST PLACE THE ORIGIN TO LOWER LEFT OF FRONT VIEW
C         WITH A CALL PLOT(?.,?.,-3), PRIOR TO THE CALL CUPID1!
C
C
C          _____                        _____
C         | TOP |                        / ISO /
C        *|_____|                        /_____/
C
C   YTRANS
C
C          _____                        _____
C         | FRT |                        | SIDE |
C         |_____|                        |_____|
C        *                XTRANS       *
C
      DIMENSION X(100),Y(100),Z(100),IPEN(100)
      DO 11 I=1,NPTS
11    READ(1,12) X(I),Y(I),Z(I),IPEN(I)
12    FORMAT(3F3.0,I2)
      IF(IPIC.EQ.3) GO TO 17
      DO 13 I=1,NPTS
13    CALL PLOT((X(I)+Z(I)*COS(ANG/57.29))+XTRANS,(Y(I)+Z(I)*SIN(ANG/57
     +.29))+YTRANS,IPEN(I))
17    DO 14 I=1,NPTS
14    CALL PLOT(X(I),Y(I),IPEN(I))
      DO 15 I=1,NPTS
15    CALL PLOT(X(I),Z(I)+YTRANS,IPEN(I))
      DO 16 I=1,NPTS
16    CALL PLOT(Z(I)+XTRANS,Y(I),IPEN(I))
      RETURN
      END
      SUBROUTINE ZARC(XP,YP,ZP,R,SANG,EANG)
C     ****************************************************************
C     *                                                              *
C     *   THIS SUBROUTINE GRAPHS CIRCULAR ARCS IN THE Z PLANE (IE    *
C     *   THE PLANE PERPENDICULAR TO THE Z-AXIS) FROM A THREE DI-    *
C     *   MENSIONAL DATA BASE IN X,Y,AND Z.                          *
C     *      XP...THE X COORDINATE OF THE CENTER OF THE ARC          *
C     *      YP...THE Y COORDINATE OF THE CENTER OF THE ARC          *
C     *      ZP...THE Z COORDINATE OF THE CENTER OF THE ARC          *
C     *       R... THE RADIUS OF THE ARC                             *
```

FIGURE 1.4 Display program for wireform objects.

```
C      *    SANG...TNE STARTING ANGLE OF THE ARC MEASURED IN DEGREES      *
C      *           CCW POSITIVE FROM THE POSITIVE Z-AXIS                   *
C      *    EANG...THE ENDING ANGLE OF THE ARC MEASURED IN DEGREES         *
C      *           CCW POSITIVE FROM THE POSITIVE Z-AXIS                   *
C      *                                                                   *
C      *********************************************************************
C
       DIMENSION P(400,3)
       PI=3.14159265
       N=IFIX(EANG-SANG)
       THETA=(EANG-SANG)/N
       THETAR=THETA*PI/180.
       SRANG=SANG*PI/180.
       DO 1 I=1,N
       DX=R*COS(SRANG)
       DY=R*SIN(SRANG)
       P(I,1)=XP+DX
       P(I,2)=YP+DY
       P(I,3)=-ZP
       SRANG=SRANG+THETAR
     1 CONTINUE
       CALL VANTAC(P,1.,N)
       RETURN
       END
       SUBROUTINE VANTAC(P,SIZE,N)
C      *********************************************************************
C      *                                                                   *
C      *    NP  =NO. OF POINTS TO BE PLOTTED                               *
C      *    NC  =NO. OF COMMANDS NECESSARY TO DRAW FIGURE                  *
C      *    NV  =NO. OF DIFFERENT VIEWS TO BE DRAWN                        *
C      *    SPACE=SPACE ALLOWED FOR EACH VIEW                              *
C      *    P(NP,3)=ARRAY CONTAINING X,Y, AND Z COORDINATES OF POINTS      *
C      *    IC(NC)=ARRAY CONTAINING PLOT COMMANDS                          *
C      *    VP(NV,3)=ARRAY CONTAINING X,Y, ANDZ COORDINATES OF VANTAGE     *
C      *           POINTS                                                  *
C      *                                                                   *
C      *********************************************************************
       DIMENSION P(400,3),IC(400),VP(100,3),PP(400,3)
       CALL FACTOR(SIZE)
       NP=N
       NC=N
       NV=1
C      WRITE(3,10)NP,NC,NV
       SPACE=8.
C      WRITE(3,101)SPACE
C      WRITE(3,102)
C      WRITE(3,103)
C      WRITE(3,104)((P(I,J),J=1,3),I=1,NP)
       DATA VP/1.,1.,1.,97*0.,2*1.,1.,97*0.,1.,1.,1.,97*0./
       WRITE(3,105)
       WRITE(3,103)
       WRITE(3,104)((VP(I,J),J=1,3),I=1,NV)
       IC(1)=-1
       DO 999 I=2,NP
   999 IC(I)=I
       WRITE(3,106)
C      WRITE(3,107)(IC(I),I=1,NC)
C      CALL PLOTS
       DO 5 I=1,NV
       A=ARTAN(VP(I,1),VP(I,3))
       SA=SIN(A)
       CA=COS(A)
       DO 6 J=1,NP
       PP(J,3)=P(J,3)*CA+P(J,1)*SA
```

FIGURE 1.4 (Continued)

```
          PP(J,1)=P(J,1)*CA-P(J,3)*SA
  6       CONTINUE
          VPP=VP(I,3)*CA+VP(I,1)*SA
          A=ARTAN(VP(I,2),VPP)
          SA=SIN(A)
          CA=COS(A)
          DO 7 J=1,NP
          PP(J,2)=P(J,2)*CA-PP(J,3)*SA
  7       CONTINUE
          DO 11 K=1,NP
          PP(K,2)=PP(K,2)+6.0
          PP(K,1)=PP(K,1)+SPACE*I
  11      CONTINUE
          DO 8 J=1,NC
          IF (IC(J).LT.0) GO TO 9
          CALL PLOT(PP(IC(J),1),PP(IC(J),2),2)
          GO TO 8
  9       K=-IC(J)
          CALL PLOT(PP(K,1),PP(K,2),3)
  8       CONTINUE
  5       CONTINUE
          XSET=(SPACE*NV)+8.
C         CALL PLOT(XSET,0.,999)
  1       FORMAT(3I5)
  2       FORMAT(F10.3)
  3       FORMAT(3F10.2)
  4       FORMAT(10I5)
  10      FORMAT('1',20X,'NUMBER OF POINTS TO BE PLOTTED=',I5,/,21X,'NUMBER
         1OF PEN MOVEMENTS REQD  =',I5,/,21X,'NUMBER OF VIEWS TO BE DRAWN
         1=',I5)
  101     FORMAT('0',20X,'SPACE PROVIDED FOR EACH VIEW  =',F6.2)
  102     FORMAT(///,30X,'POINT COORDINATES')
  103     FORMAT(/,20X,'X',20X,'Y',20X,'Z')
  104     FORMAT(/,F25.3,2F20.3)
  105     FORMAT(///,30X,'VANTAGE POINTS')
  106     FORMAT(/,30X,'PLOT COMMANDS')
C107     FORMAT(10X,10I5)
          RETURN
          END
          FUNCTION ARTAN(Y,X)
          DATA EPS/0.001/
          AX=ABS(X)
          AY=ABS(Y)
          IF(AX.GT.EPS.AND.AY.GT.EPS) GO TO 1
          IF(AX.LT.EPS.AND.AY.LT.EPS) GO TO 3
          IF(AX.LT.EPS) GO TO 2
  3       ARTAN=0.0
          RETURN
  2       ARTAN=(3.14159*AY)/(Y*2.0)
          RETURN
  1       ARTAN=ATAN2(Y,X)
          RETURN
          END
C ################################################################
C ################################################################
```

FIGURE 1.4 (Continued)

1.   Erase the line segment between two inputs made earlier by
      the operator and

2.   Display a dashed line between these data points.

This is a powerful subprogram because the programmer may select
either wireform data points or points at random from the display

surface. All known cases for the use of a hidden line can then be represented.

At this point in the construction of a display for single-line drawings, the architectural engineer needs to add any special features such as doors, windows, or the like. The procedure is the same as in the case of the hidden line just described. A list is selected, the display position is input, a scale for the display is entered, and the item is presented on the CRT. The various types of output devices (and how to use them) are the subject of Chapter 2.

Now the user has finished the task. Single-line drawings contain other information such as notes, dimensions, section views, and a bill of materials. A detailed method for these operations will be presented in later chapters, but it is important to mention in this introduction that steps in developing a single-line drawing are sequential and follow nearly the same procedure that a detailer would use.

Multiline Drawings

Multiline drawings are usually a combination of three-dimensional and single-line drawings. For this reason, a reader who has understood both the method of wireform presentation and the method for interactive generation of single-line drawings may now proceed to the generation of a multi-line drawing.[*]

Layout and Design Drawings

Layout and design drawings are usually not constructed by an architectural draftsperson. A draftsperson usually works from design drawings in the creation of other drawings. Architectural design engineers prepare design drawings and are responsible for the creation of datum references. Each datum is added to a collection called the database. It is from this database that display programs are able to generate the drawing types described earlier. Figure 1.7 is typical of a testing subprogram used by architectural design engineering during the layout phase. Here objects are not coded as simple wireforms until all surfaces have been described. In this process all surfaces are considered to be a type of wireform called a mesh network. In Figure 1.8, an output from the subprogram shown in Figure 1.7, the network is made up of straight-line segments arranged as splines forming an X-Y grid. The grid may assume any shape the designer desires. Each intersection of the grid is called

---

[*]Many excellent texts exist for studying the theory of the computer. The reader should stop and refer to the Bibliography of this book for assistance in the building of computer graphics theory.

```
C THIS DATA IS FOR THE MAIN FIGURE
 0. 0. 0.03
10. 0. 0.02
10. 0. 3.02
10. 1. 3.02
10. 1. 5.02
10. 0. 5.02
10. 0. 7.02
 0. 0. 7.02
 0. 0. 5.02
 0. 1. 5.02
 0. 1. 3.02
 0. 0. 3.02
 0. 0. 0.02
 0. 0. 3.03
10. 0. 3.02
10. 1. 3.03
 0. 1. 3.02
 0. 0. 5.03
10. 0. 5.02
10. 1. 5.03
 0. 1. 5.02
 0. 0. 7.03
 0. 8. 7.02
10. 8. 7.02
10. 0. 7.02
 0. 0. 0.03
 0. 4. 0.02
 0. 4. 0.03
 0. 4. 4.02
 0. 8. 6.03
 0. 8. 7.02
10. 0. 0.03
10. 4. 0.02
10. 4. 0.03
10. 4. 4.02
10. 8. 6.03
10. 8. 7.02
 0. 8. 6.03
10. 8. 6.02
 0. 7. 5.03
10. 7. 5.02
 0. 5. 5.03
10. 5. 5.02
 0. 4. 4.03
10. 4. 4.02
10. 8. 7.03
10. 8. 6.02
10. 7. 5.03
10. 5. 5.02
10. 4. 4.03
10. 4. 1.02
10. 3. 0.03
10. 0. 0.02
 0. 8. 7.03
 0. 8. 6.02
 0. 7. 5.03
 0. 5. 5.02
```

FIGURE 1.5 Database and output from display program.

```
 0. 4. 4.03
 0. 4. 1.02
 0. 3. 0.03
 0. 0. 0.02
 0. 4. 0.03
10. 4. 0.02

C THIS DATA IS FOR THE ZARC PROGRAM
C
3.5 12.9 9.7 2.2 110. 190.
1.0 11.82 7.75 2.2 290. 370.
13.7 16.0 13.50 2.2 110. 190.
16.125 19.95 6.65 2.2 300. 370.
```

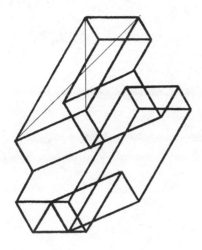

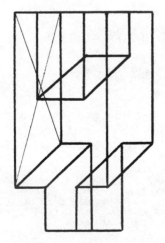

FIGURE 1.5 (Continued)

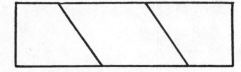

FIGURE 1.6 Working view relationship.

```
      C       PROGRAM TO TEST SURF
0001          CALL FACTOR(2.)
0002          DIMENSION X(500),Y(500),Z(500)
0003          CALL PLOTS
0004          NX=20
0005          NY=20
0006          DX=3.14159/NX
0007          DY=3.14159/NY
      C       DIX=-6.*DX
0008          DIX=-12.*DX
0009          ICNT=0
0010          DO 1 I=1,NX
0011          DIX=DIX+DX
0012          DIY=-6*DY
0013          DO 1 J=1,NY
0014          DIY=DIY+DY
0015          ICNT=ICNT+1
      C @@@@@@@@@@@@@@@@@@@@@@@@@@@@@@@@@@@@@@@@@@@@@@@@@@@@@@@@@@@@@@@@@@@@@@@@@@@
0016          Z(ICNT)=(COS(DIX)+1.)
      C @@@@@@@@@@@@@@@@@@@@@@@@@@@@@@@@@@@@@@@@@@@@@@@@@@@@@@@@@@@@@@@@@@@@@@@@@@@
      C       Z(ICNT)=(SIN(DIY)+1.)
0017          X(ICNT)=DIX
0018          Y(ICNT)=DIY
0019    1     CONTINUE
0020          NAX=2
0021          AXLX=5.
0022          AXLY=5.
0023          AXLZ=2.5
0024          LP=3
0025          XC=8.
0026          YC=5.
0027          CALL PLOT(XC,YC,-3)
0028          CALL SURF(X,Y,Z,ICNT,NX,NY,LP,NAX,AXLX,AXLY,AXLZ)
0029          YC=0.
0030          LP=2
0031          CALL PLOT(XC,YC,-3)
0032          CALL SURF(X,Y,Z,ICNT,NX,NY,LP,NAX,AXLX,AXLY,AXLZ)
0033          LP=1
0034          CALL PLOT(XC,YC,-3)
0035          CALL SURF(X,Y,Z,ICNT,NX,NY,LP,NAX,AXLX,AXLY,AXLZ)
0036          CALL PLOT(0.,0.,999)
0037          STOP
0038          END
0001          SUBROUTINE SURF(A,B,C,N,NX,NY,LP,NAX,AXLX,AXLY,AXLZ)
0002          DIMENSION A(500),B(500),C(500),BUFR(500),P(20,20)
      C
      C
      C       ****************************************************************
      C       *                                                              *
      C       *    THIS SUBROUTINE PLOTS AN ISOMETRIC PROJECTION OF A SURFACE *
      C       *    DEFINED BY AN ARRAY OF 3-D COORDINATES.  ALL CONDITIONING  *
      C       *    OF DATA SHOULD BE DONE BY THE CALLING PROGRAM.  FOR BEST   *
      C       *    RESULTS, INPUT DATA DISTRIBUTION SHOULD BE AT LEAST AS DENSE *
      C       *    AS THE NX*NY GRID TO BE PLOTTED.  Z IS DEPENDENT VARIABLE  *
      C       *    AND IS PLOTTED ALONG THE VERTICAL AXIS.                    *
      C       *                                                              *
      C       *    NOMENCLATURE:                                             *
      C       *    A    - ARRAY CONTAINING X-COORD VALUES                    *
      C       *    B    - ARRAY CONTAINING Y-COORD VALUES                    *
      C       *    C    - ARRAY CONTAINING Z-COORD VALUES                    *
      C       *    N    - NUMBER OF POINTS DEFINED                           *
      C       *    NX   - NUMBER OF GRID POINTS ALONG X-AXIS (NX.LE.20)      *
      C       *    NY   - NUMBER OF GRID POINTS ALONG Y-AXIS (NY.LE.20)      *
```

FIGURE 1.7 Typical testing program for layout phase.

```
        C      *    LP   - INDICATOR FOR SURFACE REPRESENTATION TYPF     *
        C      *              LP=1   LINES IN Z-DIRECTION ONLY           *
        C      *              LP=2   LINES IN X-DIRECTION ONLY           *
        C      *              LP=3   GRID                                *
        C      *    NAX  - REFERENCE AXIS INDICATOR                      *
        C      *              NAX.NE.1 REFERENCE AXIS NOT PLOTTED        *
        C      *              NX=1      REFERENCE AXIS PLOTTED           *
        C      *    AXLX - LENGTH OF X-AXIS (INCHES)                     *
        C      *    AXLY - LENGTH OF Y-AXIS (INCHES)                     *
        C      *    AXLZ - LENGTH OF Z-AXIS (INCHES)                     *
        C      *    SCALEING IS ACCOMPLISHED BY SPECIFYING AXIX LENGTHS  *
        C      *                                                         *
        C      ***********************************************************
        C
0003           AXLX1=AXLX+0.001
0004           AXLY1=AXLY+0.001
        C
        C      FIND MAX VALUES FOR USE IN SCALING TO FIT AXIS LENGTHS
        C
0005           XH=A(1)
0006           YH=B(1)
0007           ZH=C(1)
0008           XL=XH
0009           YL=YH
0010           ZL=ZH
0011           DO 1 I=1,N
0012           IF(XH.LE.A(I))XH=A(I)
0013           IF(YH.LE.B(I))YH=B(I)
0014           IF(ZH.LE.C(I))ZH=C(I)
0015           IF(XL.GE.A(I))XL=A(I)
0016           IF(YL.GE.B(I))YL=B(I)
0017           IF(ZL.GE.C(I))ZL=C(I)
0018      1    CONTINUE
        C
        C      SCALE DATA TO FIT AXIS LENGTHS GIVEN
        C
0019           DO 2 I=1,N
0020           A(I)=(A(I)-XL)/(XH-XL)*AXLX
0021           B(I)=(B(I)-YL)/(YH-YL)*AXLY
0022           C(I)=(C(I)-ZL)/(ZH-ZL)*AXLZ
0023      2    CONTINUE
        C
        C      FILL GRID ARRAY WITH DATA TO BE PLOTTED
        C
0024           DO 3 I=1,NX
0025           DO 4 J=1,NY
0026           P(I,J)=0.
0027      4    CONTINUE
0028      3    CONTINUE
0029           DO 5 I=1,N
0030           IX=A(I)/AXLX1*NX+1.
0031           IY=B(I)/AXLY1*NY+1.
0032           IF (C(I).GT.P(IX,IY))P(IX,IY)=C(I)
0033      5    CONTINUE
        C
        C      PLOT AXES IF REQUIRED
        C
0034           IF(NAX.NE.1) GO TO 10
0035           X=AXLX
0036           Y=0.
0037           Z=0.
0038           CALL ROTATE(X,Y,Z)
0039           CALL PLOT(X,Y,3)
0040           X=0.
0041           Y=0.
0042           Z=0.
0043           CALL ROTATE(X,Y,Z)
0044           CALL PLOT(X,Y,2)
0045           Z=AXLZ
0046           X=0.
0047           Y=0.
0048           CALL ROTATE(X,Y,Z)
```

FIGURE 1.7 (Continued)

```
0049                     CALL PLOT(X,Y,1)
0050                     X=0.
0051                     Z=0.
0052                     Y=0.
0053                     CALL ROTATE(X,Y,Z)
0054                     CALL PLOT(X,Y,3)
0055                     Y=AXLY
0056                     X=0.
0057                     Z=0.
0058                     CALL ROTATE(X,Y,Z)
0059                     CALL PLOT(X,Y,2)
0060              10     CONTINUE
                  C
                  C      PLOT SURFACE
                  C
0061                     IF(LP.EQ.1)GO TO 13
0062                     DO 6 I=1,NX
0063                     X=(I-1)*AXLX/(NX-1)
0064                     SX=X
0065                     IP=3
0066                     DO 7 J=1,NY
0067                     X=SX
0068                     Y=(J-1)*AXLY/(NY-1)
0069                     Z=P(I,J)
0070                     CALL ROTATE(X,Y,Z)
0071                     CALL PLOT(X,Y,IP)
0072                     IP=2
0073              7      CONTINUE
0074              6      CONTINUE
0075                     IF(LP.EQ.2) GO TO 14
0076              13     CONTINUE
0077                     DO 8 I=1,NY
0078                     Y=(I-1)*AXLY/(NY-1)
0079                     SY=Y
0080                     IP=3
0081                     DO 9 J=1,NX
0082                     Y=SY
0083                     X=(J-1)*AXLX/(NX-1)
0084                     Z=P(J,I)
0085                     CALL ROTATE(X,Y,Z)
0086                     CALL PLOT(X,Y,IP)
0087                     IP=2
0088              9      CONTINUE
0089              8      CONTINUE
0090              14     CONTINUE
0091                     RETURN
0092                     END
0001                     SUBROUTINE ROTATE(X,Y,Z)
0002                     DATA C1/0.707/,C2/0.808/,S1/0.707/,S2/-.587/
0003                     SY=Y
0004                     Y=Z*C2+X*C1*S2+Y*S1*S2
0005                     X=SY*C1-X*S1
0006                     RETURN
0007                     END
```

FIGURE 1.7 (Continued)

a node and is a datum that may be added to the database or discarded. A manual process of this selection is often done by the design engineer during the layout stage, but later a computer program called nodal analysis compares each intersection and *saves* or *purges* each datum.

Three closely related computer processes are often misunderstood at this point: nodal analysis, finite element analysis, and finite element modeling. To keep these straight in the design process, remember the following:

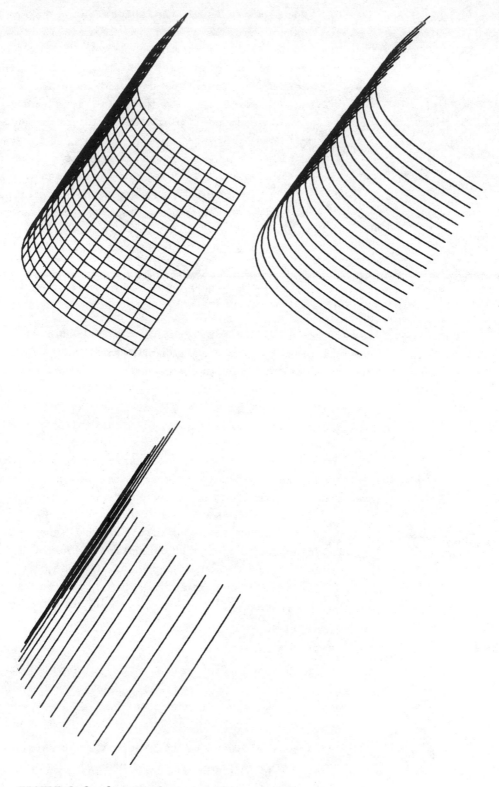

FIGURE 1.8 Output from testing program.

1. Nodal analysis is the selection or rejection of a single datum that was formed by the grid intersection of a plane surface. It is a plane surface, not a sculptured surface because a spline is made up of many tiny straight-line segments. Therefore each intersection of the grid is an intersection of two straight lines, while four intersections describe a plane surface sometimes referenced as a *patch* or *plate*.

2. Finite element analysis is the selection or rejection of entire surfaces based on the nodal analysis. Finite element analysis is almost always involved in three-dimensional objects. While this is true, remember the concept of the wireform: Objects are not solid planes. To study a 3D object, the design engineer must study each point describing that object.

3. Finite element analysis is the selection process for the entire group of surfaces that make up the object.

CHAPTER SUMMARY   Architectural engineering graphics was discussed for a very basic understanding of the fundamentals involved. Computer terms were kept to a minimum and where used were defined for the reader. Two main items of concern were discussed: (1) architectural engineering presentation techniques and (2) graphics and drafting.

The use of figures, diagrams, and tables was restricted so that the introduction centered on the possibilities available to the architectural user. Where necessary, computer instruction lists were shown, not for their understanding at this point but as examples to be studied in later chapters.

EXERCISES   1. Begin a course notebook divided into the following sections: (A) classroom notes, (B) operational instructions for computer-assisted architectural graphic devices, (C) sample sets of operational instructions for graphic devices, and (D) sample output graphics.

2. After each lecture, summarize your notes and place them in section A of your notebook.

3. Obtain handouts for section B of your notebook from your local computing center. Read each pamphlet or manual carefully and paste index tabs for easy location of each section. Subdivide section B so each device can be described separately.

4. Prepare sample sets of instructions for each of these devices.

5. Place both the instructions (input) and drawings produced (output) in sections C and D of your notebook.

6. The architectural engineer shown in Figure 1.1 is seated at a Tektronix direct-view storage terminal. List the instructions necessary to display the image shown.

7. The device shown in Figure 1.2 is a stand-alone graphics terminal found in many small architectural offices. List some of the important features of this device. How is the use of a light pen simulated with this device?

8. The image displayed in Figure 1.2 and defined in Figure 1.3 is called a wireform. Prepare a list of wireform applications which match the following list of display types:

Display Types	Wireform Applications
Pictorial illustrations	
Single-line drawings	
Multiline drawings	
Layout and design drawings	
Diagrams, charts, and graphs	

9. Input the program shown in Figure 1.4. Make the necessary changes in the program statements that begin with // so that the job can be routed to the display device of your choice.

10. Store the data listed in Figure 1.5 and input them to the program above. This produces the line drawings shown in Figures 1.5 and 1.6. Place these in your notebook.

11. Input the program shown in Figure 1.7. Add the necessary job control statements (//) so that the output may appear on the display device of your choice.

12. Place the output from the program above, shown in Figure 1.8, in your notebook.

13. Prepare a database (shown in Figure 1.5) for any common architectural object or structure.

14. Input this database to the program done for Exercise 9 and place the drawings in your notebook.

15. Prepare a database for the program done for Exercise 11 so that an architectural structural surface can be output. Place this in your notebook.

2 Automation of Routine Office Tasks

Computer-aided architectural engineering graphics is a technique that is used to express and convey ideas of shape, size, and construction of building parts or whole groups of objects of architectural importance. As outlined in Chapter 1, the format of the architectural graphics must be clear, concise, and subject to only one interpretation. To produce computer-drawn graphics that conform to accepted standards and practices, professional architects and architectural engineers make use of certain types of computer hardware, equipment, materials, and instruments. Therefore, an understanding of the tools and techniques available for architectural engineering graphics is important, if not critical, to the process of preparing graphics output. This output is usually an architectural drawing but is not limited to this format alone. In this chapter the graphics equipment, materials, and tools used by professional architects and architectural engineers to produce a drawing will be described.

REQUIREMENTS FOR OFFICE AUTOMATION
Professional architects and architectural engineers produce much of their graphics at work stations suited to the needs of the designer.* Figure 2.1 is an example of one work station available.

_____

*The term *designer* shall mean either a professional architect of an architectural engineer of either sex, male or female.

21

FIGURE 2.1   Auto-trol Technology's CC-80 Graphics Workstation as used for architecture, space planning, and facilities management. (Courtesy of Auto-trol Technology Corporation, Denver, Colorado.)

The arrangement varies somewhat from office to office. In general, these work stations contain the items in Table 2.1.

Although the number of items selected from the list in Table 2.1 may vary somewhat, each work station contains a manual and an electronic design area. This electronic area or surface is usually a tablet. Construction details vary on different tablets; some

TABLE 2.1   Items Contained in Automated Architectural Work Station

Item	Description	Use
CRT	Cathode ray tube	Refresh display area
Data tablet	Graphics tablet	Digitize objects
DISK	Rigid or floppy magnetic circles	Store programs and subprograms
DVST	Direct-view storage tube	Preview designs
HCU	Hard copy unit	Copy contents of DVST
Joystick	X-Y input device	Pointer for DVST
Light pen	X-Y input device	Pointer for CRT
MATRIX printer	Line printer	Type lines of program
Microcomputer	Smart terminal	Dynamic graphics
Minicomputer	Graphics processor	Controller for work station
Plotter	X-Y flatbed image processor	Small details
	Drum	Larger details
Tape deck	Reel-to-reel tape recorder	Store programs and subprograms

adjust to any desired working height. A twist of a knob or push of
a lever permits the top to be adjusted to any working angle.   The
most popular models of tablets adjust to a full easel position for
easy use of tablet equipment such as the devices shown in Figure
2.2.

FIGURE 2.2 Auto-trol Technology's AD/380 Automated Design and Drafting System. Left to right: CC-180 Graphics Workstation, Optec Digitizer, Mark 4 Flatbed Plotter, 16-bit graphics processor, and message center. (Courtesy of Auto-trol Technology Corporation, Denver, Colorado.)

EQUIPMENT AND MATERIALS NECESSARY

The computer-aided graphics work station is a mixture of specialized equipment designed to make the production of graphics easier and highly productive for the designer.* The designer usually elects to cover the manual design tabletop with a special sheet material. This two-sided material may be used either side up because the inside *memory layer* provides a smooth, working surface under the drawing sheet. After the designer has drawn a line on this material and caused the dent, the *memory layer* bounces the surface smooth and flat again and ready for the next drawing.

Once the table surface has been covered with a suitable covering, the engineer selects the accessories for the surface. These devices assist the designer in the production of the lines which create the drawing image. Depending on the size of the drawing surface and its location (office or field), the engineer may select from the following devices:

    1. T square, triangle, or parallel edge
    2. Drafting machine or coordinatograph
    3. Digitizer or graphics tablet

Basic Skills

The use of the T square, triangle, or straightedge should not be new
to the designer. As other manual devices become automated, however,
drafting machines may begin to appear on tablet surfaces instead of
the drawing table.

Drafting Machine. Near the middle of the twentieth century an
invention called the drafting machine became a standard piece of
equipment for drafting surfaces. It combined the best features of
the T square, parallel straightedge, and plastic triangle. It was
an extremely useful invention since it eliminated the need for
separate scale rules and a triangle, protractor, and straightedge.
All these were incorporated in a manner to permit their instant use.
The time saving was considerable because the manual operations were
combined, such as laying out horizontal or vertical lines and angles
and measuring distances. The central control allowed the designer
to accomplish all these operations with one hand, leaving the other
hand free for drawing the lines.

Operating instructions written around 1950 exclaimed the
revolutionary breakthrough whereby an operator could draw a line to
a predetermined length at any angle using one hand only! Simultaneously, setting the correct angles and without resetting
controls, parallel or perpendicular lines can be drawn anywhere on
the board.

No one at that time could envision that in 20 years the drafting machine would be used as a digitizer on an electronic table
similar to those shown in Figure 2.3.

Digitizer. The first improvement of the drafting machine was the
elimination of the pencil or pen from the designer's hand. The
designer was still at the work station and operated the drafting
machine as before. The drafting machine was called a *coordinatograph* and improved the accuracy of the graphics, usually within 8/10
of 0.001. A pointer, locator, or pen was held along the horizontal
axis and was free to move from side to side over the range of the
machine. At the same time, the entire X or horizontal assembly was
free to move vertically along the Y axis. The drawing surface was
also improved and was manufactured parallel to the motion of the
machine. Usually optically ground glass was used for the surface.
The drawing materials such as paper, nylon, scribe coat, cut and
peel, or coated materials were backlighted for easy visibility.

FIGURE 2.3 (A) Coordinatograph, (B) coordinatograph controls.

The designer moved the required amount in X and Y to create straight lines; large and small circles were made with special attachments that look like beam compasses. Irregular curves such as site profiles, street curves, cross-section shapes, and others were plotted as points in space having X and Y values. The pointer located these X-Y values as one-thousandth dots which allowed light to pass. A curve averager called a *duck* was aligned to connect the lighted dots, and then the pen holder followed the duck to create the special curve. As the designer created the line, a device called an *encoder* sensed the motion and translated this movement to nixie tubes in an electronic display. This feature saved nearly 50% of the drafting time as compared with the manual method. Another time-saving advantage of the coordinatograph was the recorder which transferred electronic readings to an automatic typewriter for storage on a paper tape. This process was called digitizing. The designer drew only once, and then a permanent record was kept on the paper tape. Changes in the design were made by editing the tape and adding new information via the typewriter. The coded tape was then played back as often as needed. Some coordinatographs were both input and output types, making this possible. However, many were

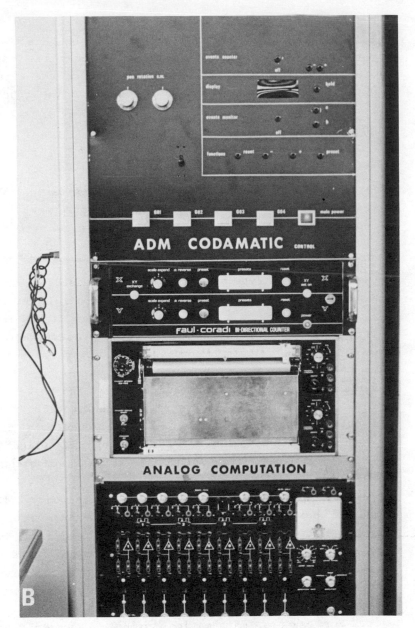

FIGURE 2.3 (Continued)

not, and an output plotter called a numerical control drafting machine was used. If the coordinatograph was used for input, the term *digitizer* was used to label this device.

Electronic Tablets. The invention of the coordinatograph eliminated the need for the designer to push and pull a triangle or T square around the drafting surface. A modern (late-twentieth-century) device called an electronic tablet or graphics tablet has given the designer an automated replacement for the coordinatograph. This device is used connected to a video display monitor. The designer holds a pencil which has an electronic cable attached through the tablet surface. When the designer touches the tablet surface, a circuit is completed, and a dot appears on the video display. The dot may be left to represent a point, or the pencil can be moved while touching the tablet surface and the dot will appear as a line on the video display.

Methods of Operation

As drawing and architectural graphics progressed toward the last 20 years of the twentieth century, many improvements and innovations took place. One of these was the addition of a keyboard to the drafting machine; the designer simply removed the X scale from the drafting machine and clipped on a small floating keyboard. One example of this type of device was introduced by Koh-I-Noor. It was a portable high-speed electronically controlled lettering machine and automated template. The keyboard was lightweight and could be clipped onto the drafting machine and moved anywhere on the drawing paper surface. The microprocessor-based system enabled the user to draw characters and symbols with liquid ink on almost any drafting surface faster and better than before. The keyboard (weighing less than 3 lb) contained 51 keys, A through Z and 39 dual function keys. A character-height selector switch allowed five different prepro-grammed heights. Also a 32-character LED (light-emitting-diode) display allowed a 5 by 7 dot matrix visual-proofing readout before the actual plotting.

The keyboard was electrically connected to 125 V through a control box. This box contained the logic circuitry required to operate the keyboard. An opening in the control box allowed tape cassettes to be played through the keyboard. The template images could be drawn from digital information stored on the tapes. At this point, the need for a large collection of plastic templates to draw special symbols became obsolete.

For example, mathematical symbols, geometric figures, arrows, architectural symbols, office and home furnishings, landscape designs, electrical and electronic symbols, power and light symbols, flowcharts, isometric values, pipe fittings, fluid power symbols, computer diagramming, operation and process flow, logic, bolts and nuts, hexes, isometric hexes and nuts, and information in English or metric terms could now be done with a single display device.

Approximate Data Gathering

Instruments like the Koh-I-Noor *auto draw* just described were very essential for producing good drawings with a minimum amount of effort in the shortest possible time. There are many different types of electronic microprocessor instruments available for approximate data gathering. Some contain numerous special accessories, while others include only the basic instrument. Most work stations have the following capabilities:

1. Adjustable size of circles from 3/16 to 8 in. in diameter or metric translation.
2. Eight-inch and larger (beam-compass-type) representation.
3. A selection of common template symbols.
4. Representation of irregular, ship, railroad, or flexible curve images.
5. A protractor which may be part of the drafting machine or a separate device. If separate, it is a semicircular form divided into units called degrees. Usually, two scales are shown each having units running from zero to 180. The outside scale is designed for laying out angles that extend to the left, and the inside scale is for angles to the right. When a graphics programmer enters these two types of angles for computer plotting, the outside reading is stored under THETA and the inside angle is stored under BETA.

When it is necessary to display curves other than standard circles or arcs, special devices called flexible curves are used. They consist of long narrow strips of flexible metal with either metal or rubber ruling edges which can be set to fit any desired curvature.

Other types of flexible curves can be used with graphic digitizers to prepare data for computer plotting. The data may be previewed on a video screen before storage in a computer file.

METHODS AND PROCEDURES The drawing surface or medium which contains the computer-aided graphics has advanced from the paper and cloth era to today's wide selection:

1. Tracing paper - pencil
2. Tracing film - ink pen
3. Electrostatic films - knife
4. Coated films - scriber
5. Photographic film - light heads

The size of the drawing sheet is determined by the project to be drawn. All offices use a variety of sheet sizes, although they often standardize on some sizes for certain types of contract work. Drawing sheets are also based on ANSI standards. This association has, over the years, undertaken the standardization of graphics practices.

The designer selects the drawing medium and sheet size for the drawing. The designer may use a drafting machine to locate points or position lines drawn by hand. Next, the drawing sheet may be removed from the table and placed on a flatbed plotter. A data file read from computer memory may add more detail to the drawing. Next, the designer may remove the drawing from the plotter and take it to a varityper and type a few notes. Figure 2.4 was produced in this manner.

The point to be made here is that the designer no longer spends long hours bent over a drawing board. Architectural engineering graphics equipment and computer programs have allowed much flexibility in how to prepare the final architectural drawing.

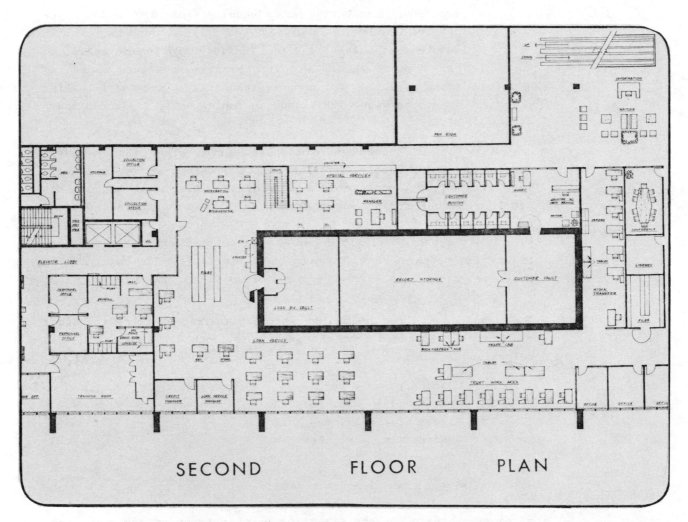

FIGURE 2.4 Diagram from mixed media I/O.

All drawings contain a logical arrangement of points, lines, and planes. How the designer chooses to produce them is not as important as the correctness of their placement. This book will introduce the reader to all the common methods for computer-generated architectural documents.

Shortcuts

When architects began to think about how to increase drawing productivity and decrease the amount of drawing time necessary to complete an architectural drawing, the first area of work that was modernized was the plotting of single lines.

Before the plotting process could be automated, a cycle was developed where a designer began and ended a specific task such as drawing a line. The cycle was as follows:

1. A command given by the operator to draw a line
2. A machine responding to this command
3. An output displaying the line image

The common forms of designer instructions or inputs were keyboard, punched tape, punched cards, plotter movement (digitizing), light pen, and CRT. All these input methods told the computer what to do and how to do it. The computer plotted the line according to the output device used; the line was drawn or shown by an X-Y plotter, high-speed printer, CRT screen, or electrostatic transfer to micro-film for storage.

Automatic line plotting systems all had certain characteristics in common. First a rough sketch was prepared, preferably on coordinate paper. The machine located lines and symbols accurately even though they were not sketched with exact coordinate locations. If a keyboard input was used, the machine was a photocomposition type which produced diagrams by passing light through glass matrices containing standardized symbols and/or characters and exposing photographic film or paper. The film or paper, when developed, was contact-printed to produce the final tracing. If, however, a control box was employed, the second most common characteristic of all systems was used, this being the identification of drafting symbols by library type number and the information retrieved from a storage device such as magnetic tape.

It was easy to see that the keyboard was limited to the symbols assigned to push buttons, whereas the storage system was unlimited as to the amounts of data but required a machine language to obtain input symbols. Third, a program of operation was written telling the machine how the output drawing was to appear. The most common form of inputting the program was by punched tape or teletypewriter.

A photoelectric tape reader and spooler processed the input data called program instructions and output directly to the automatic drafting table. The last item in the system was the type of drafting table used. The drafting table which translated complex mathematical expressions into accurate drawings at very high speeds was the most useful for its time. It was particularly suited to mirror image items, and large accurate grids and provided visual verification of computer data and program tapes. Some models were also capable of automatically drawing a third view based on data from two other views. This type of table was the X-Y plotter type and was necessary for drawings prepared before 1970. However, it was often the case where the drawing was not the desired output, and then a printer was used to type out a numerical description of each of the lines and symbols in a coordinate geometry type of listing. This was used in the automotive industry for direct machining of stamping dies. Other special applications were CRT display for the designer to change or modify and then record on microfilm, closed circuit video tape for quality control and measurement techniques, and logic signals for storage in computer memory.

Increasing Graphic Output

One of the most time-consuming tasks in architectural graphics was the change from one scale to another. If a drawing existed and the designer desired to have that same drawing at a different size or scale, the drawing had to be drawn again. Using the plotting routines just described, a designer could type

    CALL FACTOR (SIZE)

where size represents the desired scale for the drawing. The drawing would then be plotted at the new size in a fraction of the time required to redraw it. The line plotting system, coupled with a design procedure, made scaling and other corrections found on architectural engineering change orders a simple matter.

CHAPTER SUMMARY   The design procedure discussed can best be described as a method by which the designer supplies raw information to a computer and the computer in turn assists the designer in finding an answer to one or more problems (scaling, etc.). The computer is often a digital computer or special-purpose computer-related device. A systematic design procedure implies a uniform, easily understood, organized method for feeding information into and out of the design cycle.

    There are two main parts of a design cycle, data and instructions. Data consist of the numbers and characters which are to be used by the instructions to produce an architectural format. The main types of data used are numeric and alphanumeric plus special

characteristics. A list of the characters allowable in most design
cycles is as follows:

0 1 2 3 4 5 6 7 8 9

A B C D E F G H I J K L M N O P Q R S T U V W X Y Z

EXERCISES   1.   Professional architects and architectural engineers produce
much of their graphics at work stations as shown in Figure 2.1,
2.2, and 2.3. Select one of these types and locate the data
tablet surface. Place a sheet of paper on this surface as
described in the section on necessary equipment and materials
in Chapter 2. Select a device for assisting you in the production of lines and create a simple drawing.

2.   Select from the accompanying examples a sample drawing to be
entered from the drafting surface of the work station. Each of

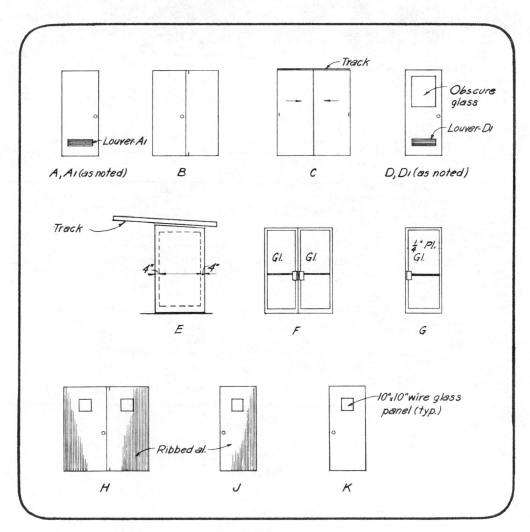

these may be created from the data tablet surface with aid of a triangle or parallel edge. (Courtesy of the US Corps of Engineers, Vicksburg, Mississippi.)

3.   Select from the accompanying example, drawings to be entered from the keyboard of the work station. (Courtesy of the US Corps of Engineers, Vicksburg, Mississippi.)

ROOM FINISH SCHEDULE EL. 512.58

ROOM	FLOOR		BASE		WAINSCOT		WALLS CONSTRUCTION	FINISH		CEILING HEIGHT	FINISH		REMARKS
Stair A *	Steel Stairs	8.04	—		—		Concrete	—	4.03	—			
Toilet	Cer. mosaic tile	9.05	Cer. tile	9.05	Cer. tile	9.05	Conc.& metal stud.	K.C.P.	4.03/9.04	10'- 0"	K.C.P.	9.04	
First aid room	Cer. mosaic tile	9.05	Cer. tile	9.05	Cer. tile	9.05	Conc.& metal stud.	Gyp. plas.	4.03/9.04	9'- 0"	Gypsum plas.	9.04	
Corridor	Terrazzo	9.05	Terrazzo	9.05	Cer. tile	9.05	Metal stud & lath	Gyp. plas.	9.04	10'- 0"	Acoustic tile	9.06	
Lobby	Terrazzo	9.05	Terrazzo	9.05	Cer. tile	9.05	Conc.& metal stud	Gyp. plas.	4.03/9.04	10'- 0"	Acoustic tile	9.06	
Women	Cer. mosaic tile	9.05	Cer. tile	9.05	Cer. tile	9.05	Metal stud & lath	K.C.P.	9.04	9'- 0"	K.C.P.	9.04	
Men	Cer. mosaic tile	9.05	Cer. tile	9.05	Cer. tile	9.05	Metal stud & lath	K.C.P.	9.04	9'- 0"	K.C.P.	9.04	
Jan. clo.	Cer. mosaic tile	9.05	Cer. tile	9.05	Cer. tile	9.05	Metal stud & lath	K.C.P.	9.04	9'- 0"	K.C.P.	9.04	
Observation rm.	Terrazzo	9.05	Terrazzo	9.05	Cer. tile	9.05	Conc.& metal stud	Gyp. plas.	4.03/9.04	10'- 0"	Acoustic tile	9.06	
Toilet	Cer. mosaic tile	9.05	Cer. tile	9.05	Cer. tile	9.05	Metal stud & lath	K.C.P.	9.04	9'- 0"	K.C.P.	9.04	
Kitchen	Cer. mosaic tile	9.05	Cer. tile	9.05	Cer. tile	9.05	Metal stud & lath	Gyp. plas.	9.04	9'- 0"	Gypsum plas.	9.04	
Comm. equip. rm.	Vinyl tile	9.05	Vinyl tile	9.05	—		Metal stud & lath	Gyp. plas.	9.04	9'- 0"	Acoustic tile	9.06	
Instr. room	Vinyl tile	9.05	Vinyl tile	9.05	—		Metal stud & lath	Gyp. plas.	9.04	9'- 0"	Gypsum plas.	9.04	
Battery room	2" Bonded conc.	4.05	Metal	9.04	—		Metal stud & lath	Cem. plas.	9.04	9'- 0"	Cement plas.	9.04	
MG. room	2" Bonded conc.	4.05	Metal	9.04	—		Conc.& metal stud	Cem. plas.	4.03/9.04	9'- 0"	Cement plas.	9.04	
Rec.& files	Vinyl tile	9.05	Vinyl tile	9.05	—		Conc.& metal stud	Gyp. plas.	4.03/9.04	9'- 0"	Gypsum plas.	9.04	
Stair C †	Steel Stairs	8.04	—		—		Conc.& metal stud	Cem. plas.	4.03/9.04	9'- 0"	Cement plas.	9.04	
Control room	Vinyl tile	9.05	Vinyl tile	9.05	—		Conc.& metal stud	Gyp. plas.	4.03/9.04	10'- 6"	Acoustic tile	9.06	
Stair B	Steel Stairs	8.04	—		—		Concrete	—	4.03	—			
Entry	Concrete	4.03	—		—		Concrete	—	4.03	9'- 6"	Cement Plas.	9.04	

K.C.P. = Keene's cement plaster

ROOM FINISH SCHEDULE EL. 527.58

ROOM	FLOOR		BASE		WAINSCOT		WALLS CONSTRUCTION	FINISH		CEILING HEIGHT	FINISH		REMARKS
Stair A *	Steel Stairs	8.04	—		—		Concrete	—	4.03	—			
Floatwell rec. rm.	Vinyl tile	9.05	Vinyl tile	9.05	—		Conc. & metal stud	Gyp. plas.	4.03/9.04	9'-0"	Gypsum plas.	9.04	
Supt. office	Vinyl tile	9.05	Vinyl tile	9.05	—		Conc. & metal stud	Gyp. plas.	4.03/9.04	9'-0"	Acoustic tile	9.06	
Asst. supt. office	Vinyl tile	9.05	Vinyl tile	9.05	—		Conc. & metal stud	Gyp. plas.	4.03/9.04	9'-0"	Acoustic tile	9.06	
Admin. office	Vinyl tile	9.05	Vinyl tile	9.05	—		Conc. & metal stud	Gyp. plas.	4.03/9.04	9'-0"	Acoustic tile	9.06	
Storage	Vinyl tile	9.05	Vinyl tile	9.05	—		Conc. & metal stud	Gyp. plas.	4.03/9.04	9'-0"	Gypsum plas.	9.04	
Women	Cer. mosaic tile	9.05	Cer. tile	9.05	Cer. tile	9.05	Conc. & metal stud	K.C.P.	4.03/9.04	9'-0"	K.C.P.	9.04	
Men	Cer. mosaic tile	9.05	Cer. tile	9.05	Cer. tile	9.05	Conc. & metal stud	K.C.P.	4.03/9.04	9'-0"	K.C.P.	9.04	
Jan. clo.	Cer. mosaic tile	9.05	Cer. tile	9.05	Cer. tile	9.05	Metal stud & lath	K.C.P.	9.04	9'-0"	K.C.P.	9.04	
Locked storage	2" Bonded conc.	4.05	Metal	9.04	—		Conc. & metal stud.	—	4.03/9.04	—			Plas. on met. stud only
Storage	2" Bonded conc.	4.05	Metal	9.04	—		Conc. & metal stud.	—	4.03/9.04	—			Plas. on met. stud only
Air cond. & vent. rm.	2" Bonded conc.	4.05	Metal	9.04	—		Conc. & metal stud.	Gyp. plas.	4.03/9.04	16'-3"	Cem. asb. bd.	906	Plas. on met. stud only
Elevator mach. rm.	2" Bonded conc.	4.05	Metal	9.04	—		Conc. & metal stud.	Gyp. plas.	4.03/9.04	16'-3"	Cem. asb. bd.	906	Plas. on met. stud only
Corridor #1	Vinyl tile	9.05	Vinyl tile	9.05	—		Metal stud & lath	Gyp. plas.	9.04	9'-0"	Acoustic tile	9.06	
Corridor #2	2" Bonded conc.	4.05	Metal	9.04	—		Metal stud & lath	Gyp. plas.	9.04	9'-0'	Cem. asb. bd.	9.06	

4.   Use the accompanying site map and enter it through the work station digitizer or coordinatograph. (Courtesy of the US Corps of Engineers, Vicksburg, Mississippi.)

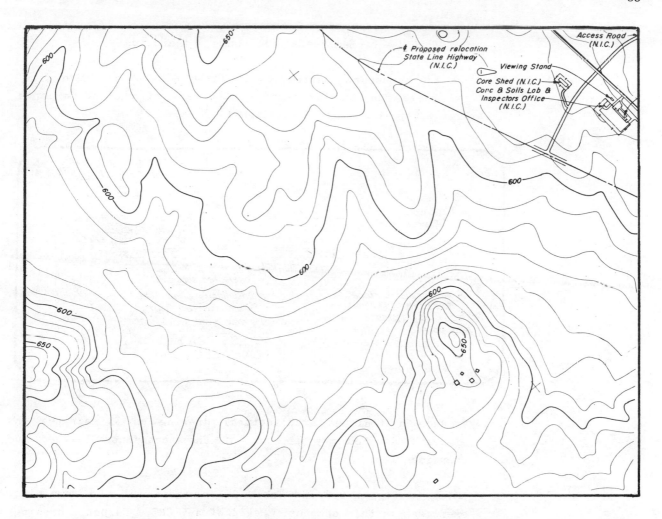

5. Use the floorplan shown and enter it so that it may be viewed on the video monitor of the work station. After viewing it,

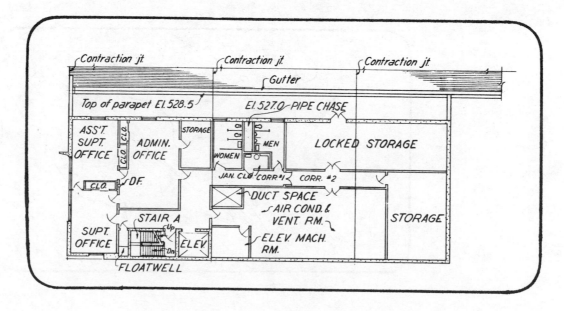

make a hard copy of an electronic data tablet. (Courtesy of the US Corps of Engineers, Vicksburg, Mississippi.)

6.   Use the necessary instruments like the Koh-I-Noor "auto draw" to create the drawing shown. (Courtesy of the US Corps of Engineers, Vicksburg, Mississippi.)

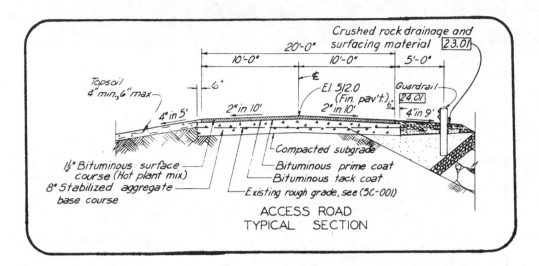

7.   Produce a finished architectural drawing as illustrated in Figure 2.4. You may use any of the techniques learned in Exercises 1-6.

8.   Refer to Figure 2.2 and Table 2.1 for each of the remaining exercises in this chapter. Begin with a CRT. Output a drawing to match that shown. (Courtesy of the US Corps of Engineers, Vicksburg, Mississippi.)

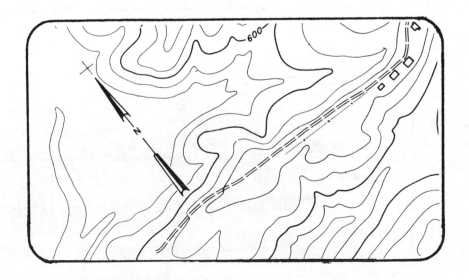

9. Choose an electronic data tablet and digitize the object shown. (Courtesy of the US Corps of Engineers, Vicksburg, Mississippi.)

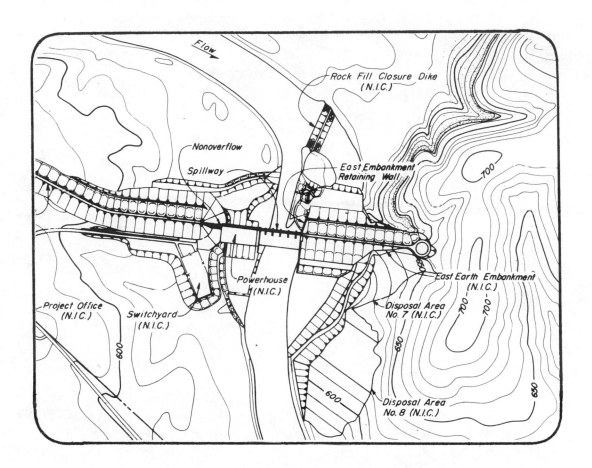

10. Locate the operational disk from Table 2.1 and list the architectural programs contained in your graphics system.

11. The direct-view storage tube display area may be used to output a digitized drawing. Use it to view Exercise 9.

12. A hard copy unit was used in Exercise 5. Any drawing on the DVST may be copied for your notebook. The joystick or thumb wheels may be used to add lines or points to an existing drawing. Use these to add a wall on the floorplan done in Exercise 5.

13. A light pen is used with a CRT. It may be used like a joystick to control a cursor on the screen. Use it to modify the drawing done in Exercise 8.

14. A matrix printer is used to list data points and program state-
     ments. Use it to provide a program listing for your notebook.

15. The plotter shown in Figure 2.2 and listed in Table 2.1 is used
     to produce high-quality inked drawings. Use it to output the
     drawing produced in Exercise 7.

3 Computer-Generated Artistic Lettering Styles

This chapter represents a new approach to computer-generated letter-ing, stylized solely for the production of architectural lettering. Whereas all former types of plotted lettering styles were suitable for mechanical drawings, none existed for free-form drawings. Using the concept discussed in this chapter, the designer may instruct the computer to remember his or her own style and reproduce it whenever needed. This of course requires the designer to hand-letter on a graphics tablet each of the alphanumeric characters desired. After just one entry, however, the computer's ability to generate "hand-drawn" lettering is possible.

The purpose of this chapter then is to develop a system which will consist of the computer requirements in both hardware (equip-ment) and software (programs), describe how to use this equipment, and finally describe how to code the lettering fonts for storage in the computer.

USE OF AUTOMATED LETTERING
In the design of free-form architectural lettering, much can be learned from the use of other types of automated lettering. For instance, the CALCOMP-generated lettering from the CALL SYMBOL instruction produces a letter font which is a 4 by 7 point grid. As illustrated in Figure 3.1, this produces a rather boxy-looking char-acter with equal spacing between characters. This is not acceptable for most architectural work. The three-point spacing between char-

39

MODULE 1 - COMPUTER ASSISTED LETTERING

FIGURE 3.1   CALCOMP-generated lettering from CALL SYMBOL.

acters should be variable for the proportional-type spacing used in architectural drawings.

Therefore, characters as listed in Table 3.1 were designed relative to a 7 by 9 point grid. As shown in Figure 3.2, this grid differs from the 4 by 7 grid in that the area between points may be enlarged or reduced independently as shown in Figure 3.3. These variable zones between grid intersections allow considerable freedom in the display of the items shown in Table 3.1. Figure 3.4 illustrates the artistic variations possible for the lowercase and uppercase letters.

Computer Requirements

Two types of computer-generated lettering have been introduced, a 4 by 7 grid matrix (CALCOMP style) also 'used by Versatec and Tektronix, and a variable 7 by 9 grid matrix designed for architects, architectural engineers, and general designers. Several design considerations were used to develop the second method:

1. The need to provide for proportional letter heights and widths.
2. The elimination of the bunching where lines join at an acute angle such as V, K, M, or W.
3. Linear elements (4 by 7 grid types) severely distort some letter shapes, so a provision for circular elements was maintained.
4. 7 by 9 characters are formed from straight lines, dots, and quarter circle areas. However, when factoring is applied to the area between the points, the arcs become elliptical, yielding a pleasing, more artistic letter form.
5. Because any combination of straight line, dot, or arc may be used, the designer must indicate the connection

TABLE 3.1 Character Generation

Special Characteristics	Numerics	Communication Code	Alpha	Notation Code
□	0	:	A	\
	1	;	B	1
△	2	<	C	
+	3	=	D	
x	4	>	E	
	5	?	F	a
	6	@	G	b
xx	7		H	c
z	8		I	d
	9		J	e
			K	f
*			L	g
			M	h
-			N	i
			O	j
!			P	k
"			Q	l
#			R	m
$			S	n
%			T	o
&			U	p
'			V	q
(			W	r
)			X	s
,			Y	t
.			Z	u
.				v
/				w
				x
				y
				z

desired. Figure 3.4 is only one possible combination. Figure 3.5 compares the letters A and S from Figure 3.4 with another connection pattern, while Figure 3.6 illustrates the placement of 7 by 9 lettering on an automated display sketch.

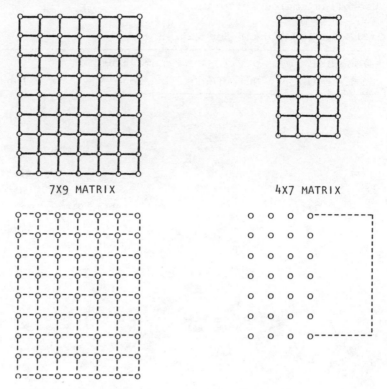

7X9 MATRIX   4X7 MATRIX

FIGURE 3.2 Comparison of 4 by 7 and 7 by 9 lettering grids.

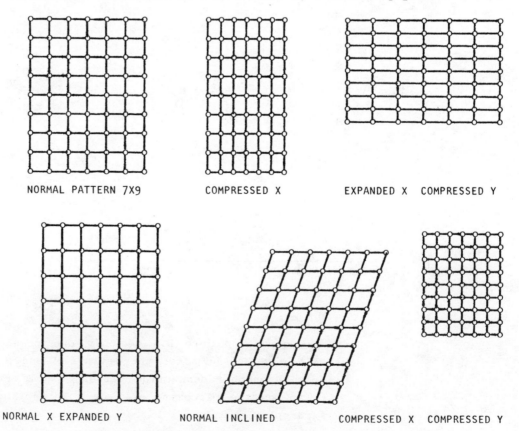

NORMAL PATTERN 7X9   COMPRESSED X   EXPANDED X COMPRESSED Y

NORMAL X EXPANDED Y   NORMAL INCLINED   COMPRESSED X COMPRESSED Y

FIGURE 3.3 Allowable variations of true 7 by 9 lettering grid.

42

FIGURE 3.4 Artistic variations possible for the lower- and uppercases.

Description of Equipment Used

An IBM 370 model 3033 with a work station similar to Figure 2.1 was used. Input and output were obtained for both 4 by 7 and 7 by 9 grid matrix lettering used as illustrations for this chapter. The lettering was displayed at the electronic work station video display direct-view storage terminal for previewing and/or modifications.

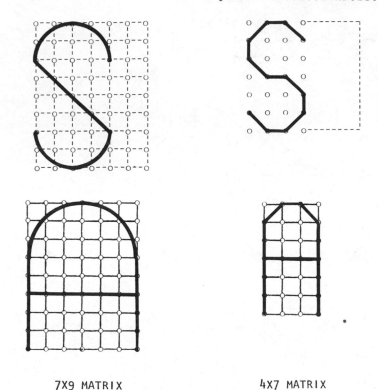

7X9 MATRIX   4X7 MATRIX

FIGURE 3.5   Comparison of A and S in different variations.

Figures for this chapter were then processed on the hard copy unit described in Chapter 2.

Codification of Lettering Fonts

Because the IBM 3033 has a great deal of storage, the fonts defining the lettering style currently being used are held in a device called a subroutine. The subroutine is read into the computer memory from its library storage location. To save more than one set of coded lettering fonts, more than one stored subroutine is required. In a general-purpose graphics software package this lettering subroutine is called SYMBOL. Because a special-purpose architectural font requires someone to specify each character line by line, it is stored under another label. Suppose the storage label LETTER is chosen for the 7 by 9 grid artistic font; the first line of the subroutine would be

    SUBROUTINE LETTER (XSCRN, YSCRN, CHT, ISTRNG, ANG, NCHRS)
where the items inside the parentheses describe the line of lettering to be displayed. First, xscrn and yscrn represent the X and Y locations on the video screen where the architectural letter-ing is to appear. Second, CHT sets the height of the 7 by 9 grid size for each character contained inside the line of lettering

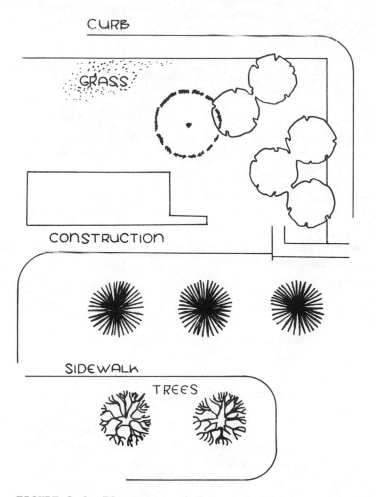

CURB

GRASS

CONSTRUCTION

SIDEWALK

TREES

FIGURE 3.6   Placement of 7 by 9 lettering on a display sketch.

called ISTRNG.   Third, ANG allows the designer to letter at any
desired angle provided the subroutine knows the number of characters
(NCHRS) inside ISTRNG.

For example, suppose two designers wish to display a typical
line of lettering below a floorplan.   The location of the line is 12
units in X and 1.5 in Y.   The lettering height should be 1/2 in. for
'FIRST FLOOR', which is to be displayed flat on the drawing sheet.
The designer types

```
CALL LETTER (1.2, 1.5, .5, 'FIRST FLOOR,' 0., 11).
```
This causes the subroutine stored under LETTER to be read and executed.   Architectural-style lettering appears on the video screen
in the proper location.

**METHOD OF
STORING
CHARACTERS**   How did the subroutine find the order of letters in the line 'FIRST
FLOOR'?   NCRS was indicated as 11 not 10; therefore the space
between the words can be found and matched.   ISTRNG is 11 characters

DATA ID(1)/1/

DATA IC (1), IC(2), IC(3), IC(4)/10606,20612,21212,21200/

DATA IC(5), IC(6), IC(7), IC(8)/20000,20012,20612,40606/

FIGURE 3.7   4 by 7 method of storing characters.

long.   Each character is located by ISTRNG (1) = F, ISTRNG (2) = I,
ISTRNG (3) = R, ISTRNG (4) = S, and ISTRNG (5) = T until all 11
storage locations have been filled.   The subroutine checks each
ISTRNG (I) location by the order of Table 3.1.   In other words, the
routine checks ISTRNG (1) under the special characters column and
does not find it; it then checks the numerics column, then the
communication column, and then the alpha column, where it locates
how to form an F.   Ten more trips through the columns of Table 3.1
and the entire line of lettering is complete.   This happens at the
speed of electronics so the designer does not have to wait - the
display appears to be instantaneous.

Two methods for storing characters present exist, the 4 by 7
and 7 by 9 grid types.   A comparison of both methods will now be
made using the first character from the first column of Table 3.1.
Figure 3.7 is the 4 by 7 method, and Figure 3.8 is the 7 by 9
method.

The 4 by 7 method of storing characters is done by data locations because the grid points never change; they are fixed in space.
The character data can therefore be compressed or packed in DATA
statements to take up less space.   The packing scheme is used
because the shape of the character is not changing and represents a
compromise between the amount of subroutine space saved and the
simplicity of the character generalized.   The 7 by 9 method requires
more lines of intersections inside the subroutine.   In fact, another
subroutine DRAWR is used by give the artistic appearance to the


```
100     Continue

        CALL DRAWR (0.,.5)

        CALL DRAWR (.5,0.)

        CALL DRAWR (.0,-1.)

        CALL DRAWR (-1.,0.)

        CALL DRAWR (0.,1.)

        CALL DRAWR (.5,0.)

        CALL DRAWR (0.,-5.)
```

FIGURE 3.8   7 by 9 method of storing characters.

letters generated. The 7 by 9 method requires seven times longer to display a simple character. The time involved is usually only a few thousandths of a second, but computer times are charges against running times (display periods), and therefore the 7 by 9 method is seven times more expensive to use.

CHARACTER PLOTTING SUBROUTINES

Both types of subroutines just described have common elements. Each uses tables of values (two index tables and one stroke table). Index Table 1 contains cross grid locations to Table 3.1 shown in this chapter. This first table is driven by the NCRS valve and sorted for Table 2. Index Table 2 contains the point locations for each of the characters in ISTRNG. And finally Table 3 contains actual stroke vectors for each single character. The third table is used as

1. Vector type (move, draw, last move, last draw)
2. X location on screen
3. Y location on screen

Generation of the display data requires that either method take place in the following stages:

1. The data for the character are located by the two outer index loops and unpacked.
2. The grid (4 by 7 or 7 by 9) is connected by predetermined individual point locations on the rows and columns of the grid pattern.
3. The width-height is computed or read from CHT.
4. Transformation ANG is calculated for rotation of the lettered line and spacing and is done by checking the preceding character in the line. If ANG = 0, this stage is omitted; if ANG > 0, then stage 4 is completed.
5. The required number of points in the stroke table is indexed, each stroke table is indexed to display multiple letters, and the last index completes the required line defining by ISTRNG.

Software Listing

It shall be pointed out that most software listings are protected by copyright laws and cannot be reproduced in a textbook. Users should contact the software vendor of their choice for detailed listings.

Grid Description

The grid for the 4 by 7 method represents equal distance points in a rectangle grid. The height of the rectangle is input through CHT.

For example, one unit is placed inside CHT, and there is 3/10 space between letters. In the case of the 7 by 9 grid method, the space between letters is contained inside the grid pattern. Initially the distances between points in the 7 by 9 method are set equal; however, these spacings may be changed rather easily. No provision for changing grid spacing is allowed in the 4 by 7 method.

Both subroutines assume that the display of the lettering is to begin at the lower left-hand corner of the line. In the 4 by 7 matrix an additional three grid spaces are spaced between letters, creating a square display area. The 7 by 9 uses as many of the grids as necessary, keeping in mind that 7 by 9 rectangles are placed side by side. The first method is quicker than the first but does not allow for proportion shaping of letters.

Character Manipulation

In addition to the obvious character manipulation such as grid height, rotation, carriage return, line feed, and space commands which both methods contain, special features for the 7 by 9 exist:

1. Factored heights. It is possible to program lettering routines where the first letter of a word is larger or smaller as follows:

ABCDEFG
HIJKLMN
OPQRSTU
VWXYZ

REFERENCE DRAWINGS:
PL 41   HA3E-008 Lighting Fixture Schedule
PL 42   HA3E-009 Conduit and Cable Schedule-Sheet 1
PL 89   HA3S-211 Outline and Details-Block 18-Sheet 2
PL 91   HA3S-213 Outline and Details-Block 18-Sheet 4
PL 137 HA3E-204 Light and Power Wiring Diagram-Sheet 2
PL 138 HA3E-205 Light and Power Conduits-Elevator
                   Tower-Sheet 1
PL 143 HA3E-212 Light and Power Conduits-Galleries
                   Sheet 1

1234567890

2.   Extension or compression of characters. The use of DFACT
     inside a stroke table causes pleasing results as illus-
     trated in Figure 3.1.

3.   Slope. The favored slope (inclined lettering) for the 4
     by 7 motif is set at $0°$ so that only upright characters
     are produced. Inclined slopes of any angle are possible
     for the 7 by 9 matrix.

4.   Rotation. A software facility provided for the DVST
     allows additional rotation of multiple lines of lettering
     and appears as follows:

```
SUBROUTINE ROTATE (DEGREE)
COMMON /TKTRNX/ TMINVX,TMINVY,TMAXVX,TMAXVY,TREALX,TREALY,
1 TIMAGX,TIMAGY,TRCOSF,TRSINF,TRSCAL,TRFACS,TRFACY,
2 TRPAR1,TRPAR2,TRPAR3,TRPAR4,TRPAR5,TRPAR6,KMOFLG(8),KPAD2,
3 KBAUDR,KGNFLG,KGRAFL,KHOMEY,KKMODE,KHORSZ,KVERSZ,KTBLSZ,
4 KSIZEF,KLMRGN,KRMRGN,KFACTR,KTERM,KLINE,KZAXIS,KBEAMX,KBEAMY,
5 KMOVEF,KPCHAR(5),KDASHT,KMINSX,KMINSY,KMAXSX,KMAXSY,KEYCON,
6 KINLFT,KOTLFT,KUNIT
  TRSINF=SIN (DEGREE/57.29578)
  TRCOSF=COS (DEGREE/57.29578)
```

5.   Weight. The thickness of a line that forms the character
     is not controlled by the subroutine but is a function of
     the display device.

6.   Spacing. Sometimes additional space is desired between
     individual letters in a line. Subroutines containing an
     enlarged space are possible by inserting a CALL MOVE
     between the first and second index tables of the subrou-
     tine letter for the 7 by 9 matrix method. No variable
     spacing is allowed for the 4 by 7.

CHAPTER SUMMARY   This chapter represented a dual approach to computer-generated
lettering. One called a 4 by 7 grid matrix method was described as
straight-line mechanical, while the second (7 by 9) was stylized
solely for the production of architectural lettering. Whereas all
former mechanical drawing styles existed in most computer graphics
software, none existed for artistic free forms. A free-form method
was developed whereby a designer could describe a unique style for
computer storage.

The purpose of this chapter was to provide basic information on
the automation of a heretofore difficult area of architectural
information. The unique lettering styles of various designers have
long been a trademark in architecture. It is now possible to cap-

ture these unique styles and reproduce them along with freehand sketches or mechanical drawing details to create a professional hand-drawn display image.

EXERCISES   1.   Architectural lettering can be computer-generated by entering the information from the work station keyboard. Each key stroke is identified by a short set of instructions for display. Choose one of the styles of lettering illustrated in this chapter and produce the lettering shown using a 4 by 7 point grid.

Dec/Hex	Glyph	Dec/Hex	Glyph	Dec/Hex	Glyph	Dec/Hex	Glyph	Dec/Hex	Glyph	Dec/Hex	Glyph	Dec/Hex	Glyph	Dec/Hex	Glyph
0 / 00	□	16 / 10	|	32 / 20	}	48 / 30	Σ	64 / 40		80 / 50	&	96 / 60	—	112 / 70	0
1 / 01	⬡	17 / 11	BS	33 / 21	{	49 / 31	÷	65 / 41	A	81 / 51	J	97 / 61	/	113 / 71	1
2 / 02	△	18 / 12	∧	34 / 22	μ	50 / 32	≤	66 / 42	B	82 / 52	K	98 / 62	S	114 / 72	2
3 / 03	+	19 / 13	≡	35 / 23	π	51 / 33	≥	67 / 43	C	83 / 53	L	99 / 63	T	115 / 73	3
4 / 04	X	20 / 14	→	36 / 24	φ	52 / 34	△	68 / 44	D	84 / 54	M	100 / 64	U	116 / 74	4
5 / 05	◇	21 / 15	CR	37 / 25	⊖	53 / 35	[	69 / 45	E	85 / 55	N	101 / 65	V	117 / 75	5
6 / 06	⧊	22 / 16	≠	38 / 26	ψ	54 / 36	]	70 / 46	F	86 / 56	Ø	102 / 66	W	118 / 76	6
7 / 07	⊠	23 / 17	±	39 / 27	×	55 / 37	\	71 / 47	G	87 / 57	P	103 / 67	X	119 / 77	7
8 / 08	Z	24 / 18	_	40 / 28	W	56 / 38	↑	72 / 48	H	88 / 58	Q	104 / 68	Y	120 / 78	8
9 / 09	Y	25 / 19	NUL	41 / 29	λ	57 / 39	√	73 / 49	I	89 / 59	R	105 / 69	Z	121 / 79	9
10 / 0A	⊠	26 / 1A		42 / 2A	∝	58 / 3A	‡	74 / 4A	¢	90 / 5A	|	106 / 6A	∞	122 / 7A	□
11 / 0B	✳	27 / 1B	∫	43 / 2B	δ	59 / 3B	‡	75 / 4B		91 / 5B	$	107 / 6B		123 / 7B	#
12 / 0C	⋈	28 / 1C	⊃	44 / 2C	∈	60 / 3C	←	76 / 4C	<	92 / 5C	×	108 / 6C	%	124 / 7C	©
13 / 0D	|	29 / 1D	∨	45 / 2D	η	61 / 3D	×	77 / 4D		93 / 5D	(	109 / 6D	—	125 / 7D	
14 / 0E	☆	30 / 1E	~	46 / 2E	SUP	62 / 3E	↑	78 / 4E	+	94 / 5E		110 / 6E	>	126 / 7E	=
15 / 0F	_	31 / 1F	≈	47 / 2F	SUB	63 / 3F	↓	79 / 4F	|	95 / 5F	¬	111 / 6F		127 / 7F	?

2. The variable 7 by 9 grid matrix designed for architects shown can be used to replace the SYMBOL-generated 4 by 7 font. Using this example, write a short list of instructions to be displayed upon a key enter of A through Z and 1 through 0.

3. Place the instructions completed in Exercise 2 into a subroutine labeled LETTER. Now two types of lettering are available for use at your work station.

4. The second type of lettering is completely variable in its shape. In this exercise and all following ones, complete the examples using the style of lettering called for.

NOTES:
1. For general notes see HA55-411.
2. Payment Items: [8.02] Miscellaneous steel, where indicated. [8.07] Transformer rail crossovers [8.08] Steel rails, splice bars, track bolts, rail clips, sole plates, and wheel stops shown in Details C and D, and Sections E-E and F-F. Exclude steel rails fabricated with removable beams shown in Section C-C.
3. Number of rail splices and approximate location are to be as shown in the plan.

5. (Courtesy of the U.S. Corps of Engineers, Vicksburg, Mississippi.)

RAIL DATA								
MARK	RAIL SIZE	RAIL CLIP		SOLE PLATE				REFERENCE DRAWINGS
		TYPE	NO. REQD.	SIZE	HOLE DIA.	D	NO. REQD.	
MK415-1	175# U.S.S.	CR175	976	4 x 3/4 x 1'-1"	1 1/4"	4 1/4"	476	HA55-024, 027, 030, 003 & 105
MK415-2	105# U.S.S.	CR128	1116	4 x 1/2 x 1'-0"	15/16"	3 1/4"	558	HA55-037, 214, 218, 220 & 222
MK415-3	40# U.S.S	114	136	4 x 1/2 x 0'-8"	11/16"	2 5/16"	68	HA55-105

6. (Courtesy of the U.S. Corps of Engineers, Vicksburg, Mississippi.)

☐ GENERAL NOTES.
1. ALL RAILING AND GRATING PANEL CONNECTIONS TO BE SHOP WELDED. ALL WELDS TO BE GROUND SMOOTH AND FINISHED TO MATCH ADJACENT SURFACES.
2. STAIR RAILING SIMILAR TO PIER RAIL. GRATING PANELS AROUND PIER AND LANDING AREA AT EL. 487.0 AND IN PANEL ON LANDWARD SIDE AT EL. 512.0 ONLY.
3. GRATING PANELS TO BE MADE OF ALUMINUM GRATING 1" DEEP WITH 15/16"(MAX) x 4" BAR SPACING, BARS 1/4" THICK. GRATING FRAMED WITH 1 1/2" x 1 1/2" ALUMINUM CHANNELS.
4. ALUMINUM TUBING TO BE HEAVY DUTY TYPE WITH MINIMUM WALL THICKNESS .125".
5. ALL POSTS TO BE SET IN SLEEVES AND ANCHORED WITH LEAD, EXCEPT STAIR RAILING.
6. PAYMENT ITEM [26.01] FISHING PIER.

7.   (Courtesy of the U.S. Corps of Engineers, Vicksburg, Mississippi.)

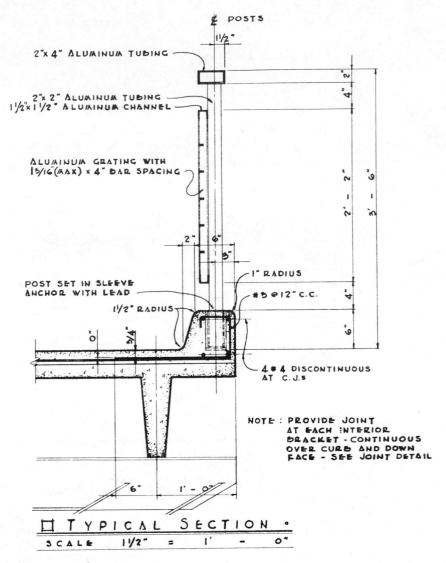

8.   (Courtesy of the U.S. Corps of Engineers, Vicksburg, Mississippi.)

| | | | DIMENSIONS | | | | | | | NO. PER BOLT | |
| | | | | | | | | | | 803 | |
COLUMN LINE	NO REQ'D	BOLT DIAM	A	B	C	D	PROJ-ECTION	PIPE SLEEVE	PLATE SIZE	NO. NUTS REQ'D.	NO. CUT WASHERS REQ'D.
4	1	$2\frac{3}{4}$"	5'-1"	4'-0"	1'-1"	0'-7"	1'-1"	$3\frac{1}{2}$	$9 \times 1\frac{1}{4} \times 1'-11$"	2	2
6a	1	$1\frac{3}{4}$"	3'-6"	2'-8"	0'-10"	0'-4"	0'-10"	3	$7\frac{1}{2} \times 1 \times 1'-3\frac{1}{2}$"	2	2
6b	1	$1\frac{1}{2}$"	3'-1	2'-3"	0'-10"	$0'-2\frac{1}{8}$"	0'-10"	$2\frac{1}{2}$	$6\frac{1}{2} \times \frac{3}{4} \times 0'-11\frac{1}{2}$"	2	2
7a	1	$1\frac{1}{2}$"	3'-4"	2'-3"	1'-1"	0'-3"	1'-1"	$2\frac{1}{2}$	$6\frac{1}{2} \times \frac{3}{4} \times 1'-0\frac{1}{2}$"	2	2
8	1	$1\frac{7}{8}$"	3'-10"	2'-10"	1'-0"	0'-4"	1'-0"	3	$8 \times 1\frac{1}{8} \times 1'-4$"	2	2
9a	1	$1\frac{1}{2}$"	3'-1"	2'-3"	0'-10"	$0'-2\frac{1}{8}$"	0'-10"	$2\frac{1}{2}$	$6\frac{1}{2} \times \frac{3}{4} \times 0'-11\frac{1}{2}$"	2	2

9. (Courtesy of the U.S. Corps of Engineers, Vicksburg, Mississippi.)

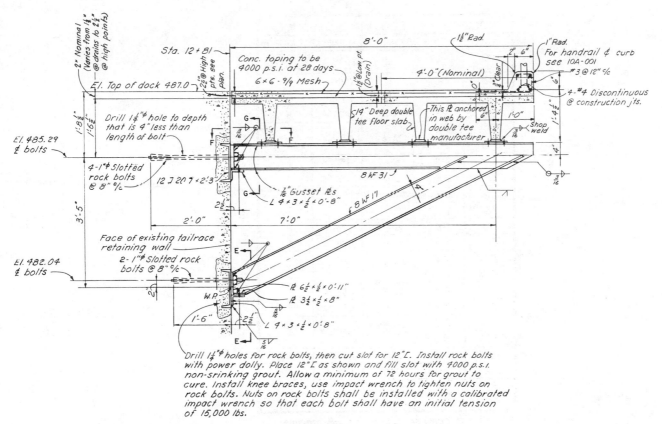

Drill $1\frac{1}{4}"\phi$ holes for rock bolts, then cut slot for 12"Ꮯ. Install rock bolts with power dolly. Place 12"Ꮯ as shown and fill slot with 4000 p.s.i. non-srinking grout. Allow a minimum of 72 hours for grout to cure. Install knee braces, use impact wrench to tighten nuts on rock bolts. Nuts on rock bolts shall be installed with a calibrated impact wrench so that each bolt shall have an initial tension of 15,000 lbs.

SECTION A-A
(TYPICAL KNEE BRACKET)
SCALE: 1" = 1'-0"

10. (Courtesy of the U.S. Corps of Engineers, Vicksburg, Mississippi.)

COLUMN AND FOOTING SCHEDULE				
COLUMN NO.	DIMENSIONS		REINFORCEMENT	
	A	B	BARS "a"	NO. OF BARS "b"
E9	2'-0"	4'-0"	7#8C1	4
E10	3'-0"	7'-6"	7#10C3	7
E11	2'-4"	6'-6"	6#11C4	6
E12	2'-0"	※5'-6"	4#10C2	5
E13	2'-0"			
E14	2'-4"	6'-6"	6#11C4	6
E15	2'-8"	6'-6"	4#11C4	6
E16	2'-0"	※5'-6"	4#10C2	5
E17	2'-0"			
E18	2'-0"	6'-6"	6#11C4	6
E19	2'-0"	6'-6"	6#11C4	6
E20	2'-0"	※5'-6"	4#10C2	5
E21	2'-0"			
E22	2'-4"	6'-6"	6#11C4	6
E23	2'-8"	6'-6"	6#11C4	6
E24	2'-0"	※5'-6"	4#10C2	5
E25	2'-0"			
E26	2'-0"	6'-6"	6#11C4	6
E27	2'-4"	6'-6"	6#11C4	6
E28	2'-0"	※5'-6"	4#10C2	5
E29	2'-0"			

※ Common footing for both columns

11. (Courtesy of the U.S. Corps of Engineers, Vicksburg, Mississippi.)

REINFORCEMENT SCHEDULE NO. 5S-250

Drawn by ..J.J...Checked by..M.A.V...   Sheet / of 3

TYPE	NO. REQD.	SIZE	LENGTH	A	B	C	D	REMARKS
K1	8	#4	3-9	1-2	1-0	1-10		Section E-E
L11	6	#4	11-0	1-0				
	13	#4	13-6					
	6	#4	10-0					
	6	#4	6-0					
	18	#4	5-6					
	8	#4	4-0					Section E-E
	24	#4	22-0					Section F-F
	8	#4	21-6					
	40	#4	16-3					
	3	#4	19-0					Section F-F
L11	13	#4	11-0	1-0				Section G-G
	17	#4	12-0					Section G-G
	13	#4	10-0					
	52	#4	2-0					Section H-H
J8	6	#4	4-9	2-0	0-10			
	14	#4	19-3					
	12	#4	12-3					
	28	#4	13-0					
	2	#4	8-0					
	2	#4	7-9					
	12	#4	6-3					
	8	#4	4-0					Section H-H

BAR BENDING DIAGRAMS

TYPE K

12. (Courtesy of the U.S. Corps of Engineers, Vicksburg, Mississippi.)

ANCHOR BOLT SCHEDULE

PAYMENT ITEMS	MARK	NO. REQD.	TYPE BOLT	BOLT DIA.	A	B	C	D	PIPE SLEEVE	PLATE SIZE	NO. PER BOLT NUTS	WASHERS	LOCATION
8.03	MK411-1	32	A	$\frac{3}{4}''$	10"	7"	3"	—	2"	$3\frac{1}{2} \times \frac{1}{4} \times 0'\text{-}3\frac{1}{2}''$	2	2	Erection Bay, Oil tanks El.466.50
8.03	MK411-2	6	B	$\frac{3}{4}''$	1'-0"	—	3"	$3\frac{1}{2}''$	—	$3 \times \frac{3}{8} \times 0'\text{-}7''$	2	2	Erection Bay, Unwatering sump
8.03	MK411-3	8	B	$\frac{5}{8}''$	10"	—	$2\frac{1}{2}''$	4"	—	$3 \times \frac{3}{8} \times 0'\text{-}7''$	2	2	Erection Bay, Station sump
8.03	MK411-4	12	A	$\frac{3}{4}''$	$6\frac{3}{4}''$	5"	$1\frac{3}{4}''$	—	2"	$3\frac{1}{2} \times \frac{1}{4} \times 0'\text{-}3\frac{1}{2}''$	1	1	Service Bay, Air receiver tanks, El. 466.50
8.02	MK411-5	60	A	1"	2'-2"	1'-6"	6"	—	2"	$4\frac{1}{2} \times \frac{1}{2} \times 0'\text{-}4\frac{1}{2}''$	2	2	Generator Bay, Gate frame
8.02	MK411-6	90	B	$\frac{3}{4}''$	$1'\text{-}8\frac{1}{2}''$	1'-0"	7"	$3\frac{1}{2}''$	2"	$3\frac{1}{2} \times \frac{1}{4} \times 0'\text{-}7''$	2	2	Generator Bay, Sill beam
8.03	MK411-7	16	A	$\frac{7}{8}''$	1'-5"	$1'\text{-}1\frac{1}{4}''$	$3\frac{1}{2}''$	—	2"	$4 \times \frac{3}{8} \times 0'\text{-}4''$	2	2	Erection Bay, Sump pump bases, El.485.50
8.03	MK411-8	2	B	$\frac{7}{8}''$	1'-5"	$1'\text{-}1\frac{1}{4}''$	$3\frac{1}{2}''$	$4\frac{1}{2}''$	2"	$4 \times \frac{3}{8} \times 1'\text{-}0''$	2	2	Erection Bay, Sump pump bases, El.485.50
8.09	MK411-9	81	D	$\frac{3}{4}''$	1'-0"	—	2"	—	—	$6 \times \frac{3}{8} \times 0'\text{-}7''$	1	1	Draft tube deck & Retaining wall guardrail
8.03	MK411-10	486	B	1"	1'-6"	$1'\text{-}1\frac{1}{4}''$	$4\frac{1}{2}''$	$8\frac{1}{2}''$	2"	$4\frac{1}{2} \times \frac{1}{2} \times 1'\text{-}1''$	2	2	Gantry crane rails El.512.0
8.03	MK411-11	24	C	1"	$2\frac{3}{4}''$	—	$1\frac{3}{4}''$	—	—	—	1	1	Gantry crane rails El.512.0
8.02	MK411-12	48	B	$\frac{3}{4}''$	1'-4"	$1'\text{-}0\frac{1}{4}''$	$1\frac{3}{4}''$	4"	2"	$3\frac{1}{2} \times \frac{1}{4} \times 0'\text{-}8''$	1	1	Service Bay, Roof beams
8.02	MK411-13	36	B	$\frac{3}{4}''$	$1'\text{-}8\frac{3}{4}''$	1'-2"	$2\frac{1}{2}''$	$5\frac{1}{2}''$	2"	$3\frac{1}{2} \times \frac{1}{2} \times 0'\text{-}9''$	2	1	Service Bay, Floor beams El.527.58
8.02	MK411-14	3	B	$1\frac{1}{2}''$	3'-0"	2'-3"	9"	7"	$2\frac{1}{2}''$	$6\frac{1}{2} \times \frac{3}{4} \times 1'\text{-}1\frac{1}{2}''$	2	2	Erection Bay, Deck beams El.512.0

13. (Courtesy of the U.S. Corps of Engineers, Vicksburg, Mississippi.)

JACK SUPPORT SETTING SCHEDULE					
NO.	X	Y	El. top of Pipe Column	El. top of Conc. Pedestal	Length of 8"ø Pipe Col.
I	-30'-11"	+48'-6"			
II	-30'-9"	+40'-9"			
III	-30'-5½"	+31'-0"	476.79	475.19	1'-7¾"
IV	-30'-4"	+21'-6"			
V	-29'-11¼"	+12'-0"			
VI	-29'-7½"	+4'-6"			
VII	-28'-9"	-3'-10"			
VIII	-26'-4"	-11'-0"			
IX	-22'-3"	-17'-1"	477.04		1'-10¼"
X	-16'-10"	-21'-10"			
XI	-10'-4"	-25'-2"			
XII	-3'-6"	-26'-4"			
XIII	+3'-4"	-25'-8"		475.54	1'-6"
XIV	+9'-7"	-23'-6"			
XV	+15'-0"	-19'-9"			
XVI	+19'-1"	-14'-10"			
XVII	+21'-9"	-9'-1"	477.54		2'-0"
XVIII	+22'-8"	-3'-0"			
XIX	+21'-3"	+4'-5"		477.54	
XX	+15'-7½"	+13'-5½"			
XXI	+7'-9"	+17'-4"			

14. (Courtesy of the U.S. Corps of Engineers, Vicksburg, Mississippi.)

ROOM	FLOOR		BASE		WAINSCOT		WALLS		CEILING	
	FINISH	PAINT	FINISH	PAINT	FINISH	PAINT	FINISH	PAINT	FINISH	PAINT
El.466.5										
Stair A †	Steel Stairs	—	—	—	—	—	Conc.	Semi-gloss	—	—
Stair B †	Steel Stairs	—	—	—	—	—	Conc.		—	—
All areas	Integral conc.		—		—		Conc. & conc. brk	—	Conc.	
El.474.5										
Stair A †	Steel Stairs		—	—	—	—	Conc.	Semi-gloss	—	—
Air Comp. Rm.	Integral conc.		—		—		Conc.		Conc.	
El.485.5										
Stair A †	Steel Stairs	—	—	—	—	—	Conc.	Semi-gloss	—	—
Stair B †	Steel Stairs	—	—	—	—	—	Conc.		—	—
All areas	2" bond conc.		—		—		Conc. & conc. brk	—	Conc.	—
El.498.5										
Stair A †	Steel Stairs	—		—		—		Conc.	Semi-gloss	—	—
Toilet	Cer. mos. tile		Cer. tile		Cer. tile		K.C.P.	Gloss	K.C.P.	Gloss
Shower	Cer. mos. tile		Cer. tile		—	—	Cer. tile		K.C.P.	Gloss
Drying	Cer. mos. tile		Cer. tile		—	—	Cer. tile		K.C.P.	Gloss
Locker	Cer. mos. tile		Cer. tile		Cer. tile		K.C.P.	Gloss	K.C.P.	Gloss
Cable tunnel	Integral conc.		—	—	—		Conc.		Conc.	
Cable spreading	2" bond conc.		—		—		Conc.	—	Conc.	
Switchgear gallery	2" bond conc.		—		—		Conc.	—	Conc.	
Stair C *	Steel Stairs		—		—		—		—	—
Stair B †	Steel Stairs		—		—		—		—	—
Turbine room	3" bond conc.		—		—		Conc.	—	Conc.	—
Corridor	2" bond conc.		—		—		Conc. & conc. brk	—	Conc.	

15. (Courtesy of the U.S. Corps of Engineers, Vicksburg, Mississippi.)

ROOM	DOOR NO.	ROUGH OP'NG WIDTH	HEIGHT	DOOR SIZE WIDTH	HEIGHT	THKNESS	DOOR TYPE	MATERIAL DOOR	FRAME	FIRE R'TG	FRAME TYPE	DOOR OPER'N
El. 466.5												
Stair A	101	3'-4½"	7'-2¼"	3'-0"	7'-0"	1¾"	K	H.M.	Pres.St.	B	A	Swing
Penstock gallery	102	5'-4½"	7'-2¼"	2.(2'-6")	7'-0"	1¾"	B	H.M.	Pres.St.		A	Swing
Stair B	103	3'-4½"	7'-2¼"	3'-0"	7'-0"	1¾"	K	H.M.	Pres.St.	B	A	Swing
Paint locker	104	3'-4"	7'-2"	3'-0"	7'-0"	1¾"	A	H.M.	Pres.St.		B	Swing
Paint locker	104A	3'-4"	7'-2"			1¾"Min.	E	H.M.		B		Sliding
Water treatment rm.	105	3'-4"	7'-2"	3'-0"	7'-0"	1¾"	A	H.M.	Pres.St.		B	Swing
Sewage treatment	106	3'-4"	7'-2"	3'-0"	7'-0"	1¾"	A	H.M.	Pres.St.		B	Swing
CO₂ room	107	3'-4"	7'-2"	3'-0"	7'-0"	1¾"	A	H.M.	Pres.St.		B	Swing
Oil purification	108	3'-6"	7'-0"			1¾"Min.	E	H.M.		B	F	Sliding
Oil purification	109	3'-6"	7'-0"			1¾"Min.	E	H.M.		B	F	Sliding
Oil storage	110	3'-6"	7'-0"			1¾"Min.	E	H.M.		B	F	Sliding
Oil storage	111	3'-6"	7'-0"			1¾"Min.	E	H.M.		B	F	Sliding
Sta. & Unwatering sumps	112	3'-4"	7'-2"	3'-0"	7'-0"	1¾"	A	H.M.	Pres.St.		B	Swing
El. 474.5												
Stair A	201	3'-4½"	7'-2¼"	3'-0"	7'-0"	1¾"	K	H.M.	Pres.St.	B	A	Swing
El. 485.5												
Stair A	301	3'-4½"	7'-2¼"	3'-0"	7'-0"	1¾"	K	H.M.	Pres.St.	B	A	Swing
Stair A	302	3'-4½"	7'-2¼"	3'-0"	7'-0"	1¾"	K	H.M.	Pres.St.	B	A	Swing
Maintenance shop	303	5'-6"	7'-2"	2(2'-7")	7'-0"	1¾"	B	H.M.	Pres.St.		A	Swing
Electrical shop	304	5'-6"	7'-2"	2(2'-7")	7'-0"	1¾"	B	H.M.	Pres.St.		A	Swing
Maintenance shop	305	8'-0"	7'-0"			1¾"	L	H.M.			F	Sliding
Maintenance shop	306	5'-4½"	7'-2¼"	2(2'-6")	7'-0"	1¾"	B	H.M.	Pres.St.		A	Swing
El. 498.5												
Stair A	401	3'-4½"	7'-2¼"	3'-0"	7'-0"	1¾"	K	H.M.	Pres.St.	B	A	Swing
Stair B	402	3'-4½"	7'-2¼"	3'-0"	7'-0"	1¾"	K	H.M.	Pres.St.	B	A	Swing
Locker room	403	3'-4"	7'-2"	3'-0"	7'-0"	1¾"	D	H.M.	Pres.St.		B	Swing
Corridor	404	5'-6"	7'-2"	2(2'-7")	7'-0"	1¾"	B	H.M.	Pres.St.		A	Swing
El. 512.0 & 515.0												
Stair A	501	3'-4½"	7'-2¼"	3'-0"	7'-0"	1¾"	K	H.M.	Pres.St.	B	C	Swing
Toilet	502	3'-4"	7'-2"	3'-0"	7'-0"	1¾"	A1	H.M.	Pres.St.		D	Swing
First aid room	503	3'-4"	7'-2"	3'-0"	7'-0"	1¾"	A	H.M.	Pres.St.		D	Swing
Corridor	504			2(2'-7½")	7'-0"	1¾"	F	Al.&glass	Al.			Swing
Lobby	505			2(2'-7½")	7'-0"	1¾"	F	Al.&glass	Al.			Swing
Lobby	506	3'-4"	7'-2"	3'-0"	7'-0"	1¾"	A	H.M.	Pres.St.		E	Swing
Women	507	3'-4"	7'-2"	3'-0"	7'-0"	1¾"	A1	H.M.	Pres.St.		D	Swing
Men	508	3'-4"	7'-2"	3'-0"	7'-0"	1¾"	A1	H.M.	Pres.St.		D	Swing
Janitor's Closet	509	3'-4"	7'-2"	3'-0"	7'-0"	1¾"	A1	H.M.	Pres.St.		D	Swing
Observation room	510			3'-0"	7'-0"	1¾"	G	Al.&glass	Al.			Swing
Toilet	511	3'-4"	7'-2"	3'-0"	7'-0"	1¾"	A1	H.M.	Pres.St.		D	Swing
Kitchen	512	3'-4"	7'-2"	3'-0"	7'-0"	1¾"	D1	H.M.	Pres.St.		D	Swing
Communication equip.	513	3'-4"	7'-2"	3'-0"	7'-0"	1¾"	A	H.M.	Pres.St.		D	Swing
Instrument room	514	3'-4"	7'-2"	3'-0"	7'-0"	1¾"	A	H.M.	Pres.St.		D	Swing
Battery room	515	3'-4"	7'-2"	3'-0"	7'-0"	1¾"	A	H.M.	Pres.St.		D	Swing
Motor generator rm.	516	3'-10"	7'-2"	3'-6"	7'-0"	1¾"	A	H.M.	Pres.St.		D	Swing
Records & files	517	3'-4"	7'-2"	3'-0"	7'-0"	1¾"	D	H.M.	Pres.St.		D	Swing
Stair C	518	7'-4"	8'-8"	2(3'-6")	8'-6"	1¾"	K	Al.	Al.		G	Swing
Control room	519	7'-4"	8'-8"	2(3'-6")	8'-6"	1¾"	B	H.M.	Pres.St.	B	H	Swing
Stair B	520	3'-4½"	7'-2¼"	3'-0"	7'-0"	1¾"	J	Al.	Al.		G	Swing

4 Computer-Assisted Sketching Techniques

Much of the design information in an architectural project file is in freehand sketch form. It would be impractical to design a structure by starting with a set of detail drawings before preliminary concepts are discussed and approved by the client (owner). It would also be even more difficult to design from purely verbal descriptions. The research and planning for a structure include idea sketches for communication to the client, site description and preliminary diagrams, notes, dimensions, and specifications. All these will be needed later in the preparation of a complete set of working drawings. Computer-assisted sketching is introduced in this chapter directly after the automated lettering so that the quality of the lettering, sketching, and working drawings will be equal.

Throughout the material in this chapter the concept of computer assistance is stressed, beginning with the tools (hardware) necessary and instructions for successful operation to the applications and purpose of speculation graphic construction. The chapter ends with sample computer-generated preliminary sketches of an office project containing floorplan layout, design sizes for work spaces, and quick planning sketches involving elevation and sections.

FREEHAND DATABASE CONSTRUCTION

Many technical reports have been written about the computer and its role in modern architectural design practice, and for the most part these studies have tried to justify or ridicule the computer as a

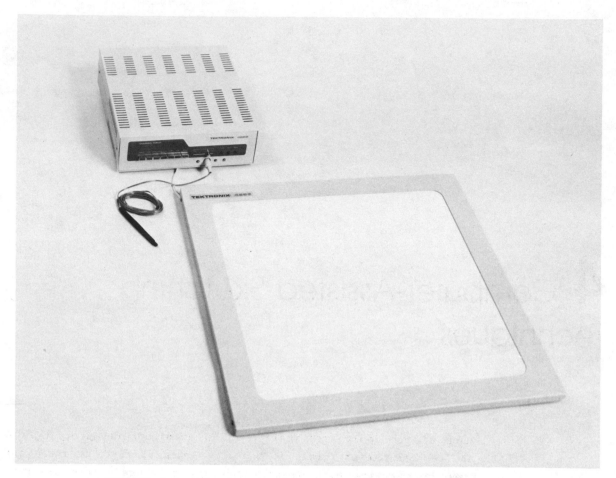

FIGURE 4.1   Electronic data tablet.   (Courtesy of Tektronix, Inc., Beaverton, Oregon.)

replacement for an artist.   In an age of increasing automation an energetic discussion has developed around the human-computer relationship.   The advent of computer graphics for engineers has underscored this relationship.   In this case the relationship has meant, "let the human do the design, and the computer will carry out the drafting work."   The results have been excellent for mechanical details requiring little freedom of line expression, freehand sketches, or shading for rendering.   The tacit assumption made by engineers is that the computer is not capable of this freedom of line expression or that the software is too difficult to write for the end results.   This chapter was written solely for the purpose of filling the gap in architectural engineering graphics known as freehand database construction.

What has been lacking is a technique which can achieve a degree of coupling for human input (sketching) and machine output (computer display and enhancement of freehand sketches).   This coupling must not force the architect, engineer, or designer to change thinking habits, language habits, or graphic response habits. In the course of the examples shown in this chapter, the reader will understand how this coupling is possible. The computer manufacturers have been striving to make this coupling by graphic input devices which attempt to give a designer an electronic medium close to the natural or professional frame of reference--this is a powerful step in the right direction. The manufacturers have done little to match an architect's habits of sketching to the electronics devices. This text is an attempt to narrow this gap. Yet even with a user's understanding of this coupling process (see Figure 4.1), some devices are ideally suited for this matching.

USE OF THE
GRAPHICS TABLET

If one studies our short but dynamic history in the computer graphics industry, it is possible to note a few manufacturers who have understood the problem of freehand database construction. This situation prompted some unnamed researcher to invert the data tablet, shown in Figure 4.1. This drawing-board-like device allowed a user to simply point at a spot on its surface and record this spot as an X and Y location in computer memory. The memory location could then be used to display a dot on a video screen or locate a pen on a plotter, and hence the name data tablet became graphics tablet out of this usage.

Several years after the invention of the data tablet the preceding graphic capabilities were recognized as having architectural value. The graphics tablet user has three techniques available:

1. DRAW2D: Freehand movements across the tablet face are read and stored as two-dimensional database.
2. DRAWSP: for tablet input of two-dimensional objects on a plane in three-dimensional space.
3. Drawings: for tablet input of contour line database.

To operate the graphics tablet shown in Figure 4.1, it must be connected to a computer terminal such as that shown in Figure 4.2. This device is called a direct-view storage terminal (DVST) and contains a video display area plus keyboard. The keyboard is the input side of the terminal, and the video screen is the output side of the terminal. By the use of a graphics tablet one can see immediately, in a sketch format, the results of touching the tablet surface. This response is immediate (less than a second), allowing an architectural designer to make corrections or monitor the results of the inputs.

These three principles of graphic input, storage, and obtaining video response are the basic ingredients of the freehand database

FIGURE 4.2   Direct-view storage terminal (DVST).   (Courtesy of
Tektronix, Inc., Beaverton, Oregon.)

column is the Y column, and the fourth column is the pen control (up
to down).

Mouse. A mouse-looking device is used when a paper sketch is not
needed. If a plastic overlay were used on the tablet surface, the
mouse could be positioned over a preprinted symbol on a menu list
and traced for input as a data file seen earlier. The mouse is
quicker than using an electric pencil in this case.

Joystick. This control stick resembles a tiny pilot's control
stick and is used to move the cursor on the DVST screen. By locating points with the cursor, the designer may locate lines of data in
a file that need to be changed or deleted. In this fashion lines
may be selected and removed from the data list and therefore selec-
tively erased when the data file is read back to the DVST or to a
pen plotter.

PURPOSE OF
SPECULATION
GRAPHIC
CONSTRUCTION

The purpose of computer-assisted sketching is to make a user ap-
proaching the study of architectural design a highly productive
individual. A user qualified in the use of a data tablet can assist
in simple research procedures and orthographic methods. The user
must have artistic ability--the computer only stores and repeats the
designer's sketch in various formats in a very fast time frame.
These elements are basic to the speculative nature of architectural
sketching.

Communication to the Client

Freehand sketching is the best means of capturing, developing, and
storing ideas in the planning stage of an architectural project.
The principle and procedures are simple, and only a few basic techniques are needed. Following the procedures from the last section
of this chapter, a user may prepare an electronics work station to
accept, modify, store, and reproduce sketches that can be shown to a
client.

Figures 4.3-4.9 represent a computer-assisted client series
beginning with the entrance to his or her office (Figure 4.3).
After entering (Figure 4.4), the client is taken to the second
floor. Leaving the escalator, the client can see the general office
arrangement (Figure 4.5). The client may move around the office

FIGURE 4.3 Client sketch (entrance).

(Figure 4.6), passing by a typical suite (Figure 4.7); he or she may
enter the suite (Figure 4.8) or may see how the boardroom is
arranged (Figure 4.9).

   If the client wishes to change anything, the sketches are
stored in data files, as described earlier, ready for modifications.
The computerized procedure is ideally suited to an inexpensive paper
for input and ease of organization of ideals as seen in the series
in Figures 4.3-4.9. The best parts of previous design sketches can
be saved, and the total sketches can be improved without tedious
redrawing.

   Good freehand client sketches look freehand. Do not try to
duplicate or trace mechanical drawings on a data tablet as sketches.
At the start, too much precision in tracing drawings wastes time.
The detailed drawing can be produced after the client's approval, as

FIGURE 4.4   Client sketch (escalator).

shown in Chapters 7 and 8.   The following are a few pointers to data
tablet users:

1.   Use free arm motion with the electric pencil.
2.   Avoid a cramped finger stroke.
3.   Do not make all corners precise, but let them cross.
4.   Make sketches fit the DVST screen as shown in Figures 4.3–
     4.9.
5.   Multiple lines are often more effective than single lines.
6.   Be careful of proportions; don't worry about the actual
     dimensions of the project.
7.   Try to avoid small details in client sketches; the overall
     effect is more important.
8.   Use pinhead or other simplified human figures, trees, etc.,
     to give depth and natural effect.

FIGURE 4.5 Client sketch (office arrangement).

Site Description

The client and the site determine the design of a structure. Do not
try to enter client sketches until all the information regarding the
site has been assembled. A structure that works well when faced
north might be unsatisfactory facing another direction. A client
may not always be a single person; more often a group of people
determine the computer-assisted sketching technique used. In Figure
4.10 a church board will decide on the site arrangement. This is a
more realistic situation. Architects and planners have many more
projects for group clients than they have for single clients. The
largest part of the site description problem lies in executing the

FIGURE 4.6 Client sketch (work area).

half-formed ideas of the group. They usually know approximately
what they want and can afford, but not how to develop, refine, or
express their ideas.

Research and Planning

A site planning checklist is sometimes used with the clients to
determine types of parking, plantings, sidewalk placement, and
building orientation. This method helps to avoid change, extra
visits to the site, extra meetings with the clients, or unnecessary
work. It sometimes forces the clients to organize their thoughts
and in the final analysis be happier with their planning task.

FIGURE 4.7 Client sketch (suite).

The client's needs and desires must be the starting point in research and planning an architectural project. As in Figure 4.10, some of the factors involved are simple and need no explanation, while others are more subtle:

1. The size of the church membership determines the size of the site and structure.
2. The distribution by age and family units will determine the number of automobiles that will enter and exit the site.

FIGURE 4.8   Client sketch (inside of suite).

3.   The amount of money available for land purchase and con-
     struction of structures will affect the quality and size
     of the project.

4.   Religion practices of church membership will determine if
     special-purpose rooms are needed in structures.

5.   The educational preference of church membership will
     determine if daily or weekly school facilities are re-
     quired. (School-plant planning is a field by itself.)

6.   Special interests or social habits of the church member-
     ship, such as maintaining a church library, will determine
     the need for this area.

FIGURE 4.9   Client sketch (boardroom).

7.   The client board ideas, such as number of restrooms, architectural style, and colors, should be worked into the planning before sketches are input for computer storage.

THE PRELIMINARY SKETCH   When designing a structure such as shown in Figure 4.10, the first sketches are called preliminary study sketches. They may be pictorials or orthographic sketches. The purpose of this type of sketch is to experiment with possible solutions to the research and planning data sheet problems. These solutions do not usually come to mind in a finished detailed drawing form. They instead develop through knowledge of the client's desires and the research into space requirements, building site, structure orientation, and other factors listed earlier.

Although the floorplan is usually the first sketch started, it is a good idea to study how the building slope and site size are interrelated. The remainder of this chapter discusses this inter-

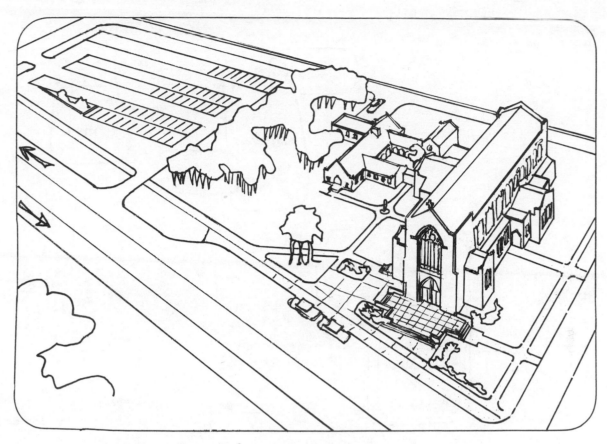

FIGURE 4.10 Site description for church.

relationship and how to generate quick elevation or section sketches.

Floorplan Layout

When all data from architect and client meetings have been gathered, work may begin on the preliminary sketch of the floorplan. This process must be as complete and detailed as possible to avoid back-tracking and wasted effort.

The technique for preliminary sketching is recommended. Sketch the desired floor areas as balloons on the data tablet (see Figure 4.11). Use approximate position and avoid straight lines or measurement for this step. Straight lines as in sharp rectangles tend to discourage experiment and make it difficult to flow one area into another. The relative areas of the balloons can be established from the checklist or client estimates. Use the erase function of DRAW2D to manipulate different balloon arrangements. When the shape and organization of the overall plan begin to look right, then start to

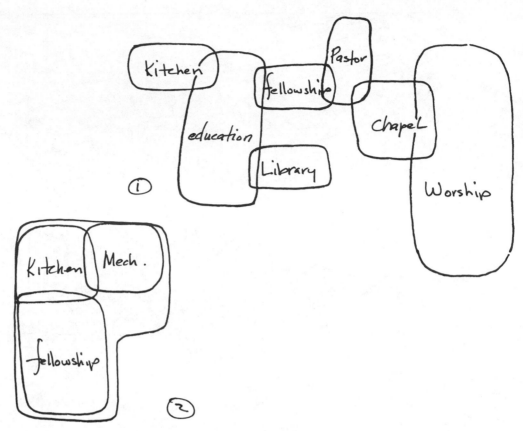

FIGURE 4.11   Balloon sketch of floor area.

straighten lines and square off corners as shown in Figure 4.12.
Try more than one solution. Once the sketch reaches this stage, the
client chooses the scheme liked best.

     The refinement is a one-line floor plan, at a small scale,
where the thickness of walls is not shown. When used as an outside
wall, the single line will represent the outside of the wall. As an
inside wall the line will represent the centerline of the wall.

Determining Building Slope and Size

After the floor plan for the structure has been entered into DRAW2D,
the user may begin to decide how the structure will fit the site. A
preliminary plot plan sketch is a plan view of the site, the building, and all outside work in connection with the project. The outside work includes all concrete and paving work, location of utilities, determination of building slope, and site structure, such as
covered walks or arbors.

     Before starting the determination of the building slope and
site plan, the data tablet user should be familiar with the use of
contour lines and lot lines and the problems of setbacks and ease-

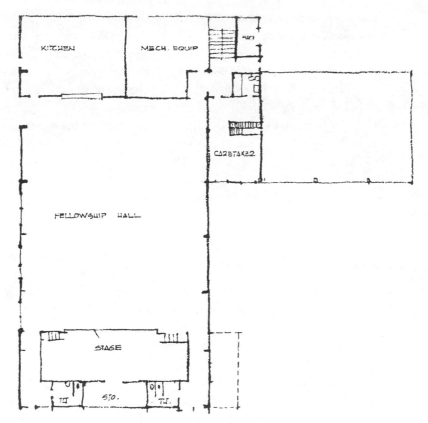

FIGURE 4.12   Refinement of balloon concepts.

ments.   A contour line is represented on the preliminary site plan
as an intersection of an imaginary horizontal plane with the surface
of the ground.   The vertical distance between contour lines is
called the contour interval.

     Building slope is determined after the building is placed on
site so that groundwater will drain away from the structure.   A
simple way of visualizing contours which describe the building slope
is to imagine the water level of a lake; as the water level drops,
it leaves marks on the slope line.   When these marks are viewed from
an airplane, they would represent contour lines.   All the marks
together would represent a contour map of the shore around a lake.
Suppose the building is the lake and the reverse process takes
place.   The water would run away from the building and not into it.

Quick Elevation and Sections

At this point some sketches of the exterior elevations of the church
should be input from the data tablet.   To do this, it will be necessary to determine the type of structural system to be used.   The
first step is to establish the type of framing system, especially

floor framing. Most church groups have strong ideas about interior elevations, what they can see, but care little about the invisible parts of the structure. Wood versus concrete exposure in the worship (nave) area of the structure is often discussed.

However, the type of floor construction will affect the overall height of the church above the ground level. Generally, a concrete floor will be 6 to 8 in. above the building slope contours, while a wood floor will be anywhere from 16 to 20 in. above. Concrete floors, either poured in place, precast, or prestressed slabs, are used because of economy and durability.

Many types of framing systems are also used; some of the more common types for churches are the following:

1.   Walls:
     a.   Masonry unit with brick or stone face
     b.   Metal stud, sheet material, and facing
     c.   Modular post and beam
2.   Roofs:
     a.   Wood with A-frame
     b.   Concrete for hyperbolic paraboloid shells
     c.   Flat tar and gravel over built-ups
     d.   Slat, stone, metal, etc.
3.   Floors:
     a.   Concrete, ceramic tile, masonry veneers
     b.   Wood sheathing
     c.   Metal joist, wood covering
     d.   Metal joint, lightweight concrete

Many different combinations of these materials can be used for the quick elevation or section sketch. The tablet user must combine them in a way that will suit the client and the conditions of the site.

CHAPTER SUMMARY   The object of completing a set of preliminary sketches using computer-assisted techniques is to provide information required for a complete set of working details. At this stage the computer-stored sketches are a structural section, exterior elevations, site plan, and a single-line floorplan, plus many client ideas. These sketches were produced from a data tablet and the following computer program.

```
C...............................................................
C
C     DRAW2D   -   A   FORTRAN   PROGRAM   FOR   TABLET   INPUT   OF
C              TWO-DIMENSIONAL DATABASES
C
C...............................................................
      LOGICAL IEND
      COMMON /IOFILE, INTERM,IOTERM,IPTR,INP1,INP2,INP3,INP4,
     +                IOUTP1,IOUTP2,IDEBUG
      COMMON /TAB2DC/ CANG,SCALEC,IOXC,IOYC
      COMMON /WINDOC/ WXMING,WXMAXC,WYMINC,WYMAXC,WXR,WXC,WYR,WYC
      COMMON /VPORTC/ VXMINC,VXMAXC,VYMINC,VYMAXC,VXR,VXC,VYR,VYC
      COMMON /TRANWC/ XA,WB,WC,WD
      DIMENSION ITITLE(72)
      DATA DELIM/-999.0/,IXYPL/4HXYPL/,IENDD/4HENDD/,ISMIC/4H;   /
C
C  INITIALIZE NUMBER OF RECORDS IN DATAFILE "IOUTP1"
      NR=0
C
C  INITIALIZE THE NAMED COMMON "IOFILE".
      INTERM= 1
      IOTERM= 3
      IPTR  =20
      INP1  =11
      INP2  =12
      INP3  =13
      INP4  =14
      IOUTP1=21
      IOUTP2=22
C
C  WRITE PROGRAM HEADER TO TERMINAL.
      CALL ANMODE
      WRITE(IOTERM,1000)
1000 FORMAT(/////,
     +      /,'<<<<<<<<<<<<<<<<<<<<<<<<<>>>>>>>>>>>>>>>>>>>>>>>>',
     ;      //,'          START OF CREATE 2-D.',
     +      //,'<<<<<<<<<<<<<<<<<<<<<<<<<>>>>>>>>>>>>>>>>>>>>>>>>')
C
C  INITIALIZE DEBUGGING OUTPUT LEVEL.
      CALL QDEBUG
```

```
      IF(IDEBUG .GT. 0) WRITE(IPTR,1000)
      IF(IDEBUG .GT. 0) WRITE(IPTR,1001)IDEBUT
1001 FORMAT(' ',2I)
C
C  PROMPT THE USER FOR THE BAUD RATE.
      CALL QBAUD(IBAUD)
C
C  INITIALIZE THE TEKTRONIX CONTROL SYSTEM.
      CALL INITT(IBAUD)
C
C  INITIALIZE THE NAMED COMMON "TAB2DC" AND ASSOCIATED VARIABLES.
   10 SCALEC=0.0
      IXOC=0.0
      IXOC=0.0
      CALL BELL
C
C  CLEAR THE SCREEN AND RETURN THE ALPHANUMERIC CURSOR TO HOME.
      CALL NEWPAG
C
C  PROMPT USER FOR THE DATABASE NAME OR IDENTIFIER.
      CALL INAME(ITITLE)
C
C  WRITE THE DATABASE TYPE TO DATAFILE.
      WRITE(INP3,1004) IXYPL,ISEMIC
1004 FORMAT(2A4)
C
C  PROMPT USER SCALE OF THE DRAWING TO BE TRACED.
      CALL TSCALE(SCALE,RADANG)
      SCALEC=SCALE
      CANG=RADANG
C
C  PROMPT USER FOR THE LOCATION OF THE ORIGIN ON THE DRAWING
      CALL TORGIN(IOX,IOY)
      IOXC=IOX
      IOYC=IOY
C
C  PROMPT USER FOR THE WINDOW LIMITS FOR THE TERMINAL DISPLAY OF
C  THE DATA RECEIVED.
      CALL WLIMIT
C
C  PROCEED WITH THE CREATION OF THE DATABASE.
      CALL INTAB2(IEND,NR)
      WRITE(INP3,1002) DELIM
```

```
1002 FORMAT(F10.4)
     IF(.NOT. IEND) GO TO 10
     CALL TABOFF
     WRITE(INP3,1003) IENDD,ISEMIC
1003 FORMAT(2A4)
     CALL FINITT(770,0)
C
C........................................................................
     STOP
     END
C
C
     SUBROUTINE QDEBUG
C***********************************************************************
C    THIS ROUTINE ASKS THE USER IF HE WOULD LIKE TO HAVE PRINT-OUT
C    FOR DEBUGGING.
C----------------------------------------------------------------------
     LOGICAL ITEST
     DIMENSION IMESS(72)
     COMMON /IOFILE/ INTERM,IOTERM,IPTR,INP1,INP2,INP3,INP4,
    +                IOUTP1,IOUP2,IDEBUG
     DATA IBLANK/1H /
C
C ISSUE PROMPT TO USER FOR INPUT.
  10 WRITE(IOTERM,1000)
1000 FORMAT(/,' DO YOU WISH PRINT-OUT AS A DEBUGGING AID?',
    +       /,' ENTER 0, 1, 2, OR 3 FOR LEVEL OF DEBUGGING -')
C
C INPUT THE RESPONSE.
     READ(INTERM,1001) (IMESS(I),I=1,72)
1001 FORMAT(72A1)
     WRITE(IOTERM,1002)
1002 FORMAT(/,'       ')
C
C FIND THE FIRST CHARACTER IN THE MESSAGE, CONVERT THE CHARACTER
C ARRAY TO A INTEGER NUMBER AND STORE THE VALUE FOUND.
     LOC=0
  11 LOC=LOC+1
     IF(LOC .EQ. 72) GO TO 99991
     IF(IMESS(LOC) .EQ. IBLANK) GO TO 11
     CALL INTNUM(IMESS,LOC,IDEBUG,ITEST)
     IF(ITEST) GO TO 99991
     RETURN
```

```
C
C   ISSUE WARNING MESSAGE AND ALLOW USER TO RE-SPECIFY THE INPUT
99991 CALL ANMODE
      WRITE(IOTERM,99992)
99992 FORMAT(/,' WARNING - FAULTY INPUT RECEIVED, RE-ENTER INPUT.')
      GO TO 10
C
C***************************************************************************
      END
C
C
      SUBROUTINE QBAUD(IBAUD)
C***************************************************************************
C     THIS ROUTINE PROMPTS THE USER FOR THE TERMINAL BAUD RATE AND
C     RECEIVES THE RESPONSE FOR THE PROMPT.
C     ENTERED+  NONE
C     RETURNED+  IBAUD - THE TERMINAL BAUD RATE.
C
C
C---------------------------------------------------------------------
      LOGICAL IEND,INOCMD,ITEST,IDUMP
      DIMENSION IMESS(72)
      COMMON /IOFILE/ INTERM,IOTERM,IPTR,INP1,INP2,INP3,INP4,
     +                IOUTP1,IOUTP2,IDEBUG
      COMMON /IOBUGG /ICARD(72),ILINE(132),ISIZE,ICURSR,IFIN,IFOUT,
      IDUMP
      DATA IBLANK/1H /
C
C   ISSUE PROMPT FOR USER INPUT.
      WRITE(IOTERM,1000)
1000 format(' ENTER THE TERMINAL BAUD RATE -')
C
C   INPUT THE RESPONSE.
   10 READ(INTERM,1001) (IMESS(Z), Z=1,72)
 1001 FORMAT(72A1)
      WRITE(IOTERM,1002)
 1002 FORMAT(/,'          ')
C
C   FIND THE FIRST CHARACTER IN THE MESSAGE, CONVERT THE CHARACTER
C   ARRAY TO AN INTEGER NUMBER AND RETURN VALUE.
      LOC=0
   20 LOC=LOC+1
      IF(LOC .EQ. 72) GO TO 99991
      IF(IMESS(LOC) .EQ. IBLANK) GO TO 20
      CALL INTNUM(IMESS,LOC,IBAUD,ITEST)
```

```
       IF (ITEST) GO TO 99991
       IBAUD=IBAUD/10
       RETURN
C
C     FAULTY INPUT RECEIVED, ISSUE WARNING MESSAGE AND ALLOW USER TO
C     RE-ENTER THE RESPONSE.
99991 CALL WARN(17)
       GO TO 10
C
C******************************************************************
       END
C
C
       SUBROUTINE INNAME(INAME)
C******************************************************************
C     THIS ROUTINE IS USED TO PROMPT THE USER FOR THE DATABASE NAME
C     OR IDENTIFYER.
C          RETURNED: INAME - THE CHARACTER ARRAY CONTAINING THE NAME.
C-----------------------------------------------------------------
       COMMON /IOFILE/ INTERM,IOTERM,IPTR,INP1,INP2,INP3,INP4,
      +                IOUTP1,IOUTP2,IDEBUG
       DIMENSION INAME(72)
       DATA IBLANK/1H /
C
C  PROMPT THE USER FOR NAME.
       CALL ANMODE
       WRITE(IOTERM,1000)
1000 FORMAT(/,' ENTER DATABASE NAME OR IDENTIFYER -')
C
C  RECEIVE THE USER#S REPLY TO PROMPT.
   10 CALL ANMODE
       READ(INTERM,1001) (INAME(I),I=1,72)
1001   FORMAT(72A1)
C
C     FIND THE FIRST CHARACTER IN THE MESSAGE AND CONVERT THE
C     CHARACTER ARRAY TO A FLOATING POINT NUMBER.
       LOC=0
   11 LOC=LOC+1
       IF(LOC .GT. 72) GO TO 99991
       IF(INAME(LOC) .EQ. IBLANK) GO TO 11
C
C     OUTPUT THE NAME TO THE 'CREATE' DATABASE & ECHO ON LINEPRINTER.
       CALL ANMODE
       WRITE(INP3,1002) (INAME(I),I=1,68)
```

```
1002 FORMAT('OBJT:',68A1)
     IF(IDEBUG .GT. 0) WRITE(IPTR,1003) (INAME(I),I=1,68)
1003 FORMAT(//////,' DATABASE NAME ......................... ',72A1,/)
     RETURN
C
C    INVALID OR MISSING RESPONSE, ISSUE WARNING.
99991 CALL ANMODE
     WRITE(IOTERM,1004)
1004 FORMAT(/,' WARNING - INVALID OR MISSING NUMERICAL RESPONSE,
     RE-ENT +ER.')
     GO TO 10
C
C******************************************************************
     END
C
C
     SUBROUTINE TSCALE(SCALE,CANGLE)
C******************************************************************
C    THIS ROUTINE IS USED TO PROMPT THE USER FOR THE NECESSARY
C    INFORMATION TO ESTABLISH A SCALE FACTOR FOR TABLET INPUT
C    AND THEN CALCULATES THE FACTOR.
C         RETURNED: SCALE - THE ESTABLISHED SCALE FACTOR.
C
C
C-----------------------------------------------------------------
     LOGICAL ITEST
     COMMON /IOFILE/ INTERM,IOTERM,IPTR,INP1,INP2,INP3,INP4,
     +               IOUTP1,IOUTP2,IDEBUG
     DATA EPS/0.0001/,EPSS/-0.0001/
     DATA IBLANK/1H /
C
C  INITIALIZE VARIABLES.
     SCALE=0.0
C    ISSUE PROMPT.
     CALL ANMODE
  10 WRITE(IOTERM,1001)
1001 FORMAT(/,' ENTER THE LENGTH OF THE SCALE INDICATOR -')
C
C  RECEIVE USER'S NUMERICAL RESPONSE TO THE PROMPT.
     CALL RECNUM(SLEN)
C
C  PROMPT USER FOR THE BEGINNING POINT OF SCALE INDICATOR.
C    ISSUE THE PROMPT.
     CALL ANMODE
     WRITE(IOTERM,1003)
```

```
1003 FORMAT(/,' INPUT THE BEGINNING POINT OF THE SCALE INDICATOR -')
C      RECEIVE POINT FROM TABLET.
       CALL TABINT(1,0,0)
       CALL ONEPNT(IX1,IY1)
       CALL BELL
       CALL TABOFF
C
C  PROMPT THE USER FOR THE ENDING POINT OF THE SCALE INDICATOR.
C      ISSUE THE PROMPT.
       CALL ANMODE
       WRITE(IOTERM,1004)
1004 FORMAT(/,' INPUT THE ENDING POINT OF THE SCALE INDICATOR -')
C      RECEIVE THE POINT FROM THE TABLET.
       CALL TABINT(1,0,0)
       CALL ONEPNT(IX2,IY2)
       CALL BELL
       CALL TABOFF
C
C  CALCULATE THE ROTATION CORRECTION.
       X1=FLOAT(IX1)
       Y1=FLOAT(IY1)
       X2=FLOAT(IX2)
       Y2=FLOAT(IY2)
       XX=X2-X1
       YY=Y2-Y1
       CALL RPOLAR(XX,YY,DIST,RADS)
       CANGLE=RADS
C
C  CALCULATE THE SCALE FACTOR.
       IF(DIST .EQ. 0.0) GO TO 99991
       SCALE=SLEN/DIST
       IF((SCALE .GT. EPSS) .AND. (SCALE .ST. EPS))  GO TO 99991
C
C  WRITE OUT STATISTICS.
       CALL ANMODE
       IF(IDEBUG .GT. 1) WRITE(IPTR,1005) SLEN,DIST,SCALE,CANGLE
1005 FORMAT(/,' LENGTH OF SCALE INDICATOR .......... ',F10.4,
     +        /,' TABLET GRID DISTANCE .............. ',F10.4,
     +        /,' SCALE FACTOR ...................... ',F10.4,
     +        /,' ANGULAR CORRECTION (RADIANS)....... ',F10.4,/)
     RETURN
C
C  ISSUE WARNING MESSAGE AND ALLOW USER TO RESPECIFY THE INPUT.
99991 CALL ANMODE
       WRITE(IOTERM,99992)
```

```
99992 FORMAT(/,' WARNING - FAULTY INPUT RECEIVED, RE-ENTER INPUT.')
C
C**************************************************************************
      END
C
C
      SUBROUTINE RECNUM(RNUM)
C**************************************************************************
      LOGICAL ITEST
      DIMENSION IMESS(72)
      COMMON /IOFILE/ INTERM,IOTERM,IPTR,INP1,INP2,INP3,INP4,
     +                IOUTP1,IOUTP2,IDEBUG
      DATA IBLANK/1H /
C
C  RECEIVE THE USER'S REPLY TO THE PROMPT.
   10 CALL ANMODE
      READ(INTERM,1000) (IMESS(I),I=1,72)
 1000 FORMAT(72A1)
C
C     FIND  THE  FIRST  CHARACTER  IN  THE  MESSAGE  AND  CONVERT  THE
C     CHARACTER ARRAY TO A FLOATING POINT NUMBER.
      LOC=0
   11 LOC=LOC+1
      IF(LOC .GT. 72) GO TO 99991
      IF(IMESS(LOC) .EQ. IBLANK) GO TO 11
      CALL RELNUM(IMESS,LOC,RNUM,ITEST)
      IF(ITEST) GO TO 99991
      RETURN
C
C     INVALID OR MISSING RESPONSE, ISSUE WARNING.
99991 CALL ANMODE
      WRITE(IOTERM,1001)
 1001 FORMAT(/,' WARNING - INVALID OR MISSING NUMERICAL RESPONSE,
      RE-ENT +34.')
      GO TO 10
C
C**************************************************************************
      END
C
C
      SUBROUTINE RPOLAR(X,Y,RAY,RAD)
C**************************************************************************
C     THIS SUB CONVERTS CARTESIAN COORDINATES(X,Y) TO POLAR
C     COORDINATE SYSTEM(RAY,ANGLE).  RAY IS OF THE SAME CONVENTION
```

```
C     AS X&Y BUT THE ANGLE IS RETURNED IN RADIANS.
C           ENTERED:  X - CARTESIAN COORDINATE FOR THE X-AXIS.  C
                Y - CARTESIAN COORDINATE FOR THE Y-AXIS.  C
RETURNED:  RAY - POLAR RAY VALUE.
C                     RAD - POLAR ANGULAR VALUE IN RADIANS.
C-------------------------------------------------------------------
C
C   POINT ON Y-AXIS?
C   POINT ON X-AXIS?
      IF (X .EQ. 0.0) GO TO 170
      IF (Y .EQ. 0.0) GO TO 260
C COMPUTER POLAR COORDINATES.
      RAY=SQRT(X**2+Y**2)
      RAD=ATAN(Y/X)
      RETURN
  170 IF (Y .EQ. 0.0) GO TO 240
      RAY=ABS(Y)
C   IS POINT ABOVE OR BELOW ORIGIN?
      IF (Y .LT. 0.0) GO TO 220
      RAD=1.5708
      RETURN
  220 RAD=4.7124
      RETURN
  240 RAY=0.0
      RAD=0.0
      RETURN
C   POINT IS ON X-AXIS
  260 RAY=ABS(X)
C IS POINT TO LEFT OR RIGHT OF ORIGIN?
      IF(X .LT. 0.0) GO TO 300
      RAD=0.0
      RETURN
  300 RAD=3.1415

C**********************************************************************
      RETURN
      END
C
C
      FUNCTION DIST2D(A1,A2,B1,B2)
C**********************************************************************

C     THIS ROUTINE CALCULATES THE DISTANCE BETWEEN TWO POINTS IN
C     TWO-DIMENSIONAL SPACE DE.G. X1=A1,Y1=A2,X2=B1,Y2=B2].
C     USES PYTHAGARON THEOREM TO DERIVE HYPOTENUSE.
```

```
C            ENTERED:  A1      - THE COORDINATE OF THE FIRST POINT WITH
C                                THE SAME AXIS CONVENTION AS B1.
C                      A2      - THE COORDINATE OF THE FIRST POINT WITH
C                                THE SAME AXIS CONVENTION AS B2.
C                      B1      - THE COORDINATE OF THE SECOND POINT
C                                WITH THE SAME AXIS CONVENTION AS A1.
C                      B2      - THE COORDINATE OF THE SECOND POINT
C                                WITH THE SAME AXIS CONVENTION AS A2.
C            RETURNED: DIST2D  - THE DISTANCE BETWEEN TWO POINTS IN
C                                TWO-DIMENSIONAL SPACE.
C------------------------------------------------------------------
      DATA EPS/0.0001/
C
      DIST2D=0.0
      ADELTA=ABS(A1-A2)
      BDELTA=ABS(B1-B2)
      IF(((ADELTA .LT. EPS) .AND. (ADELTA .GT. EPS)) .AND.
     +   ((BDELTA .LT. EPS) .AND. (BDELTA .GT. EPS))) RETURN
      DIST2D=SQRT(ADELTA**2+BDELTA**2)
C******************************************************************
      RETURN
      END
C
C
      SUBROUTINE  TORGIN(IXO,IYO
C******************************************************************
C    THIS ROUTINE PROMPTS THE USER FOR THE ORIGIN OF THE DRAWING
C    TO BE TRACED ON THE TABLET
C            RETURNED: IXO     - THE X-AXIS COORDINATE OF THE ORIGIN.
C                      IYO     - THE Y-AXIS COORDINATE OF THE ORIGIN.
C
C------------------------------------------------------------------
      COMMON /IOFILE/ INTERM,IOTERM,IPTR,INP1,INP2,INP3,INP4,
     +                IOUTP1,IOUTP2,IDEBUG
C
C  PROMPT THE USER FOR THE LOCATION
      CALL ANMODE
      WRITE(IOTERM,1000)
 1000 FORMAT(/,' INPUT THE ORIGIN LOCATION FOR THE INPUT DATA -')
C
C  RECEIVE THE POINT FROM THE TABLET.
      CALL TABINT(1,0,0)
      CALL ONEPNT(IXP,IYO)
      CALL BELL
      CALL TABOFF
```

```
C
C  WRITE-OUT STATISTICS.
      CALL ANMODE
      IF(IDEBUG .GT. 1) WRITE(IPTR,1001) IXO,IYO
1001 FORMAT(/,' X-AXIS ORIGIN VALUE ................. ',I5,
     +       /,' Y-AXIS ORIGIN VALUE ................. ',I5,/)
C
C*****************************************************************************
      RETURN
      END
C
C
      SUBROUTINE WLIMIT
C*****************************************************************************
C     THIS ROUTINE SPECIFIES THE WINDOW LIMITS FOR THE TERMINAL
C     DISPLAY OF THE DATA GIVEN THE UPPER RIGHT-HAND CORNER AND
C     LOWER LEFT-HAND CORNER OF THE AREA ON THE TABLET SURFACE
C     WHICH IS TO BE DISPLAYED.  THE USER IS PROMPTED FOR A POINT
C     FOR EACH OF THE CORNERS.
C
C---------------------------------------------------------------------
      COMMON /IOFILE/ INTERM,IOTERM,IPTR,INP1,INP2,INP3,INP4,
     +                IOUTP1,IOUTP2,IDEBUG
      COMMON /TAB2DC/ CANG,SCALEC,IOXC,IOYC
      DATA XPIX/1023.0/,YPIX/780.0/
C
C  ISSUE THE PROMPT AND RECEIVE THE DATA FOR THE UPPER LEFT-HAND
C  CORNER.
      CALL ANMODE
      WRITE(IOTERM,1000)
1000 FORMAT(/,; INPUT THE UPPER LEFT-HAND CORNER OF THE DISPLAY
      WINDOW +-')
      CALL TABINT(1,0,0)
      CALL ONEPNT(IXMIN,IYMAX)
      CALL BELL
      CALL TABOFF
C
C  PROMPT THE USER AND RECEIVE THE POINT FOR THE LOWER LEFT-HAND
C  CORNER.
      CALL ANMODE
      WRITE(IOTERM,1001)
1001 FORMAT(/,' INPUT THE LOWER RIGHT-HAND CORNER OF THE DISPLAY
      WINDOW +-')
      CALL TABINT(1,0,0)
      CALL ONEPNT(IXMAX,IYMIN)
```

```
      CALL BELL
      CALL TABOFF
C
C   TRANSLATE THE WINDOW BOUNDRIES.
      WXMIN=SCALE*FLOAT(IXMIN-IOXC)
      WXMAX=SCALE*FLOAT(IXMAX-IOXC)
      WYMIN=SCALE*FLOAT(IYMIN-IOYC)
      WYMAX=SCALE*FLOAT(IYMAX-IOYC)
C
C   SET THE VIEWPORT-WINDOW SPECIFICATIONS, RETAINING ORIGINAL
C   PROPORTIONS.
      CALL PPORTW(WXMIN,WXMAX,WYMIN,WYMAX,XPIX,YPIX)
C
C   WRITE OUT STATISTICS.
      CALL ANMODE
      IF (IDEBUG .GT. 1) WRITE(IPTR,1010) IXMIN,IXMAX,IYMIN,IYMAX
1010 FORMAT(/,' THE TABLET WINDOW X-AXIS MINIMUM ... ',I5,
     +       /,' THE TABLET WINDOW X-AXIS MAXIMUM ... ',I5,
     +       /,' THE TABLET WINDOW Y-AXIS MINIMUM ... ',I5,
     +       /,' THE TABLET WINDOW Y-AXIS MAXIMUM ... ',I5,/)
      IF(IDEBUG .GT. 1 WRITE(IPTR,1011) VXMN,VXMX,VYMN,VYMX
1011 FORMAT(/,' THE VPORT WINDOW X-AXIS MINIMUM ....', F10.4,
     +       /,' THE VPORT WINDOW X-AXIS MAXIMUM ....', F10.4,
     +       /,' THE VPORT WINDOW Y-AXIS MINIMUM ....', F10.4,
     +       /,' THE VPORT WINDOW Y-AXIS MAXIMUM ....', F10.4,/)
      IF(IDEBUG .GT. 1) WRITE(IPTR,1012) WXMN,WXMX,WYMN,WYMX
1012 FORMAT(/,' THE WINDO WINDOW X-AXIS MINIMUM .... ',F10.4,
     +       /,' THE WINDO WINDOW X-AXIS MAXIMUM .... ',F10.4,
     +       /,' THE WINDO WINDOW Y-AXIS MINIMUM .... ',F10.4,
     +       /,' THE WINDO WINDOW Y-AXIS MAXIMUM .... ',F10.4,/)
C
C****************************************************************
      RETURN
      END
C
C
      SUBROUTINE INTAB2(IEND,NREC)
C****************************************************************
C   THIS ROUTINE IS USED TO CREATE A TWO-DIMENSIONAL DATABASE
C   USING THE TEKTRONIX GRAPHICS TABLET.  INPUT FROM THE TABLET
C   IS RECEIVED FILTERED FOR VALID POINTS, TRANSFORMED ACCORDING
C   TO THE SCALE FACTOR AND ORIGIN, OUTPUT TO A DATABASE, AND
C   ECHOED TO THE TERMINAL SCREEN FOR VISUAL INSPECTION.  DATA
C   IS  OUTPUT  IN  THE  FORM:  X-COORDINATE,  Y-COORDINATE,  PEN
C   SPECIFICATION USING A FORTRAN FORMAT OF 2F10.4,I5.
```

```
C     THE PEN SPECIFICATION INDICATES A MOVE WHEN A NEGATIVE VALUE
C     IS PRESENT, A DRAW WHEN THE VALUE IS POSITIVE.  DATA ECHOED
C     TO SCREEN OCCURS CONCURRENTLY WITH DATA INPUT FROM THE TABLET.
C
C------------------------------------------------------------------
      LOGICAL IEND
      DIMENSION IHBUFF(500),IXBUFF(500),IYBUFF(500),IMESS(72)
      COMMON /IOFILE/ INTERM,IOTERM,IPTR,INP1,INP2,INP3,INP4,
     +                IOUTP1,IOUTP2,IDEBUG
      DATA IS/83/,IE/69/,IC/67/,IQ/81/IT/84/
C
C  INITIALIZE VARIABLES.
      IEND=.FALSE.
      NWANT=500
C
C  ERASE THE TERMINAL SCREEN.
      CALL ERASE
C
C  PROMPT THE USER FOR TABLET INPUT & WRITE-OUT HEADER.
      CALL ANMODE
      WRITE(IOTERM,1001)
1001 FORMAT(/,' WHEN CURSOR APPEARS ON THE TERMINAL SCREEN,
          ENTER',/,
     +          /,' AN "S" TO START 2-D INPUT SESSION,',
     +          /,' AN "E" TO ERASE THE TERMINAL SCREEN,',
     +          /,' A "C" TO CONTINUE CREATION OF CURRENT 2-D
             DATABASE,',
     +          /,' A "Q" TO QUIT 2-D DATABASE CREATION,',
     +          /,' A "T" TO TERMINATE 2-D INPUT SESSION.')
      WRITE(IOTERM,1006)
1006 FORMAT(/,' ENTER ANY KEYBOARD CHARACTER DURING TABLET INPUT,
     +          /,' MODE AND DATA BUFFER WILL BE DUMPED TO DATABASE',
     +          /,' FILE AND DISPLAYED ON TERMINAL SCREEN.',/)
C
C  DISPAY CURSOR ON TERMINAL SCREEN, ACCEPT INPUT CHARACTER, AND
C  PROCESS THE CHARACTER COMMAND.
   20 CALL SCURSR(ICH,IXS,IYS)
      IF(ICH .EQ. IS) GO TO 40
      IF(ICH .EQ. IE) GO TO 30
      IF(ICH .EQ. IC) GO TO 40
      IF(ICH .EQ. IQ) RETURN
      IF(ICH .EQ. IT) GO TO 99999
C
C  CHARACTER COMMAND NOT FOUND, ISSUE WARNING AND ACCEPT NEW INPUT.
      CALL ANMODE
```

```
      WRITE(IOTERM,1002)
1002 FORMAT(/,'WARNING - COMMAND NOT FOUND, RE-ENTER INPUT.')
      GO TO 10
C
C  ERASE TERMINAL SCREEN.
   30 CALL ERASE
      GO TO 20
C
C  PLACE SESSION IN TABLET MODE AND RECEIVE DATA.
   40 CALL BELL
      CALL TABINT(1,0,0)
      CALL MULPNT(NWANT,NFOUND,IHBUFF,IXBUFF,IYBUFF)
      CALL BELL
      IF(NFOUND .LE. 1) GO TO 20
C
C  LIMIT THE NUMBER OF RECORDS IN DATABASE FILE TO 2000, CHECK FOR
C  OVERFLOW OF DATABASE FILE.
      NREC=NREC+NFOUND
      IF(NREC .GT. 2000) NFOUND=NFOUND-(NREC-2000)
      IF(NFOUND .LE. 1) GO TO 99991
C
C  IF DEBUGGING OPTIONS ARE IN EFFECT, ECHO DATA ON LINE PRINTER.
      CALL ANMODE
      IF(IDEBUG .GT. 0) WRITE(IPTR,1003) NFOUND,NREC
1003 FORMAT(/,' THE NUMBER OF POINTS RECEIVED WAS .. ',I5,
     +      /,' THE TOTAL NUMBER OF RECORDS IS ..... ',I5)
      IF(NFOUND .LE. 1) GO TO 20
      DO 100 I=1,NFOUND
      IF(IDEBUG .GT. 2) WRITE(IPTR,1004) IHBUFF(I),IXBUFF(I),IYBUFF
     (I)
  100 CONTINUE
1004 FORMAT(3(I5,5X))
C
C  PASS THE DATA RECEIVED ON TO A ROUTINE WHICH WILL FILTER THE DATA
C  FOR OUTPUT AND PROMPT USER WITH CURSOR FOR FURTHER INSTRUCTIONS.
      CALL FILTR2(IHBUFF,IXBUFF,IYBUFF,NFOUND)
C     CHECK TO SEE IF DATABASE FILE IS FULL.
      IF(NREC .GT. 2000) GO TO 99991
      GO TO 20
C
C  ISSUE ERROR MESSAGE AND TERMINATE ROUTINE.
99991 CALL ANMODE
      WRITE(IOTERM,1005)
      IF(IDEBUG .GT. 0) WRITE(IPTR,1005)
```

```
1005 FORMAT(/,' ERROR - DATABASE FILE FULL, SESSION TERMINATION,')
C
99999 IEND=.TRUE.
C**********************************************************************
      RETURN
      END
C
      SUBROUTINE FILTR2(IHA,IXA,IYA,NA)
C**********************************************************************
C    THIS ROUTINE FILTERS THE DATA FOR VALID POINTS AND TRANSFORMS
C    THE DATA ACCORDING TO THE ROTATION CORRECTION, SCALE FACTOR,
C    AND ORIGIN LOCATION.
C
C--------------------------------------------------------------------
      DIMENSION IHA(500),IXA(500),IYA(500)
      COMMON /TAB2DC/ CANG,SCALEC,IOXC,IOYC
C
C  INPUT THE DATA FROM THE TEMPORARY STORAGE.
      I=1
      NAA=0
   10 NAA=NAA+1
      IF(NAA .GT. NA) RETURN
      IF(IHA(NAA) .EQ. 29) GO TO 20
      IF(IHA(NAA) .EQ. 26) GO TO 30
      I=1
      GO TO 10
C
C  IF HEADER WAS "29", THEN A MOVE COMMAND WAS INDICATED.
   20 IX=IXA(NAA)
      IY=IYA(NAA)
      CALL OUTMOV(IX,IY,I)
      GO TO 10
C
C  IF HEADER WAS "29", THEN A DRAW COMMAND WAS INDICATED.
   3
   0 IX=IXA(NAA)
      IY=IYA(NAA)
      CALL OUTDRW(IX,IY,I)
      GO TO 10
C
C**********************************************************************
      END
C
C
```

```
      SUBROUTINE OUTMOV(IXPT,IYPT,II)
C*******************************************************************
C     THIS ROUTINE IS USED TO TRANSFORM THE POINT ACCORDING TO
C     THE SCALE FACTOR AND ORIGIN, OUTPUT THE POINT TO THE
C     DATAFILE, AND ECHO THE DATA TO THE TERMINAL SCREEN.
C     THE PEN SPECIFICATION AND ECHO OF DATA ARE REPRESENTED AS
C     A MOVE.
C          ENTERED:   IXPT    - THE X-AXIS COORDINATE RECEIVED FROM
C                              THE TABLET.
C                     IYPT    - THE Y-AXIS COORDINATE RECEIVED FROM
C                              THE TABLET.
C                     II      - A VARIABLE USED TO TEST FOR THE
C                              OCCURRENCE OF THE FIRST COORDINATE.
C                              THE PEN SPECIFICATION FOR THIS POINT
C                              MUST BE A MOVE.
C
C-----------------------------------------------------------------
      COMMON /IOFILE/ INTERM,IOTERM,IPTR,INP1,INP2,INP3,INP4,
     +                IOUTP1,IOUTP2,IDEBUG
      COMMON /TAB2DC/ CANG,SCALEC,IOXC,IOYC
      DATA IP/-1/
C
C   TRANSLATE THE POINT RELATIVE TO THE ORIGIN
      IX=IXPT-IOXC
      IY=IYPT-IOYC
      CALL ANMODE
      IF(IDEBUG .GT. 2) WRITE(IPTR,1001) IX,IY,IP
1001 FORMAT(//,3(I5,5X
C
C   SCALE THE POINT FROM TABLET SIZE TO USER'S SCALE SIZE.
      XPT=SCALE*FLOAT(IX)
      YPT=SCALE*FLOAT(IY)
      CALL ANMODE
      IF(IDEBUG .GT. 2) WRITE(IPTR,1002) XPT,YPT
1002 FORMAT(2F10.4)
C
C   CORRECT THE ANGULAR ERROR BETWEEN THE TRACINGS HORIZONTAL AND
C   THE TABLETS HORIZONTAL.
      XX=XPT*COS(CANG)+      YPT*SIN(CANG)
      YY=XPT*(-1*SIN(CANG))+YPT*COS(CANG)
C
C   OUTPUT THE POINT TO THE DATAFILE AND ECHO ON LINE PRINTER.
      CALL ANMODE
      WRITE(INP3,1001) XX,YY,IP
      IF(IDEBUG .GT. 0) WRITE(IPTR,1001) XX,YY,IP
```

```
1000 FORMAT(2F10.4,I5)
     II=0
C
C   ECHO THE DATA ON THE TERMINAL SCREEN.
     CALL COORDW(XX,YY,XC,YC)
     IX=INT(XC)
     IY=INT(YC)
     CALL MOVABS(IX,IY)
C
C*******************************************************************
     RETURN
     END
C
C

     SUBROUTINE OUTDRW(IXPT,IYPT,II)
C*******************************************************************
C     THIS ROUTINE IS USED TO TRANSFORM THE POINT ACCORDING TO
C     THE SCALE FACTOR AND ORIGIN, OUTPUT THE POINT TO THE
C     DATAFILE, AND ECHO THE DATA TO THE TERMINAL SCREEN.
C     THE PEN SPECIFICATION AND ECHO OF DATA ARE REPRESENTED AS
C     A DRAW.
C          ENTERED:  IXPT    - THE X-AXIS COORDINATE RECEIVED FROM
C                              THE TABLET.
C                    IYPT    - THE Y-AXIS COORDINATE RECEIVED FROM
C                              THE TABLET.
C                    II      - A VARIABLE USED TO TEST FOR THE
C                              OCCURRENCE OF THE FIRST COORDINATE.
C                              THE PEN SPECIFICATION FOR THIS POINT
C                              MUST BE A MOVE.
C
C
C------------------------------------------------------------------
     COMMON /IOFILE/ INTERM,IOTERM,IPTR,INP1,INP2,INP3,INP4,
    +                IOUTP1,IOUTP2,IDEBUG
     COMMON /TAB2DC/ CANG,SCALEC,IOXC,IOYC
     DATA IP/1/
C
C   CHECK TO SEE IF FIRST DISPLAY GENERATION IS TO BE A MOVE.  IF
C   SO, THEN ERROR HAS OCCURRED AND TERMINATE ROUTINE.
     IF(II .EQ. 1) RETURN
C
C   TRANSLATE THE POINT RELATIVE TO THE ORIGIN
     IX=IXPT-IOXC
     IY=IYPT-IOYC
     CALL ANMODE
```

```
      IF(IDEBUG .GT. 1) WRITE(IPTR,1001) IX,IY,IP
1001 FORMAT(//,3(I5,5X))
C
C  SCALE THE POINT FROM TABLET SIZE TO USER'S SCALE SIZE.
      XPT=SCALE*FLOAT(IX)
      YPT=SCALE*FLOAT(IY)
      CALL ANMODE
      IF(IDEBUG .GT. 1) WRITE(IPTR,1002) XPT,YPT
1002 FORMAT(2F10.4)
C
C  CORRECT THE ANGULAR ERROR BETWEEN THE TRACINGS HORIZONTAL AND
C  THE TABLETS HORIZONTAL.
      XX=XPT*COS(CANG)+      YPT*SIN(CANG)
      YY=XPT*(-1*SIN(CANG))+YPT*COX(CANG)
C
C  OUTPUT THE POINT TO THE DATAFILE AND ECHO ON LINE PRINTER.
      CALL ANMODE
      WRITE(INP3,1001) XX,YY,IP
      IF(IDEBUG .GT. 0) WRITE(IPTR,1000) XX,YY,IP
1000 FORMAT(2F10.4,I5)
C
C  ECHO THE DATA ON THE TERMINAL SCREEN.
      CALL COORDW(XX,YY,XC,YC)
      IX=INT(XC)
      IY=INT(YC)
      CALL DRWABS(IX,IY)
C
C*********************************************************************
      RETURN
      END
C
C
C  *****************************************************************
C *                                                                 *
C *  NOCONV: A FORTRAN SOFTWARE SYSTEM FOR ALPHANUMERIC TO          *
C *          INTEGER OF FLOATING POINT NUMBER REPRESENTATION.       *
C *                                                                 *
C *                                                                 *
C *                                                                 *
C *                                                                 *
C *                                                                 *
C *  NOCONV CONSISTS OF THE FOLLOWING ROUTINES:                     *
C *                                                                 *
C *  RELNUM - CONVERSION OF AN ALPHANUMERIC ARRAY INTO A            *
C *           FLOATING POINT NUMBER.                                *
```

```
C *    INTNUM - CONVERSION OF AN ALPHANUMERIC ARRAY INTO A            *
C *             INTEGER NUMBER.                                       *
C *                                                                   *
C *                                                                   *
C *                                                                   *
C *                                                                   *
C *                                                                   *
C *    DESCRIPTION:                                                   *
C *                                                                   *
C *         THESE ROUTINES PROVIDE FOR THE CONVERSION OF THAT PART    *
C *    OF A CHARACTER ARRAY WHICH CONTAINS THE REPRESENTATION         *
C *    OF A NUMBER TO A REAL OR INTEGER NUMBER.  OFTEN, IN AN         *
C *    INTERACTIVE PROGRAM, MIXED CHARACTER AND NUMERIC INPUT         *
C *    MUST BE RECEIVED.  AFTER THE NUMBER HAS BEEN LOCATED           *
C *    WITHIN THE RECORD RECEIVED, THIS SYSTEM OFFERS A WAY OF        *
C *    CONVERTING THE NUMBER TO A FORM WHICH CAN BE USED BY           *
C *    THE COMPUTER FOR MATHEMATICAL COMPUTATION.  THE                *
C *    CHARACTER REPRESENTATION OF THE NUMBER MUST BE IN              *
C *    FORTRAN "A1" FORMAT.                                           *
C *                                                                   *
C *                                                                   *
C *                                                                   *
C *                                                                   *
C *    IMPLEMENTATION:                                                *
C *                                                                   *
C *         NO SPECIAL REQUIREMENTS FOR IMPLEMENTATION ARE REQUIRED.  *
C *                                                                   *
C *                                                                   *
C ********************************************************************
C
C

       SUBROUTINE RELNUM(MESS,IPOINT,RNUM,IERROR)
C ********************************************************************
C    THIS ROUTINE CONVERTS A CHARACTER ARRAY INTO A REAL (FLOATING
C    POINT) NUMBER.  THE CHARACTERS, STARTING AT "IPOINT", ARE
C    EXAMINED TO ENSURE THAT ONLY VALID 'NUMBER' CHARACTER (0-9,
C    DECIMAL POINT) ARE PRESENT.  "RELNUM" USES ROUTINE " INTNUM' TO
C    CONVERT THE PART OF THE REAL NUMBER LEFT OF THE DECIMAL POINT.
C    THE RIGHT PART RIGHT OF THE DECIMAL POINT IS ALSO CONVERTED BY
C    "INTNUM" BUT MUST BE DIVIDED BY A FACTOR WHICH CONVERTS THE
C    INTEGER NUMBER INTO ITS CORRECT DECIMAL EQUIVALENT.  THE RIGHT
C    AND LEFT PARTS ARE THEN ADDED TOGETHER TO FORM THE CONVERTED
C    REAL NUMBER "RNUM".
```

```
C           ENTERED:  MESS   - THE CHARACTER ARRAY CONTAINING THE
C                             REAL NUMBER.
C                     IPOINT - THE BEGINNING POINT OF THE CHARACTER
C                             NUMBER IN ARRAY "MESS".
C           RETURNED: IPOINT - THE UPDATED MESSAGE ARRAY POINTER.
C                     RNUM   - THE REAL NUMBER FOUND.
C
C
C-------------------------------------------------------------------
      LOGICAL IERROR,NSIGNC
      COMMON /NOCNVC/ NSIGNC
      DIMENSION MESS(72)
      DATA IBLANK /1H /
C
C INITIALIZE VARIABLES.
      RNUM=0.0
      NSIGNC=.FALSE.
C
C SAVE ORIGINAL POINTER.
      IP1=IPOINT
C
C CONVERT INTEGER PART OF NUMBER.
      CALL INTNUM(MESS,IPOINT,INUM,IERROR)
      IF(IERROR) RETURN
      IP2=IPOINT
C
C  CHECK FOR BLANK FOLLOWING INTEGER PART OR A BLANK AFTER THE
C DECIMAL POINT. IF TRUE THEN A SPECIAL CASE HAS OCCURRED AND NO
C DECIMAL PART EXISTS.
      IF(MESS(IPOINT  ) .EQ. IBLANK) GO TO 10
      IF(MESS(IPOINT+1) .EQ. IBLANK) GO TO 10
C NUMBER AND CONVERT DECIMAL PART.
      IPOINT=IPOINT+1
      CALL INTNUM(MESS,IPOINT,INUM,IERROR)
      IF(IERROR) RETURN
      IP3=IPOINT
      GO TO 20
C
C  SPECIAL CASES FOR REAL NUMBERS:  1) NUMBERS THAT END WITH A
C DECIMAL POINT (I.E. '12345.') 2) NUMBERS THAT END WITHOUT A
C DECIMAL POINT (I.E. '12345').
   10 IDNUM=0
      IPT3=IPOINT
C
```

```
C   DECREMENT "IP3" BY ONE PLACE TO ACCOUNT FOR DECIMAL POINT AND
C   CALCULATE DIVISION FACTOR "FACT" FOR DECIMAL PART.
   20 IP3=IP3-1
      NDECPL=IP3-IP2
      FACT=10.0*NDECPL
C
C   CONVERT "IDNUM" INTO DECIMAL FORM AND ADD TWO PARTS TOGETHER.
C   IF INUM WAS NEGATIVE, CONVERT IDNUM TO A NEGATIVE.
      IF(NSIGNC) IDNUM=1*IDNUM
      RNUM=FLOAT(INUM)+(FLOAT(IDNUM)/FACT)
C
C*****************************************************************
      RETURN
      END
C
C
      SUBROUTINE INTNUM(MESS,IPOINT,INUM,IERROR)
C*****************************************************************
C   THIS ROUTINE CONVERTS A CHARACTER ARRAY INTO AN INTEGER NUMBER.
C   THE CHARACTERS STARTING AT "IPOINT" THRU "ICOUNT" CHARACTERS
C   "ICOUNT" CHARACTERS, STARTING AT "IPOINT", ARE EXAMINED TO
C   ENSURE THAT ONLY VALID 'NUMBER' CHARACTERS (0-9, DECIMAL POINT)
C   ARE PRESENT.  IF INVALID CHARACTERS ARE FOUND, THEN A WARNING
C   MESSAGE IS PRODUCED AND THE ROUTINE TERMINATED.  IF A CHARACTER
C   IS A VALID ONE THEN THE CURRENT INTEGER NUMBER ("INUM") IS
C   MULTIPLIED BY TEN (TO INCREMENT THE DECIMAL PLACES BY ONE
C   PLACE) AND THE NEWLY CONVERTED CHARACTER IS ADDED TO "INUM".
C          ENTERED:  MESS    - THE ARRAY CONTAINING THE NUMBER TO BE
C                               CONVERTED.
C                    IPOINT  - THE BEGINNING POINT, IN ARRAY MESS, OF
C                               THE NUMBER.
C                    ICOUNT  - THE NUMBER OF CHARACTERS, STARTING AT
C                               "IPOINT", INCLUDED IN THE NUMBER.
C          RETURNED+ IPOINT  - THE UPDATED MESSAGE ARRAY POINTER.
C                    INUM    - THE INTEGER NUMBER.
C
C
C-----------------------------------------------------------------
      LOGICAL IERROR,NSIGN,NSIGNC
      COMMON /NOCNVC/ NSIGNC
      DIMENSION MESS(72),NUMS(10)
      DATA NUMS01H0,1H1,1H2,1H3,1H4,1H5,1H6,1H7,1H8,1H9/
      DATA IDECPT/1H./
      DATA IBLANK/1H /
      DATA INSIGN/1H-/
```

```
C
C   INITIALIZE THE VARIABLES.
      INUM=D
      IERROR=.FALSE.
      NSIGN=.FALSE.
C
C  CHECK FOR NEGATIVE NUMBER.
      IF(MESS(IPOINT) .NE. INSIGN) GO TO 10
      NSIGN=.TRUE.
      NSIGNC=.TRUE.
      IPOINT=IPOINT+1
C
C  LOOK FOR VALID CHARACTERS.  IF VALID, STORE CONVERSION IN "INO"
C  IF NOT VALID, ISSUE WARNING AND TERMINATE ROUTINE.
   10 INO=99
C     IF A DECIMAL POINT OCCURS TERMINATE ROUTINE NORMALLY.  THIS
C     CHECK OCCURS SO THAT "INTNUM" MAY BE USED BY ROUTINE "RELNUM".
      IF(MESS(IPOINT) .EQ. IDECPT) GO TO 20
      IF(MESS(IPOINT) .EQ. IBLANK) GO TO 20
      DO 100 I=1,10
  100 IF(MESS(IPOINT) .EQ. NUMS(I)) INO=I-1
      IF(INO .EQ. 99) GO TO 99991
C
C  PUSH CURRENT NUMBER UP ONE DECIMAL PLACE AND ADD CONVERTED
C  CHARACTER TO THE CURRENT NUMBER.
      INUM=(INUM*10)+INO
      IPOINT=IPOINT+1
      GO TO 10
C
C  IF NEGATIVE SIGN WAS FOUND, CONVERT NUMBER TO NEGATIVE.
   20 IF(NSIGN) INUM=-1*INUM
      RETURN
C
C   INVALID  CHARACTER  WAS  FOUND.   PRODUCE   WARNING   MESSAGE  AND
C  TERMINATE ROUTINE.
99991 IERROR=.TRUE.
C     CALL WARN(19)
C
C*************************************************************************
      RETURN
      END
C
C
C  *************************************************************************
```

```
C *
C *   VINDOW: A FORTRAN SOFTWARE SYSTEM FOR WINDOWING X-Y DATA.   *
C *                                                              *
C *                                                              *
C *                                                              *
C *                                                              *
C *                                                              *
C *   VINDOW CONSISTS OF THE FOLLOWING ROUTINES:                 *
C *                                                              *
C *   VPORT   - INITIALIZATION OF THE OUTPUT DEVICE VIEWPORT     *
C *             SPECIFICATIONS.                                  *
C *   SEEVPT  - RETURNS THE CURRENTLY SPECIFIED VIEWPORT BOUNDS. *
C *   WINDO   - INITIALIZATION OF THE USER'S DATA WINDOW
*
C *             SPECIFICATIONS.                                  *
C *   SEEWIN  - RETURNS THE CURRENTLY SPECIFIED WINDOW BOUNDS.   *
C *   TRANSW  - COMPUTATION OF THE VIEWPORT-WINDOW TRANSFORMATION *
C *             VALUES.                                          *
C *   COORDW  - TRANSLATION OF "DATA" COORDINATES INTO "OUTPUT   *
C *             DEVICE" COORDINATES.                             *
C *   PPORTW  - INITIALIZATION OF THE VIEWPORT AND WINDOW        *
C *             SPECIFICATIONS, RETAINING WINDOW PROPORTIONS.    *
C *             SETS VIEWPORT XMIN AND YMIN TO THE ORIGIN (0,0)  *
C *             OF THE DISPLAY DEVICE.                           *
C *                                                              *
C *                                                              *
C *                                                              *
C *                                                              *
C *                                                              *
C *   DESCRIPTIONS:                                              *
C *                                                              *
C *   THESE ROUTINES PROVIDE FOR THE TRANSLATION OF THE USER     *
C *   DATA INTO A PHYSICAL LOCATION ON THE TERMINAL SCREEN OR    *
C *   PLOTTER BED.  ANY PART OF THE USER DATA MAY BE VIEWED      *
C *   AT ANY TIME BY A TECHNIQUE OF WINDOWING.  A RECTANGLE IS   *
C *   SPECIFIED IN USER DATA COORDINATE SYSTEM AS A MAXIMUM      *
C *   AND MINIMUM OF THE X AND Y AXES.  THIS RECTANGULAR AREA    *
C *   CAN BE FITTED INTO A SIMILAR AREA ANYWHERE ON THE SCREEN   *
C *   (THE SCREEN RECTANGULAR AREA IS CALLED THE VIEWPORT).      *
C *                                                              *
C *                                                              *
C *                                                              *
C *                                                              *
C *                                                              *
```

```
C *   IMPLEMENTATION:                                                      *
C *                                                                        *
C *   AFTER SPECIFICATION OF THE WINDOW AND VIEWPORT HAS BEEN              *
C *   MADE AND BEFORE THE ACTUAL PLOTTING THE DATA, THE                    *
C *   TRANSFORMATION VALUES MUST BE ACCOMPLISHED IN ORDER TO SAVE          *
C *   EXECUTION TIME DURING DATA PLOTTING.  ROUTINE "TRANSW" IS            *
C *   USED FOR THIS PURPOSE.  DURING PLOTTING OF THE DATA ROUTINE          *
C *   "COORDW" IS CALLED TO PERFORM THE ACTUAL TRANSFORMATION              *
C *   FROM USER DATA TO SCREEN OR PLOTTER COORDINATES.                     *
C *                                                                        *
C *   THESE ROUTINES CAN GENERALLY BE CONSIDERED DEVICE                    *
C *   INDEPENDENT, BUT CARE SHOULD BE TAKEN WHEN SPECIFYING THE            *
C *   VIEWPORT ON DIFFERENT DEVICES.  TERMINAL SCREENS ARE                 *
C *   ADDRESSED IN PIXELS (I.E. VXMIN > 0, VXMAX < 1023, VYMIN             *
C *   > 0, AND VYMAX < 780).  INCREMENTAL PLOTTERS MUST BE                 *
C *   ADDRESSED IN A REAL MEASUREMENT SUCH AS INCHES OR                    *
C *   CENTIMETERS.                                                         *
C *                                                                        *
C *   THREE LABELED COMMON STATEMENTS MUST BE DECLARED IN THE              *
C *   CONTROLLING PROGRAM, THEY ARE:  "WINDOC", THE WINDOWING              *
C *   TRANSFORMATION VALUES USED BY ROUTINE "COORDW".                      *
C *                                                                        *
C *   INITIALIZATION OF THE COMMON AREAS SHOULD BE PERFORMED AT            *
C *   THE BEGINNING OF ANY PROGRAM SEGMENT WHICH USED THE                  *
C *   VIEWPORT-WINDOW TRANSFORMATIONS.                                     *
C *                                                                        *
C *                                                                        *
C *                                                                        *
C *                                                                        *
C *                                                                        *
C *                                                                        *
C *                                                                        *
C ************************************************************************
C
C

      SUBROUTINE VPORT(VXMIN,VXMAX,VYMIN,VYMAX)
C************************************************************************
C   THIS ROUTINE IS USED TO SPECIFY THE VALUES DEFINING
C   THE VIEWPORT BOUNDS.  IF NO BOUNDS WERE SPECIFIED THE
C   DEFAULT VALUES DECLARED DURING INITIALIZATION ARE USED.
C   ENTERED:  VXMIN   - THE MINIMUM HORZ COORDINATE TO BE DISPLAYED
C                       (THE LEFT BOUND).  SET TO ZERO IF CURRENT
C                       VPORT VALUES ARE TO BE RETURNED.
```

```
C              VXMAX    - THE MAXIMUM VERT COORDINATE TO BE DISPLAYED
C                        (THE RIGHT BOUND).   SET TO ZERO IF CURRENT
C                        VPORT VALUES ARE TO BE RETURNED.
C              VYMIN    - THE MINIMUM VERT COORDINATE TO BE DISPLAYED
C                        (THE BOTTOM BOUND).
C              VYMAX    - THE MAXIMUM VERT COORDINATE TO BE DISPLAYED
C                        (THE TOP BOUND).
C
C
C----------------------------------------------------------------
      COMMON /VPORTC/ VXMINC,VXMAXC,VYMINC,VYMAXC,VXR,VXC,VYR,VYC
C
C   INITIALIZE VARIABLES.
      VXMINC=VXMIN
      VXMAXC=VXMAX
      VYMINC=VYMIN
      VYMAXC=VYMAX
C
C   FIND X AND Y-AXES RANGES AND THE CENTER OF THE RANGES.
      VXR=(VXMAX-VXMIN)/2.0
      VXC=(VXMIN+VXMAX)/2.0
      VYR=(VYMAX-VYMIN)/2.0
      VYC=(VYMIN+VYMAX)/2.0
C
C   INITIALIZE THE WINDOW BOUNDS THE SAME AS THE VIEWPORT BOUNDS.
      CALL WINDO(VXMIN,VXMAX,VYMIN,VYMAX)
C
C****************************************************************
      RETURN
      END
C
C
      SUBROUTINE (VXMIN,VXMAX,VYMIN,VYMAX)
C
C****************************************************************
C  THIS SUB IS USED TO:  (1) CALL FOR THE PRESENT VALUES
C  DEFINING THE VIEWPORT BOUNDS, AND (2) SPECIFY THE VALUES
C  DEFINING THE VIEWPORT BOUNDS.  IF NO BOUNDS WERE SPECIFIED THE
C  DEFAULT VALUES DECLARED DURING INITIALIZATION ARE USED.
C  RETURNED:  VXMIN - THE CURRENT LEFT BOUND.
C             VXMAX - THE CURRENT RIGHT BOUND.
C             VYMIN - THE CURRENT BOTTOM BOUND.
C             VYMAX - THE CURRENT TOP BOUND.
```

```
C
C
C-------------------------------------------------------------
      COMMON /VPORTC/ VXMINC,VXMAXC,VYMINC,VYMAXC,VXR,VXC,VYR,VYC
C
      VXMIN=VXMINC
      VXMAX=VXMAXC
      VYMIN=VYMINC
      VYMAX=VYMAXC
C*******************************************************************
      RETURN
      END
C
C
      SUBROUTINE WINDO(WXMIN,WXMAX,WYMIN,WYMAX)
C*******************************************************************
C     THIS ROUTINE IS USED TO SPECIFY THE VALUES
C     DEFINING THE WINDOW BOUNDS.  IF NO BOUNDS WERE SPECIFIED THE
C     DEFAULT VALUES DECLARED DURING INITIALIZATION ARE USED.
C     ENTERED:  WXMIN - THE MINIMUM HORZ COORDINATE TO BE DISPLAYED
C                         (THE LEFT BOUND).  SET TO ZERO IF CURRENT
C                         WINDO VALUES ARE TO BE RETURNED.
C               WXMAX - THE MAXIMUM VERT COORDINATE TO BE DISPLAYED
C                         WINDO VALUES ARE TO BE RETURNED.
C               WYMIN - THE MINIMUM VERT COORDINATE TO BE DISPLAYED
C                         (THE BOTTOM BOUND).
C               WYMAX - THE MAXIMUM VERT COORDINATE TO BE DISPLAYED
C                         (THE TOP BOUND).
C
C
C-------------------------------------------------------------
      COMMON /WINDOC/ WXMINC,WXMAXC,WYMINC,WYMAXC,WXR,WXC,WYR,WYC
C
C  INITIALIZE VARIABLES.
      WXMINC=WXMIN
      WXMAXC=WXMAX
      WYMINC=WYMIN
      WYMAXC=WYMAX
C
C  FIND X AND Y-AXES RANGES AND THE CENTER OF THE RANGES.
      WXR=(WXMAX-WXMIN)/2.0
      WXC=(WXMIN+WXMAX)/2.0
      WYR=(WYMAX-WYMIN)/2.0
      WYC=(WYMIN+WYMAX)/2.0
```

```
C
C   INITIALIZE THE VEIWPORT-WINDOW TRANSFORMATION VALUES.
      CALL TRANSW
C
C***********************************************************************
      RETURN
      END
C
C
      SUBROUTINE SEEWIN(WXMIN,WXMAX,WYMIN,WYMAX)
C***********************************************************************
C    THIS SUB IS USED TO (1) CALL FOR THE PRESENT VALUES
C    DEFINING THE WINDOW BOUNDS, AND (2) SPECIFY THE VALUES
C    DEFINING THE WINDOW BOUNDS.  IF NO BOUNDS WERE SPECIFIED THE
C    DEFAULT VALUES DECLARED DURING INITIALIZATION ARE USED.
C
C    RETURNED: WXMIN - THE CURRENT LEFT BOUND.
C              WXMAX - THE CURRENT RIGHT BOUND.
C              WYMIN - THE CURRENT BOTTOM BOUND.
C              WYMAX - THE CURRENT TOP BOUND.
C
C
C----------------------------------------------------------------
      COMMON /WINDOC/ WXMINC,WXMAXC,WYMINC,WYMAXC,WXR,WXC,WYR,WYC
C
      WXMIN=WXMINC
      WXMAX=MXMAXC
      WYMIN=MYMINC
      WYMAX=MYMAXC
C***********************************************************************
      RETURN
      END
C
C
      SUBROUTINE TRANSW
C***********************************************************************
C    THIS SUB DERIVES THE WINDOW VIEWPORT TRANSFORMATION VALUES.
C    PLACES THE VALUES IN COMMON AREA "TRANWC".  THESE VALUES ARE
C    USED BY ROUTINE "COORDW" WHICH APPLIES THE TRANSFORMATION.
C
C----------------------------------------------------------------
      COMMON /WINDOC/ WXMINC,WXMAXC,WYMINC,WYMAXC,WXR,WXC,WYR,WYC
      COMMON /VPORTC/ VXMINC,VXMAXC,VYMINC,VYMAXC,VXR,VXC,VYR,VYC
      COMMON /TRANWC/ WA,WB,WC,WD
```

```
C
C  WINDOW-VIEWPORT TRANSFORMATIONS FOR HORZ COORDINATES.
      WA=(VXMAXC-VXMINC)/(WXMAXC-WXMINC)
      WB=VXMINC-(WXMINC*WA)
C
C  WINDOW-VIEWPORT TRANSFORMATIONS FOR VERT COORDINATES.
      WC=(VYMAXC-VYMINC)/(WYMAXC-WYMINC)
      WD=VYMINC-(WYMINC*WA)
C
C**********************************************************************
      RETURN
      END
C
C
      SUBROUTINE COORDW(XP,YP,TWXP,TWYP)
C**********************************************************************
C   THIS SUB TAKES A 2-D POINT AND APPLIES THE WINDOW-VIEWPORT
C   TRANSFORMATIONS AS DERIVED IN ROUTINE "TRANSW".
C   ENTERED:  XP - USER HORZ. COORDINATE TO BE TRANSFORMED.
C             YP - USER VERT. COORDINATE TO BE TRANSFORMED.
C   RETURNED: TWXP - THE TRANSFORMED HORZ. COORDINATE.
C             TWYP - THE TRANSFORMED VERT. COORDINATE.
C
C
C--------------------------------------------------------------------
      COMMON /TRANWC/ WA,WB,WC,WD
C
      TWXP=WA*XP+WB
      TWYP=WC*YP+WD
C
C**********************************************************************
      RETURN
      END
C
C
      SUBROUTINE PPORTW(XMIN,XMAX,YMIN,YMAX,XPIX,YPIX)
C**********************************************************************
C
C--------------------------------------------------------------------
C
C  CALCULATE THE WINDOW RANGES.
      XRANGE+ABS(XMAX-XMIN)
      YRANGE=ABS(YMAX-YMIN)
C
```

```
C  CALCULATE A SCALE FACTOR BETWEEN THE VEIWPORT (XPIX,YPIX) AND THE
C  WINDOW (XMIN,XMAX,YMIN,YMAX) SPECIFICATIONS FOR THE X AND Y AXES.
     SX=XPIX/XRANGE
     SY=YPIX/YRANGE
C
C  DETERMINE WHICH OF THE SCALE FACTORS WILL PRESERVE THE RATIO OF
C  HEIGHT TO WIDTH BETWEEN THE VIEWPORT AND WINDOW.
     IF(SX .LE. SY) SF=SX
     IF(SX .GT. SY) SF=SY
C  CALCULATE THE VIEWPORT SPECIFICATIONS USING THE WINDOW SPECS
C  AND THE PROPER SCALE FACTOR.
     XSET=(XPIX-(SF*XRANGE))/2.0
     YSET=(YPIX-(SF*YRANGE))/2.0
     VXMN=XSET
     VXMX=XPIX-XSET
     VYMN=YSET
     VYMX=YPIX-YSET
C
C  ESTABLISH THE VIEWPORT SPECIFICATIONS.
     CALL VPORT(VXMN,VXMX,VYMN,VYMX)
C
C  ESTABLISH THE WINDOW SPECIFICATIONS.
     CALL WINDO(XMIN,XMAX,YMIN,YMAX)
C
C*********************************************************************
     RETURN
     END
C
C

     SUBROUTINE WARN(IWKEY)
C*********************************************************************
C     THIS ROUTINE PROVIDES FOR THE OUTPUT OF WARNING MESSAGES.
C          ENTERED:  IWKEY   - THE WARNING KEY (I.E. WHICH WARNING
C                               MESSAGE IS TO BE ISSUED).
C
C
C-------------------------------------------------------------------
     COMMON /TOFILE/ INTERM,IOTERM, IPTR,INP1,INP2,INP3,INP4,
    +                IOUTP1,IOUTP2,IDEBUG
C
C  THE TEKTRONIX PACKAGE REQUIRES A CALL TO T.C.S. ROUTINE "ANMODE"
C  TO CORRECT THE DISCREPANCY BETWEEN STORED BEAM POSITION AND
C  THE ACTUAL BEAM LOCATION CAUSED BY NON T.C.S. OUTPUT TO THE
C  TERMINAL.
```

```
      CALL ANMODE
C
      GO TO (1,2,3,4,5,6,7,8,9,10,11,12,13,14,15,16,17,18,19,20,21,22
     +),IWKEY
C
    1 RETURN
C
    2 WRITE(IOTERM,9001)
 9002 FORMAT(/,' WARNING - THE VALUE GIVEN FOR X-SCALING IS NEAR
      ZERO,',+/,'        (-0.0001 < SCALE FACTOR > 0.0001).',/)
      RETURN
C
    3 WRITE(IOTERM,9003)
 9003 FORMAT(/,' WARNING - THE VALUE GIVEN FOR Y-SCALING IS NEAR
      ZERO,',+/,'        (-0.0001 < SCALE FACTOR > 0.0001).',/)
      RETURN
C
    4 WRITE(IOTERM,9004)
 9004 FORMAT(/,' WARNING - THE VALUE GIVEN FOR Z-SCALING IS NEAR
      ZERO,',+/,'        (-0.0001 < SCALE FACTOR > 0.0001).',/)
      RETURN
C
    5 WRITE(IOTERM,9005)
 9005 FORMAT(/,' WARNING - THE TEXT CHARACTER NOT PLOTABLE.',/)
C
    6 WRITE(IOTERM,9006)
 9006 FORMAT(/,' WARNING - THE VALUE GIVEN FOR SCALING IS NEAR
      ZERO,',/,+'        (-0.0001 < SCALE FACTOR > 0.0001).',/)
    7 RETURN
C
    8 WRITE(IOTERM,9008)
 9008 FORMAT(/,' WARNING - PARAMETER PASSED TO "WINDO3" WAS NEAR
      ZERO,',+/,        (-0.0001 < PARAMETER > 0.0001).',/)
      RETURN
C
    9 RETURN
C
   10 RETURN(IOTERM,9010)
 9010 FORMAT(/,' WARNING - PARAMETER PASSED TO "PAGE" WAS NEAR
      ZERO,',/,+'        (-0.0001 < PARAMETER > 0.0001).',/)
      RETURN
C
   11 WRITE(IOTERM,9011)
 9011 FORMAT(/,' WARNING - INVALID TOPOLOGY FOR AN OBJECT,
      VIOLATION',/,+'      OF THE EULER FORMULA.',/)
      RETURN
```

```
C
      12 WRITE(IOTERM,9012)
9012 FORMAT(/,' WARNING - OVERFLOW OF TOPOGRAPHY ARRAY (NUMBER
     OF',/,+'        MEMBERS MUST BE LESS THAN OR EQUAL TO 100.',/)
     RETURN
C
      13 WRITE(IOTERM,9013)
9013 FORMAT(/,' WARNING - OVERFLOW IN CONNECTIVITY ARRAY (NUMBER
     OF',/,+'        CONNECTION MUST BE LESS THAN OR EQUAL TO
     100).',/)
     RETURN
C
      14 WRITE(IOTERM,9014)
9014 FORMAT(/,' WARNING - OVERFLOW OF 3-D SUBSCRIPTED POINT
     LIST',/,+'        (MAXIMUM NUMBER OF POINTS IS 100).',/)
     RETURN
C
      15 WRITE(IOTERM,9015)
9015 FORMAT(/,' WARNING - NUMBER OF VERTICIES READ IS LESS THAN
     THE',/,+'        NUMBER OF POINT COORDINATES READ.',/)
     RETURN
C
      16 WRITE(IOTERM,9016)
9016 FORMAT(/,' WARNING - COMMAND NOT FOUND.',/)
     RETURN
C
      17 WRITE(IOTERM,9017)
9017 FORMAT(/,' WARNING - INVALID OR MISSING PARAMETERS.',/)
     RETURN
C
      18 WRITE(IOTERM,9018)
9018 FORMAT(/,' WARNING - TOPOLOGY FOR OBJECT NOT FOLLOWED BY THE
     GEOMETRY.',/)
     RETURN
C
      19 WRITE(IOTERM,9019)
9019 FORMAT(/,' WARNING - INVALID CHARACTERS IN NUMERIC STRING.',/)
     RETURN
C
      20 WRITE(IOTERM,9020)
9020 FORMAT(/,' WARNING - NUMBER OF COLUMNS IN ROW WAS MORE
     THAN',/,'        THE LENGTH ESTABLISHED BY FIRST ROW INPUT.')
     RETURN
C
      21 WRITE(IOTERM,9021)
9021 FORMAT(/,' WARNING - NUMBER OF COLUMNS IN ROW WAS LESS
```

```
      THAN',/,'         THE LENGTH ESTABLISHED BY FIRST ROW INPUT.')
      RETURN
   22 WRITE(IOTERM,9022)
 9022 FORMAT(O,' WARNING - NO DATA EXISTS IN OBJECT BUFFER.')
      RETURN
C
C**************************************************************************
      END
```

EXERCISES   1.   The use of the graphics tablet for freehand sketching has been
                 explained in detail in this chapter. Select the DRAW2D mode
                 and enter the sketches shown. A freehand motion across the
                 tablet face will be read and stored as a two-dimensional data-
                 base.

2. Now select the DRAWSP mode and enter any type of planning sketch desired. Figures 4.3-4.9 are good examples.

3. Computer-assisted freehand sketching can be done with an electric pencil, mouse, or joystick; choose one of these devices and develop a sketch that can be used in a communication to a client.

4. Change pointing devices and develop a site description similar in nature to Figure 4.10.

5. Select the electric pencil and data tablet to try a balloon sketch for research and planning a new house construction.

6. From the balloon sketch just done and demonstrated in Figure 4.11, develop a preliminary sketch. Follow the suggestions contained in Chapter 4 and shown in Figure 4.12.

7. Input a sample floorplan for this project. Try more than one solution. Once the sketch has reached this stage, it is easy to modify using DRAW2D.

8. After the floorplan has been approved by the client and entered into DRAW2D, lay out and determine the building slope and plan view of the site.

9. From the information stored in Exercise 4, develop a quick elevation of the new house developed in Exercises 5-8.

10. Next lay out a general cross section of the project as described in the text. Represent construction materials such as wood, concrete, steel, and so forth.

11. From the general section, develop wall sections for four different framing systems as shown.

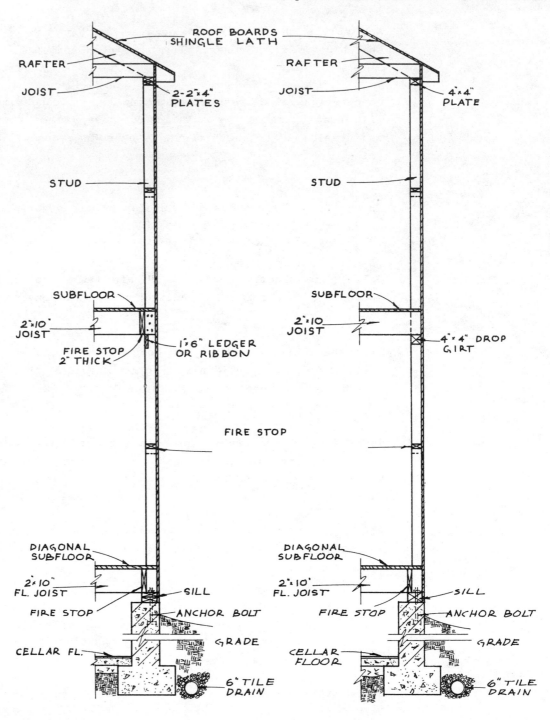

ROOF BOARDS
SHINGLE LATH

RAFTER

JOIST

2-2"x4"
PLATES

STUD

SUBFLOOR

2"x10"
JOIST

FIRE STOP
2" THICK

1"x6" LEDGER
OR RIBBON

FIRE STOP

DIAGONAL
SUBFLOOR

2"x10"
FL. JOIST

FIRE STOP

SILL

ANCHOR BOLT

CELLAR FL.

GRADE

6" TILE
DRAIN

RAFTER

JOIST

4"x4"
PLATE

STUD

SUBFLOOR

2"x10"
JOIST

4"x4" DROP
GIRT

FIRE STOP

DIAGONAL
SUBFLOOR

2"x10"
FL. JOIST

FIRE STOP

SILL

ANCHOR BOLT

CELLAR
FLOOR

GRADE

6" TILE
DRAIN

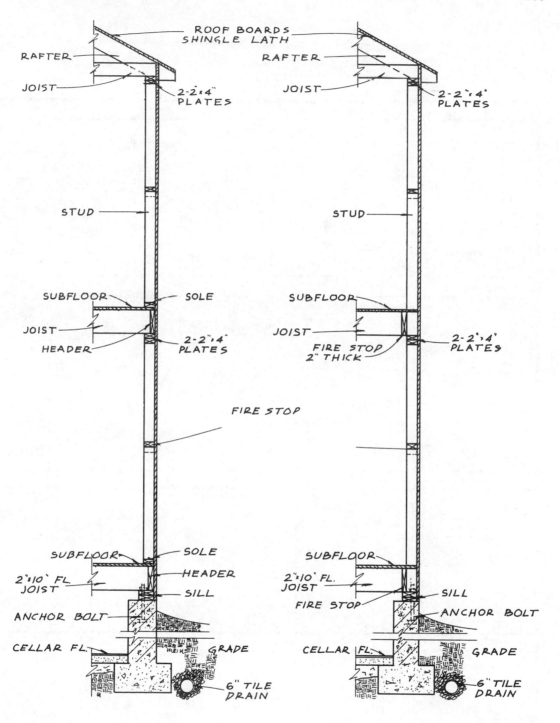

12. Individual rooms may now be planned and entered as sketches. Develop a series of sketches for the kitchen; suggestions are shown.

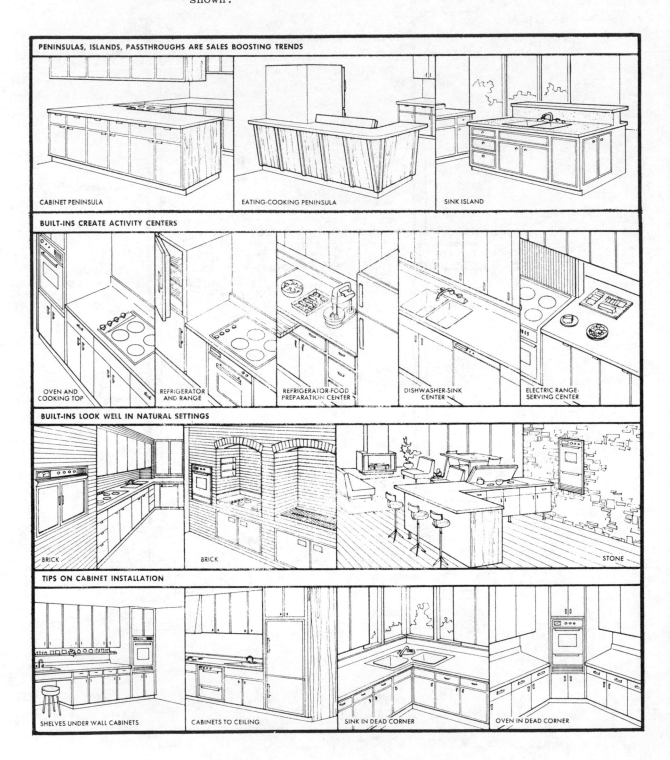

PENINSULAS, ISLANDS, PASSTHROUGHS ARE SALES BOOSTING TRENDS

CABINET PENINSULA

EATING-COOKING PENINSULA

SINK ISLAND

BUILT-INS CREATE ACTIVITY CENTERS

OVEN AND COOKING TOP

REFRIGERATOR AND RANGE

REFRIGERATOR-FOOD PREPARATION CENTER

DISHWASHER-SINK CENTER

ELECTRIC RANGE-SERVING CENTER

BUILT-INS LOOK WELL IN NATURAL SETTINGS

BRICK

BRICK

STONE

TIPS ON CABINET INSTALLATION

SHELVES UNDER WALL CABINETS

CABINETS TO CEILING

SINK IN DEAD CORNER

OVEN IN DEAD CORNER

13. Bathrooms often reflect a lack of planning; develop a set of
sketches for the bath as shown.

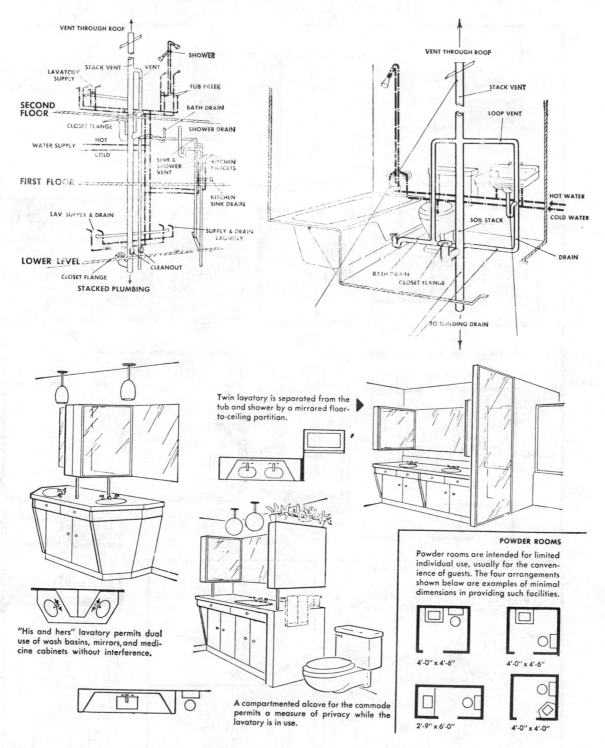

Twin lavatory is separated from the
tub and shower by a mirrored floor-
to-ceiling partition.

"His and hers" lavatory permits dual
use of wash basins, mirrors, and medi-
cine cabinets without interference.

A compartmented alcove for the commode
permits a measure of privacy while the
lavatory is in use.

POWDER ROOMS

Powder rooms are intended for limited
individual use, usually for the conven-
ience of guests. The four arrangements
shown below are examples of minimal
dimensions in providing such facilities.

4'-0" x 4'-6"   4'-0" x 4'-6"

2'-9" x 6'-0"   4'-0" x 4'-0"

14. Plan and execute sketches for the design of a utility room as shown.

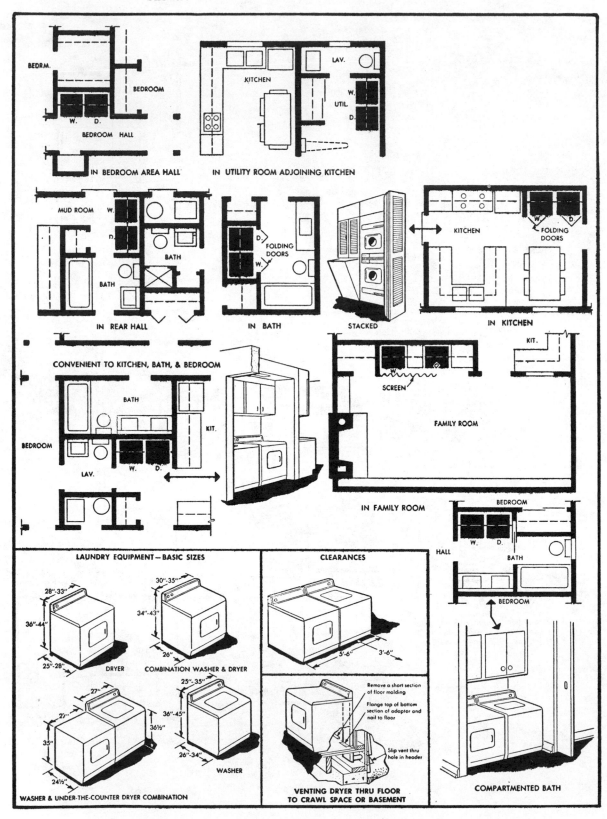

5 Geometric and Template Image Processing

Geometric and template image processing for architectural applications is generally thought of as being either passive or active in nature. When a designer selects a computer mode rather than manual documentation, a decision is made if the graphics can be done with computer memory modules. The latter is referred to as computer-assisted (Chap. 6) rather than computer-aided. The two terms aided and assisted do not carry the same meaning. Computer-aided (this chapter) is an *active* process because it appears that the computer has the ability to solve graphic problems without prior input by humans. Types of hardware in this class are referred to as *smart*. A smart terminal has a microprocessor built into it for computer-aided instruction of graphics.

Computer-assisted graphics systems are referred to as *passive*. Passive graphic solutions are also done by a computer but are referred to as *offline*. An example of this type of graphic display for architecture is the designer who has graphic routines stored outside the computer and calls the computer with a set of instructions whenever there is need for a particular graphic solution. There may or may not be time delay when passive systems are used; however, in an active system the answer is immediate and is referred to as *real-time* graphics. In the last few years real-time graphics for architects have been used in connection with an interactive graphics system (IGS). The IGS is manufactured especially for

113

active graphics problems falling into one of four major application lines: drafting, mapping, image processing, or business analysis.

The standard products of an IGS are detailing symbols, piping, electrical, figure construction, or useful curves and surfaces. These IGSs generate more accurate drawings and patterns at a lower cost and in less time. The IGS processor or computer handles the repetitive aspects of drafting, freeing the operator to focus on the creative side of the work.

The problem will be given in most cases but has to be identified as IGS possible or not. The term *computer valuable* or IGS possible means that the designer will make a decision about whether the extent and complexity of the design warrants the time and expense of the IGS process. If the answer is yes, then a sketch of the problem as shown in Chapter 4 is constructed to determine if this particular design is unique or if it fits into a larger or more universal design problem. Whenever possible the designer writes the program so that not only the problem at hand can be solved but also any other of that type. The ability to correctly formulate the problem is the key to the success or failure of an IGS in a design office.

GRAPHIC SYMBOLS   Before plunging into a detailed description of the many types of graphic symbols that an IGS can produce, it seems fitting to devote some explanation to how the digital computer is programmed for a host-IGS environment. Programming for an IGS design station falls into two logical groups. The first is the designer who knows very little about computers or how high-level languages are used to create subroutines or subprograms. This kind of user wants to be able to draw standard parts, as described in Chapter 6, and is therefore concerned with learning how to use a programmer's set of instructions in order to plot a detailed drawing containing graphic symbols.

The second interest in programming is from the designer who wishes to go farther than the computer programmer and link the input (picture-type information) with the output such that each input is immediately fed back to an operator via a display. This combination best uses the interactive part of the IGS. This type of operation requires more knowledge of programming than either the casual user or the computer programmer. It is true that the IGS was unheard of several years ago. When we consider what the computer is and how it has helped in the design field of architecture, it was only natural that gradually the computer would be used to document as well as design. The computer of then, and the IGS of now, was and still is an extremely fast and accurate slide rule, sorter, data processor, simulated rememberer, logic organizer, *comparer*, evaluator, electronic drafting machine, and specification writer. The IGS will do whatever a human directs it to do more accurately and faster than any human alive. The real danger of such a wonder machine is that we tend to use the IGS as a crutch. We must continue to think; the IGS will handle the long manual routine items such as listing data points or drawing lines.

How, then, can the IGS be put to immediate use in the classroom or architect's office to do symbol drawing? First, do not fear the machine; study how it works and how to communicate with the particular model that you have chosen. Second, consider how much of your daily routine is taken up with symbols or highly repetitive nonthinking drafting tasks. If this is more than one-third, these types of tasks can be done by the computer and release over 30% of the work force to do design tasks. Thirty percent will return the cost of the IGS in 1 year for a large office.

If a small office is involved, maybe a time-sharing renting technique will work effectively. Third, begin by automating the simplest tasks first to gain understanding and confidence in IGS usage. If possible, choose a reoccurring problem that must be solved by a different set of data each time and requires 1 or more hours to solve by a draftsperson. Chances are the time required to computerize the problem will take a couple of hours also, but the program can be used over and over again by inserting different data and solving the problem in milliseconds after that. Once a task has been set up and stored, the time required to repeat it is 1/100,000 of manual. Naturally one-time jobs are not done on an IGS.

IGS Detailing Symbols

IGS detail symbols on plan-type drawings and construction sections are most important for the new user to understand and properly apply. These symbols guide the reader, and therefore the builder, throughout the construction drawing package. A typical set of drawings making up a construction contract may include 100 or more sheets having over 100 separate details; therefore it is important that each detail be identified (properly labeled) for easy location within the package. Common symbols found on computer-generated drawings can include such things as piping as shown in Figure 5.1. Figure 5.1 is called a catalog sheet. It contains 40 symbols that can be used in single-line connection or double-line diagrams. Additional symbols appear in Figure 5.2 and are used to indicate heating, ventilating, and air conditioning for buildings.

Other miscellaneous symbols are also shown in Figure 5.2 and will be used later in the chapter, for now it is important to know

TYPE OF FITTING		SINGLE-LINE CONVENTION					DOUBLE-LINE CONVENTION					FLOW DIAGRAM
		Flanged	Screwed	B.&S.-H.&S.	Welded	Soldered	Flanged	Screwed	B.&S.-H.&S.	Welded	Soldered	
1	Joint											
2	Joint-Expansion											
3	Union											
4	Sleeve											
5	Reducer											
6	Reducer-Eccentric											
7	Reducing Flange											
8	Bushing											
9	Elbow-45°											
10	Elbow-90°											
11	Elbow-Long radius											
12	Elbow-(turned up)											
13	Elbow-(turned down)											
14	Elbow-Side outlet (outlet up)											
15	Elbow-Side outlet (outlet down)											
16	Elbow-Base											
17	Elbow-Double branch											
18	Elbow-Reducing											
19	Lateral											
20	Tee											
21	Tee-Single sweep											

FIGURE 5.1 Piping symbols available by number.

how these detailing symbols are stored and used by the IGS operator
in a meaningful way. An IGS has the ability to store preprogrammed
symbols so that an operator may work at a video preview station
called a direct-view storage tube (DVST). This DVST work station
has a keyboard for entering commands to the graphics processor, a
set of cross hairs which appear on the screen, and a graphics tablet

TYPE OF FITTING		SINGLE-LINE CONVENTION					DOUBLE-LINE CONVENTION					FLOW DIAGRAM
		Flanged	Screwed	B.&S.–H.&S.	Welded	Soldered	Flanged	Screwed	B.&S.–H.&S.	Welded	Soldered	
22	Tee –Double sweep											
23	Tee –(outlet up)											
24	Tee –(outlet down)											
25	Tee–Side outlet (outlet up)											
26	Tee–Side outlet (outlet down)											
27	Cross											
28	Valve–Globe											
29	Valve–Angle											
30	Valve–Motor operated globe											motor operated
31	Valve–Gate											
32	Valve–Angle gate											
33	Valve–Motor operated gate											motor operated
34	Valve–Check											
35	Valve–Angle check											
36	Valve–Safety											
37	Valve–Angle safety											
38	Valve–Quick opening											
39	Valve–Float operated											
40	Stop Cock											

FIGURE 5.1 (Continued)

as explained in Chapter 4. In addition to the freehand sketch mode, a graphics tablet may be used to move the cursor on the screen. An IGS user may choose to move the cursor by this method or use a

HEATING, VENTILATING, AND AIR CONDITIONING

Item	Symbol	Item	Symbol
Ceiling Air Diffuser (Supply Outlet)	12" throat-1000 cfm	Deflecting Vanes at supply outlet	
Butterfly Damper (Hand operated, unless noted motor operated)	Plan View Side View	Splitter Damper at branch takeoffs	
Automatic Louver or Damper (Plan View)	M	Register, Sidewall (Plan) or Ceiling (Edge view) (Supply outlet, exhaust inlet, and return inlet) SR=Supply Register SG=Supply Grille ER=Exhaust Register EG=Exhaust Grille RR=Return Register RG=Return Grille	SR, ER or RR 20×12-700 cfm
Direction of Air Flow — Supply / Return / Exhaust		Register, Sidewall (Elevation)	
Duct Section (Exhaust or Return)		Register, Ceiling (Plan) or Sidewall (Far side of duct)	
Duct Section (Supply)		Turning Vanes	
Duct Size in Inches (First figure, side shown; second figure, side not shown)	12 x 20	Unit Heater	UH-7
Electric Duct Heater	DH-2	Inclined Rise in Respect to Air Flow	R
Flexible Connection		Inclined Drop in Respect to Air Flow	D
Access Door (Indicate size)	AD-12 x 18	Damper	
Louver (Inlet and End Views) (Indicate type and motor location if power operated)			

FIGURE 5.2   Additional symbols for IGS.

MISCELLANEOUS   PIPE   FITTINGS

Type of fitting	Symbol	Type of fitting	Symbol
Control valve – pressure reducing		Strainer – Y pattern	
Eductor		Strainer – double	
Filter – oil		Strainer – single	
Fire hose cabinet		Tank (Designate type)	REC
Fire hydrant	F	Thermometer	
Flow meter		Trap – air	T
Flow meter – totalizing		Valve – flap	
Hose bibb		Valve – lockshield	
Hose coupling – quick connecting		Valve – sample	Label
Orifice plate		Pipe cap	
Plug valve		Pipe plug	
Pump (Indicate type such as vacuum)		Flexible connection (Both double and single line)	
Pressure gauge with cock		Mechanical joint (Double line)	
Sight flow indicator		Mechanical joint (Single line)	
Sight funnel		Dresser coupling (Double line)	
Hose bibb valve		Dresser coupling (Single line)	

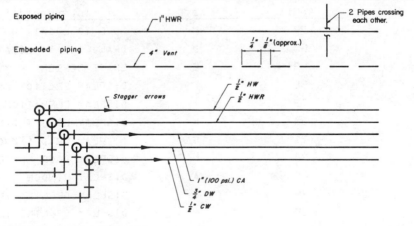

Exposed piping   ⌐1" HWR   2 Pipes crossing each other.

Embedded piping   4" Vent   ¼" ⅛" (approx.)

Stagger arrows   ½" HW
                        ½" HWR

1" (100 psi.) CA
¾" DW
½" CW

FIGURE 5.2 (Continued)

joystick control or a set of thumb wheels. Before the cursor can be moved, however, it must first appear on the screen from storage. The IGS operator may display a cursor by typing

　　　CALL SCURSOR(IX,IY)

where IX and IY are the screen coordinates for the intersection of the cross hairs. Once the cursor is visible on the screen, it may be moved by the joystick, tablet, or thumb wheels. The cursor is displayed in refresh graphics mode so it is dynamic and is free to float around the screen face. Most IGS work stations are limited to cross hairs refresh only.

　　　After the cursor is moved to a desired location, the IGS operator may send this location back to the graphics processor or store this location as a point in the database memory module. This is done by typing

　　　CALL SCURSOR(KEY,IXTO,IYTO)

where IXTO and IYTO are returned to the IGS as screen locations and KEY represents the desired function. For example, suppose an operator wanted to send a "move to INTO, IYTO" to the graphics processor. In this case KEY is set equal to 77 which is the ASCII signal sent to the graphics processor when the M key from the keyboard is depressed. Numerical (ASCII) signals from 0 to 127 may be sent to the graphics processor for interpretation and translation into a move, draw, display symbol, erase, make copy, letter, or end session. The number of interpretations are limited to the number of keys on the keyboard. A typical keyboard arrangement and ASCII numerical codes are shown in Table 5.1.

　　　To represent the detailing symbols which can be used, let's assign the following keys from the Table 5.1:

ASCII	Key	Interpretation
77	M	MOVE TO LOCATION
68	D	DRAW LINE TO LOCATION
69	E	ERASE SCREEN
70	F	DISPLAY SECTION SYMBOL
73	I	DISPLAY ELEVATION SYMBOL
88	X	DISPLAY LONGITUDINAL SECTION SYMBOL
71	G	DISPLAY GRID SYMBOL
78	N	DISPLAY DOOR NUMBER SYMBOL
65	A	DISPLAY WINDOW TYPE SYMBOL
79	O	DISPLAY OPENING IN PLAN SYMBOL
80	P	DISPLAY OPENING IN WALL SYMBOL
85	U	DISPLAY OPENING IN CEILING SYMBOL
72	H	MAKE A HARD COPY OF SCREEN
76	L	LETTER NOTES ON SCREEN
71	Q	END SESSION AT IGS

TABLE 5.1 ASCII Code Chart

CONTROL				HIGH X & Y GRAPHIC INPUT		LOW X		LOW Y	
NUL 0		DLE 16		SP 32	0 48	@ 64	P 80	` 96	P 112
SOH 1		DC1 17		! 33	1 49	A 65	Q 81	a 97	q 113
STX 2		DC2 18		" 34	2 50	B 66	R 82	b 98	r 114
ETX 3		DC3 19		# 35	3 51	C 67	S 83	c 99	s 115
EOT 4		DC4 20		$ 36	4 52	D 68	T 84	d 100	t 116
ENQ 5		NAK 21		% 37	5 53	E 69	U 85	e 101	u 117
ACK 6		SYN 22		& 38	6 54	F 70	V 86	f 102	v 118
BEL 7 BELL		ETB 23		' 39	7 55	G 71	W 87	g 103	w 119
BS 8 BACK SPACE		CAN 24		(40	8 56	H 72	X 88	h 104	x 120
HT 9		EM 25		) 41	9 57	I 73	Y 89	i 105	y 121
LF 10 LINE FEED		SUB 26		* 42	: 58	J 74	Z 90	j 106	z 122
VT 11		ESC 27		+ 43	; 59	K 75	[91	k 107	{ 123
FF 12		FS 28		, 44	< 60	L 76	\ 92	l 108		124
CR 13 RETURN		GS 29		- 45	= 61	M 77	] 93	m 109	} 125
SO 14		RS 30		. 46	> 62	N 78	∧ 94	n 110	~ 126
SI 15		US 31		/ 47	? 63	O 79	— 95	o 111	RUBOUT (DEL) 127

121

To make the list of keys just assigned function as desired, an interactive program that can be used over and over again is written and stored in the IGS for any architectural use. The first statement in the program activates the DVST through the processor key:

```
CALL INITT(JBAUD)
```

where JBAUD is set equal to the transmission speed of your IGS. Next the keys that are to be used are entered as

```
DATA IMOVE/77/,IDRAW/68/,IERASE/69/,ISECTN/70/
DATA IELEVN/73/,ILONGS/88/,IGRID/71/,INDOOR/78/
DATA IWINDW/65/,IOPENG/79/,IWALLO/80/
DATA ICEILG/85/,ICOPYS/72/,LETTER/76/,IQUIT/71/
```

where the ASCII numerical values are assigned computer storage locations. At this point the program statement CALL SCURSOR (KEY, IXTO,IYTO) can be used to find which of the keys was depressed by the IGS operator by

```
IF(KEY.EQ.77) CALL MOVARS(IXID,IYTO)
IF(KEY.EQ.68) CALL DRWAR(IXTO,IYTO)
IF(KEY.EQ.69) CALL ERASE
IF(KEY.EQ.70) CALL SECSYM(IXTO,IYTO)
IF(KEY.EQ.73) CALL ELESYM(IXTO,IYTO)
IF(KEY.EQ.88) CALL LONGSC(IXTO,IYTO)
IF(KEY.EQ.71) CALL GRID(IXTO,IYTO)
IF(KEY.EQ.78) CALL CIRCL(IXTO,IYTO)
IF(KEY.EQ.65) CALL CIRCL(IXTO,IYTO)
IF(KEY.EQ.79) CALL XMARK(IXTO,IYTO)
IF(KEY.EQ.80) CALL YMARK(IXTO,IYTO)
IF(KEY.EQ.85) CALL ZMARK(IXTO,IYTO)
IF(KEY.EQ.72) CALL HCOPY
IF(KEY.EQ.76) CALL LETTER
IF(KEY.EQ.71) CALL FINITT(0,0)
```

where the series of IF statements asks if KEY is equal to the ASCII list 77 through 71 in the order indicated. When the numerical value of KEY equals or matches the ASCII equivalent, then the CALL command following the IF portion is executed. How to write these call routines will be explained in Chapter 6.

Equipment Identification

The recognition and proper use of equipment used in commercial building construction is a must for the IGS user. Figure 5.3 illustrates various pieces of equipment and how they might appear if used in a construction detail. Note that in Figure 5.4 equipment in plan views is shown differently from the same equipment in elevation views.

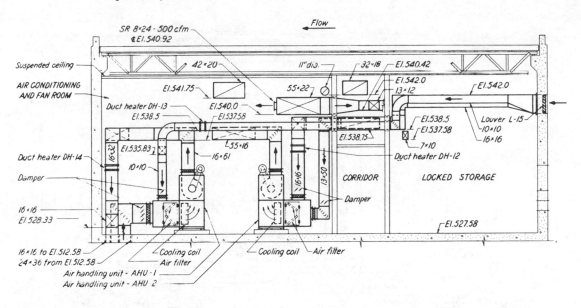

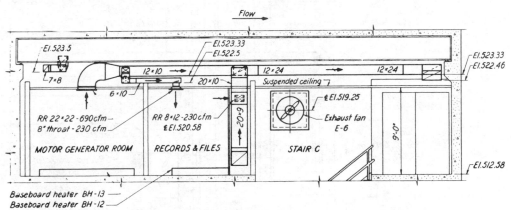

FIGURE 5.3   Equipment items for IGS.

An IGS user prepares working plans and detailed drawings that require equipment identification from notes, verbal instructions, and rough or detailed sketches for architectural or construction purposes. Freehand sketching is one of the best means of translating notes and verbal instructions into meaningful data. This type of sketching should not be confused with the design sketching done in Chapter 4; it is rather a method of procedure for the IGS detailer to use when organizing the material for a working drawing sheet.

An inexpensive squared paper that will fit on the graphics tablet is suitable for detail sketching to the required scale. Sketches are always done to the scale that will be used in the working drawing so several sketches may be layered for trial arrangement

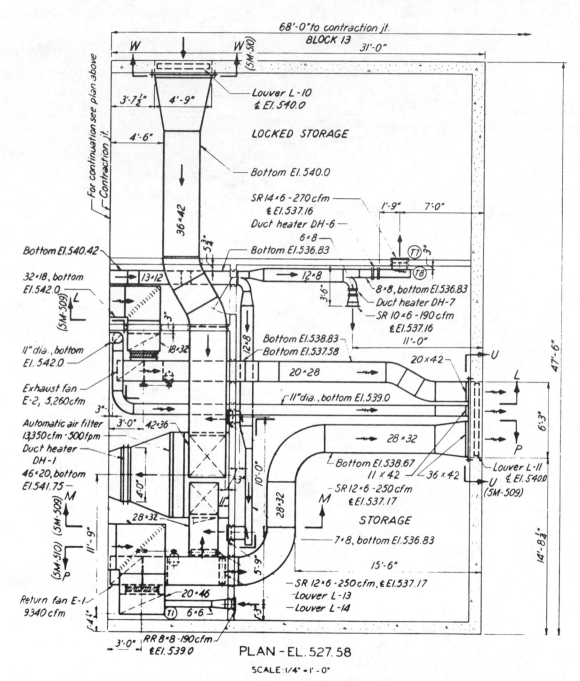

FIGURE 5.4   Equipment layout in PLAN view.

before formal drafting is done. Sketching techniques are faster
than programming, and changes can be made because the CRT screen
face is easy to erase. The project architect will approve the
sketches and arrangement as the detailer develops them, thereby

saving the need for hard copies to be changed at this early project stage.

The IGS detailer may be responsible for plan-type sketches or other details including trial elevations. The ability to sketch with precision and some degree of speed is required of most architectural detailers. Certain methods for developing sketching skills were covered in Chapter 4.

Piping, Plumbing, Heating, and Ventilating

Piping, heating and ventilation (HV) systems, and the many components that make up air handling ductwork are of interest to a great many IGS users. This area of architectural graphics is largely ignored in conventional textbooks. It is of primary concern in a large number of offices due to the lack of qualified detailers and is one of the easiest areas to computer-automate. Although each group is specialized, all are directly concerned with various forms of piping, hose, ducts, and the fittings that connect these components into workable systems.

This section is about piping and HV systems. The term system means a complete network of pipes, ducts, and other parts designed to do a specific job in a structure or building. In this section the user will be introduced to piping symbols and how to display them. Building operations are so tied into these systems that a piping or duct breakdown in one part of a building can bring operations in another section to an almost immediate halt.

Piping carries fluids from one part of the building to another as shown in Figure 5.5. In addition to carrying liquids such as hydraulic fluids or oils, piping systems carry gas and compressed air (shown in Figure 5.6), which are considered to be fluids because they flow. Fluids travel through a system at various temperatures, pressures, and speeds.

Before looking at these more involved networks of pipes, consider a typical section of a system. Figure 5.7 shows a common arrangement of pipes in a building. They control the flow of the fluids through the floor. The fittings connect the sections of pipe.

To permit the pipeline to make the turn as shown in detail A of Figure 5.7, a fitting called an elbow is displayed. This is done by a subroutine called ELBOW. Another fitting is displayed by calling TEE, because it resembles the letter T. Gate valves are drawn by the computer through the use of call GATE. The subroutine ELBOW is a routine that the author has used to display this fitting and would appear as the following lines of call routine:

```
C ** ** ** ** ** ** ** ** ** ** ** ** ** ** ** ** ** ** ** ** ** ** ** **
C * THIS SUBROUTINE DRAWS AN ELBOW FITTING ANYWHERE ON THE   *
C * PLOTTER SURFACE.  FOUR POSSIBLE POSITIONS ARE USED       *
C *                                                          *
C *          1=ZERO DEGREES ROTATION                         *
C *          2=90 DEGREES ROTATION                           *
C *          3=180 DEGREES ROTATION                          *
C *          4=270 DEGREES ROTATION                          *
C ** ** ** ** ** ** ** ** ** ** ** ** ** ** ** ** ** ** ** ** ** ** ** **

      SUBROUTINE ELBOW(XXX,YYY,SIZE,POS)
      CALL PLOT(XXX,YYY,3)
      XL=SIZE*7
      YY=YYY-SIZE
      XC=XXX+SIZE*6
      R=SIZE*6.
      Y=YYY+SIZE
      IF(POS.EQ.1)GOTO1
      IF(POS.EQ.2)GOTO2
      IF(POS.EQ.3)GOTO3
      IF(POS.EQ.4)GOTO4
    1 CALL RECT(XXX,YY,SIZE,XL,0.,3)
      CALL RECT(XXX,YYY,SIZE,XL,90.,3)
      CALL CIRCL(XC,YYY,0.,90.,R,R,0.)
      GOTO10
    2 CALL RECT(XXX,YYY,SIZE,XL,180.,3)
      XOFF=XXX+SIZE
      CALL RECT(XOFF,YYY,SIZE,XL,90.,3)
      YR=YYY+SIZE*6
      CALLCIRCL(XOFF,YR,90.,180.,R,R,0.)
      GOTO10
    3 CALL RECT(XXX,YYY,SIZE,XXL,270.,3)
      CALL RECT(XXX,Y,SIZE,XL,180.,3)
      XR=XXX-SIZE*6.
      CALL CIRCL(XR,YYY,180.,270.,R,R,0.)
      GOTO10
    4 CALL RECT(XXX,YYY,SIZE,XL,0.,3)
      X=XXX-SIZE
      CALL RECT(X,YYY,SIZE,XL,270.,3)
      YR=YYY-SIZE*6.
      CALL CIRCL(XXX,YR,270.,360.,R,R,0.)
   10 RETURN
      END
```

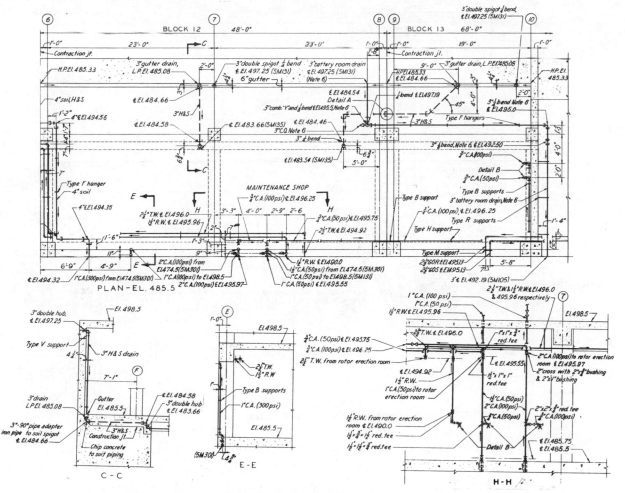

FIGURE 5.5 Typical piping diagram

Pipe fitting (like elbows) are preprogrammed as template symbols and
are the parts used to connect section of pipe, section of tube, and
ductwork. Those shown in Figure 5.7 are threaded fittings. When
the system is first set up, the pipe symbols are located by a grid
placement technique known as *push button template parts*. The next
call draws are used to connect the fittings, and call letters are
added to label each section of the system.

   This piping example illustrates the fact that a piping diagram
and the actual system perform a particular job. The sole purpose of
the piping in the display is to show the piping leading to and from
various sections of the building. Regardless of how complicated the
system may seem to be, the display is simply a network of components
which carry a liquid or gas from one point to another. With the

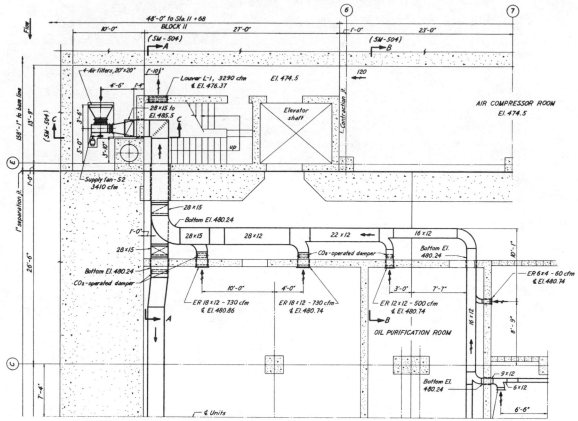

FIGURE 5.6 Typical ducting diagram.

introduction of an automatic method of drawing the diagram, the architectural user who is knowledgeable in piping assembly can now produce excellent diagrams for documentation and later installation. Actually, it is not that piping diagrams are more complicated than other forms of CAD drafting; it is just that it may have many elements in it in order to accomplish its function.

The drawing represented in Figure 5.5 was done by an IGS detailer a window at a time. Each window such as PLAN, ELEVATION, TYPICAL SECTIONS, and details filled the DVST screen. The process began with a plan generation; after checking, it was routed to the upper left-hand corner of a plotter bed. Likewise, the elevation and various details were done one at a time; hard copies were made for the checker and then routed to their proper plotter locations. Finally, block notes were typed and checked on the IGS and sent to the plotter, completing the representation shown in Figure 5.5.

Display diagrams done in this fashion have many components, as indicated in Figure 5.6, all related to the single function of moving fluids from one point to another for a particular purpose. The ways in which such components are designed and displayed depend on the fluids themselves and the pressures and the temperatures to be expected in the system.

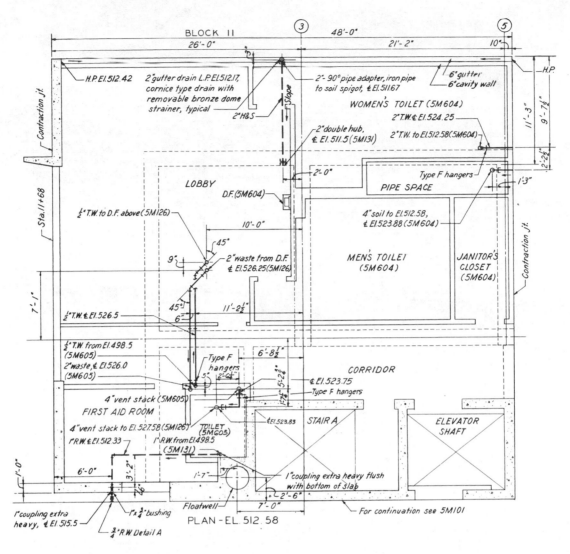

FIGURE 5.7   Arrangement for pipes in a building layout.

The components represented by symbols have two purposes: (1) to help keep the fluid moving freely and smoothly through the system and (2) to help keep the system and fluid in good condition. Ductwork (Figure 5.6) is an example, and filters are another. Because equipment needs protection, filters are used. Such symbols are especially important because the fluids carried through a system may be damaging to the building occupants. HV under pressure, various types of waste products, and paint are all good examples of such fluids. The filters keep these fluids free from harmful contaminants to protect both the equipment that the system serves and people. Well-designed system diagrams have various features to minimize maintenance and wear and tear. Figure 5.8 is a good example of this. Here a piping diagram is shown as it appears in a

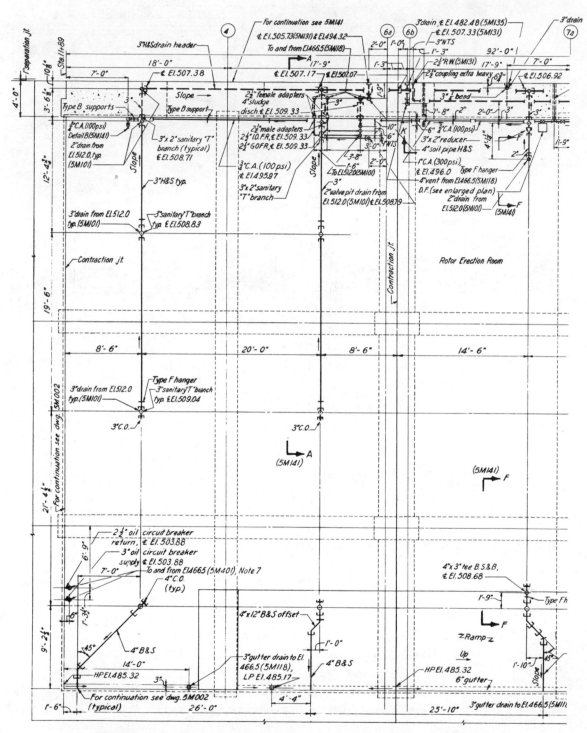

FIGURE 5.8   Piping for section 4 through 7a of a building.

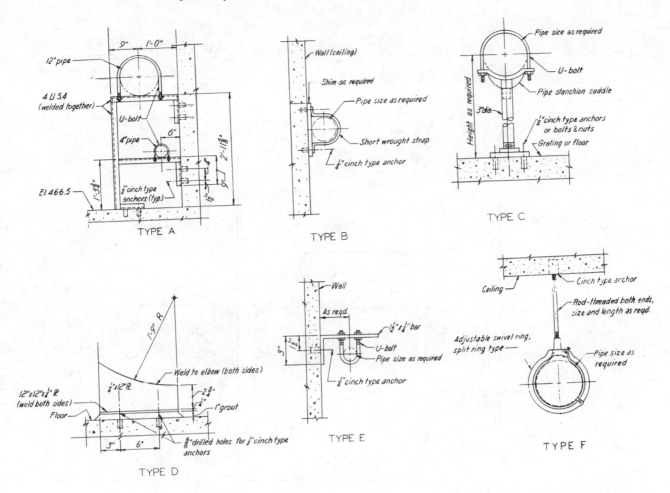

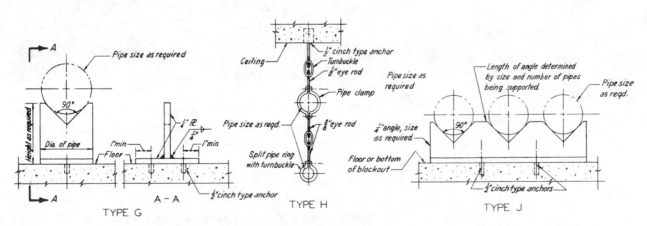

FIGURE 5.9 Pipe support details.

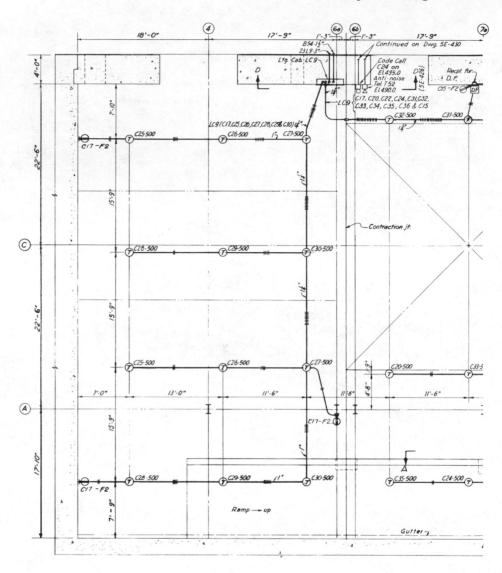

PLAN EL. 485.5

FIGURE 5.10   Electrical layer related to Figure 5.8.

building. Both lines and connections are displayed by the IGS user.
In this example five windows were used at the DVST. The plan window
was developed first and then elevations I-I, J-J, K-K, and L-L were
developed from push button template parts.

Piping must be supported to keep the line straight and to pre-
vent sagging. A rigid pipe that sags excessively will strain its
connections. A pipeline may be designed to run at a slight angle
and will be supported at suitable intervals. To some extent, rigid
piping is self-supporting because it has a certain amount of mechanical strength. Yet it must be supported by being fastened to the
walls, ceiling, or floor as shown in Figure 5.9.

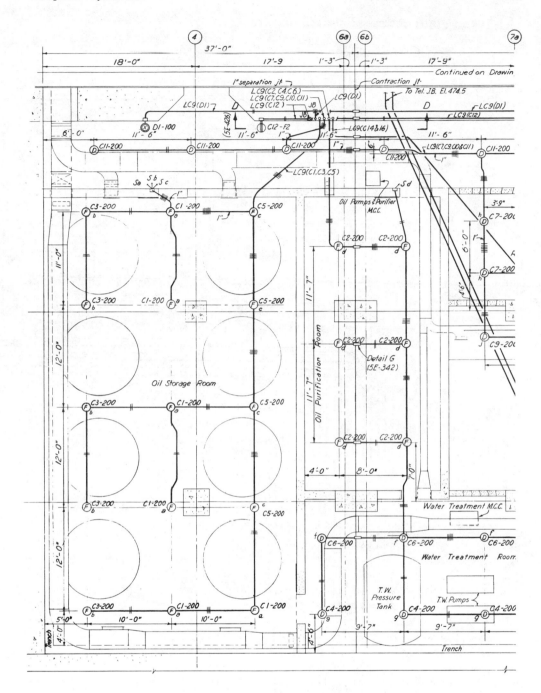

FIGURE 5.11 Electrical layer related to Figure 5.6.

Nearly all materials, and metals in particular, expand as the temperature increases and contract or become smaller in size as the temperature decreases. To allow for this expansion and contraction in piping systems, expansion joints must be included in the piping diagram between sections of rigid pipe. As these sections expand or

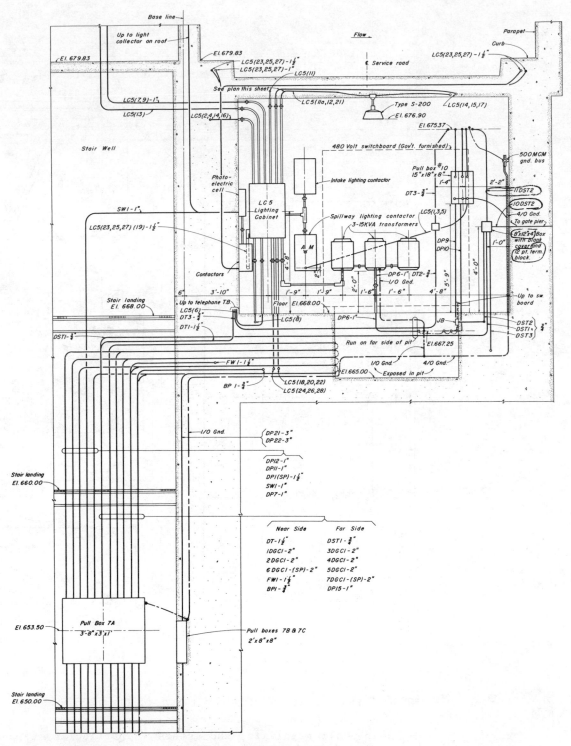

FIGURE 5.12　Electrical highway diagram.

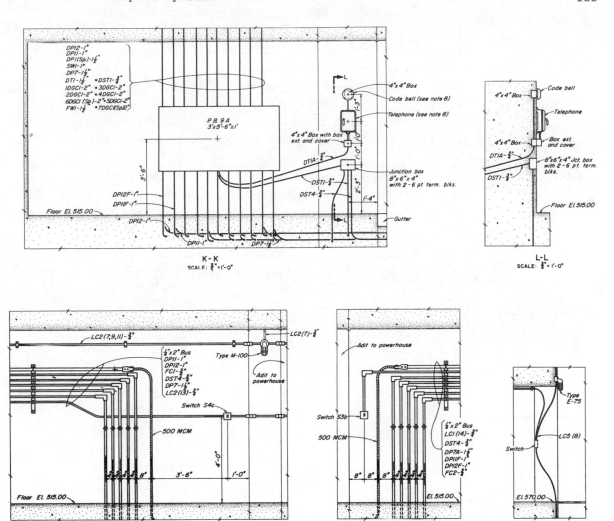

FIGURE 5.13 Support details for highway runs.

contract, the expansion joint compresses or expands accordingly. The design of a pipe hanger or support device must take into account the pipe size. See Tables 1 and 2 or Figure 5.9.

Electrical

Another useful area that can be put on IGS-type standard push button template parts is the electrical diagram used in the design of buildings. Like piping, electrical diagrams require special knowledge in their design, but the display of these diagrams can now be done rather easily on an IGS. Figure 5.10 represents the electrical portion of the piping and equipment diagram displayed in Figure 5.8. While Figure 5.11 is the counterpart to Figure 5.6, note the relationship of Figure 5.10 to Figure 5.8 and Figure 5.11 to Figure 5.6.

Electrical diagrams supply power through flexible connections, while fluids travel through more rigid pipes and ducts.

A more typical type of electrical diagram is called the *highway* shown in Figure 5.12. It cannot be compared with earlier displays because it represents the logic of the electrical power flow in a building. Figure 5.13, also an electrical diagram, can be compared with Figure 5.9 because both are placement and support diagrams.

USEFUL CURVES AND SURFACES

The last item that might be useful to be assigned to a push button template keystroke is the family of architecture curves and surfaces. Avoiding the keys already assigned, the IGS operator might use

ASCII	Key	Interpretation
112	P	PARABOLA
101	L	ELLIPSE
104	H	HYPERBOLA
99	C	CATENARY
121	Y	CYCLOID
116	T	TROCHOID
115	S	SINE CURVE
103	G	GEOMETRICAL MEAN
113	Q	SPIRALS
107	K	SHEW CURVES
108	L	CYLINDERS AND PRISMS
110	N	POLYGONS
118	V	CONES
114	R	RHOMBUS
111	O	SPHERES
117	U	POLYHEDRA
109	M	GEODESIC DOMES
106	J	HYPERBOLIC PARABOLOID
105	I	ELLIPSOID
98	B	ELLIPTIC PARABOLOID
97	A	HYPERBOLOIDS

While it is not the intention of the writer to provide the call routines for each of these 21 useful curves or surfaces, a selected set of examples should provide the basis for how to write these routines.

Parabola-Paraboloid

Curves formed by the intersection of a plane with a right circular cone make up a family of architectural curves called the parabola-paraboloid group. These include the hyperbola, ellipse, and many others. When the IGS operator depresses the p key, the program compares

```
IF(KEY.EQ.P) CALL FIT(IXTO,IYTO,IXA,IYA,IXB,IYB)
```

where CALL FIT is a routine stored as

```
       SUBROUTINE FIT(IXTO,IYTO,IXA,IYA,IXB,IYB)
       XA=IXTO
       YA=IYTO
       XB=IXA
       YB=IYA
       XC=IXA
       YC=IYB
       XC=IXB
       YC=IYB
       DIMENSION S8(8,9),THE(2)
       M=2
       DY=YC-YA
       DX=XC-XA
       Z3=SQRT(DY**2+DX**2)
       IF (Z3) 20,20,2L
21     DO 8 I=1,2
       IF (ABS(DX)-ABS(DY)) L,2,2
 1     THE  (I)=1.5708-ATAN(ABS(DX/DY))
       GO TO 3
 2     THE  (I)=ATAN(DY/DX))
 3     IF (DX) 25,26,26
25     IF(DY) 5,4,4
26     IF(DY) 4,5,5
 4     THE  (I)=-THE  (I)
 5     IF (DX) 6,7,7
 6     THE  (I)=THE  (I)+3.1416
 7     DX=XB-XA
 8     DY=YB-YA
       Z2=SQRT(DY**2⬛DX**2)*COS(THE  (2)-THE  (1))
       IF (Z2) 20,20,22
22     S8(1,3)=XA-XC
       S8(2,3)=XA-XB
       KTRA=1
       GO TO 13
16     A=S8(1,3)
       B=S*(2,3)
       S8(1,3)=YA-YC
       S8(2,3)=YA-YB
       KTRA=2
       GO TO 13
17     CALL SEELOC(IX,IY,IDTH)
       DZ=0.01/FCTR
       Z=DZ
       CALL PLOT(XA,YA,3)
       C=S8(1,3)
```

```
          D=S8(2,3)
18        X=(A*Z+B)*Z+XA
          Y=(C*Z+D)*Z+YA
          CALL PLOT(X,Y,2)
          Z=Z+DZ
          IF (Z-Z3) 18,19,19
19        CALL PLOT(XC,YC,2)
          RETURN
13        S8(1,1)=Z3*Z3
          S8(1,2)=Z3
          S8(2,1)=Z2*Z2
          S8(2,2)=Z2
          CALL SOLUT(SS,M)
          IF(M) 20,20,14
14        GO TO(16,17),KTRA
20        CALL PLOT(XA,YA,3)
          CALL PLOT(XB,YB,2)
          GO TO 19
          END
```

Ellipse-Ellipsoid

A variation of the conic section curve described earlier is the
ellipse.   When the IGS operator depresses the e key, the program
compares

```
          IF(KEY.EQ.E) CALL ELIPS(IXTO,IYTO,A,B,ALP,THET,THE,IV)
```

where CALL ELIPS is a routine stored as

```
          SUBROUTINE ELIPS(XO,YO,A,B,ALP,THET,THE,IV)
          XO=IXTO
          YO=IYTO
          IF (ABS(A)+ABS(B)) 4,20,4
 4        ALP=ALP/57.2958
          THEO=THET/57.2958
          D=A*B/SQRT((A*SIN(THEO))**2+ (B*COS(THEO))**2)
          XC=XO-D*COS(THEO+ALP)
          YC=YO-D*SIN(THEO+ALP)
          BSQ=B*B
          ABSQ=A*A-BSQ
          AB=A*B
          CALL PLOT(XO,YO,IV)
          CALL SEELOC(DTHE,DTHE,FCTR)
          DTHE=0.03/(ABS(A)+ABS(B))/FCTR
          N=(THEF-THEO)/DTHE
          IF (N) 6,5,7
 5        N=-1
 6        N=-N
          DTHE=-DTHE
 7        THEN=THEO+DTHE
```

```
          DO 10 I=1,N
          ST=SIN(THEN)
          D=AB/SQRT(ABSQ*ST*ST+BSQ)
          XF=XC+D*COS(THEN+ALP)
          YF=YC+D*SIN(THEN+ALP)
          CALL PLOT(XF,YF,2)
10        THEN+THEN+DTHE
          ST=SIN(THEF)
          D=AB/SQRT(ABSQ*ST*ST+BSQ)
          XF=XC+D*COS(THEF+ALP)
          YF=YC+D*SIN(THEF+ALP)
          CALL PLOT (XF,YF,2)
          RETURN
20        CALL PLOT(XO,YO,IV)
          RETURN
          END
```

Hyperbola-Hyperboloids

When the IGS operator positions the cursor and presses the h key, the program compares

```
     IF(KEY.EQ.H) CALL SOLUT(IXTO,IYTO)
```

where CALL SOLUT is used by CALL FIT to produce a hyperbolic curve.

Geodesic Domes

The best example of the use of a perfect sphere is the development of the geodesic dome by Buckminster Fuller. Combining the tetrahedron and the sphere, it is composed of all regular convex polyhedra. The tetrahedron encloses the minimum of space with the maximum of surface and is the best form against external and tangential pressures. The geodesic dome encloses the maximum of space with a minimum of surface and is the strongest form against internal or radical pressures.

When the IGS operator positions the cursor and presses the m key, the program compares

```
     IF(KEY.EQ.M) CALL FIT4(IXTO,IYTO)
```

where FIT4 is used by another routine called FLINE to display the geodesic dome.

CHAPTER SUMMARY   Geometric and template image processing is a technique used by interactive programs to provide the architectural user with a simple push button method of creating diagrams and drawings. Not every architectural drawing is ideally suited to this type of image processing, but for those items such as

1. Detailing symbols
2. Material identification
3. Piping and heating-ventilation
4. Electrical

    5.   Human figure generation

    6.   Useful curves and surfaces

an IGS method can be ideally suited.

    During the discussion for this chapter the reader was intro-
duced to the theory of programmable function keys (PFKs) whereby an
operator can point and place a template object on the face of the
DVST.   Six different examples as listed were used throughout the
chapter; 127 keys on a standard keyboard were preprogrammed for ease
of diagram construction.

EXERCISES   1.   Interactive graphics systems (IGSs), when properly programmed,
            allow the architect or engineer the freedom to construct many
            diagrams with relative ease.   Many of the figures used in this

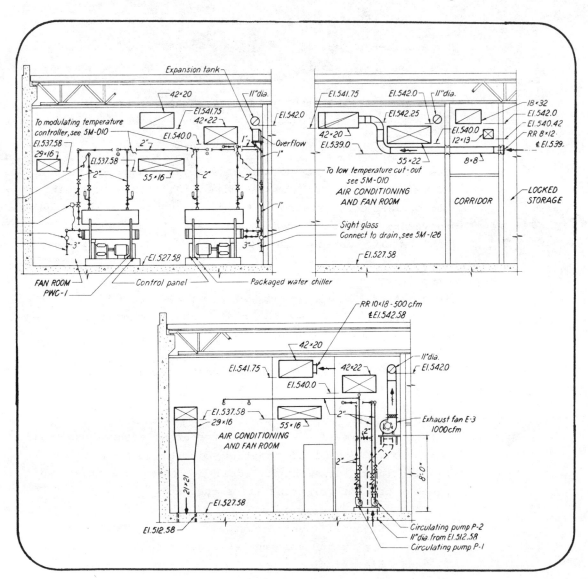

chapter were only partially constructed; complete Figure 5.3 as shown. (Courtesy of the U.S. Corps of Engineers, Vicksburg, Mississippi.)

2. Complete Figure 5.5 as shown. (Courtesy of the U.S. Corps of Engineers, Vicksburg, Mississippi.)

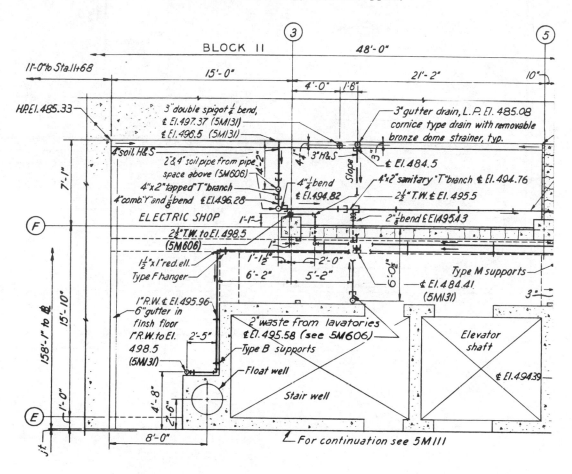

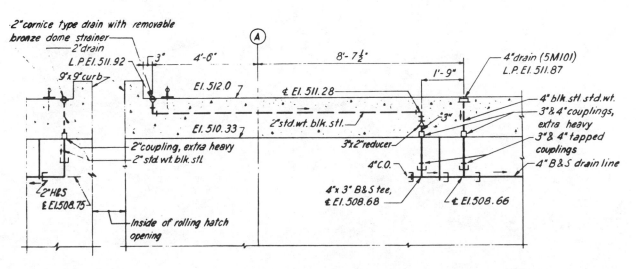

3.   Complete Figure 5.6 as shown. (Courtesy of the U.S. Corps of
     Engineers, Vicksburg, Mississippi.)

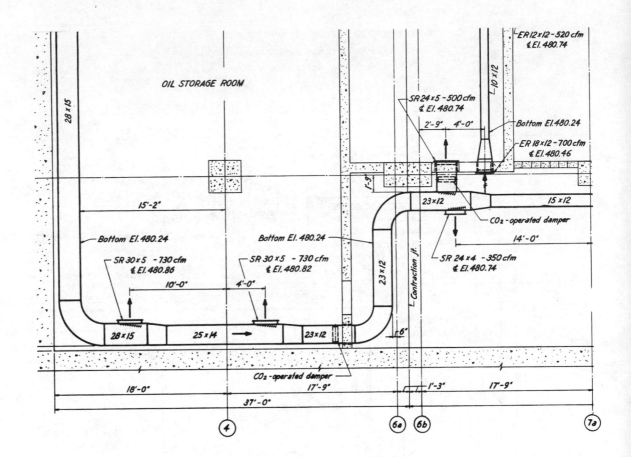

4.   Complete Figure 5.8 as shown.

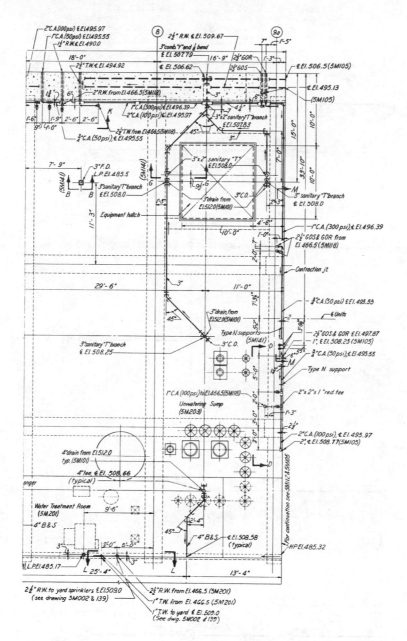

5.   Complete Figure 5.10 as shown. (Courtesy of the U.S. Corps of
      Engineers, Vicksburg, Mississippi.)

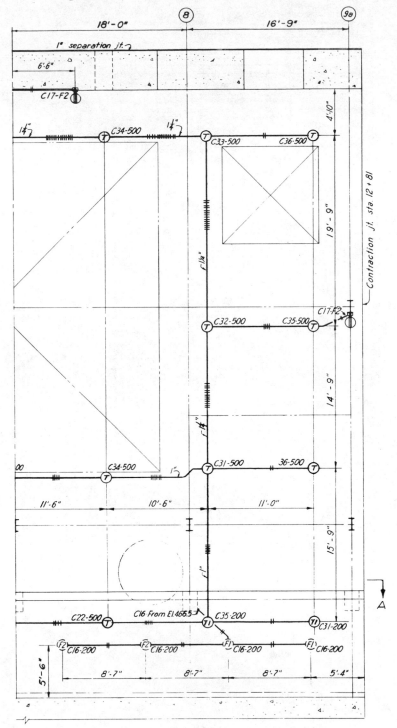

6. Complete Figure 5.11 as shown. (Courtesy of the U.S. Corps of
   Engineers, Vicksburg, Mississippi.)

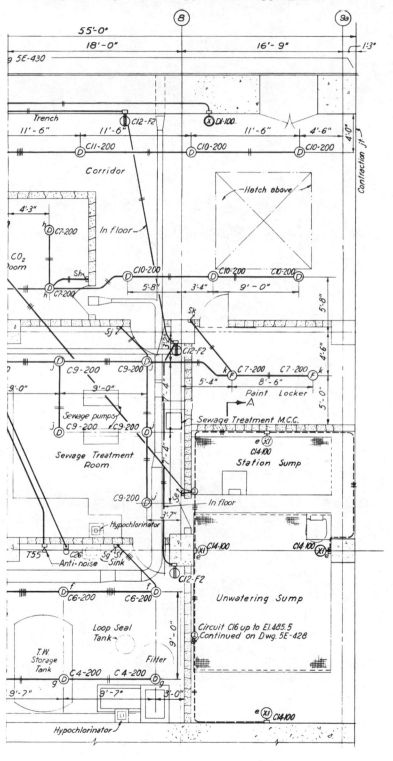

7. Complete Figure 5.12 as shown. (Courtesy of the U.S. Corps of Engineers, Vicksburg, Mississippi.)

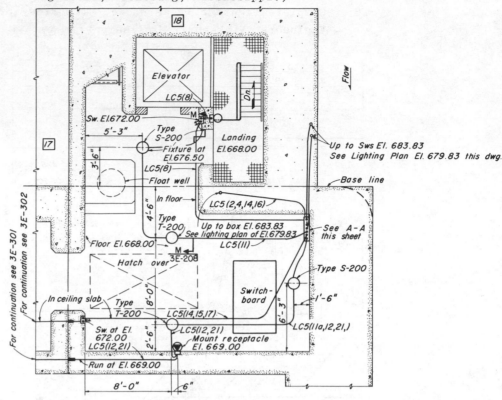

LIGHTING CONDUITS – EL. 668.00
SCALE: $\frac{1}{4}$" = 1'-0"

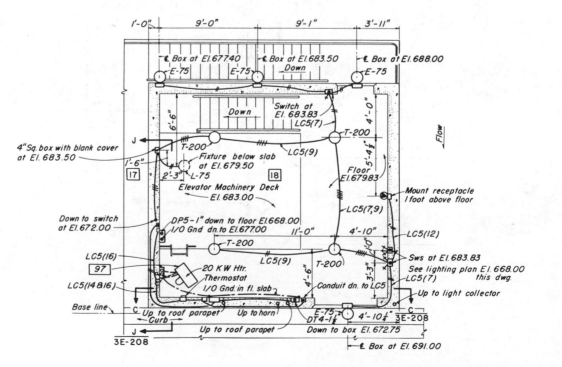

146

6 Storing Architectural Details

The basic techniques for storing architectural details are essentially the same as those for the other forms of computer-aided architectural graphics presented in earlier chapters except that special symbols, conventions, and usually construction methods and details are involved. The purpose of storing details is related to the concept of layering.[*] Different layers are the contributions of a team of specialists, which include the architect, designer, computer programmer, detailer, and illustrator. In some examples, one person may often function in several capacities and develop ideas for more than one layer, particularly in a small design project. On large projects, the practice is to isolate design functions and activities to a single layer. An example of separate stored layers for a large project might be as follows:

1. Site description for an office building (see Figure 6.1)
   a. Property description
   b. Topo drawing
   c. Excavation plans
   d. Footing plans and critical path method diagrams
2. Floorplans and horizontal sections (see Figure 6.2)
   a. Working drawings showing floor patterns

---

[*]See Chapter 15 for layering concepts.

147

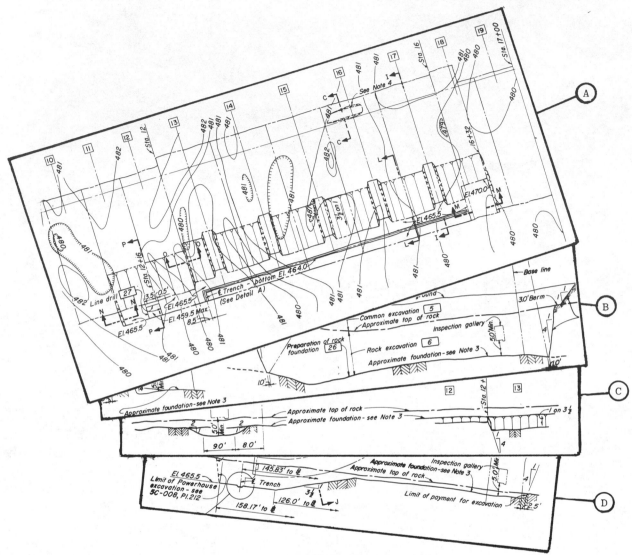

FIGURE 6.1 Site description and related diagrams stored in common. (Data from the U.S. Corps of Engineers, Graphic Compatibility System, Vicksburg, Mississippi.)

b. Placing drawings for concrete, steel, or wood

c. Erection plans

3. Elevations or vertical sections (see Figure 6.3)

a. Heating and air conditioning

b. Electrical, plumbing

4. Design drawings (see Figure 6.4)

a. Shop details

b. Interior modifications (as built)

Each of these layers is stored using a window detail approach.

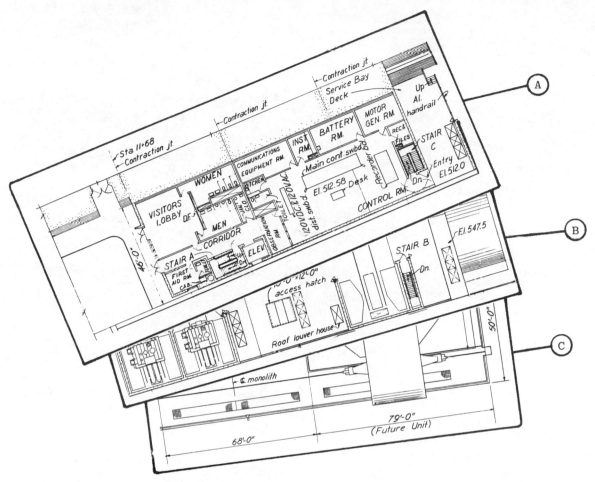

FIGURE 6.2 Floorplans and horizontal sections stored in common. (Data from the U.S. Corps of Engineers, Graphic Compatibility System, Vicksburg, Mississippi.)

Because of the extensive education and experience with layering and windowing methods, the designer and programmer act as team leaders with the advice and representation of the project owner throughout the layering stages. The mechanical group leader is responsible for the planning and layering of the project plumbing, heating, ventilating, and other mechanical systems. The electrical group leader produces the layering for the necessary circuits and fixtures for power, lighting, fire alarm and clock systems, the intercom, and the telephone system.

The team leaders, under the guidance of the architect and approval of the owner, prepare the site data to begin the layers as needed. From these data, detailers will prepare other layers for the entire project. The concept of layering and its speed of production by computer assistance are extremely important since this system, if properly executed, will reduce the costs for the entire building program.

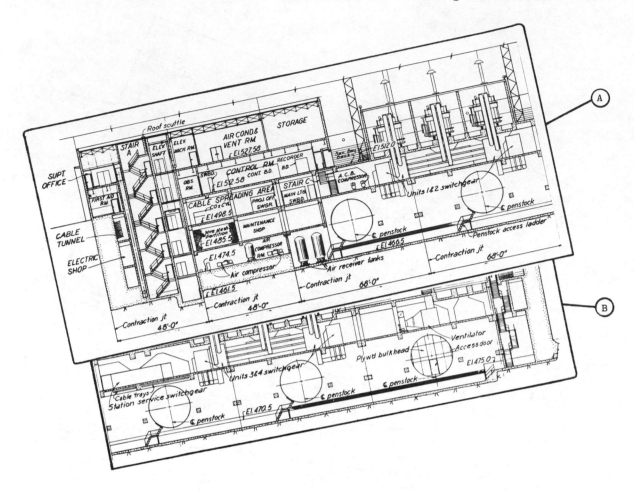

FIGURE 6.3 Elevations and vertical sections stored in common. (Data from the U.S. Corps of Engineers, Graphic Compatibility System, Vicksburg, Mississippi.)

Most building projects involved four layering stages:

1. Preliminary planning
2. Storage of window details
3. Preparation of specifications, dimensions, or descriptions of the stored details
4. Scheduling and management of the actual construction

Further project advantages exist with layering because the architect will always have details other than those of construction, for example, plans for the use of construction equipment, site development such as grading and paving, storage of materials, and the like. To assist the designers in storing these details, a computer approach is used for layering as follows:

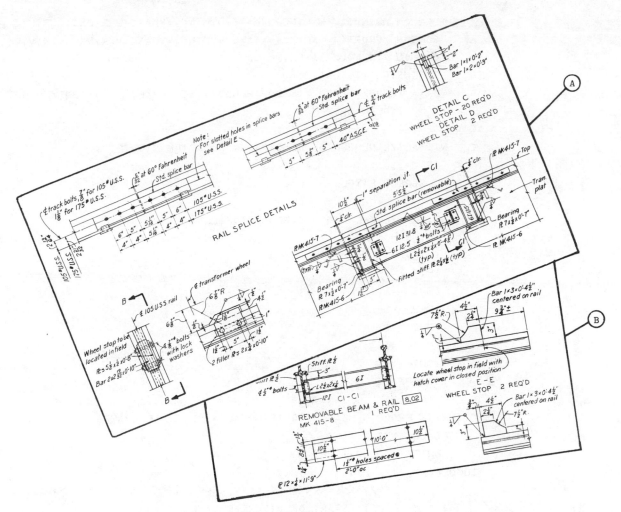

FIGURE 6.4 Design drawings stored in common. (Data from the U.S. Corps of Engineers, Graphic Compatibility System, Vicksburg, Mississippi.)

```
C.........................................................................
C
C    CREATESP - A FORTRAN PROGRAM FOR STORAGE OF TWO-DIMENSIONAL
C             DATABASES INTO DISCRETE LAYERS.
C
C.........................................................................
     LOGICAL IEND
     COMMON /IOFILE, INTERM,IOTERM,IPTR,INP1,INP2,INP3,INP4,
    +             IOUTP1,IOUTP2,IDEBUG
     COMMON /TAB2DC/ CANG,SCALEC,IOXC,IOYC
```

```
      COMMON /WINDOC/ WXMINC,WXMAXC,WYMINC,WYMAXC,WXR,WXC,WYR,WYC
      COMMON /VPORTC/ VXMINC,VXMAXC,VYMINC,VYMAXC,VXR,VXC,VYR,VYC
      COMMON /TRANWC/ WA,WB,WC,WD
      DIMENSION ITITLE(72)
      DATA IENDD/4HENDD/,IENDO/4HENDO/,ISEMIC/4H;   /,IOBJT/RHOBJT/,
     +     ICOLAN/1H:/
C
C  INITIALIZE NUMBER OF RECORDS IN DATAFILE "IOUTP1".
      NR=0
C  ONE SCREEN PIXEL.
C
C  INITIALIZE THE NAMED COMMON "IOFILE".
      INTERM= 1
      IOTERM= 3
      IPTR  =20
      INP1  =11
      INP2  =12
      INP3  =13
      INP4  =14
      IOUTP1=21
      IOUTP2=22
C
C  WRITE PROGRAM HEADER TO TERMINAL AS USED IN DRAW2D.
      CALL ANMODE
      WRITE(IOTERM,1000)
1000 FORMAT(/////,
     +         /,'<<<<<<<<<<<<<<<<<<<<<<<<<<<<<<<<<<<>>>>>>>>>>>>>>>>>>>>>>>',
     +        //,' START OF DISCRETE LAYER.;
     +        //,'<<<<<<<<<<<<<<<<<<<<<<<<<<<<<<<<<<<<<<>>>>>>>>>>>>>>>>>>>>>>>')
C
C  INITIALIZE DEBUGGING OUTPUT LEVEL USED IN DRAW2D.
      CALL QDEBUG
      IF(IDEBUG .GT. 0) WRITE(IPTR,1000)
      IF(IDEBUG .GT. 0) WRITE(IPTR,1001)IDEBUG
1001 FORMAT(' ',I1)
C
C  PROMPT THE USER FOR THE BAUD RATE USED IN DRAW2D
      CALL QBAUD(IBAUD)
C
C  INITIALIZE THE TEKTRONIX CONTROL SYSTEM USED IN DRAW2D.
      CALL INITT(IBAUD)
      CALL BELL
C
C  CLEAR THE SCREEN AND RETURN THE ALPHANUMERIC CURSOR TO HOME AS
```

```
      DRAW2D.
   10 CALL NEWPAG
C
C  PROMPT USER FOR THE DATABASE NAME OR IDENTIFIER AND OUTPUT IT AS
      DRAW2D.
      CALL QTITLE(ITITLE)
      WRITE(INP3,1002) IOBJT,ICOLAN,(ITITLE(1),1=1,67)
 1002 FORMAT(A4,A1,67A1)
C  PROMPT THE USER FOR THE Z-PLANE COORDINATE....SEE NEW SUBROUTINE.
      CALL QELEV(ZCOORD)
C  PROMPT THE USER FOR THE SCALE FACTOR AND THE ROTATION CORRECTION
C  BETWEEN THE TABLET AND THE USER DRAWING...LIKE TSCALE.
      CALL QSCALE(SCALEC,CANG)
C
C  PROMPT USER FOR THE WINDOW LIMITS FOR THE TERMINAL DISPLAY OF
C  THE DATA RECEIVED(WLIMIT)
      CALL QWINDO(FINE)
C
C  PROCEED WITH THE CREATION OF THE DATABASE.
      CALL INTAB2(FINE,IEND,NR)
      WRITE(INP3,1003) IENDO,ISEMIC
 1003 FORMAT(2A4)
C
C  CHECK TO SEE IF PROGRAM TERMINATION IS TO OCCUR, OR CREATION
C  OF NEXT 2-D OBJECT IS TO OCCUR.
      IF (.NOT. IEND) GO TO 10
C
C  END OF PROGRAM, WRITE "ENDD" COMMAND ON THE END OF THE DATABASE
C  FILE AND TERMINATE PROGRAM.
      CALL ANMODE
      WRITE(INP3,1004) INEDD,ISEMIC
 1004 FORMAT(2A4)
      CALL FITITT(770,0)
C
C...................................................................
      STOP
      END
      SUBROUTINE QELEV(ZCOORD)
C*****************************************************************
C    THIS ROUTINE PROMPTS THE USER FOR THE Z-AXIS COORDINATE OF
C    THE X-Y PLANE.
C
C
C
```

```
C
C---------------------------------------------------------------------
      LOGICAL ITEST
      COMMON /IOFILE/ INTERM,IOTERM,IPTR,INP1,INP2,INP3,INP4,
     +                IOUTP1,IOUTP2,IDEBUG
C
C PROMPT THE USER FOR THE Z-COORD.
      CALL ANMODE
   10 WRITE(IOTERM,1000)
 1000 FORMAT(/,' ENTER THE Z-AXIS COORDINATE FOR THE X-Y PLANE -')
C
C  RECEIVE USER'S NUMERICAL REPLY TO THE PROMPT.
      CALL RECNUM(ZCOORD)
C
C*********************************************************************
      RETURN
      END
C
C

      SUBROUTINE EDITDA(FINE)
      COMMON /IOFILE/ INTERM,IOTERM,IPTR,INP1,INP2,INP3,INP4,
     +                IOUTP1,IOUTP2,IDEBUG
      COMMON /IN2DIM/ XP(500),YP(500),ZP(500),IP(500),NDATA
      COMMON /TAB2DC/ CANG,SCALEC,IOXC,IOYC,ZCOORD
      DATA JP/80/,IR/82/,ID/68/,IA/65/,IG/71/,IQ/81/,IH/72/
C
C  ISSUE THE HELP MESSAGE.
   10 CALL NEWPAG
      CALL ANMODE
      WRITE(IOTERM,1000)
 1000 FORMAT(/,' WHEN CURSOR APPEARS ON THE TERMINAL SCREEN, ENTER',/
     +       /,' AN "P" TO ESTABLISH THE POINT AT THE CROSSHAIR',
     +       /,' AS THE CURRENT POINT,',
     +       /,' AN "P" TO REPLACE CURRENT POINT IN EDIT WITH THE',
     +       /,' POINT AT THE CROSS-HAIR LOCATION,',
     +       /,' AN "A" TO ADD A LINE,',
     +       /,' A "D" TO DELETE A LINE,',
     +       /,' A "G" TO GRID EDIT THE DATABASE,',
     +       /,' A "Q" TO QUIT EDIT MODE AND RETURN TO CREATE MODE,',
     +       //,' ENTER A NULL LINE TO BEGIN-')
      CALL ANMODE
      READ(INTERM,1001) IDUMMY
 1001 FORMAT(A1)
      CALL ECHODA
```

```
C
C   GET THE POINT LOCATION AND PROCESS THE COMMAND, "ICHAR".
    20 CALL BELL
       CALL CURSR(XLOC,YLOC,ICHAR)
       IF(ICHAR .EQ. JP) GO TO 1
       IF(ICHAR .EQ. IR) GO TO 2
       IF(ICHAR .EQ. ID) GO TO 3
       IF(ICHAR .EQ. IA) GO TO 4
       IF(ICHAR .EQ. IG) GO TO 5
       IF(ICHAR .EQ. IH) GO TO 10
       IF(ICHAR .EQ. IQ) RETURN
C
C   CHARACTER COMMAND NOT FOUND, ISSUE WARNING AND ACCEPT NEW INPUT.
       CALL HOME
       CALL ANMODE
       WRITE(IOTERM,1002)
1002 FORMAT(/,' WARNING - COMMAND NOT FOUND, RE-ENTER INPUT.')
       GO TO 20
C
C   THE POINT IS TO BE EDITED, FIND ITS LOCATION IN THE BUFFER.
     1 ZLOC=ZCOORD
       ILOC=IFINDA(XLOC,YLOC,ZLOC,FINE)
       IF(ILOC .EQ. 0) GO TO 99991
       GO TO 20
C
C   THE COORDINATES RECEIVED FROM THE CURSOR ARE TO REPLACE CURRENT
C   POINT LOCATION "ILOC".
     2 XP(ILOC)=XLOC
       YP(ILOC)=YLOC
       ZP(ILOC)=ZCOORD
       CALL ERASE
       CALL ECHODA
       GO TO 20
C
C   THE COORDINATES RECEIVED FROM THE CURSOR ARE TO BE DELETED WITHIN
C   THE BUFFER.
     3 ILOC=IFINDA(XLOC,YLOC,ZLOC,FINE)
       IF(ILOC .EQ. 0) GO TO 99991
       IP(ILOC)=-1*IP(ILOC)
       CALL ECHODA
       GO TO 20
C
C   ADD A LINE TO THE DATABASE.
     4 NDATA=NDATA+1
```

```
            XP(NDATA)=XLOC
            YP(NDATA)=YLOC
            ZP(NDATA)=ZLOC
            IP(NDATA)=-1
            CALL HOME
            CALL ANMODE
            WRITE(IOTERM,1003)
1003 FORMAT(/,' ENTER THE ENDING POINT-')
      CALL BELL
      CALL CURSR(XLOC,YLOC,ICHAR)
      NDATA=NDATA+1
      XP(NDATA)=XLOC
      YP(NDATA)=YLOC
      ZP(NDATA)=ZLOC
      IP(NDATA)=1
      CALL ECHODA
      GO TO 20
C
C  EDIT THE DATABASE USING THE GRID METHOD.
    5 CALL EDITG
      GO TO 20
C
C  POINT WAS NOT LOCATED IN DATA BUFFER, ISSUE WARNING.
99991 CALL ANMODE
      WRITE(IOTERM,1009)
1009  FORMAT(/,' ERROR - POINT NOT LOCATED IN OBJECT BUFFER,
      RE-ENTER.')
      GO TO 20
C
C**************************************************************
      END
C
C
      SUBROUTINE CURSR(XCOORD,YCOORD,ICHAR)
C**************************************************************
C     THIS ROUTINE MAY BE USED TO SPECIFY (OR INPUT)
C     COORDINATES DIRECTLY FROM THE TERMINAL.  THE SCREEN
C     COORDINATES RECEIVED FROM TEKTRONIX CONTROL SYSTEM
C     ROUTINE "SCURSR" ARE TRANSFORMED INTO DATA COORDINATES
C     THROUGH AN INVERSE OF THE WINDOW-VIEWPORT TRANSFORMATION.
C          ENTERED:       NONE
C          RETURNED:  XCOORD - THE HORIZONTAL COORDINATE OF
C                              THE POINT RECEIVED IN DATA
C                              (WORLD) COORDINATES.
```

```
C                   YCOORD - THE VERTICAL COORDINATES OF THE
C                            POINT RECEIVED IN DATA (WORLD)
C                            COORDINATES.
      COMMON /TRANWC/ WA,WB,WC,WD
C
C  GENERATE THE CROSSHAIRS AND RECEIVE THE COORDINATES.
      CALL SCRUSR(ICHAR,IX,IY)
      XCOORD=FLOAT(IX)
      YCOORD=FLOAT(IY)
C
C   TRANSFORM  THE  COORDINATES  RECEIVED  FROM  SCREEN  TO  DATA
C  COORDINATES.
      XCOORD=(XCOORD-WB)/WA
      YCOORD=(YCOORD-WD)/WC
      RETURN
      END
C
C

      SUBROUTINE EDITG
      COMMON /IN2DIM/ XP(500),YP(500),ZP(500),IP(500),NDATA
C
C  ASK THE USER FOR THE GRID MODULE FOR EDITING.
      CALL QGRID(XO,YO,ZO,FINE)
      CALL QGRID(XO,YO,FINE)
C
C  FIND THE MINIMUM AND MAXIMUM VALUES FOR THE RANGE OVER WHICH
C  THE GRID MUST BE IMPOSED.
      FCHECK=FINE/2.0
      XLOC=AMIN(XP,NDATA)
      YLOC=AMIN(YP,NDATA)
      ZLOC=AMIN(ZP,NDATA)
      XMAX=AMAX(XP,NDATA)
      YMAX=AMAX(YP,NDATA)
      ZMAX=AMAX(ZP,NDATA)
C
C  CALCULATE THE STARTING (MINIMUM) VALUES FOR THE GRID INCREMENTING
C  USING THE ORIGIN LOCATIONS AS A REFERENCE
      XDELT=AXDIST(XLOC,XO)
      IXDELT=INT(XDELT/FINE)
      XLOC=FLOAT(IXDELT)*FINE
      YDELT=AXDIST(YLOC,YO)
      IYDELT=INT(YDELT/FINE)
      YLOC=FLOAT(IYDELT)*FINE
C     ZDELT=AXDIST(ZLOC,ZO)
```

```
C     IZDEL=INT(ZDELT/FINE)
C     ZLOC=FLOAT(IZDELT)*FINE
C
  10 DO 100 I=1,NDATA
 100 IF(ABS(XP(I)-XLOC) .LT. FCHECK) XP(I)=XLOC
     XLOC=XLOC+FINE
     IF(XLOC .LT. XMAX) GO TO 10
C
  20 DO 200 I=1,NDATA
 200 IF(ABS(YP(I)-YLOC) .LT. FCHECK) YP(I)=YLOC
     YLOC=YLOC+FINE
     IF(YLOC .LT. YMAX) GO TO 20
C
C 30 DO 300 I=1,NDATA
 300 IF(ABS(ZP(I)-ZLOC .LT. FCHECK) ZP(I)=ZLOC
     ZLOC=ZLOC+FINE
     IF(ZLOC .LT. ZMAX) GO TO 30
     CALL ECHODA
     RETURN
     END
```

The preparation of window details for storage in a discrete layer involves two steps. First a rough freehand sketch is made on a graphics tablet; the procedure for this was described in detail in Chapter 4, and typical outputs were shown in Figures 4.3-4.9. Second, this output is refined into a display drawing as shown in Figure 4.10.

Display drawings are often preliminary drawings which are embellished in order to make them more attractive to the client. As demonstrated in Chapter 4, they are often rendered in a combination of pencil, ink, and water color. In addition to the use of perspective for main floor and front elevations, as shown in Figure 4.3, they frequently include imaginary backgrounds such as trees, shrubbery, and other features to achieve a more realistic effect.

Elevations

Elevations are either internal or external views of the upright walls of the structure projected on a vertical plane. Normally four windows are contained in a single layer each having a separate storage area labeled north, east, west, and south elevations. See Chapters 12 and 13. Each storage location is called a window, and by calling north window, a single view of the north elevation will appear on the layer. The number of windows used depends on the complexity of the structure. Windows are not duplicated if the elevations are similar in description. A structure that is symmetrical about a centerline may include an elevation showing adjacent half elevations of the rear and front. In this case a vertical centerline separates the two halves, and each half is then windowed.

Elevation window details show the exact shape and size of the height and width of each wall and opening. They can also represent the finish such as brick or glass by adding standard material symbols from computer memory as in Chapter 5. These memory modules contain special arrangements of building materials that are necessary to construct the desired display pattern. Memory modules are used instead of subroutines such as dashed line or dimensioning packages. Invisible lines are rarely used on elevations except to indicate the outline of the structure below the grade line or possibly a roofline which may be concealed. Likewise very few dimensions are displayed on elevations. Height locations of openings or ceilings are noted. Usually no horizontal dimensions are included. All other dimensionings are placed either on the floorplan or section views.

Elevation window drawings will generally include the diagram for roof slope. This is stored just above the roofline. Other lines in elevation displays are sometimes highlighted by a shading technique called tone.

The basic steps in preparing an exterior elevation layer are the following:

1. Locate the footing and foundation layer from computer memory. Make a hard copy of this window as described in Chapter 1.

2. Locate one wall section layer and scale it to match step 1.

3. Tape the hard copies of the top and side views in their proper positions on the surface of the graphics tablet as shown in Chapter 4. Lines now can be projected from both the top and side views for creating the elevation storage layer.

4. Show the foundation below the grade level with dashed lines. All other lines should be solid. Select material patterns from memory modules for the surface finish.

5. Note finished floor and grade elevations. Locate doors, roof drains, and other features to be shown on the elevations. Store these in the normal manner.

Plan and Site Descriptions

The foundation plan used to construct the exterior elevations is a
horizontal drawing representation. A foundation plan is a top view
of the foundation showing the size of footings, various distances
from reference and boundary points, locations of columns, and other
pertinent details.

The foundation plan as well as all floorplans are oriented on
the layer so that the front of the structure is facing the bottom of
the page. If the structure has a basement, the foundation plan is
stored on one layer, and all the necessary units to be installed
there will be located on a separate layer. This second layer would
also contain partition walls and the equipment location of heating
and cooling units.

The final horizontal layer is the site description. This layer
is used to develop size-related drawings such as the topo plan. A
topo plan is usually the cover sheet in a set of working drawings
and gives the overall picture of the location of the structure and
its orientation to the site. A typical topo plan storage output is
shown in Figure 6.1A. If the ground is uneven or hilly or contains
unusual features such as a draining ditch, contour lines show the
extent of grading changes which the contractor must make. The topo
plan also includes provisions for water supply sewer groundwater
drainage, utilities, walls, and drives.

Working Drawings

From the preliminary database construction and the display drawings,
the project team now stores a complete set of working drawings on
separate layer storage locations. These layers must provide enough
information so that along with the specifications no design decisions are left to the contractor. The layers will therefore include
all necessary building details such as

    1. Topo plan (Figure 6.1A)
    2. Foundation plan (Figure 6.1D)
    3. Floorplans (Figure 6.2A)
    4. Elevations (Figure 6.3A)
    5. Sections (Figure 6.3B)
    6. Connection diagrams as necessary

Placing drawings in storage deals specifically with the storage
of layers for the fabrication of commercial buildings, industrial
plants, schools, hospitals, bridges, or large structures. This type
of database differs in some respects from the orthographic representation introduced in Chapter 5 and used thus far in this chapter.

Special techniques are used to present structure form and shape before storage on an information layer in the computer.

The structural engineer determines the design of the structure and the drawing layer information stored. While preparing the layer data, the engineer takes into consideration such factors as code requirements, availability of materials, ease of erection, and site condition. From this database detailers may store drawing layers for

1. Concrete, steel, or wood construction (Figure 6.4A)
2. Special symbols (Figure 6.4B)
3. Erection plans (Figure 6.2C)

CONSTRUCTION
METHODS
AND DETAILS

The two most common stored types of structural details are for reinforced concrete and steel. Few structural applications include heavy timber or wood members. Wood and steel beams are used with masonry and construction; however, some represent stored details involving reinforced concrete, columns, beams, floor slabs, and stairways and are made of poured concrete with an exterior facing of brick or other masonry materials backed up with lightweight concrete blocks.

Steel framing details use standard steel members as the principal framing elements. The elements are joined in several ways. Usually shop connections are welded together. The exterior facing is also of brick or some other masonry material backed up with concrete blocks.

Steel and Concrete Placement

To ensure that the steel elements in the details are properly fabricated and erected in the correct position, each steel piece is given an ID symbol. This marking is placed on the detail and painted on the steel member.

While no uniform system of building symbols exist, small structures use a capital letter followed by a number. The number designates the drawing layer containing the details of the steel member. The letter indicates the shape of the member, such as B = beam, C = column, G = girder, and L = lintel. Therefore B4 would identify a beam whose detail appears on layer 4.

Building symbols for larger, multistory structures often identify the members with a beam digit followed by an encircled number. This number identifies the story of framing where the member is to be placed during erection. For example, a number 4 beam which is used for both second and fourth floors would be marked $B4^2$ and $B4^4$.

A similar system is used for concrete building symbols. The various parts of a concrete building are indicated by symbols which assign the floor, the type of concrete member, and the location layer of the member detail. Therefore 3B3 would mean third floor beam number 3. The coding for concrete members is B = beams, C = columns, D = dowels, F = footings, G = girders, J = joists, L = lintels, S = slabs, T = ties, Y = stirrups, and W = wall portions.

Building Orientation and Erection Plans

Erection drawings, which are stored by the fabricator, are also called placing drawings for foundations, floors, and framing systems. Erection drawings show the location, shape, and size of components in the structure, or the where of the questions how (construction details), what (building symbols), and where (erection plans).

The responsibility of the designer in preparing erection drawings is limited to carrying out all instructions on the engineering specifications and where nothing specific is stated in regard to building codes. It is not our intention in this section to discuss all the design factors involved in storing and erecting building plans but we do intend to introduce the user to one of the many uses for window drawings.

Stored details used for erection include all the essential windows from any layer required for the completion of a structure. A complete layering will contain foundation details, room arrangement on floorplans, elevations, and sections.

Another important function of erection plans is to show the framing system used for the building. A framing system not only presents the layout of the members but also indicates the shape, size, and location of each member. A typical framing program is as follows:

```
C.........................................................................
C
C     DRAWSP - A FORTRAN PROGRAM FOR TABLET INPUT OF TWO-DIMENSIONAL
C              OBJECTS ON A PLANE IN THREE-DIMENSIONAL SPACE.  USED
C              WITH CREATESP TO STORE FRAMING PLANS FOR MULTISTORY
C              BUILDINGS.
C.........................................................................
      LOGICAL IEND
      COMMON /IOFILE/ INTERM,IOTERM,IPTR,INP1,INP2,INP3,INP4,
     +                IOUTP1,IOUTP2,IDEBUG
      COMMON /TAB2DC/ CANG,SCALEC,IOXC,IOYC
      COMMON /WINDOW/ WXMINC,WXMAXC,WYMINC,WYMAXC,WXR,WXC,WYR,WYC
      COMMON /WPORTC/ VXMINC,VXMAXC,VYMINC,VYMAXC,VXR,VXC,VYR,VYC
```

```
      COMMON /TRANWC/ WA,WB,WC,WD
      COMMON /TELEVC/ PELEV,NELEV
      DIMENSION ITITLE(72)
      DATA DELIM/-9999.0/,IXYZP/4HXYZP/,IENDD/4HENDD/,ISEMIC/4H;   /
C
C  INITIALIZE NUMBER OF RECORDS IN DATAFILE "IOUTP1".
      NR=0
C
C  INITIALIZE THE I/O FILES.
      INTERM= 1
      IOTERM= 3
      IPTR  =20
      INP1  =11
      INP2  =12
      INP3  =13
      INP4  =14
      IOUTP1=21
      IOUTP2=22
C
C  WRITE PROGRAM HEADER TO TERMINAL AS USED IN CREATESP.
      WRITE IOTERM,1000
1000 FORMAT(/////,
     +        /,' <<<<<<<<<<<<<<<<<<<<<<<<<<<>>>>>>>>>>>>>>>>>>>>>>>>>>>',
     +       //,'           START OF CREATE PLANE FOR FRAMING.',
     ;       //,' <<<<<<<<<<<<<<<<<<<<<<<<<<<>>>>>>>>>>>>>>>>>>>>>>>>>>>',
C
C  INITIALIZE DEBUGGING OUTPUT LEVEL IN CREATESP.
      CALL QDEBUG
      IF(IDEBUG .GT. 0) WRITE(IPTR,1000)
      IF(IDEBUG .GT. 0) WRITE(IPTR,1001) IDEBUG
1001 FORMAT(' ',I1)
C
C  PROMPT THE USER FOR THE TERMINAL BAUD RATE USED IN CREATESP.
      CALL QBAUD(IBAUD)
C
C  INITIALIZE THE TEKTRONIX CONTROL SYSTEM USED IN CREATESP.
      CALL INITT(IBAUD)
C
C  INITIALIZE THE NAMED COMMON "TAB2DC" AND ASSOCIATED VARIABLES.
   10 SCALEC=0.0
      IOXC=0.0
      IOYC=0.0
      PELEV=0.0
      NELEV=0
      CALL BELL
```

```
      C
      C  CLEAR THE SCREEN AND RETURN THE ALPHANUMERIC CURSOR TO HOME AS
      C  CREATESP
         CALL NEWPAG
      C
      C  PROMPT USER FOR THE DATABASE NAME OR IDENTIFYER.
         CALL INNAME(ITITLE)
      C
      C  WRITE DATABASE TYPE COMMAND TO DATAFILE.
         WRITE(INP2,1002) IXYZP,ISEMIC
 1002 FORMAT
      C
      C  PROMPT USER SCALE OF THE FRAMING TO BE STORED.
         CALL TSCALE(SCALE,RADANG)
         SCALEC=SCALE
         CANG=RADANG
      C
      C  PROMPT USER FOR THE LOCATION OF THE ORIGIN ON THE STORED DRAWING
         CALL TORIGIN(IOX,IOY)
         IOXC=IOX
         IOYC=IOY
      C
      C  PROMPT USER FOR THE WINDOW LIMITS FOR THE TERMINAL DISPLAY OF
      C  THE DATA RECEIVED.
         CALL WLIMIT
      C
      C  PROCEED WITH THE CREATION OF THE DATABASE FOR FRAMING LAYER.
         CALL INTABE(IEND,NR)
         CALL TABOFF
         WRITE(INP2,1003) DELIM
 1003 FORMAT(F10.4)
         IF(.NOT. IEND) GO TO 10
         WRITE(INP2,1004) IENDD,ISEMIC
 1004 FORMAT(2A4)
         CALL FINITT(770,0)
      C
      C......................................................................
         STOP
         END
```

SUBPICTURE TECHNIQUES FOR BUILDING DETAILS

Design drawings are made from merging layers of the computer database called subpictures by the use of working programs. Design drawings must be complete to the extent that every bit of information contained in these chapter sections is contained either by a diagram, description, note, or reference to a building code.

It is not necessary for the designer to make new layers of data for each structural or architectural member of the project. The designer merges enough information from various layers to include in every set of building plans a typical design drawing for such things as slabs, beams, column design, and the like.

While design drawings show the general layout of structural members, shop drawings represent how the various parts are to be fabricated or assembled. All features that are specifically related to the connection of individual structural or architectural members have to be clearly illustrated. The details of the members can be fabricated offsite (in a shop) and transported to the building project. Diagrams for items fabricated onsite are called construction diagrams or field drawings.

The most common practice of fabricating steel structural members in the field is by welding or bolting with high-strength machine bolts. The placement of bolts for connecting members is controlled by gage lines. The location of these lines has been standardized to fit a text format called a schedule.

A schedule is a summary of all the bolt locations, drilled holes, or welding notes in the structure in the order of their use, complete with the number of items required. One of the important concepts of computer-aided design drawings for shop details is the automatic generation of a schedule or bill of materials. These are often referred to as a *shop bill* which lists all the items required for fabrication and shipment to the site.

In some cases shop bills are output directly alongside the detail of the member or are included as an 8 $\frac{1}{2}$ by 11 spec size sheet. With computer database layering a list is easy to generate at the same time a plotter or CRT is diagramming the graphic shape of the shop detail.

CHAPTER SUMMARY   Stored drawings are extremely useful in the industrial marketplace and therefore are subject to the latest technological advancements with regard to how they are produced. This chapter contained the types of window details, what they look like, and how they are stored by the architectural team. One of these team members is the computer-aided graphics programmer. This member operates the many related pieces of hardware explained in Chapter 1. For stored drawings the operator has three techniques available:

1. <u>Read</u> from a graphics terminal the current database information about each of the layers for a design project.
2. <u>Write</u> by pointing a light pen or using a data tablet to cause input commands to be accepted without computer-language-type programs.

3. Obtain a <u>drawing</u> <u>response</u> for each read or write action. The operator will see immediately, in window form, the result of the request in 15 sec or less, and the operator may make corrections or modify the design immediately.

The three principles of graphic reading, writing, and obtaining a drawing response are the basic ingredients of a computer-aided architectural graphics system. An operator processes a drawing using this system and recalls from memory, library, or files any other information pertaining to the drawing. By correlation and combination new information is created which can take its place in memory as a document, drawing, memory word, or verbal expression.

EXERCISES 1. Prepare a series of drawings to be stored in common. Select a storage location label such as CONCET with space for 10 windows. In the first window, place the concrete section shown. (Courtesy of the U.S. Corps of Engineers, Vicksburg, Mississippi.)

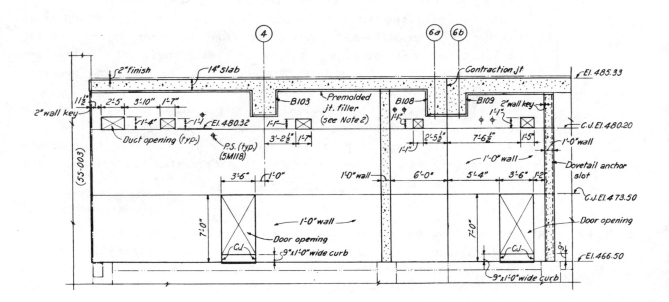

2. In the second window, show the expansion of the section as shown. (Courtesy of the U.S. Corps of Engineers, Vicksburg, Mississippi.)

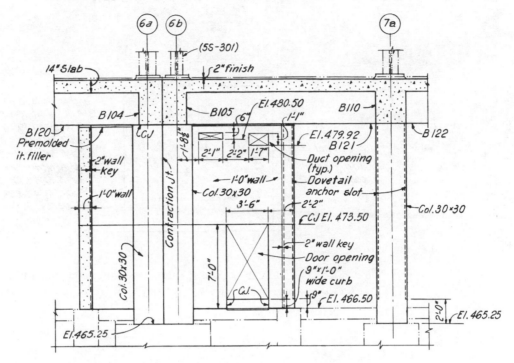

3. In the third window, show a further expansion of the section as shown. (Courtesy of the U.S. Corps of Engineers, Vicksburg, Mississippi.)

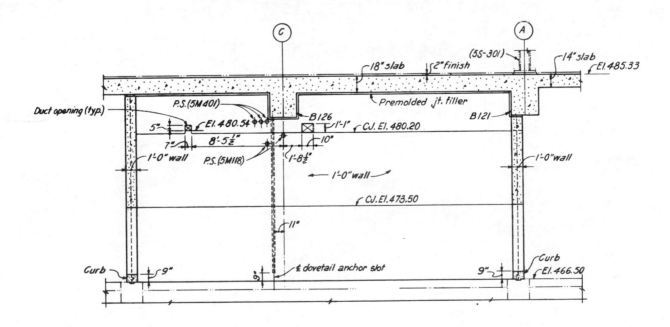

4. In the fourth window, show a detail of A in plan view as shown.
    (Courtesy of the U.S. Corps of Engineers, Vicksburg,
    Mississippi.)

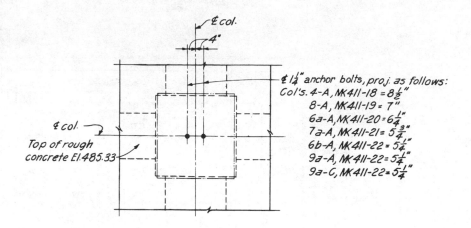

5. In the fifth window, show a vertical section through detail A
    as shown. (Courtesy of the U.S. Corps of Engineers, Vicksburg,
    Mississippi.)

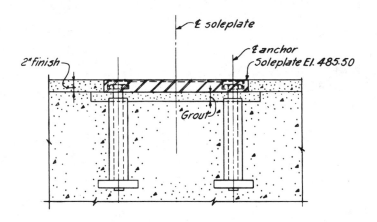

6. In the sixth window, show an enlargement of A from window 3 as shown. (Courtesy of the U.S. Corps of Engineers, Vicksburg, Mississippi.)

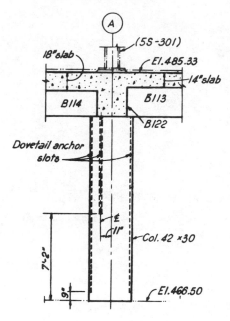

7. In the seventh window, show a slab detail around a column; provide for a vertical section to the taken through this detail. Show this as section L-L. (Courtesy of the U.S. Corps of Engineers, Vicksburg, Mississippi.)

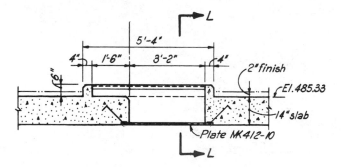

8. In the eighth window, display the section L-L as shown.
(Courtesy of the U.S. Corps of Engineers, Vicksburg,
Mississippi.)

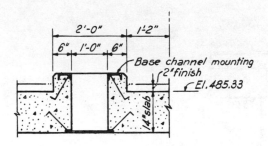

9. In the ninth window, show a floor slab and wall connection as
shown. (Courtesy of the U.S. Corps of Engineers, Vicksburg,
Mississippi.)

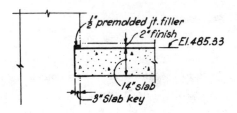

10. In the tenth window, show a modification of this as shown.
(Courtesy of the U.S. Corps of Engineers, Vicksburg,
Mississippi.)

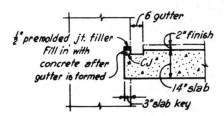

7 Computer Displays for Working Drawings

A complete study of computer-aided architectural graphics must include something about the computerization of working drawings and how if affects work done by a designer or architect. The human is smart, creative, and slow, while the computer is stupid, uncreative, and very fast. The problem then is to allow the human and computer to work well together as a team. Certainly their characteristics complement each other, but their languages are very different. We think in symbols and pictures, while the computer understands only simple electrical impulses. Computer graphics is playing an increasingly large part in our lives. Over the past decade, particularly for computer-aided design, computer graphics has been justified because it can save money and time and can improve the quality of a working drawing. Dollar savings of from 3:1 to 6:1 and time savings of from 20:1 to 50:1 are typical of those quoted for applications explained in this text.

Computer graphics is a way of converting the computer's impulses into engineering documents, and conversely, to translate the operator's instructions into electronic data. In many of the more sophisticated systems, we need know little about computer programming in order to control the human-machine effort. In general, computer graphics includes any device which converts computer language to people language, or any device that converts people language to computer language, with the intent of solving problems by creating graphical images.

171

RECALL OF
STORED DRAWINGS

Most recall systems are easy-to-operate, self-contained, automated systems for the direct production of high-quality finished ink on vellum drawings. The system is designed for simple, real-time operation by draftspersons or designers and is particularly useful for producing working drawings containing repetitive symbology and text. It can be installed in an architectural drafting room since it does not depend on an outside processing source. Applications include the ones shown in this chapter plus technical illustrations, electrical and electronics schematics, piping and hydraulic layouts, CPM and PERT charts, and many other drawings where speed and accuracy are a must.

An example of a recall system and how it works can be studied by examining the many figures shown in this book. Most of the illustrations, diagrams, and drawings used in this book were recalled from a computer with the help and instructions of a human operator. A recall method, then, would be the combination of these two elements to produce synergy, or united action. The logical basis for this concept lies in the fact that the human mind tends to solve problems heuristically (trial and error), while a mechanical system solves by the use of algorithms (error-free sequence of logic). By letting each (mind-machine) work to its best capacity, a new and better method can be automated.

Another time-saving advantage was the data recorder, which transferred electronic readings corresponding to X-Y positions to a storage device for later recall. This process was called digitizing. Digitizing was so basic in the 1970s for building computer databases that people were employed by business and industry, 8 hr a day, as digitizer operators. The person operating a digitizer drew only once, and then a permanent electronic record was kept in computer storage. In addition an off-line record was kept as a backup database. These techniques included punched cards, paper tape, magnetic tape, and floppy disk. Change in the design were made by editing the storage medium and adding new information on a cathode ray tube (CRT), digitizer, or microfilm. The architect could choose to send the information by telephone to another office before it was displayed and while it was still in a form of computer data. The electronic information was received at the new location and then displayed.

Theory of Drawing Sheet Arrangement

Now that the computer contains the stored instructions for architectural drawings, a procedure for recalling the views of a working drawing may be employed. This technique, called subpicturing, is one of the basic methods whereby a designer may select views for a working drawing. All the graphic conventions for the selection of working views still hold. The normal viewing orientation is selected for elevation views. One or more section views are then selected. Depending on the complexity of the object to be drawn, a plan view is selected, the most common selection being the floor, site, and foundation views. Designers use planning formats for ease of subpicturing. A rough sketch is prepared. Many times the designer will sketch a line, stop and write the recall statement which will provide that line, and code it in the space provided. The sketch allows the designer to "play computer" or display the computer instruction for error sensing.

In general, the following is the suggested procedure for selecting views to be recalled. Drawings and graphs, like computer listings, require some planning to achieve a pleasing and effective appearance.

1. The initial position of the pen when plotting operation begins is assumed to be the origin (X,Y=0.0). This location is set by CALL PLOTS or CALL BEGIN. A designer can also select another location anywhere on the plotter surface (CALL PLOT(XLINE,YLINE, -3)). When selecting views for a working drawing, the obvious thing is to make sure that when summed the distances from plotter origin to drawing origin, the size of views, and the distance between views will fit the display device selected. In the case of a plotter containing a roll of drafting paper, the length of the paper roll determines the height of the drawing. The Y axis of the plotter is limited to the size of paper roll selected. If 18-in. paper is selected, only about 16 in. will be used for display purposes. The inch at the top and bottom is used by the plotter and is not available for plotting the drawing. The initialing CALL PLOTS sets the starting position; if the designer called for a new origin, subtract this amount from the remaining space of 16 in. Now add the height of the front view, the space between the front and top views, and the depth of the top view. Test this distance against the space available. A larger roll size may be needed, or the drawing may be scaled to fit the space.

2. The X axis is controlled by a rotating drum, the X direction of the flat bed, or the size of the CRT. In the preceding case, the roll of paper provides for drawings up to 144 in., or J size drawings. Most drawings will fit the X direction easier than they will in the Y axis.

3. Determine if a CALL FACTOR is needed. Remember that this subroutine reduces both the X and Y dimensions. If the Y direction needs to be reduced to fit the roll and X is left full size, then CALL DFACT(1.,REDUCE) should be called after CALL PLOTS. REDUCE should be less than 1.

The alternative to subpicturing for the selection of working views would be the use of a computer main-line program. This program would allow the designer to choose the views desired. The spacing between views would be variable so that different arrangements and spacings could be tried. This method of view selection requires that the drawing data be provided for the program. Remember that in the case of recall for views only the starting points of figures need be known. The program method of view selection is very fast, but the geometry must be fairly simple, usually straight-line segments only.

Usually the two methods are not mixed. The drawing data are prepared as a series of points, each having X, Y, and Z coordinates. The number of these points to be plotted is read into the program first. The number of pen movements required to draw the object or connect the points is read next. The number of views to be drawn is specified along with the space provided for each view. The point coordinates are used by the program to draw the various views. A frontal view can be constructed by plotting the X and Y coordinates, while the horizontal view would require the X and Z coordinates. To plot a profile, the Z and then Y coordinates are used.

Changes in Stored Drawings

The geometric subroutine SCALE checks the entire list of commands and converts or scales the list of fit a particular unit size. The reader will note that the number of units called for in the subroutine SCALE explained earlier was 10. In other words, the dimensions of the object to be represented in the working drawing could be any number of units but would be plotted a maximum of 10. Each dimension was scaled in proportion to a maximum of 10.

A unit may be set equal to an English inch or a convenient metric unit. Nearly 50% of all plotting is now being done on a metric scale. American manufacturers of recall hardware are supplying either method of scaling. Scaling does not mean the conversion from English to metric measurement. Scaling means what it has always meant, the ability to represent large *real-world* sizes on a small piece of paper called an architectural drawing. The use of the computer has made changes in stored drawings easier. The architect may think in full sizes which are related to the design and not have to worry if they will fit on the plotter.

The scale is selected to match the physical limits of the display device. In the case of the interactive plotter a plotting area of 10 units by 10 units was set inside SCALE. It can easily be seen that other applications of scaling would require similar routines. Variations of SCALE have now been developed to determine scale factors of a data array. SCALG, for instance, is used for data on a logarithmic scale.

One of the important features of many of the recall systems available today is the ability to store drawing files. In the plumbing, heating, and ventilating field schematic symbols are stored in memory and used as subpicture elements to create a drawing. Much developmental work has been done in this area. Mechanical work has included the standardization of piping symbols so that similar drawings can be done in the hydraulics and pneumatics areas. All the architectural documentations that require control devices can be preprogrammed and used in this manner.

It is beyond the scope of this book to include the theory of these template symbols for special fields. The reader should be aware that they exist and should not be surprised when another area is added. The concept of a drawing file that can be moved from location to location on the working drawing is important. This concept works just like the draftsperson using a plastic template, rotate it to an angle, and even flip it over. The computer has the same capability but can normally generate an entire drawing in the same time it takes the draftsperson to draw one symbol. When designing a file for use, the designer considers ease of use by a draftsperson or detailer.

To put a system in the drawing room, we must find a way to translate the designer's ideas or sketch directly to a finished drawing. In a search for such a means, we must also not overlook human considerations. Draftspersons and designers are not computer operators or computer programmers and resist any attempt to translate their art to the computer field. A more satisfactory approach might therefore be to conceive a system with which the draftsperson could communicate directly without recourse to computer languages or data processing. This can be done by the selection of drawing files.

A drawing file system having two modes of operation is usually used. The first, an on-line method, is intended to be operated by a draftsperson. This does not require knowledge of computers, their operation, or their programming. Further, no off-line computer processing or subsequent operations are involved. No punched tapes, magnetic tapes or punched cards need be handled. No photographic processes are used. No off-line symbol or aperture preparation is required. The output from this system is a completed master tracing ready for blueprinting, microfilming, or filing.

The second method of operation provides for off-line preparation of a batch program. The formats of these programs are identi-

cal to those used in on-line operation, except the computer will not
prompt or ask questions of the user. The off-line programs are fed
to the self-contained template drafting master program. The template system consists of a plotter controlled by a real-time computer based on mini- or microcontrol. For operation of this system a
magnetic tape cartridge memory is added to the configuration. Pre-
stored on tape are complete descriptions of each template symbol to
be used. Many symbols may be stored, each containing lines, circles, and alphanumeric characters.

Relationship of Various Sheets in the File

Input to the file system for preparation of a finished ink drawing
is a crudely drawn sketch preferably, but not necessarily, on 10
squares to the inch grid paper. This sketch is translated by the
system operator into a series of coded commands. These commands are
typed directly into the system via the keyboard when operating on
line, or they are stored on magnetic disk for later drawing when
operating off line.

File symbols are located by means of X-Y coordinates visually
taken from the grid background. For sketches on plain paper a film
grid overlay is used. A simplified system provides for rapid specification of the type and location of each symbol. All symbols are
initially sequentially numbered and referenced as to type and location. All further reference to a symbol for locating interconnect-
ing lines or test messages can now be made by simply calling the
symbol number. The computer will look up its type and location.

Upon completion of symbol entry the operator proceeds to enter
all line data. Each line is quickly recorded and stored. Provision
is included for lines to exactly butt on symbol terminals even
though the symbol was crudely drawn or inaccurately located. This
is possible since the computer knows the exact location of each connection point of each symbol without regard to sketch accuracy.
After the line work is completed, the operator starts on the last
phase of the data preparation, text insertion. Text material includes symbol designation notes, dimensions, and any other alphanumeric data not previously included as part of a symbol. Text
messages are entered via the keyboard at the drawing point indicated
by a grid coordinate or by reference to a particular symbol point.
Text may be called in a variety of sizes, and the message may be
specified to be left, right, or centered on this position.

Plotting is begun as soon as data input is complete. Drawing
time of an average B size drawing is about 8 min. The finished
product will be a mechanically drawn vellum master with perfect

symbology and with lettering quality superior to LeRoy types, produced in a fraction of the time a skilled draftsperson would have required. The drafting process can be automated by establishing a cycle where we, the designers, begin and end a specific task such as drawing a line. The cycle should be as follows: (1) A command is given by the designer to recall an image, (2) the computer responds to this command, (3) an output device displays the image, and (4) the designer may modify the image displayed. The common types of equipment that a designer may use to issue a command are keyboard, magnetic tape reader, digitizer, graphic tablet, light pen, and joystick. All these input methods tell the computer what to do and how to do it. The drafting machine draws or displays the image according to the output device used; whether by plotter, matrix printer, CRT (alphanumeric or graphic), or hard copy unit.

Automatic drafting and design systems all have certain characteristics of operation or use. If a keyboard input is used, the computer-automated drafting machine will be a function-generated, photocomposition type which produces diagrams by a single press of a preprogrammed character key. Each recalls from computer storage or off-line storage a unique set of data points for displaying the desired image. It can easily be seen that the keyboard is limited to the amount of graphics assigned to push buttons. The designer wants more freedom of shape and more possibilities to create engineering drawings. Therefore, subprograms are read from magnetic disks or other suitable input methods. Now the designer must input a group of subprograms that the computer will connect and display as a finished drawing. The designer writes a program that *calls* the subprograms in the order desired. The push button keyboard is extremely easy to operate but has limited use. The storage of subprograms is unlimited as to the amount of graphic shapes but requires a computer language to obtain the desired drawing.

Halfway between the two extremes is the low-cost CRT graphics terminal. With the aid of an interactive graphing package an English command structure can be used by nonprogrammers. It is a conversational relationship with the computer. By using a library of prompt messages, the draftsperson can launch a straightforward system of database construction. Although elementary in its execution, this type of graphics software has a lot of computing power backing it up. Examples of these types of packages were discussed in Chapters 4 and 5.

From these three types of equipment (passive, active, and interactive) a system for doing drafting and design work can be built. An ideal system would contain one or more of the following items:

1.   A host computer for construction of a database and storage
2.   A digital plotter, drum, or flatbed for finished drawings
3.   A graphic display terminal for preview of design intent:
     a. A hard copy unit for CRT copies of design stages
     b. A joystick or light pen for graphic manipulation
     c. A graphic tablet or digitizer for existing drawings
4.   A matrix printer for shadow plots and a preview of plotter output
5.   A digital cartridge tape drive for off-line storage

The last classification to be added is the interactive graphics system (IGS). They are self-contained graphics systems usually containing one or more of the following items:

1.   General-purpose 32-bit minicomputer
2.   Microprocessor-based CRT terminal
3.   Ten-megabyte disk storage units
4.   36 x 48 in. graphics tablet (digitizer)
5.   Small flatbed plotter
6.   Hard copy unit for CRT
7.   High-level language compiler
8.   Database management software systems

It would be impossible, within the framework of this text, to give a detailed working description of each of the many manufactured IGS systems. The author has selected those he is familiar with and presents them as typical working drawing formats.

Drawing and Display Formats

The IGS is the most advanced of the computer graphics systems now available. It combines the latest in interactive graphics hardware technology with a full range of powerful, easy-to-use software designed to minimize the time and effort required to tailor the capability of the system to the user's particular application. The IGS produces high-speed, cathode ray tube display of interactive graphical images specified by data structures resident in the main memory of the digital processor. The IGS is comprised of the following standard subsystems:

1.   Digital graphics controller
2.   High-speed stroke generator
3.   Host computer interface
4.   Remote console interface
5.   Maintenance control panel

These subsystems are connected to the host computer, and from one to four remote display consoles are used to form a complete interactive graphics system.

The subsystems are mounted in a single standard 19-in. housing located physically adjacent to the processor. A separate remote console interface is located beneath the operator worktables at each display console. From early punched card plotting machines, automated drafting and design have progressed dramatically to today's completely self-contained IGS graphic systems. Today's system is far and away the most advanced of its kind. Its interactive capabilities permit drawings to be electronically produced and modified under full designer control. Design alternatives are resolved quickly and easily. Drawing repetitious patterns no longer consumes valuable work-hours. And architects can put the power of the computer to work to solve complex problems.

Computer Output to Microfilm (COM). William Porter, director of marketing for Datagraphix, was quoted by Computerworld as saying, "COM is an inexpensive peripheral system from the point of view of total capital outlay, but the savings which can be derived from its use can be quite significant. So, if users look at the savings, there is a high priority for its installation."

In the field of architectural drafting and design, COM is a natural output medium. Architectural graphics has used microfilm to record and store drawings for years. With the introduction of computer automation for microfilm the automated drawing is now stored at the same time. Computer-produced magnetic tapes are fed through a tape-to-film recorder. Electronic impulses are converted to visual images on microfilm at speeds 10 to 20 times faster than line printing.

The microfilm is processed in an automated film developer. Duplicators make as many copies of the developed microfilm as needed. A 4 by 16 in. microfiche can hold up to 690 11 by 14 in. drawings plus indexing, depending on reduction. Draftspersons can easily locate desired drawings through oversize titles and indexing along the top of columns. The retrieval of information can be done in a matter of seconds with a standard desk-top viewer. When paper copies are required, a reader-printer provides full-size prints at minimal cost.

One of the advantages of COM is that a user can make as many high-quality prints as needed, so it is possible for companies with small printing jobs and big distribution problems to justify a COM unit on less than 100,000 original drawings a month.

CRT Interactive Graphic Displays. Hughes. This graphics terminal provides powerful image manipulations such as rotation, scaling, zoom and pan, offsetting, line texturing, and windowing without relying on software for these functions. This type of equipment is an excellent example of modern engineering graphics-oriented terminal devices.

Tektronix. The family of Tektronix terminals is the largest single manufactured item that can be found in nearly every computer graphics application. For this reason Tektronix terminals are included as the major example of CRT interactive displays. The range of devices manufactured is excellent, from an inexpensive 4006 model to the system-designed 618: CRT peripherals such as joysticks, hard copy units, data tablets, small interactive plotters, and added storage make this line of products extremely flexible and useful for the architect.

Peripheral Devices. Strictly speaking, a digital plotter is a peripheral device because the operator cannot interact with the computer to modify the design drawing. The majority of manufacturers make several per᠎pheral devices such as plotters, digitizers, direct-view storage tubes, and matrix printers. The number of manufacturers is increasing almost at a daily rate. The reader should be aware that any listing is representative of the total number of companies involved in the computer graphics industry, not the total.

As we progress through this textbook, many examples of input and output peripheral devices will be explained in detail. The CALCOMP plotter is a classic example of a well-known computer graphics peripheral device. It is not designed for architectural graphics use solely. It is a general-purpose device. The author makes use of it throughout the text by modification to the basic, general-purpose software. Whenever a change has been made, it has been noted with comment statements before the software listing.

Earlier an example of an interactive plotter was chosen; to avoid confusion at that point, the plotter was connected to an interactive terminal. It was the terminal that made the two devices interactive, not the plotter. The designer communicates with the computer through the terminal, and the plotter displays the drawing. The designer may interrupt the computer output and change a drawing, but the plotter paper must be changed by the operator.

Peripheral devices describe the character of the automated graphics system chosen. Automated graphics systems are used for drafting, mapping image analysis, or business applications. The scope of this text is limited to architectural applications. The manufactured systems outlined thus far include all aspects of automated graphics. Therefore a detailed description of architectural drafting systems is given next.

Now the user must decide how he or she is to communicate with the system he or she has chosen to be the ADM (architectural drafting machine). The most common types of languages used in programming ADM systems are mathematical-formula-based ones. FORTRAN is the most popular, and the following section of this chapter is based on a sound understanding of FORTRAN.

No matter which type of language is chosen, the steps in problem solving remain the same:

1. Formulate the problem.
2. Construct a mathematical model by the use of graphical methods.
3. Set up the model in the form of one or more equations that satisfy the model constraints.
4. Draw a flowchart of the logical problem solution.
5. Write the language required, such as FORTRAN or BASIC.
6. Prepare the data for input to the program.
7. Trial-run the program and data on the ADM.
8. Analyze the results and modify the program.

LANGUAGES FOR
ARCHITECTURAL
GRAPHICS

A design language can best be described as a method by which we, the designers, supply raw information to a machine and the machine in turn assists us in finding an answer to one or more problems. The machine is often a computer or special-purpose computer-related device. A language for architectural graphics implies a uniform, easily understood, organized procedure for feeding information into and out of the design cycle. The design cycle would involve setting up the goal, defining the task to be done, constructing a certain concept of analysis, and then utilizing the routine for solution and documentation. This indicates that a designer produces a program. It is inside of this program that the design language is most useful, for here the speed and accuracy of the computer can be harnessed.

The two main parts of a design program are data and instructions. Data consist of the numbers and characters which are to be used by the instructions to produce an architectural drawing. The main types of data used are numeric and alphanumeric, plus special characteristics. Each line of the program is divided into positions, each of which may contain one character or space. Positions 1 through 5 are used for line numbers, which are labels to identify a particular line. If no statement number is assigned, then the first five spaces are left blank. The design command is entered in positions 7 through 72. A character C in position 1 indicates that the command on that line is a designer comment. Comments do not affect the program and may be used for explanatory purposes. Each of the lines that are used by a designer is one of the following types:

1. Arithmetic: specified computation to be completed
2. Control: commands which specify flow of machine operations
3. Input/output: governs the movement of data between human and machine
4. Declaration: supply of descriptive information about programs

The designer uses the language to produce a series of commands which move the pen in such a manner that the end result is a properly drawn design or working drawing. The particular graphic display device accepts these commands only when received in the proper sequence and in a specific format. The designer must be able to write a computer program in a language such as FORTRAN or BASIC and must also know how to construct subroutines for the display of the standard drawing parts.

Arithmetic Quantities

The three basic arithmetic elements used in coding calculations are constants, variables, and functional references, all of which represent numerical quantities. The two modes of numerical quantities allowed are integer and real. Integer quantities represent whole-number values and are treated as fixed-point numbers within the computer. They may have a value between 0.99999999999 and 99,999,999,999. Real quantities represent real numbers, i.e., those which may have a fractional component. They are treated as floating-point numbers within the computer and have a range between $10^{**}(-150)$ and $10^{**}(147)$. Both integer and real quantities carry 11 significant digits.

Identifiers are used to name the variables, subprograms, or subroutines which appear in a coded program. An identifier is a string of letters or digits, the first of which must be a letter. The string may be any desired length, but only the first six characters will be used. Identifiers are implicitly declared to be one of two types (integer or real), according to the following:

1. Identifiers beginning with the character I, J, K, L, M, or N are assigned integer type.
2. Identifiers not included in the preceding classification are assigned real type.

Constants

Constants are integers or real numbers which appear in a source program in explicit form. Integer constants are written as a string of decimal digits. Leading zeros are ignored, e.g., 0,1,123. Real constants are written as a string of decimal digits which include a decimal point, e.g., 1.0,1.,2.768. Real constants may be given a scale factor by appending an E, followed by an integer constant, which indicates the power of 10 by which the number is to be multiplied. This scale factor may be preceded by a plus or minus sign to indicate positive or negative powers of 10. If no sign is given, it is assumed to be positive; e.g., 1.E-5 means 0.00001, or .00314E+3 means 3.14.

Variables

Variables represent quantities which may assume many different values during the execution of a program. Each variable has a name and a type. The type of variable corresponds to the type of quantity it represents. Variables of either type may be scalar or array variables.

Scalar Variables. A scalar variable represents a single quantity and is written as a simple identifier, e.g., AMOUNT, X, K2.

Array Variables. An array variable represents a single element in an array of quantities. An array variable is denoted by the array identifier followed by a subscript list enclosed in parentheses. The subscript list is a sequence of arithmetic expressions separated by commas. Each expression corresponds to a subscript, and the values of the expressions determine which element of the array is referenced, e.g., X(1), K2(M), LINE(INDEX,LINE (Y)+(Y). Any valid expression may also be used as a subscript. The value of each subscript expression will be converted to an integer value before it is used as a subscript. The value of a subscript must lie within the limits specified for the array.

Function References

A function is a subprogram which acts upon one or more quantities, called arguments, and produces a single quantity, called the function value. Function references are denoted by the identifier which names the function followed by an argument list enclosed in parentheses.

Function type is assigned by the type of identifier which names the function. The type of function is independent of the types of its arguments. A function references represents a quantity, namely, the function value, and will act as a variable. The type of the function corresponds to the type of the function value, e.g., SIN(X), BESSEL(N,Z*SQRT(ALPHA)), DAY(6,7,41).

Arithmetic Expressions

An expression is a sequence of elements separated by operational symbols and/or parentheses in accordance with conventional mathematical notation. An expression has a single numeric value equaling the result of the calculation specified by the numeric quantities and arithmetic operations comprising it. The arithmetic operational symbols are +, -, *, /, and **, denoting addition, subtraction, multiplication, division, and exponentiation, respectively.

An expression may be as simple as a single element, e.g., -3.146, OMEGA(T), COS(THETA). Compound expressions may be formed by using arithmetic operational symbols to combine basic elements, e.g., -Z+2, SUM/N, SQRT(B**2+A). Any expression may be enclosed in parentheses and considered as a basic element, e.g., -A*(3.14*-THETA). Any expression may be preceded by a plus or minus sign, e.g., +TEN, -(A+B), -SIN(THETA). However, no two operational symbols may appear in sequence. The expression X*-Y is not allowed in a computer language. The use of parentheses will give the correct form, X*(-Y).

If the precedence of arithmetic operations is not included explicitly by parentheses, it is implicitly interpreted to be as follows, in order of decreasing precedence:

Symbol	Operation
**	Exponentiation
* and /	Multiplication and division
+ and -	Addition and subtraction

For example, the expression U*V+W/X**Y+Z is taken to be (U*V)+ (W/(X**Y)+Z. Since sequences of operations of equal precedence can result in ambiguities, they are resolved by grouping from the left. Thus A**B**C and X/Y/Z are interpreted as (A**B)**C and (X/Y)/Z.

The numerical value of any expression may be integer or real as determined by the types of its elements. There are three possible combinations: All elements are integer (integer expression), all elements are real (real expression), or both real and integer elements occur (mixed expression). All combinations are permissible.

Integer Expressions

An integer expression is evaluated using integer operations throughout to give an integer result. Fractional parts arising in division are truncated, not rounded; e.g., 5/3 gives 1, and 4/7 forms 0.

Declaration Statements

A declaration describes certain properties of a coded program. Several statements are reserved for the purpose of supplying the system with declarative information. These statements are primarily concerned with the interpretation of identifiers occurring in the source program and with memory allocation in the object program.

Each identifier in a source program is classified in accordance with the element it identifies. Four main classifications are recognized: (1) scalar, (2) array, (3) subprogram, and (4) dummy. Classification is made according to the context in which the identifier makes its first physical appearance in the source program. This first appearance amounts to a declaration, explicit or implicit, of the proper interpretation of the identifier throughout the program.

Allocation Statements

Memory allocation statements are used to supply the graphics system with supplemental information regarding the storage of scalar variables and arrays.

Dimension Statements

The dimension statement is used to declare an identifier to be an array identifier and to specify the number and limits of the array subscripts. As many arrays may be declared in a dimension statement as will fit one line of coded program. Any number of dimension statements may be used in a program. The information provided by a dimension statement is required for allocation of storage for arrays. Each array variable appearing in a program must represent an element of an array declared in a dimension statement. The array variable must have a number of subscripts equal to (or less than) those declared for the array, and the total number of each subscripted variable must not exceed those specified by the dimension statement; e.g., DIMENSION X(10),Y(10),Z(10) gives the array name and the maximum number of storage locations each may assume. Therefore LINE(25,50) is a two-dimensional array named line having a maximum storage of 25 locations in one direction and 50 in the other. If LINE(I,J) were to be plotted and storage location I contained 1 to 25 sets of data and J contained 1 to 50 sets of data, a minimum of 25 plotted lines would appear on the printout.

Common Statements

The identifiers in a common statement may be either scalar or array identifiers. The common statement specifies that the scalar and array identifiers appearing in the list are to be stored in an area that will also be available to other graphic users. By using the common statement, the same storage area may be shared by a program and its graphic subroutine.

Each array name appearing in a common statement must also appear in a dimension statement in the same program. Quantities whose identifiers appear in common statements are allocated storage cells in the same sequence in which their identifiers appear in the common statement, beginning with the first common statement in the program.

Storage allocation for identifiers appearing in a common statement begins at the same location for all programs. This allows the programmer to establish a one-to-one correspondence between quantities used in several programs even when those quantities have different identifiers within various programs. For example, if a

graphics program contains COMMON X,Y,Z as its first common statement, X and XPAGE will refer to the same storage location. A similar correspondence will hold for the pairs Y and YPAGE and Z and
ZPAGE. Identifiers that are linked through the common statement
must agree in type (real or integer).

Equivalence Statements

The equivalence statement allows more than one identifier to represent the same quantity, e.g., EQUIVALENCE(R1,R2,...,Rn), where R
denotes a location reference. The location references of an equivalence statement may be simple scalar or array identifiers appended
by an integer constant enclosed in parentheses. All location references enclosed within the same parenthetical expression share the
same storage location; such a group is known as an equivalence set;
e.g., EQUIVALENCE(RADIUS,ARC) states that the identifiers RADIUS and
ARC refer to the same storage location.

To reference a specific location in an array, that location
must be appended to an array identifier as an integer constant. For
example, if A is a scalar variable and B is an array, the statement
EQUIVALENCE(A,B(5)) specifies that A and the fifth location of the
array B share the same location.

Subprogram Definition Statements

The subprogram is classified as external to the main graphics program and is defined separately from the graphics program calling
them. Subprograms are complete and autonomous programs within themselves. There are two types of subprograms which may be declared:
function subprograms and subroutine subprograms.

Any subprogram may call other subprograms; however, recursion
is not allowed. All subroutines constitute closed subroutines;
e.g., they appear only once in the source program regardless of the
number of times they are called.

Assignment Statements

An assignment statement specifies an expression to be evaluated and
a variable, called the statement variable, to which the expression
value is to be assigned, e.g., VARIABLE=EXPRESSION.

Note that the equals sign does not mean equality but replacement. Consider the following examples:

    Y=2*Y   M=M-S*(M-1)   Z(I)=SIN(THETA)

These examples are not equations but valid assignment statements.
The first example means take the value of Y, double it, and assign
the resulting value to Y. In the second example, 1 is subtracted
from M, the result is multiplied by S, and that quantity is sub-

tracted from M; the total result is assigned to a storage location called M. In the third example, the sine function is operated on the variable THETA, and this result is assigned to a subscripted variable Z.

Control Statements

In a coded graphics program, control normally passes sequentially from one statement to the next in the order in which they are presented to the computer. Control statements allow the designer to alter this normal program flow. To implement this, source statements may be given statement numbers which are referenced by control statements. A statement number consists of an unsigned integer constant comprised of up to five digits.

Although statement numbers appear in the source program in integers, they must not be confused with numeric quantities. They represent a distinct type of quantity in a graphics program, and no two statements may have the same number. The most common form of control statement is the unconditional GOTO statement. It is used as GOTO n, where n is a statement number. This statement transfers control to the statement numbered n, e.g., GOTO 41.

If Statements

Another type of control statement is the if statement. The if may be used to test a true or false state (logical if) or test the value of an expression for negative, null, or positive responses, e.g., IF(X-1)n1,n2,n3, where n1, n2, and n3 are statement numbers. This statement transfers control to statement n1 if the operation X-1 has a negative result. n2 would receive control if the operation X-1 were also zero, while n3 would receive control if the operation were positive in its result. Any valid expression may be used as the test IF(EXPRESSION), and any statement number arrangement can be used, e.g., IF(TEST+SUM)1,4,4. Here both the zero and positive results are sent to the same statement number.

Do Statements

The do statement allows a series of statements to be executed repeatedly under the control of a variable whose value changes between repetitions, e.g., DO N scalar variable = integer1,integer2,integer3. N is a statement number, and the scalar variable is in integer form. The do statement causes the following statements up to and including statement N to be executed repeatedly. This group of statements is called the range of the do and is located where integer2 is shown. Integer1 is the location of the index or starting point of the do, while integer3 is the incremental value of the index. The values of integers 1, 2, and 3 are called the index, range or limit, and increment.

The initial execution of all statements within the range is always performed with the initial value assigned to the index, regardless of the value of the limit and increment. After each execution of the range the increment is added to the value of the index and the result compared to the limit. If the result is not greater than the limit, the statements within the range are again executed using the new value of the index. After the last execution, program control passes to the statement immediately following statement N.

Continue Statements

The general rules of graphics programming state that the range of a do statement cannot end with a transfer instruction. The continue statement is a dummy, or no-operation, statement that may be used to end the range of a do statement.

Stop Statements

A stop statement terminates execution of the graphics program and returns control to the designer for other functions of the ADM system.

Call Statements

The call statement is used to call, or transfer control to, a graphic subroutine or subprogram. The identifier is the name of the subroutine. The arguments may be given as constants or subscripted variables. Unlike a function, a subroutine has more than one result and may use one or more of its arguments to return these results to the calling program (the main line). A subroutine may require no arguments at all, e.g., CALL TITLE, where the sole function of the subroutine is to plot a title block for a drawing sheet. However, the general use is with an argument list, e.g., CALL PLOT(XLINE,- YLINE,IPEN), where the XLINE is the data required to plot a straight line in the x direction, YLINE is the data required to plot a straight line in the y direction, and IPEN contains an integer for pen control.

Return Statements

The return statement returns control from an external graphics sub- routine to the calling or graphics main-line program. Therefore, the last statement executed in a subroutine will be a return state- ment.

Data Statements

A data statement provides a quick method for inputs of limited amounts of the database for a graphics procedure, e.g., DATA X/3.14,8.9,5.6/. This statement provides for X_1 to contain 3.14, X_2 to contain 8.9, and X_3 to contain 5.6. X must be contained in a dimension statement in order for the main data statement to take effect. Any number of pieces of data may be entered in this manner, provided the variable is an array.

Read Statement

For large amounts of data the read statement is most useful. It causes information to be read from batch, or interactive, sources. It is used in several different ways, e.g., READ(n1,n2) (an IBM method, where n1 is a reader control and n2 is a format statement), READ n,VARIABLE (where n is the format statement), and READ VARIABLE (called a free-format method where data are separated by commas and are not formatted into spaces).

Write Statement

A write statement can also be used as PRINT. The write statement provides a method for output of data in the reverse manner from a read statement. It is used in graphics programs to provide a database for plotting points as finished geometry.

CHAPTER SUMMARY   The sample programs illustrated throughout this book show how design language would appear on a standard computer printout sheet. The purpose of the programs is to call a series of subprograms from computer storage to draw a design on a digital plotter. The mechanics of recalling graphics programs was introduced. It was presented here only to indicate the manner in which a designer may use the language needed to operate a graphics system.

This chapter was developed for use with a digital computer, CRT graphic terminal, and digitally controlled plotter. These basic pieces of hardware can be operated together to form either an automated recall or a design system. The sample recalls were given so that the host computer may be any of the following:

1. DEC PDP 11
2. Interdata 7/32, 8/32
3. D/G Nova series
4. HP 2100, 3000, 9810, 9825, 9830
5. IBM 370 with ASCII Interface
6. CDC 6000 series
7. UNIVAC 1108
8. Wang 2200

Undoubtedly, other host-plotter arrangements are possible. The author recommends the CALCOMP 500, 836, 936, or 960 to ensure compatibility.

EXERCISES   1.   Stored drawings may be recalled and viewed on a CRT, DVST, or other type of video monitor. The graphics system command CALL is used to view existing drawings, while SAVE is used to store the instructions for the drawing images. Begin by recalling the drawings saved in Exercise 1 in Chapter 6 under CONCET. Page through the windows and check the viewed drawings with the input sketches.

2.   After window checking, arrange the 10 windows to be plotted on a digital plotter. The general arrangement is as shown.

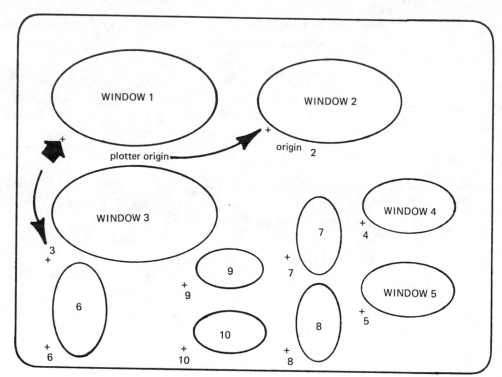

3.   Changes in stored drawings can be made by rearranging the placement of the windows or by the modification of the data in a single window. Repeat Exercise 2 using a different arrangement.

4.   Recall window 1 stored in Exercise 1 in Chapter 6 under the label CONCET; rename this EQCET1. Add the piping and equipment as described in Chapter 5 (IGS) and according to the example shown. (Courtesy of the U.S. Corps of Engineers, Vicksburg, Mississippi.)

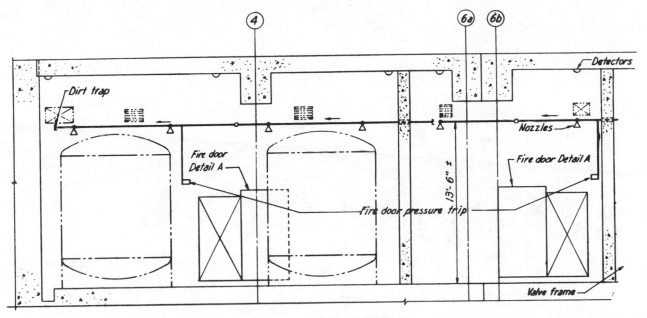

5.   Recall window 2 stored in Exercise 2 in Chapter 6 and rename it EQCET2. Add the piping and equipment as shown. (Courtesy of the U.S. Corps of Engineers, Vicksburg, Mississippi.)

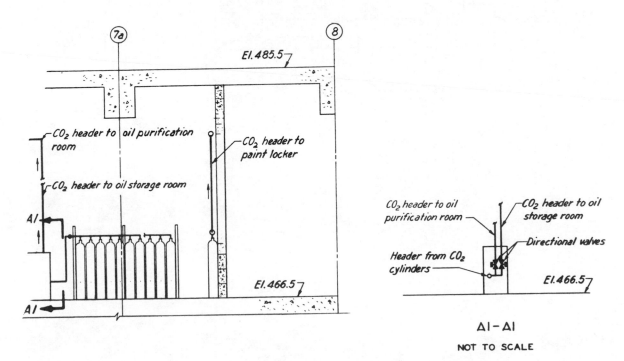

6.   It is possible to use stored drawing information to create new
     drawing files. Use window 3 of Exercise 3 in Chapter 6 to
     obtain the information to create a plan view as shown. Add the
     piping and equipment as shown and provide three sections A-A,
     B-B, and C-C. (Courtesy of the U.S. Corps of Engineers,
     Vicksburg, Mississippi.)

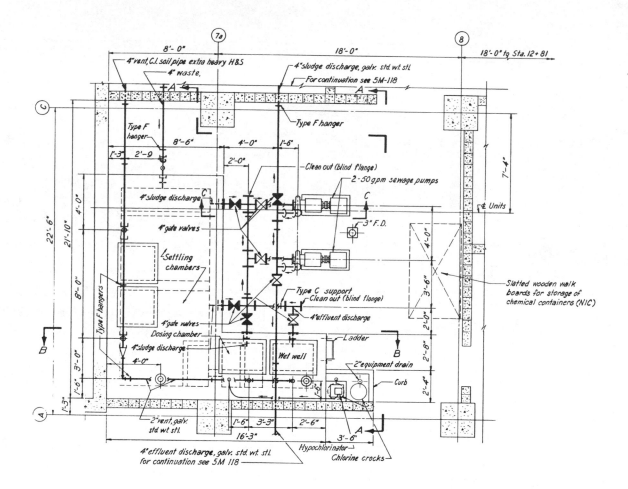

7. Set up a separate window for detail section A-A as shown. (Courtesy of the U.S. Corps of Engineers, Vicksburg, Mississippi.)

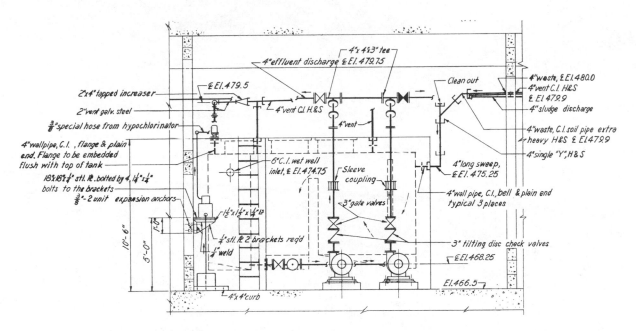

8. Set up a separate window for detail section B-B as shown. (Courtesy of the U.S. Corps of Engineers, Vicksburg, Mississippi.)

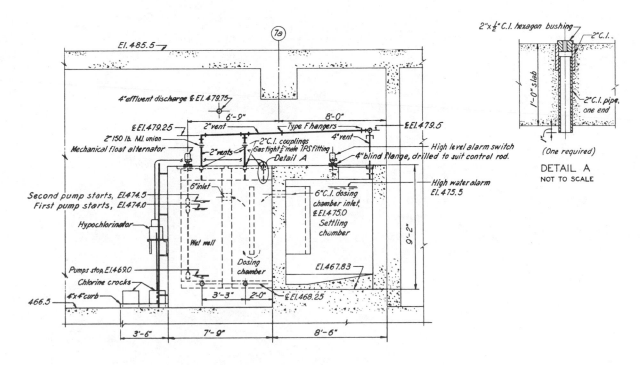

9. Set up a separate window for detail section C-C as shown. (Courtesy of the U.S. Corps of Engineers, Vicksburg, Mississippi.)

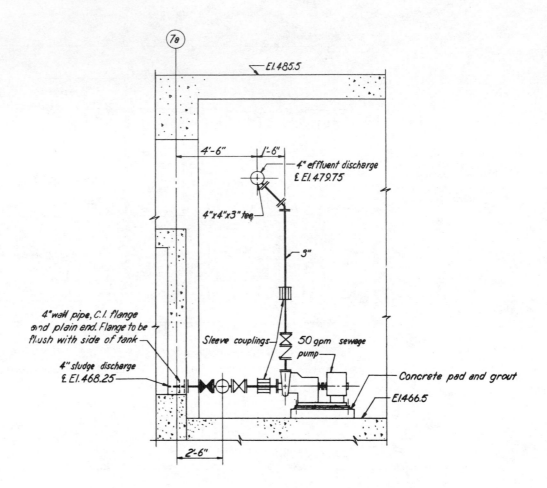

10. Arrange the newly created windows to repeat Exercise 2. This will test your ability to manipulate the relationship of various sheets in a file.

11. Output the arrangement done for Exercise 10 so that it can be stored on microfilm or previewed on a CRT interactive graphics terminal.

12. Develop a new display program that will produce a plan view of
    Exercise 1 in Chapter 6. The output of this program should
    produce the drawing shown.

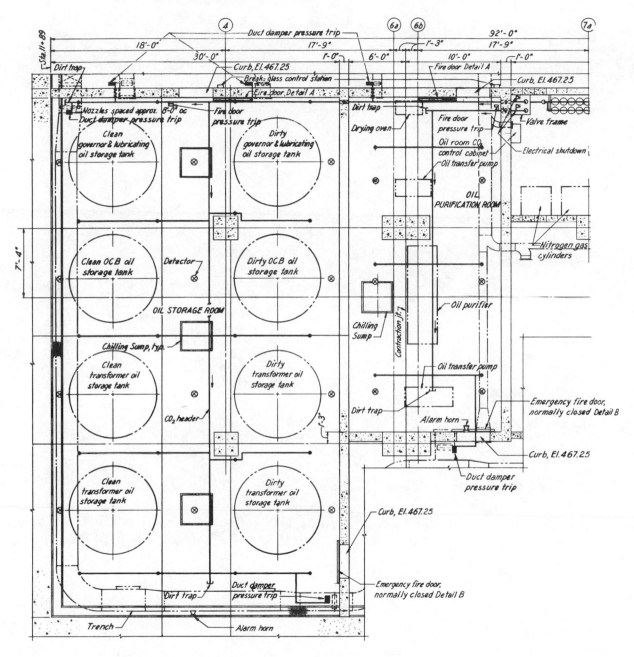

8 Floorplan Generation

The most important drawing in a set of computer-generated architectural drawings is the floorplan, since all other drawings are derived from the database constructed from this source. For example, the geometry for the foundation plan is taken from the floorplan database. Elevations are projected from it also. The sizes of roof and ceiling members are taken from data for spans between walls on the floorplan. The interrelationship of database is diagrammed in Figure 8.1. By studying this diagram of computer displays, it becomes apparent that no computer-generated drawings can be designed in isolation from the others. Neither can changes in the database for one be made without considering the effects of the data on the other outputs. The major drawings of a set such as floorplan, foundation, structural sections, exterior and interior elevations, and framing plans must all agree and are presented in Chapters 8 through 14 respectively.

Other drawings such as electrical, plumbing, heating, and ventilation are closely related to each other and to the floorplan. Some sheets in a set of architectural drawings, such as construction details, are related closely to only one or two other sheets. The preliminary planning outlined in Chapter 4 is the basis for presentation drawing as well as working drawings, while the specifications are supplements to all architectural drawings.

197

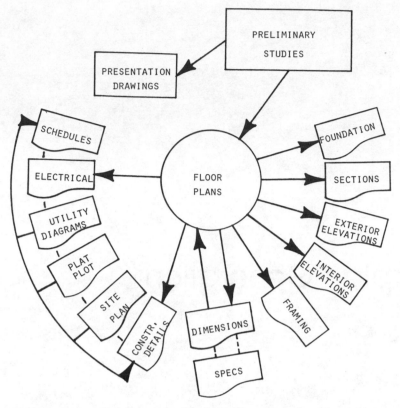

FIGURE 8.1 Database relationship for drawings in an architectural set.

AUTOMATED FLOORPLAN DESIGN

Before starting the design of any sheet in a set of computer-generated architectural drawings, an analysis of the preliminary study should be made. This will indicate the primary data gathered, the various symbols and conventions to be used for that particular sheet (in this case the floorplan). This will shorten the design layout time considerably and reduce the number of preview sessions and data modifications (erasing and redrawing time for manual preparation). Always check the overall dimensions for the floorplan in order to select a proper display scale. Next, space the floorplan in the display area for general appearance, leaving room for dimensions and notes. A large floorplan in a display area will be more pleasing to the eye if it is spaced equally at the sides with slightly more space at the bottom than at the top. This will frame the floorplan effectively and leaves room for title strips and scale notation.

Begin the layout process with the overall dimensions from the database. Place these in the display area first to see if the preceding procedure has been followed. The order of line generation suggested next depends on the size of the database and how the

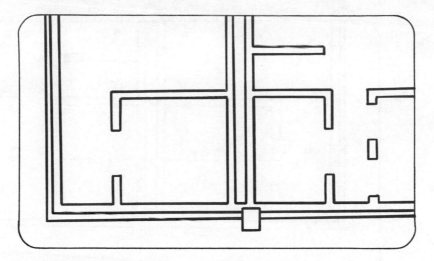

FIGURE 8.2   DVST display of major outlines for a floorplan.

arrays are stored in the computer. Variations in the procedure will always be possible depending on varying situations. For most floorplans the following is used:

1.   Display all major outlines of the floorplan as shown in Figure 8.2.
2.   Call CNTRL to locate centerlines and edge lines of important features such as walls, doors, and openings as shown in Figure 8.3.
3.   Display smaller details such as window openings, doors, and features located by the centerlines as shown in Figure 8.4.

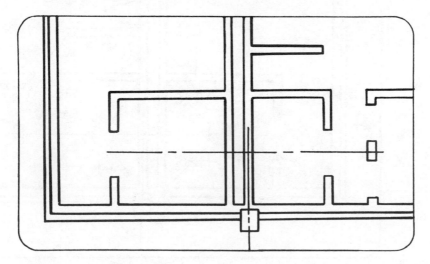

FIGURE 8.3   Centerlines are placed on important features.

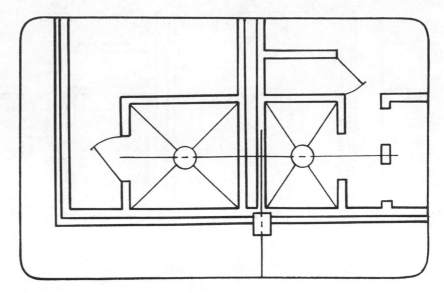

FIGURE 8.4 Display of doors and features located by centerlines.

4. Display cabinets and all built-in portions of the floor-
    plan as shown in Figure 8.5

5. Display all minor objects that will be located on the
    floorplan (unusual features of this design only).

6. Add all dimensioning for items 1 through 5 as shown in
    Figure 8.6.

7. Add all lettered notes as described in Chapter 3.

8. Preview the entire display program for checking by the
    architect as follows:

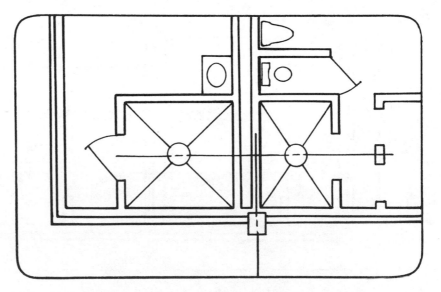

FIGURE 8.5 Display of cabinets and built-ins.

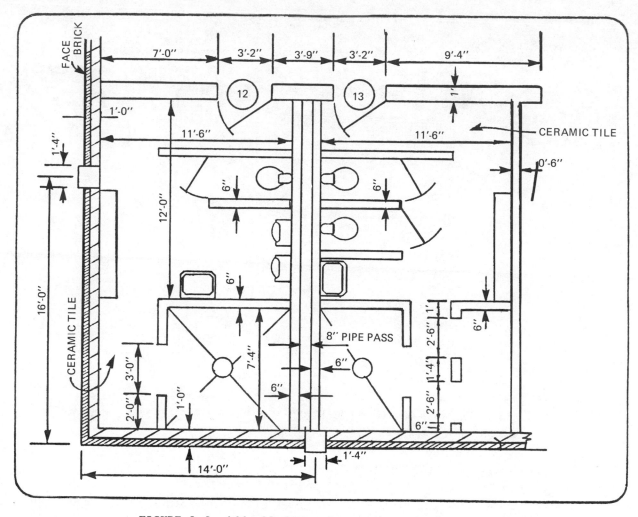

FIGURE 8.6   Add all dimensions and notes for the floorplans.

```
C   FLOORPLAN PROGRAM FOR PREVIEW AND CHECKOFF BY ARCHITECT.
        INTEGER FOOT(3),TITLE(17),XGRID,YGRID
        REAL LOC
        DATA FOOT/' SQU','ARE ','FEET'/
        DATA IFOOT/'FOOT'/
C   WHEN PLOT IS SPECIFIED,POS1 IS WALLS****************
C   POS1 8BLACK***************************************
C   POS2 4GREEN**************************************
C
C   READ IN THE 2 PARAMETER CARDS - FIRST THE TITLE CARD
C       SECOND THE PLOT SIZE FACTOR AND GRID SIZE
C
        READ(1,20) NUMT,TITLE
20      FORMAT(I2,17A4)
```

```
      READ(1,*) FACT,SGRID
C
C  SET UP THE PARAMETERS FOR THE CALL TO GRID - INCLUDES THE SIZE
C     OF THE SQUARES AND THE OVERALL SIZE OF THE GRID AS WELL AS
C     PROVIDING THE NUMBER FOR THE GRID LEGEND
C
      IF(SGRID.NE.1.) GO TO 2
      XGRID=53.
      YGRID=28.
      GSIZE=16.
      GO TO 4
2     IF(SGRID.NE..5) GO TO 3
      XGRID=106.
      YGRID=56.
      GSIZE=4.
      GO TO 4
3     IF(SGRID.NE..25) GO TO 998
      XGRID=212.
      YGRID=112.
      GSIZE=1.
      FOOT(3)=IFOOT
C
C  INITIALIZE THE PLOTTER AND SET THE PLOT SIZE SCALE FACTOR
C
4        CALL PLOTS
         CALL FACTOR(FACT)
C
C  DRAW THE LEGEND IN THE LOWER LEFT HAND CORNER OF THE PLOT
C
C        THE HEADING
C
      CALL SYMBOL(0.,2.,.5,'LEGEND',0.,6)
      CALL SYMBOL(0.,1.73,.25,'************',0.,12)
C
C        THE SAMPLE GRID SQUARE
C
C
      LOC=1.73-SGRID-.2
      CALL PLOT(.5,LOC,3)
      CALL PLOT(.5+SGRID,LOC,2)
      CALL PLOT(.5+SGRID,LOC+SGRID,2)
      CALL PLOT(.5,LOC,2)
C
C        THE LABEL FOR THE SAMPLE GRID SQUARE
C
```

```
        CALL NUMBER(.5+SGRID+.25,LOC,.25,GSIZE,0.,-1)
        CALL SYMBOL(.5+SGRID+.5,LOC,.25,FOOT,0.,12)
C
C       THE SCALE IN INCHES
C
        SCALE=.25*FACT
        CALL NUMBER(.5+SGRID+.25,LOC-.4,.25,SCALE,0.,4)
        CALL SYMBOL(.5+SGRID+2.,LOC-.4,.25,'INCHES = 1 FOOT ,0.,15)
C
C  RESET THE ORIGIN FOR DRAWING THE GRID AND TITLE
C
        CALL PLOT(0.,3.,-3)
C
C  DRAW THE TOP TITLE FOR THE PLOT
C
        XTITL=(53.-(.75*NUMT))/2.
        CALL SYMBOL(XTITL,29.,.75,TITLE,0.,NUMT)
C
C  CHANGE PEN COLORS AND DRAW THE GRID
C
        CALL NEWPEN(2)
        CALL GRID(0.,0.,SGRID,SGRID,XGRID,YGRID)
C
C  RESET THE ORIGIN AND CHANGE PEN COLOR TO DRAW THE FLOOR PLAN
C       THE ORIGIN IS NOW THE LOWER LEFT HAND CORNER OF THE BUILDING
C
        CALL PLOT(1.5,1.75,-3)
        CALL NEWPEN(1)
C
C  EXERCISE THE PEN BEFORE DRAWING THE FLOOR PLAN
        CALL PLOT(-4.,0.,3)
        CALL PLOT(-4.28,.2)
        CALL PLOT(-3.95,0.,2)
        CALL PLOT(-3.85,0.,2)
        CALL PLOT(-3.8,28.,2)
        CALL PLOT(-3.75,0.,2)
C
C  LOOP TO READ THE DATA POINTS AND DRAW THE FLOOR PLAN
C
1       READ(1,*,END=999) X, Y, INC
        CALL PLOT(X,Y,INC)
        GO TO 1
C
C  ERROR MESSAGE FOR INVALID GRID SIZE ON PARAMETER CARD
C
```

```
998   WRITE(3,10)
10    FORMAT(' ','INVALID GRID SIZE SPECIFIED, CORRECT AND RESUBMIT',
      *' *** VALID SIZES ARE 1., .5, AND .25')
C
C  CLOSE THE PLOTTAPE AND END THE PROGRAM
C
999   IF(INC.NE.999) CALL PLOT(0.,0.,999)
      STOP
      END
```

9.   List the database for the display program as follows:

```
00000010  45CLEMSON UNIVERSITY EXAMPLE FLOOR PLAN
00000020    0.45         0.25
00000030    0.0          0.0       3    OUTSIDE WALLS (GOING CLOCKWISE)
00000040    0.0         24.5000     2
00000050   48.4375      24.5000     2
00000060   48.4375      19.3750     2
00000070   48.0000      19.3750     2
00000080   48.0000      18.1250     2
00000090   48.4375      18.1250     2
00000100   48.4375      17.8125     2
00000110   48.4375      17.0625     3
00000120   47.4365       0.0        2
00000130   40.2000       0.0        2
00000140   38.8000       0.0        3
00000150   35.7500       0.0        2
00000160   34.2500       0.0        3
00000170   31.0625       0.0        2
00000180   31.0625       0.3300     2
00000190   28.8125       0.3300     2
00000200   28.8125       0.0        2
00000210   24.7500       0.0        2
00000220   24.7500       2.1250     2
00000230   21.3125       2.1250     2
00000240   21.3125       0.0        2
00000250    0.0          0.0        2
00000260   48.4375       3.0000     3    MACHINE ROOM (GOING CLOCKWISE)
00000270   45.0625       3.0000     2
00000280   45.0625       3.1875     2
00000290   45.0625       3.1875     2
00000300   44.3125       3.0000     3
00000310   41.3125       3.0000     2
00000320   41.3125       3.1875     2
00000330   44.3125       3.0000     2
00000340   44.3125       3.0000     2
00000350   40.5625       3.0000     3
```

```
00000360   40.2500    3.0000   2
              .
              .
              .
00000940   42.1875   19.3750   2
00000950   30.1250   13.0625   3   LOBBY AREA
00000960   30.1250   16.9375   2
              .
              .
              .
00001480   42.0625   12.5625   2
00001490   42.0625   12.0625   2
00001500   30.0000    4.1250   3   RIGHT SIDE OF HALLWAY
              .
              .
00001860   26.8750   10.5000   2
00001870   24.8125   16.2500   3   LEFT SIDE OF HALLWAY
00001880   21.8125   16.2500   2
              .
              .
              .
00003250   30.0000   24.5000   2
00003260   30.0000   21.5000   3   BACK HALLWAY
00003270   24.1250   21.5000   2
              .
              .
              .
00003790   24.3750   18.0625   2
00003800   24.3750   18.3750   2
00003810   21.6250    5.0000   3   STORAGE AREA
              .
              .
              .
00004260    2.3750   20.5000   2
00004270   11.7500   23.4375   3   STORAGE AREA POSTS
00004280   12.0000   23.4375   2
              .
              .
              .
00004820    5.7500    0.2500   2
00004830    5.7500    0.0      2
00004840    6.0000    0.0      2
00004850    6.0000    0.2500   2
END OF DATA
```

Simple Floorplans from Preliminary Sketches

The floorplan is displayed from the final preliminary notes and from presentation sketches discussed in Chapter 4. The procedure for making this transfer is quite straightforward, consisting of the following:

1. A dual line plan is displayed on a DVST. Lines on the screen for outside walls indicate the facing material such as masonry, wood, or concrete. Lines for interior walls show the centerlines. If possible arrange the main entrance to appear at the bottom of the screen as in Figure 8.7.

2. The standard section symbol for wall materials may be added (refer to Chapter 5 to refresh how this is done) as displayed in Figure 8.7.

3. Such things as steps, landings, and stairwells are shown in dashed outline and noted as illustrated in Figure 8.7.

4. Plumbing fixtures are displayed along with callouts and notes as shown in Figure 8.6. Often these are shown in

FIGURE 8.7 4054 Graphic Computing System. (Courtesy of Tektronix, Inc., Beaverton, Oregon.)

cabinet outlines. Insulation around fixtures and pipes and in walls is indicated by a serpentine display and noted.

5. Where space is reserved for building equipment supplied by vendors, the equipment is displayed by a dashed line and noted (NIC, not in contract).

Multistory Plans

In a multistory structure floorplans are generated for each floor. In the case of a high rise with 100 stories, 100 floorplans are generated. Since much duplication exists, a computer file containing similar data will produce the finished drawing in 1/10,000 of the time required to draw the plans and reproduce them on sepia copies. Even with time saving, there are unique items on each floor: electrical, heating and air conditioning, plumbing, and placement schedules. On small jobs, this information may be placed on a single floorplan. In multistory projects the variations between floors cause the designer to consider the following.

Electrical runs, outlets, switches, and switch legs are displayed by symbols. The entrance point location for switchgear should be shown and the sizes of the main fuses and number of branch circuits noted. Be sure to follow the template methods described in Chapter 5. Heating and air conditioning runs and units are displayed in their proper location along with notes about manufacturer, catalog number, type of unit, and capacity. Register outlets are shown in phantom line on the screen while return-air vents are located by notes. Plumbing fixtures are displayed in their proper location, as mentioned earlier. For additional information, see Chapter 5.

Placement schedules locate windows, doors, and other objects as well as describe the room finish for each room in the building. Type, brand, and unusual callouts should be included in the display of the schedule. Schedules are usually placed on separate sheets but may appear as part of a floorplan display if the project is small.

DIMENSIONING AND NOTATION

Dimensioning, like lettering, should be consistent. Earlier the steps for the display of a floorplan were given; in addition to the shape of a building, information such as the space between wall surfaces, locations of features, the type of material, openings required, and the kind of finish must be included. The technique for including this information on a floorplan is called dimensioning and notation. When an architectural detailer dimensions a floorplan of a building, engineering and design judgment is exercised. This judgment indicates a thorough knowledge of construction practices.

The techniques of automatically dimensioning a floorplan do not differ from conventional methods. In architectural practice, dimension lines are continuous, with the notation above the line. This will speed the display output. Notation is read from the bottom or right-hand edge of the display printout. The floorplan must be described systematically by dividing it into simple geometric shapes. The rules learned in earlier experiences hold true. The dimensioning of a floorplan is accomplished by specifying each elemental form to indicate its size and relationship relative to a centerline or finished surface.

The procedure for using automated dimensioning and notes are outlined in the following steps:

1. Divide the floorplan to be dimensioned into geometric shapes and decide which are size and which are location dimensions.

2. Call DIMEN for placement of the size dimensions on each geometric shape.

3. Select the locating centerlines and call CNTRL for the proper placement.

4. Call DIMEN for the plotting of the location dimensions.

5. Add the final overall dimensions by CALL PLOT and CALL DIMEN in combination.

6. Call LABEL for adding notes that must be placed on the floorplan.

7. All leaders and special symbols are placed on the floorplan.

The subroutine DIMEN will be described in detail in Chapter 11 and should be referred to in order to place dimensions where they will be most easily understood. The extension, dimension lines, and arrowheads are displayed at the same time. The actual length of the dimension line is the product of DIME (the labeled length) and SCALER. If the actual length is 1.2 in. after scale conversion, the annotation is printed in the middle of the dimension line. If the dimension line is between 0.8 and 1.2 in. after scale conversion, the annotation is placed after the line. If the line is less than 0.8 in. after conversion, the arrowheads are placed outside along with the notation. Before conversion, distances are always expressed in feet and inches. Whenever distances are in even feet, 0 in. is displayed. For distance dimensions less than 1 ft., a zero is displayed before the number of inches in the notation. Each continuous row of dimensions must add to the overall dimension.

Room Labels

The room labeling is done automatically with room in the hundred
series assigned to the first story. Any basement labels are two
digit beginning with 10 and ending with 99. Second-story rooms
begin with 200 and end with 299. Each story then has a hundred numbered sequence keyed to the room finish schedule. The room finish
schedule may be arranged in a way similar to a door schedule, where
items are labeled opposite the room numbers. Typical labeling
schemes are used together with the floorplan, room finish schedule,
and interior elevations.

Special Symbols

Special symbols may be used on the floorplan. These include conventional arrows, small circles, or slant lines (hash marks) through
the intersection of the dimension line with the centerline or extension line. Hash marks are used with some stand-alone architectural
detailing equipment. Circles and arrows have special meaning in
modular dimensioning.

One important symbol, the north arrow, should be placed at a
convenient location. Place an entrance symbol at the main entrance.
Review the other special symbols introduced in Chapter 5 and study
their placement on the floorplan.

Linear Dimensions and Notes

There are many variations in the placement of linear dimensions and
notes; however, the following order can be used from a wall line:

1. Dimension between door and window center and the outside
    of the end walls
2. Dimension between centerlines of interior walls and the
    outside of end walls
3. Dimension between wall breaks and the outside of end walls
4. Overall size dimensions from the outside wall to the out-
    side wall

It is common to dimension to the surface of wall studs or other
structural components, not to the surface finish. All centers of
openings or walls are displayed with centerlines. Short interior
partitions like dividers are displayed inside the floorplan, not
outside with the other linear dimensions. Other features inside the
floorplan are usually dimensioned on the construction detail display
areas.

INTRODUCTION TO
SECTION SYMBOL
GENERATION

In Chapter 5 a considerable amount of discussion centered around how to generate symbols. One of these symbols, shown in Figure 5.1, was called the section symbol. When this symbol appears on a floorplan as shown in Figure 8.8, it means that a layer of information contains the graphic details for describing a section cut from the footings through the roof line. Chapter 5 described how to display this particular symbol by pressing the F key from the keyboard. This chapter introduces what the symbol represents in computer storage.

Page Reference Techniques

In the case of Figure 8.8 a two-part symbol was used. The symbol itself contains two important segments. The bulb or circle is divided into two compartments. The first compartment is formed by dividing the bulb into two parts (top and bottom). The top contains a number. This number is the layer number which contains the picture of the section. Since several section cuts are placed on one layer, it is common to have the layer number repeated on the floorplan section symbols. When a layer contains enough details to fill a page of output, another layer is chosen for storage. Layers contain windows, with usually one detail to a window; therefore, a single section is easy to recall using the techniques learned in Chapter 6.

A window can be found by referring to the lower half of the bulb. While it is common to repeat layer numbers (numbers in the top half), it is not possible to repeat window numbers. Therefore each window is unique. Figure 8.6 represents a window display, while Figure 8.8 represents a layer display.

Longitudinal Notation

The second segment of the section symbol contains a straight line with an arrow placed at 90°. The arrow indicates how the detail was stored in the computer memory. If the arrow faces away from the reader, the detail is stored in the normal manner. However, if the arrow faces toward the reader, then the detail is a mirror image. This keeps the right and left sides of objects separated later during construction.

The length of the line from the arrow to the bulb may be any length. Whatever the line crosses on the floorplan is shown as a section detail. For example, Figure 8.8 shows a floorplan where the section symbol passes through the entire floorplan (Section 1/18). This causes an entire cross section of the building to be stored in a separate window detail. These types of sections are called longitudinal sections. Usually special notes are used to define the longitudinal section of the building.

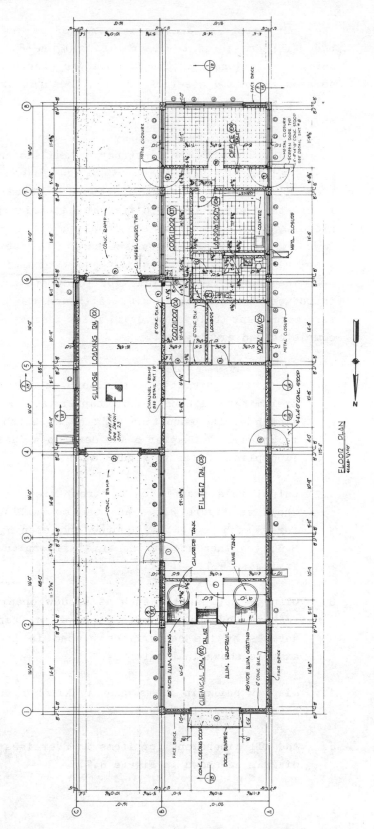

FIGURE 8.8. Final floorplan (typical electrostatic plotter output). (Courtesy of the U.S. Corps of Engineers, Vicksburg, Mississippi.)

CHAPTER SUMMARY   The most important drawing in computer memory is the floorplan and
                  the database stored to create it. Figure 8.1 illustrated this im-
                  portant relationship. The first seven chapters of this text can now
                  be used to create a series of architectural drawings. Using Figure
                  8.1 as a guide, the reader can follow the formation of the next
                  several chapters.

                       A series of DVST displays, Figures 8.2-8.7, illustrated the
                  steps involved with the construction and storage of a typical floor-
                  plan. Floorplans vary from project to project, depending on several
                  factors. Multistory plans of course require additional layers of
                  information and slightly different dimensioning and notation tech-
                  niques. Small items like the labeling of rooms for individual win-
                  dows within layers were discussed. In fact the series of DVST
                  displays 8.2-8.6 dealt with only one window of a floorplan layer.

                       The use of layer information to create working details was then
                  introduced through Figure 8.8. Although the contents of this chap-
                  ter were kept brief, several ideas using earlier chapters were
                  completed and displayed.

      EXERCISES   1.   Begin the automation of floorplan drawings by referring to
                       preliminary sketches in Chapter 4. Recall the single-line
                       sketch of the education wing of a church design. Use the IGS
                       techniques of Chapter 5 and develop a dual line diagram for the
                       floorplan. Refer to Figure 8.2

                  2.   Output this example on a direct-view storage tube display as
                       shown in Figure 8.7. Add the centerlines for important fea-
                       tures such as walls, doors, and openings as shown in Figure
                       8.3, and then output the trial floorplan on the plotter shown
                       in Figure 8.7.

                  3.   Display all details such as window openings, doors, and other
                       features by the IGS method shown in Chapter 5. Locate these
                       details by the centerlines placed in Exercise 2. Follow the
                       example shown in Figure 8.4.

                  4.   Display built-in items such as kitchen cabinets for the floor-
                       plan as shown in Figure 8.3.

                  5.   Add all dimensions for items in Exercises 1-4. Plot a finished
                       diagram as shown in Figure 8.7.

6. Store the floorplan shown in Figure 8.8 in three windows. The first is to contain blocks 1, 2, and 3; the second blocks 3, 4, and 5; and the third blocks 5, 6, 7, and 8.

7. Recall window 1 and develop a detail for a 3/18 section symbol.

8. Recall window 2 and develop a detail for a 2/18 section symbol.

9. Recall window 2 and develop a detail for a 4/18 section symbol.

10. Recall window 3 and develop a detail for a 3/18 section symbol.

11. Store the details completed in Exercises 7-10 on a single layer (sheet).

12. Recall and arrange the various windows as shown in Figure 8.7; direct the output to a digital plotter.

13. Floorplans and many other types of computer-generated drawings are stored by data blocks. In Figure 8.8, the data blocks are labeled by numbers across the top of the sheet and letters down the left side. Using Figure 8.8 as a guide, lay out a floorplan for block 11 as shown. (Courtesy of the U.S. Corps of Engineers, Vicksburg, Mississippi.)

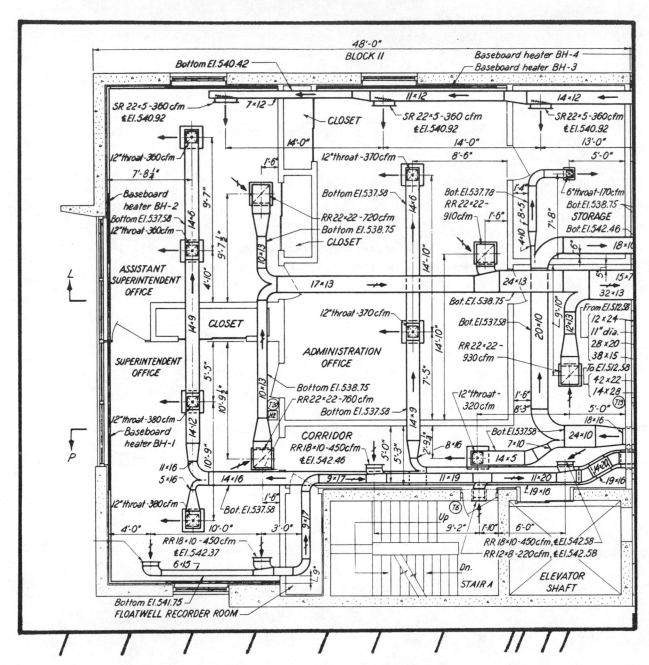

14. Repeat Exercise 13 for block 12 as shown. (Courtesy of the
     U.S. Corps of Engineers, Vicksburg, Mississippi.)

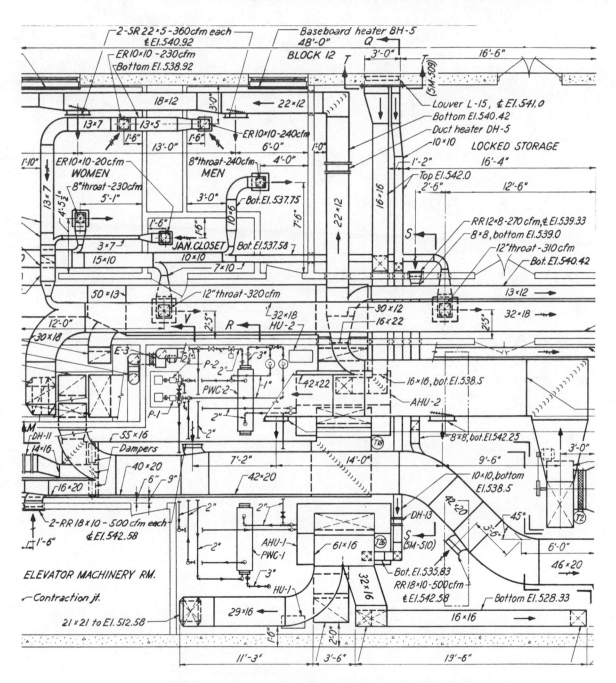

15. Recall blocks 11 and 12 as a single floorplan.

9 Foundation Plan Generation

Computerized methods for foundation plans are generated from a computer-automated system which manipulates three-dimensional databases. This has provided the designer with an effective tool for satisfying the graphical as well as the quantitative demands that occur in the design process. The advantages of using a system to fully use the information that is available during the early stages of the design process are explored in this chapter. Also discussed are the more obvious features of a system for constructing, modifying, viewing, and analyzing spatial relationships.

The introduction of a system which can meet the requirements for the design, documentation, analysis, and construction of a building is the main thrust of this chapter. The rapid rate of system usage for these tasks in many offices closely parallels similar developments in the more conventional interactive graphics system described in Chapter 5. A further parallel has been the discovery that the most effective way to use the capabilities of this method was to institute database management devices at the early stages of the design process. Just as was the experience with floorplans, meeting this objective reduces the amount of effort required to bring a project from conception to fruition.

RELATIONSHIP
TO FLOORPLAN
GENERATION
The bulk of work done on a system involves the storage of points, lines, planes, and solids. Figure 9.1 illustrates a collection of system hardware. This system consists of a graphics display, alpha-

FIGURE 9.1 Collection of system hardware. Input: (A) keyboard, (B) joystick, (C) digitizer. Output: (D) plotter, (E) DVST, (F) CRT.

218

numeric keyboard, alphanumeric console, and hard copy device. In addition a high-quality pen plotter is used to produce ink on vellum drawing. The console portion contains a menu display of frequently used graphical functions that the user may wish to implement. Several graphics terminals may be added to a single facility where the manipulation of the drawing is accomplished. In this fashion, up to four work stations may be used to store graphic images.

The operator of a typical work station uses a light pen in his or her right hand to select menu items. The left hand is free to use a function box, which contains 32 lighted push buttons. A typical work procedure is to select image functions with the left hand (a depressed button activates firmware) and position them with the right hand. This method of using a system consists of hardware, firmware, and software that set the basic graphics-handling potential of the system. The manner in which a user will approach a foundation layout problem will be determined by the hardware-software that is backing up each of the push buttons.

It really is not important in this section of the text whether hardware or software is used more, as both are featured by different system manufacturers. Both the software (light pen controlled) and hardware (push button controlled) are needed to provide a complete system. With the advent of programmable microprocessors and the introduction of firmware, the gray area at the interface between software and hardware has narrowed.

To input or store points, lines, or planes in a system, any one of three types of commands may be employed. The first type, composed of system commands, is the set of instructions that are standard to any computer graphics operating system, and examples were shown in Chapters 1-8. These instructions usually consist of all the basic graphics-handling operations common to all applications. Instructions to move, copy, rotate, dimension lines, store, and plot are all part of the system command repertoire. These commands are preprogrammed by the vendor of the system.

The second type, user commands, is commonly thought of as programs that are written by a user to enhance the basic capabilities of the system for unique needs. Every office has its own unique and special needs. For example, Figure 9.2 is a typical foundation plan in which such items as footing notes, footing details, and dimensions are displayed and plotted within a single layer. The information is displayed in a descriptive manner and as a series of sections. Another display option might be just a single window of a footing detail or typical foundation wall footing as shown in Figure 9.3. Therefore the user may wish to create windowed programming in house. By writing a user command (usually in a common programming language such as FORTRAN), the architect has complete control of its

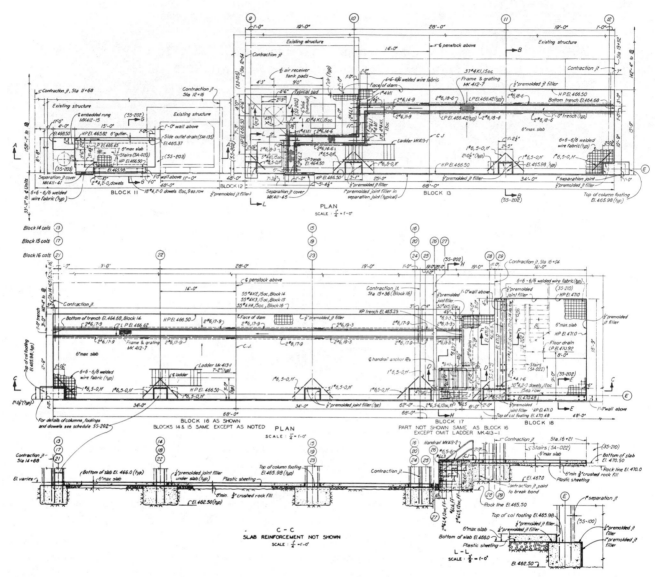

FIGURE 9.2 Typical foundation plan. (Courtesy of the U.S. Corps of Engineers, Vicksburg, Mississippi.)

use. In addition, he or she has added a powerful tool to the system that greatly increases its productivity.

To ensure the integrity of the operating system (system commands), it is important to keep the user command software separated from the general operating system. This is done by providing "handles" in the operating system to allow the user commands to

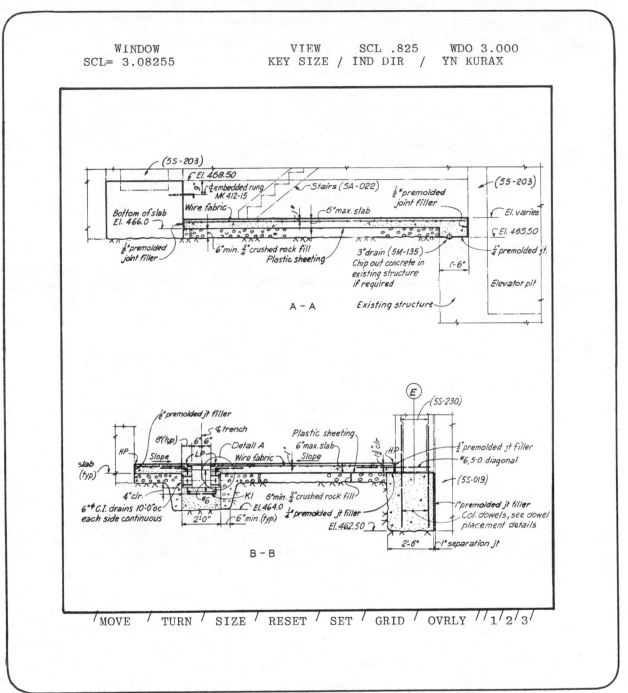

FIGURE 9.3 Window details of sections A-A and B-B from Figure 9.2.
(Courtesy of the U.S. Corps of Engineers, Vicksburg, Mississippi.)

access and modify the drawing database but not modify the operating
system software.

The third method is known as <u>macros</u>. They are system and user
commands combined to form more powerful commands. In addition, a
macro may involve the use of graphics language to increase its capability. The main difference between a macro and a user command is
the ease of implementation. Draftspersons and designers, as well as
programmers, write macros. Macros are often written and implemented
within 5 min. of conceptualization. They provide the user with a
flexible tool that permits quick creation of a command language
sometimes referred to as quick draw commands.

DIMENSIONING
AND NOTATION
TECHNIQUES

A system for dimensioning foundations is simply an organizational
scheme that allows a drawing to be represented in a numerical form.
In Chapters 1-5 databases were restricted to two-dimensional
straightline drawings. The X-Y coordinates of each line were stored
in a table. In Chapter 6 we became more sophisticated; the databases evolved to handle more complex geometries more efficiently.
Three-dimensional arcs, curves, surfaces, and parts were just a few
of the component types that these programs could handle.

Dimensioning an existing drawing may be compared to making a
tracing. The drawing is taped onto a graphics tablet. The user
then indicates with an electric pencil the beginnings, corners, and
ends of dimension lines. Predefined template parts may be used to
add dimension symbols to memory.

A relatively fast method of getting dimensioning into a computer database, foundation dimensioning is a very successful application. Whenever the design data lie on a grid, it is a very popular
method of inputting dimensions. If grids are not used and the drawing is dimensioned at full scale, the actual hardware accuracy of a
graphics tablet is about 0.025 mm. However, the ability of a good
draftsperson to consistently position a pen on a drawing in a typical production environment is about 0.50 mm. Drawings for foundations usually lie on grid; therefore accurate database and three-
dimensional models can be displayed using this method. Some design
firms have experimented with dimensioning a nongrid drawing onto a
grid overlay and then increasing the accuracy via geometric dimensioning routines.

Dimensioning, given elevation views, may be achieved with the
tablet and pen by interactively declaring the third dimension for
dimensioned geometry. Three-dimensional details constructed in this
manner will contain sufficient accuracy for placement location. A
location database is used to represent a dimensioned object in detail form. To accomplish this in an efficient manner, a windowed

representation of the object is often used. This window consists of dimension lines in space that are used to note the edges of details. A cube therefore can be dimensioned by three lines. This method of dimensioning is acceptable for placement details but can be awkward to use when representing complex shapes such as might be found in a longitudinal section. For these types of objects, more sophisticated systems for dimensioning have now been developed.

Footing Notes

Before a dimensional database can be utilized for an image, it must be placed in a system memory. The method of dimensioning just explained is only one method of obtaining a database. Another method is known as interactive construction. This method of constructing a database is the most natural to a user familiar with dimensioning skills. True, it is done at the work station and not at the drawing board, but the similarities are remarkable. By using the electronic pen, tablet, alphanumeric keyboard, and function box, the designer constructs a dimensioning procedure in much the same way that is used at a conventional drawing board.

First, the user "turns the key" that activates his or her work station. This is usually a set of procedures and alpha codes that allows the operator to use the work station. Doing the "housekeeping" jobs is also referred to as a manner of turning on or starting up the system. Next the user enters a single string command such as

    FOOTING NOTES

or depresses a single function button. This *sets the page* on the CRT for the following:

1. All walls, piers, and columns shall center on the footing unless otherwise noted on the drawings.
2. All footings shall rest on firm, undisturbed soil; i.e., the top of footings shall be 3.5 ft below finished grade or 2.5 ft below existing grade, whichever is deeper, unless otherwise noted on the drawings.
3. All corner bars in all footings shall be provided. Lap footing reinforcing bars or a minimum of 1 ft at splices. Reinforcing in footings, between column pads, shall extend into the column pad a minimum of 2 ft.
4. All slabs on grade shall be reinforced with 6 by 6 10/10 mesh unless otherwise noted.
5. Masonry and poured concrete bearing walls, which will be backfilled one side only, shall be shored until full roof and floor load construction has been placed on the wall.

6. All poured concrete walls shall be doweled to the footings
    with reinforcing equal to the concrete wall vertical rein-
    forcing.

7. Provide 2 #5 continuous around openings in concrete walls.

8. Minimum poured concrete wall reinforcement (unless other-
    wise noted):

	Horizontal	Vertical
8-in. wall at centerline of wall	#4 at 10 in.	#4 at 16 in.
10-in. wall (each face)	#4 at 16 in.	#4 at 18 in.
12-in. wall (each face)	#4 at 12 in.	#4 at 18 in.
14-in. wall (each face)	#4 at 10 in.	#4 at 18 in.
16-in. wall (each face)	#4 at 10 in.	#4 at 16 in.

9. If no soil boring tests have been made on the site, the
    general contractor shall make posthole examination of the
    soil 4 ft below the footing elevation. One hold should be
    made at each exterior corner of the building.

Special Symbols

Once enough information is displayed on the CRT page, the user may
select a single working view space to add more detailed bits of
graphics. This single view space will be framed with a rectangular
box to indicate the window size. A menu bar is placed below a viewing surface for each touch of the light pen. See Figure 9.4 (single
window).

    / MOVE / TURN / SIZE / RESET / SET / GRID / OVERLY / 1 2 3

This philosophy carried through the design and placement of footing
notes will greatly increase the productivity of the system. If the
user wishes to "go back" to a layer relationship, the added lines
from the single window are now located in the foundation plan shown
in Figure 9.2.

A menu bar should also have a comprehensive set of geometric
construction routines to allow the user to build onto the foundation
drawing by geometric relationships. A dimensional set of geometric
construction routines similar to those described in Chapter 5 is
available.

The modification of the output to yield a detail can be done by
the use of menu items. The draftsperson may want to relocate a section of output; the following item is touched with the light pen:

    / MOVE /   /   /   /   /   /   /   /

Then the portion of graphics to be moved is touched by the pen. The

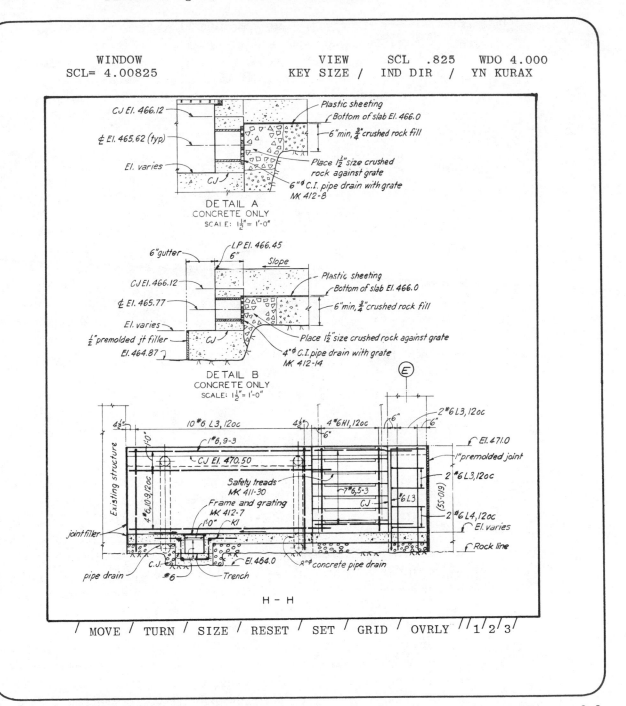

FIGURE 9.4 Added detail information and detail H-H from Figure 9.2 (Courtesy of the U.S. Corps of Engineers, Vicksburg, Mississippi.)

draftsperson is now free to position the graphics at will. To use menu items and construct a variety of information, the draftsperson's direction must now be given. Additional engineering drawing requirements such as cross-hatching, notes, and dashed lines may also have to be added to the detail. The answer is to allow the draftsperson to interact with the database to produce footing details.

Placement Details

Placement details are a special case of this general freedom of interaction with the system. Simply, it is the desire to make those details appear that will be necessary in the proper placement of the footings. Placement details show the extent and location of all concrete footings, flat work, and underpinnings of the architectural plan. Placement details are located directly on the foundation plan for ease of reference. Usually separate windows are used for each placement detail. The individual windows are then arranged on the free space of the foundation layer. These details must represent how the loads from above are transmitted from the floorplan through the footings to the soil.

In concrete floor construction, wall loads are carried through the footings to the soil; the floor slabs are carried by compacting the soil beneath the concrete slab. Wood floor systems use outside foundation walls and interior supports designed to carry the load from the floorplan. The foundation plan and the placement details are based on the database collected for the floorplan as are all other viewing layers for the architectural plans. The best procedure is to display the database for the outline of the building from the floorplan database. Show the centerlines of any bearing walls on the display console, the locations of all outside entrances, and any isolated columns. These will be used for placing dimensions and locating details later. Next display the inside basement wall footings, foundations for fireplaces or other structural elements, and the location for underground piping and ductwork. It is important to display these items at an early stage so that placement details are generated for the proper pouring of concrete, building of forms, or placement of steel reinforcement.

At this point the designer may leave the database for the floorplan and begin adding information unique to the foundation plan. Usually a checklist is used. Most foundation plans include the following (see Figure 9.5):

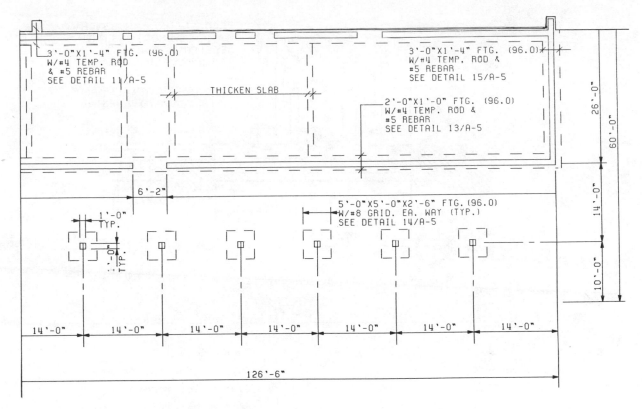

FIGURE 9.5 Plan view of footings and walls.

1. Plan views of

    a. Footings and walls
    b. Piers and pads
    c. Walls below grade
    d. Girders and beams used for support
    e. Placement details for walks, driveways, and paved outdoor areas
    f. Footings outside the building, curbs, gutters, and areaways

2. Complete dimensioning and notes to go with the placement details (see Figure 9.2)

3. Cross-sectional details of all foundation work

INTRODUCTION TO SECTION GENERATION By using the same general sectioning techniques explained in Chapter 8, several cross-sectional details may now be developed. Figures 9.6-1.12 are parts of a layer display of a cross section of Figure 9.6. Seven display windows are used:

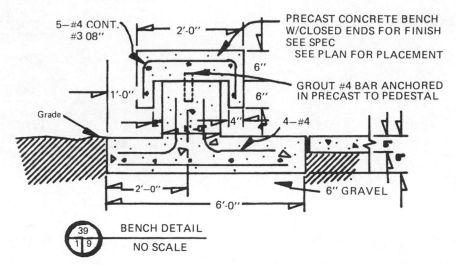

FIGURE 9.6 Window 39: bench detail.

Figure	Window	Title of section detailed
9.6	39	Bench detail
9.7	46	Typical footing detail
9.8	49	Slab reinforcement
9.9	51	Bottom bar reinforcement at flat slab opening
9.10	59	Sill
9.11	63	Exterior masonry expansion joint
9.12	64	Exterior masonry expansion joint for inside corner

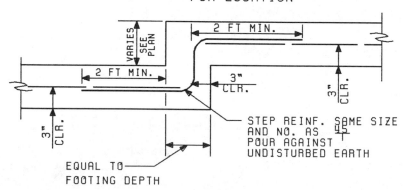
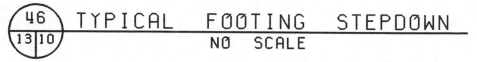

FIGURE 9.7 Window 46: typical footing stepdown.

NOTE: MAXIMUM RATIO OF FOOTING
STEPS – 1 VERTICALLY TO
2 – HORIZONTALLY

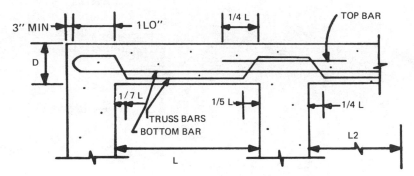

FIGURE 9.8   Window 49:   slab reinforcement.

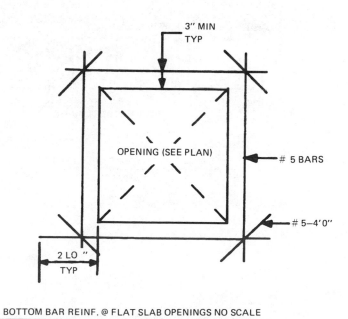

FIGURE 9.9   Window 51:   bottom bar reinforcement at flat slab opening.

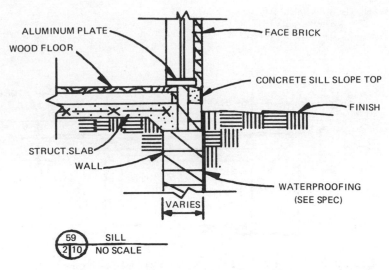

FIGURE 9.10 Window 59: sill detail and foundation wall.

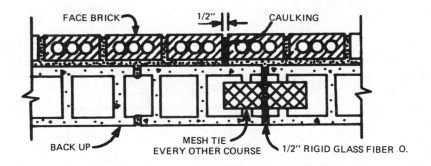

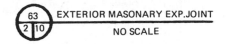

FIGURE 9.11 Window 63: exterior masonry expansion joint.

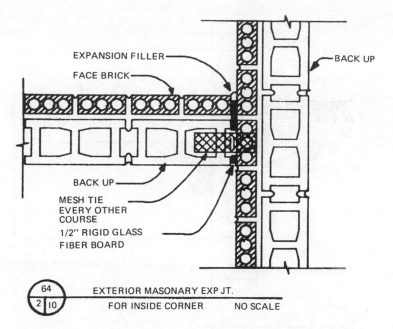

FIGURE 9.12   Window 64:   exterior masonry expansion joint for inside corner.

Figures 9.13 and 9.14 form a layer display of a cross section of Figure 9.3.   Two display windows are used:

Figure	Window	Title of section detailed
9.13	31	Freestanding curb
9.14	32	Integral curb

Figures 9.15 through 9.19 are parts of a layer display of gutters and steps, containing five windows:

Figure	Window	Title of section detailed
9.15	40	Terrazzo step
9.16	42	Ceramic tile step
9.17	43	Ceramic tile gutter
9.18	44	Concrete step
9.19	45	Concrete gutter

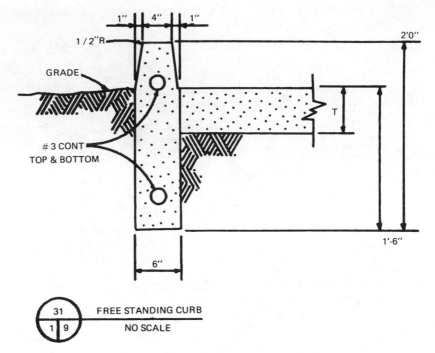

FIGURE 9.13   Window 31:   freestanding curb.

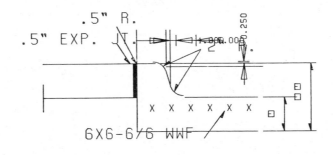

FIGURE 9.14   Window 32:   integral curb.

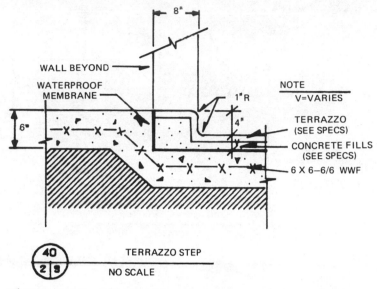

FIGURE 9.15 Window 40: terrazzo step.

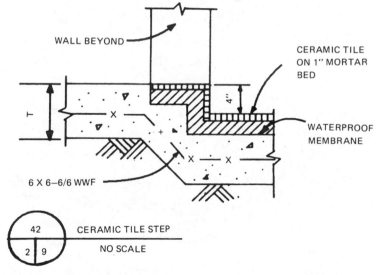

FIGURE 9.16 Window 42: ceramic tile step.

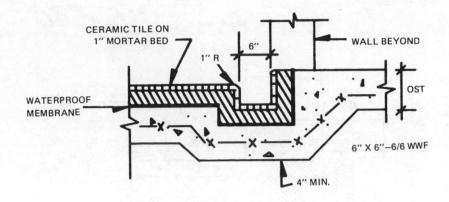

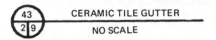

FIGURE 9.17 Window 43: ceramic tile gutter.

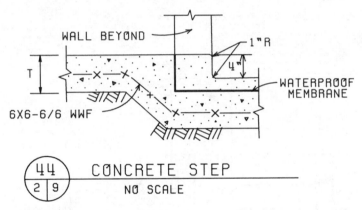

FIGURE 9.18 Window 44: concrete step.

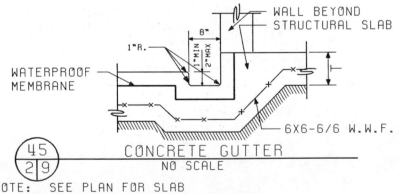

NOTE: SEE PLAN FOR SLAB
        THICKNESS (T)
        SEE SPECS FOR BASE
        REQUIRED. USE AN APPROVED
        DOWEL PLACEMENT REINFORCING
        AS SPECIFIED

FIGURE 9.19 Window 45: concrete gutter.

CHAPTER SUMMARY   The foundation plan is generated in a manner similar to the floor-plan. This chapter has many illustrations and recommendations for the reader:

1. The use of database layers is encouraged.

2. Design work stations are demonstrated

3. User commands were discussed.

4. Dimensioning techniques were outlined.

5. Footing notes were entered through the design work station.

6. Special symbols from menu bars were manipulated by a light pen.

7. Placement details were windowed with 18 examples given for further study.

EXERCISES   1.   Output a foundation detail D-D shown in Figure 9.2 on the CRT in the format shown. (Data from the U.S. Corps of Engineers, Graphic Compatibility System, Vicksburg, Mississippi.)

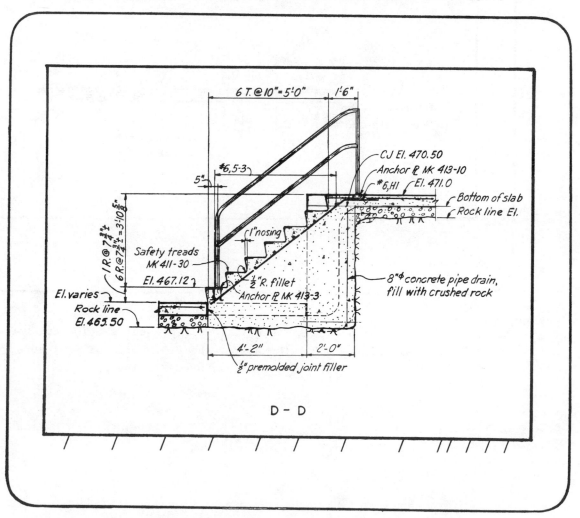

2. Output a foundation detail E-E shown in Figure 9.2 on the CRT
    in the format shown. Locate E-E so that detail F-F can be
    shown below it. (Data from the U.S. Corps of Engineers,
    Graphic Compatibility System, Vicksburg, Mississippi.)

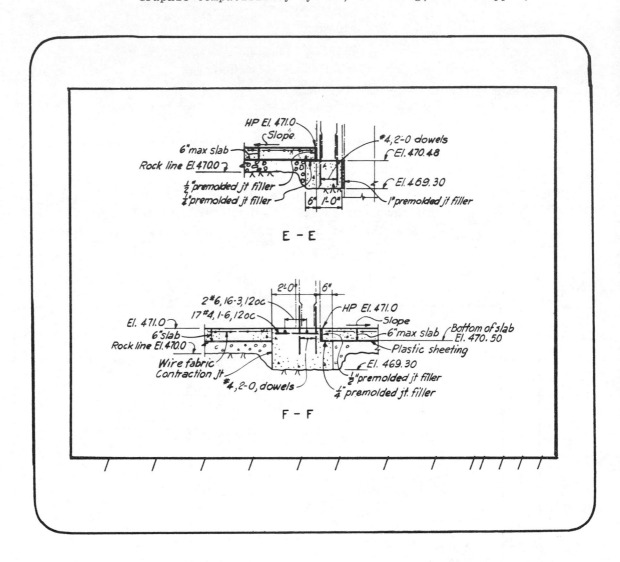

3. Output a foundation detail to represent section cut G-G and J-J
    in Figure 9.2. (Data from the U.S. Corps of Engineers, Graphic
    Compatibility System, Vicksburg, Mississippi.)

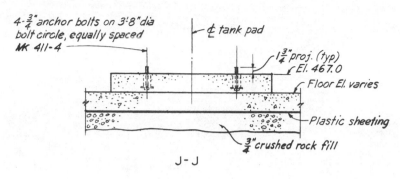

J - J

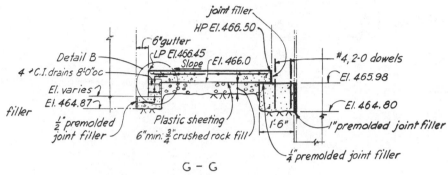

G - G

4. Practice footing notes by preparing the footing details shown. (Data from the U.S. Corps of Engineers, Graphic Compatibility System, Vicksburg, Mississippi.)

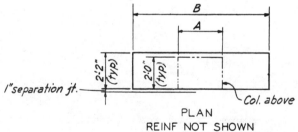

PLAN
REINF NOT SHOWN

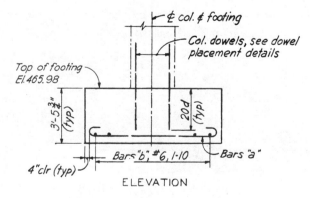

ELEVATION

FOOTING DETAILS

5. Continue the footing notations by preparing the dowel placement details shown. (Data from the U.S. Corps of Engineers, Graphic Compatibility System, Vicksburg, Mississippi.)

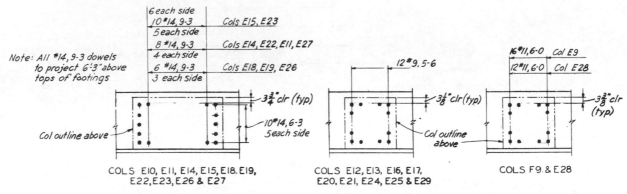

DOWEL PLACEMENT DETAILS

6. Placement details C-C and D-D can be output to a CRT as shown. (Data from the U.S. Corps of Engineers, Graphic Compatibility System, Vicksburg, Mississippi.)

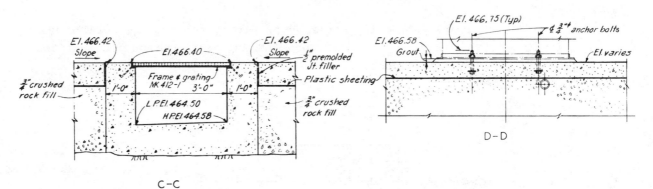

7. Section generations from foundation plans can be shown on a CRT; build a database for the simple section shown. (Data from the U.S. Corps of Engineers, Graphic Compatibility System, Vicksburg, Mississippi.)

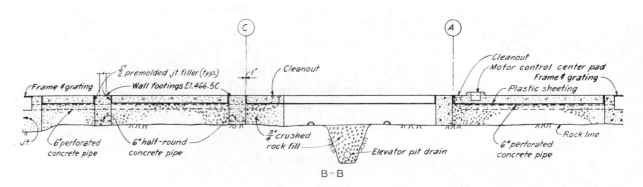

8. Section details can be designed from the database in Exercise 7. Look at the "frame & grating" detail at the right side of the section. Increase the display size and present a construction detail as shown. (Data from the U.S. Corps of Engineers, Graphic Compatibility System, Vicksburg, Mississippi.)

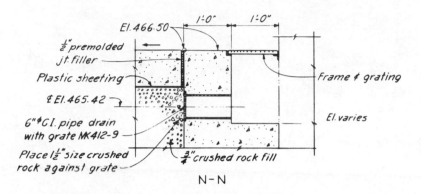

N–N

9. Now look at the motor control center pad shown in Exercise 7. Repeat Exercise 8 as shown. (Data from the U.S. Corps of Engineers, Graphic Compatibility System, Vicksburg, Mississippi.)

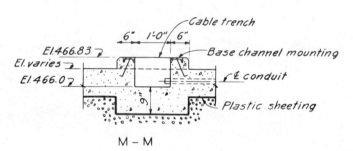

M – M

10. Repeat Exercise 9 for the cleanout shown in Exercise 7; follow the example shown. (Data from the U.S. Corps of Engineers, Graphic Compatibility System, Vicksburg, Mississippi.)

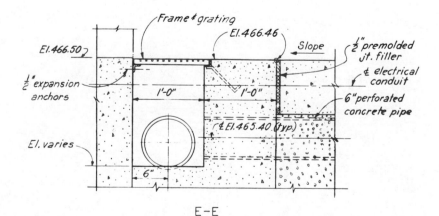

E–E

10 Section Generation and Profile Drawings

The creation of sections and profiles for architectural display is a prime case of a user who wants to deal with three-dimensional graphic structures. The graphic structure represents the entire architectural project in basic geometric forms. Figure 10.1 is a computer display of architectural structure. From this three-dimensional representation called a wireform, a number of sections and/or profiles can be displayed. The problem of using computer graphics in this manner for architectural sections has been limited by two basic shortcomings in our ability to display and program as described in Chapter 1:

1.   Graphical display (sections and profile are the worst case) is a convention all its own. Translating architectural sectioning techniques into computer language by hand is tedious, error prone, time consuming, and normally more difficult than creating the original drawing.

2.   Translation of a concept from the architect's mind into graphics is complex. It is a series of intricate steps which eventually converge as an architect brings many individual and sometimes unrelated ideas into the complete and final design.

This chapter deals with a practical system to meet these two basic limitations by providing capability such that

241

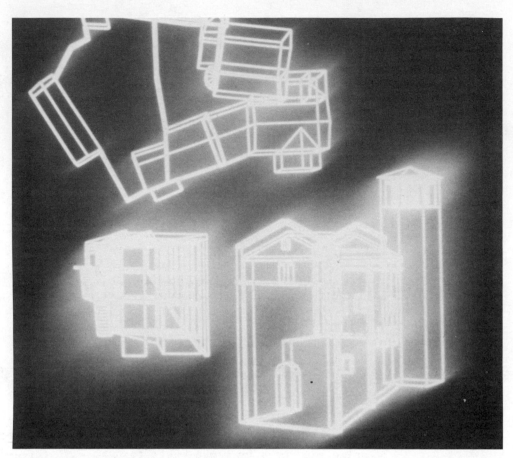

FIGURE 10.1   CRT display of an architectural structure. (Courtesy of
Evans and Sutherland, Salt Lake City, Utah.)

1.   The user deals directly in a graphic language rather than
     in an artificial coding language normally associated with
     computer-based automated devices.   The user is not a pro-
     grammer; a typical user is a student designer, architect,
     or draftsperson.   This type of system provides a highly
     automated tool to permit the work of design to be done
     faster, more accurately, and more economically.

2.   The user of this type of system proceeds with the design
     as always.   Now, however, each time a design step is
     taken, the system allows evaluation of the result in rela-
     tion to what has gone before.   The designer now has an
     automated tool for aid, directly and in realtime, with the
     design process.   In later sections of this chapter, exper-
     ience with this system will indicate that this method will
     increase performance significantly; it is introduced here
     only to set the stage for later applications.

This system of section generation also accepts graphic data directly. The user enters the data with a pencil-like electric pen and
tablet. To the user, it appears as if the pen is actually writing
on the face of the CRT when the pen is brought in contact with the
surface of the graphics tablet. Actually, the pen and tablet are
giving instructions to the computer, which in turn is creating a
data sequence causing the tube to respond graphically. The computer
immediately produces a precise picture of what is understood the
user to mean.

When a user draws a line, the system immediately produces a
picture of that line on the tube face. The picture shows the user
what the computer did in response to the request. The response is
what the computer interpreted the designer to mean, not a mere copy
of the input. If the user approves of what the computer presented
on the CRT, he or she continues; if not, any misinterpretation is
immediately corrected. Thus, the user has a continual running review of what he or she is doing; he or she is in real time communication with a computer. The process of drafting and displaying a
part is controlled in real time. The pen and tablet and the real
time feedback are the two powerful, unique features.

When a display system like Figure 10.2 is applied to lines,
planes, curves, profiles, and sections in an orderly fashion, it
uses real time communication with a computer to create and revise
drawings--the basic starting point for almost all architectural
design. If, in the conventional drafting sequence, a horizontal or
vertical line is desired, the draftsperson uses the T-square and
triangle or standard drafting machine. With this display system,
the user pushes a button which tells the computer the architect is
using the graphics tablet to draw such a line.

Real time process control tells the computer to draw only the
specified component (straight, vertical, or slant line) no matter
how the pen deviates as it is moved across the tablet. In the case
of lettering for real time the computer must wait for the draftsperson to complete each letter in a character string. In cases such
as this *faster than real time* is needed to speed up the display
time. Similarly, a user can instruct the computer to display
curves, profiles, and sections without tracing the entire path of
the specified element. The user then has a choice of two modes
(real time and faster than real time) in which to operate:

1. Real time tablet and pen on paper to create drawings, or
2. Pen and tablet like a pointer to activate controls in the
   software which quantitatively define end points of lines,
   centers of surfaces, and other boundary conditions as
   shown in Figure 10.3. These controls are usually menu

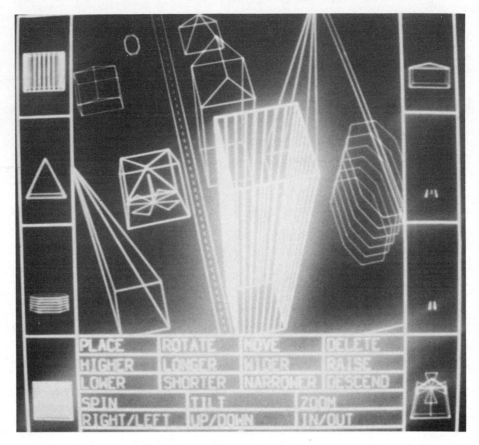

FIGURE 10.2   Interactive architectural display system.   (Courtesy of
Evans and Sutherland, Salt Lake City, Utah.)

items, appropriately labeled, on a portion of the CRT not
used for drawing. The user simply touches his or her pen
to an appropriate menu item location on the tablet to
initiate a variety of graphic responses, as was shown in
Figure 10.2.

Single Wall Sections

Section views like single wall sections can best be described by a
set of working exercises. These exercises can be followed if the
reader has the system shown in Figures 10.2 and 10.3. Exercises are
shown first as program statements, as they might appear on the face
of the CRT, and then as output (drawings), as they might appear on a
plotter bed.

Commonly used section displays are generally grouped into three
areas:

1. Sections taken from plan views
2. Sections that appear on the same pages
3. Special sections

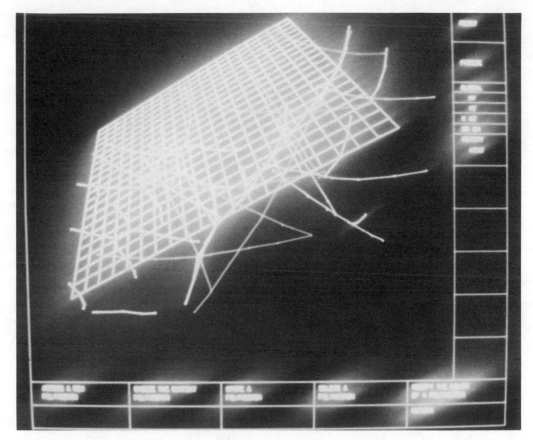

FIGURE 10.3 Boundary conditions displayed on CRT from tablet input.
(Courtesy of Evans and Sutherland, Salt Lake City, Utah.)

To perform any of these types of section exercises, the user of
graphics software must understand the job control language (JCL) for
the host processor. For example,

```
//PLOTTER JOB(ACCOUNT NUMBER, TIME REQUESTED, LINES OF OUTPUT)
//STEP 1 EXEC FORTCLG, PLOT = 1812
//C. SYSIN DD *
     CALL PLOTS

     / PROGRAM STATEMENTS/

     CALL PLOT(18.,0.,999)
     STOP
     END

/*
//G.SYSIN DD *

     / DATA /

/*
//
```

represents the JCL for a large host processor such as the IBM 370/3033. These statements may be punched on cards or typed from a keyboard. Their purpose is to activate an automatic spooling program which operates at the system level. For example,

```
//LICHEN1 JOB(0923-2-001-00- ,#02,1),'LIHWA BOX 22',    JOB 5908
//       TIME=(0000,02),REGION=256K
//STEP1 EXEC FTG1CLG,PLOT=0812
//C.SYSIN  DD *
//G.SYSIN  DD
//
```

is the output from the JCL statements plus the program statements. The program statements must be included before complete processing will take place. The second page of the output from a graphics program contains any warning messages and the job statistics and appears as

```
J E S 2   J O B   L O G

18,14,17, JOB 5908 IEF677I WARNING MESSAGE(S) FOR JOB LICHEN1 ISSUED
18,14,18, JOB 5908 SHASP373 LICHEN1 STARTED - INIT 87 - CLASS B -
     SYS 3033
18,14,31, JOB 5908 MYS0011 LICHEN1 .C   001 IGIFORT COND CODE 0000..
18,L4,59, JOB 5908 MYS0011 LICHEN1 .L   002 IEWL    COND CODE 0000..
18,15,05, JOB 5908 MYS0011 LUCHEN1 .G   003 MAIN    COND CODE 0000..
18,15,06, JOB 5908 SHASP395 LICHEN1 ENDED


----------JES2 JOB STATISTICS----------

03 DEC 80 JOB EXECUTION DATE

   45 CARDS READ

  254 SYSOUT PRINT RECORDS

   54 SYSOUT PRINT RECORDS

 0.82 MINUTES EXECUTION TIME
```

The fourth page of the output contains the program statements and is called the *main* program. It appears as

```
FORTRAN IV G1 RELEASE 2.0  MAIN  DATE=80338   18/14/23    PAGE 0001

     CALL PLOTS
     CALL TITLE(.5)
     CALL PLOT(18.,0.,999)
     STOP
     END
```

Any subprograms called from the main program are listed on separate
pages. In this case, only one subprogram called title has been
written by the graphics program. It would appear on the fifth page
of the printed output as

FORTRAN IV G1 RELEASE 2.0   TITLE DATE=80338 18/14/23 PAGE 0001

```
      SUBROUTINE TITLE(SIZE)
      CALL RECT(0.,11.25,17.,0.0,3)
      CALL RECT(0.,,750,1.,0.0,3)
      CALL RECT(1.,0.,,750,3.5,0.0,3)
      CALL RECT(4.5,0.,,375,2.5,0.0,3)
      CALL RECT(7.0,0.,,375,3.5,0.0,3)
      CALL RECT(7.0,,375,,375,3.5,0.0,3)
      CALL RECT(10.5,,0.,,750,5.25,0.0,3)
      CALL RECT(15.75,0.,,750,5.25,0.0,3)
      CALL SYMBOL(.1,,1.,08,12HDRAWING NO.,0.,12)
      CALL SYMBOL(.375,.25,.25,1H1,0.,1)
      CALL SYMBOL(1.875,.5,,09,22HARCHITECTURAL GRAPHICS,0.,22)
      CALL SYMBOL(1.625,.3125,.1,20HSINGLE WALL SECTIONS,0.,20)
      CALL SYMBOL(4.625,,12,.1,6HSCALE:,0.,6)
      CALL SYMBOL(4.625,,45,.1,5HDATE:,0.,5)
      CALL SYMBOL(5.25,,45,.1,6H9-6-80,0.,6)
      CALL SYMBOL(5.50,,12,.1,4HFULL,0.,4)
      CALL SYMBOL(7.125,,12,.1,7HCOURSE:,0.,7)
      CALL SYMBOL(8.,,12,.1,6HEG 310,0.,6)
      CALL SYMBOL(7.125,,45,.1,7HDR BY:,0.,7)
      CALL SYMBOL(7.9,,45,.1,              ,0.,10)
      CALL SYMBOL(11.75,.1,.1,18HTITLE OF DRAWING,0.,18)
      CALL SYMBOL(12.5,,32,0.25,11HTITLE BLOCK,0.,11)
      CALL SYMBOL(16.125,.1,.1,5HGRADE,0.,5)
      RETURN
      END
```

The graphical image produced is a borderline and title strip
format. No drawing is produced. One could be produced by the
addition of a few program statements and another subprogram. Note
the following example:

FORTRAN IV G1 RELEASE 2.0   MAIN   DATE=80339   11/15/16

```
      DIMENSION X(100),Y(100),1PEN(100)
      DATA X/2.,2*7.,2*3.,2*2.,2*5.,2*6.5,2.,2*5.,2*6.5,2*7.,3*2.,2.,
     2.,+3*3.,10.,2*13.5,12.5,11.,3*10.,13.5/
      DATA X/2*2.,2*3.,2*5.,2*2.,3.,2.,3.,2*6.5,2*7.5,2*6.5,2*10.,
     6.5,+2*9,2*7.5,10.,6.5,2*2.,4*5.,2.,2*3./
```

```
        DATA 1PEN/3.6*2,3.2,3.2,3.8*2,3.2,3.2,3.2,3.3*2,3.2*2,3.2/
        CALL PLOTS
        CALL TITLE(.5)
        CALL DRAW2D(X,Y,1PEN,35)
        CALL CIRCL(11.,5.,180.,360.,0.75,0.75,0.)
        CALL PLOT(18.,0.,999)
        STOP
        END
```

A presorted location in computer memory is requested by the DIMEN-
SION statement.   There are 100 possible locations available for the
subprogram DRAW2D.   Next the data are entered by use of the DATA
statement.   And finally a system subroutine called CIRCL has been
used in the image display to identify the section member.   The subprogram DRAW2D is listed as

FORTRAN IV G1 RELEASE 2.0   DRAW2D   DATE=80339   11/15/16   PAGE 0001

```
        SUBROUTINE DRAW2D(X,Y,IPEN,NDATA)
        DIMENSION(100),Y(100),IPEN(100)
        DO 100 1=1,NDATA
100     CALL PLOT(X(1),Y(1),1PEN(1))
        READ(1,4)NDASHP
  4     FORMAT(12)
        DO 5 1=1 NDASHP
        READ(1,*)X1,Y1,Z,W
        CALL PLOT(X1,Y1,3)
  5     CALL DASHP(Z,W,.15)
        RETURN
        END
```

This subprogram is useful for plotting any 2D data such as a
single wall section.   The architectural user must remember to set
aside the proper amount of storage by the use of a DIMENSION statement before the CALL DRAW2D statement.   If, for example, 250 X and Y
data points were used to describe the wall section, then a minimum
of 250 storage locations should be provided.   Also in this example,
250 is too large for the use of DATA statements.   The introduction
of a data error is probable at this point.   The data are therefore
placed after the //G.SYSIN DD * JCL statement and are read into the
main program by a READ statement.   Either method of input may be
used for the data.   If the database is small, it is more convenient
to enter it as a DATA statement.   DRAW2D is used to connect
straight-line segments only.   If circles or arcs are required in the
2D image display, they are usually entered directly in the main program.

Building Cross Sections

Figure 10.4 is the output of the graphical-structural components for the subprogram and main programs if 3D data are used. These 3D image displays are useful for building section representations but do little to represent single section drawings.

Three-dimensional data are needed to display automatic cross-section representations. The main program is modified as

```
FORTRAN IV G1 RELEASE 2.0     MAIN        DATE=80275      08/58/19

    DIMENSION X(100),Y(100),Z(100),IPEN(100)
    DATA X/0.,3*0.5,3*1.5,6*0.,2*3.5,4*2.,4*3.4,4*0.5,1.5/
    DATA Y/2*0.,4*1.5,2*0.,2*0.5,4*1.5,2*0.,1.5,2*0.,2*0.5,1.5,
   +4*0.5,+4*0.,1.5,2*0./
    DATA Z/3*-1.5,2*-0.5,6*01.5,2*-0.,2*01.5,7*-0.,+-1.5,-0.,-1.5,
   +-0.,-1.5,4*-0.5/
```

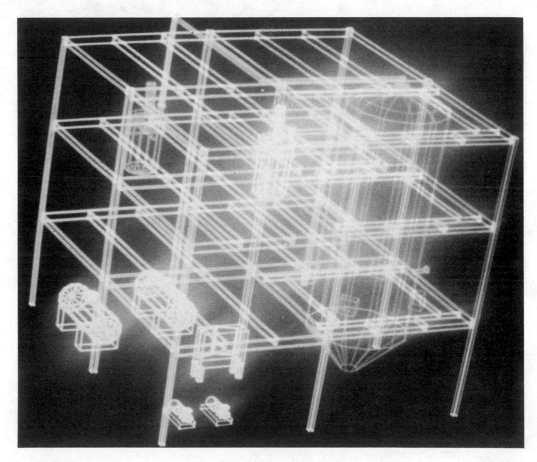

FIGURE 10.4 Output of the graphical-structural components. (Courtesy of Evans and Sutherland, Salt Lake City, Utah.)

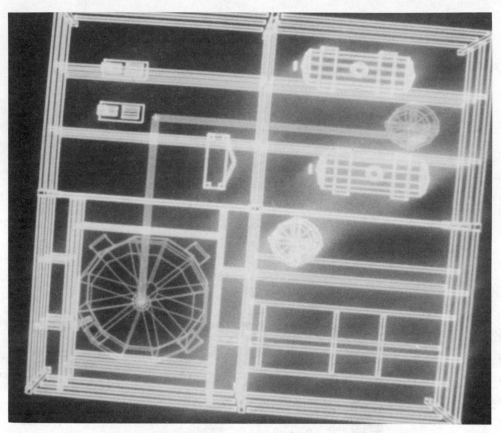

FIGURE 10.5   Plan rotation of Figure 10.4.   (Courtesy of Evans and Sutherland, Salt Lake City, Utah.)

```
      DATA IPEN/3,16*2,3,4*2,3,2,3,2,3,2,3,2*2,3,2/
      CALL PLOTS
      CALL TITLE(S)
      CALL PLOT (3,5,2,5,-3)
      CALL CUPID(X,Y,Z,IPEN,8,5,6,5,33,30,,11)
      CALL PLOT(18,0,0,0,999)
      STOP
      END
```

In this program the addition of a subprogram displays the three-dimensional data that are contained in the DATA statements as

```
FORTRAN IV G1 RELEASE 2,0      CUPID      DATE=80275      08/58/19
```

```
      SUBROUTINE CUPID(X,Y,Z,IPEN,XTRANS,YTRANS,NADT,ABG,SF)
      DIMENSIONX(100),Y(100),Z(100),IPEN(100),
```

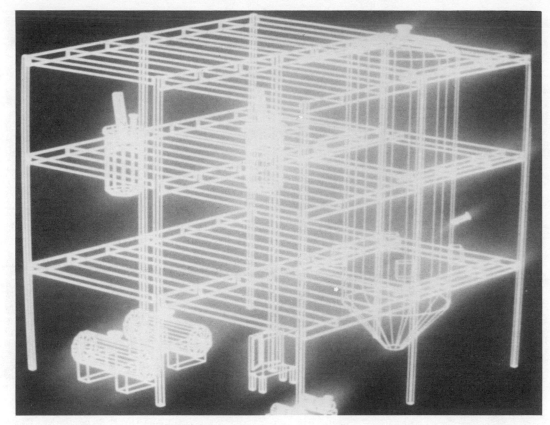

FIGURE 10.6 Rotation of Figure 10.5 into elevation. (Courtesy of
Evans and Sutherland, Salt Lake City, Utah.)

```
      +XPLOT(100),YPLOT(100)
       COSA=COS(ANG/57.3)
       SINA=SIN(ANG/57.3)
       DO 1 K=1,NDAT
       XPLOT(K)=(X(K)+Z(K)*SF*COSA)+8.2
       YPLOT(K)=(Y(K)+Z(K)*SF*SINA)+5.2
    1  CALL PLOT(XPLOT(K),YPLOT(K),IPEN(K))
       DO 10 J=1,NDAT
   10  CALL PLOT(X(J),Y(J),IPEN(J))
       DO 20 I=1,NDAT
       Z(I)+Z(I)+YTRANS
   20  CALL PLOT(X(I),Z(I),IPEN(I))
       DO 30 I=1,NDAT
       Z(I)=(Z(I)+XTRANS)-YTRANS
   30  CALL PLOT(Z(I),Y(I),IPEN(I))
       RETURN
       END
```

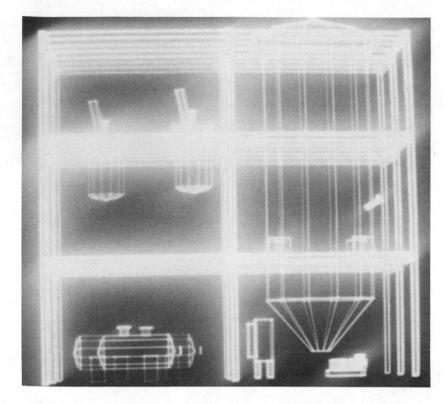

FIGURE 10.7 Elevation rotation before longitudinal section is taken. (Courtesy of Evans and Sutherland, Salt Lake City, Utah.)

Figure 10.5 is the graphical image produced by the main program and subprogram. Note that the cross-section view has been produced by rotating the wireform pictorial shown in Figure 10.4.

To use this display later, selective erase and hidden line selection must be employed. The wireform must appear as the solid object that it represents. Figure 10.6 is the graphical image of this modification. Figure 10.7 is another cross section taken as a longitudinal section instead of a horizontal (Figure 10.5). By a

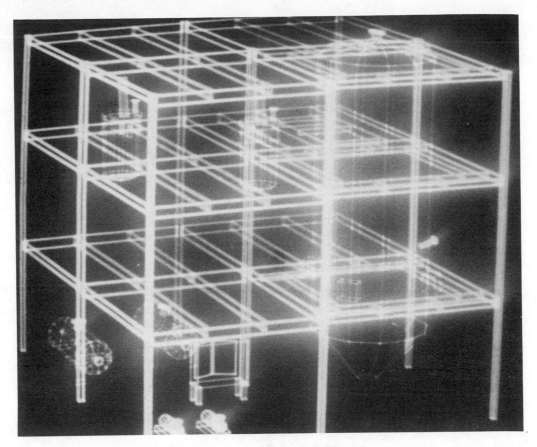

FIGURE 10.8   Two-level data presentation for longitudinal section cut.   (Courtesy of Evans and Sutherland, Salt Lake City, Utah.)

combination rotation, as shown in Figure 10.8, the viewer senses the three-dimensional database used in longitudinal section generation. Figure 10.9 is a combination rotation of the three-dimensional database for the horizontal cross-section viewing.   And finally, Figure 10.10 represents three-axis rotation of the three-dimensional database.

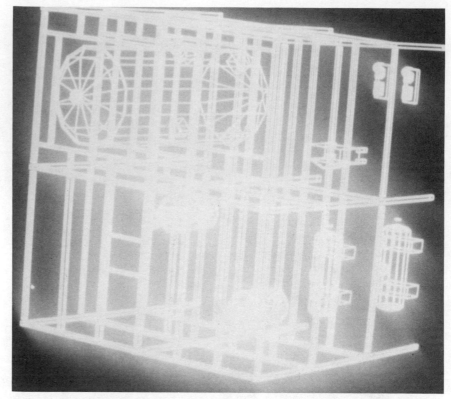

FIGURE 10.9 Combination rotation for the horizontal cross-section viewing. (Courtesy of Evans and Sutherland, Salt Lake City, Utah.)

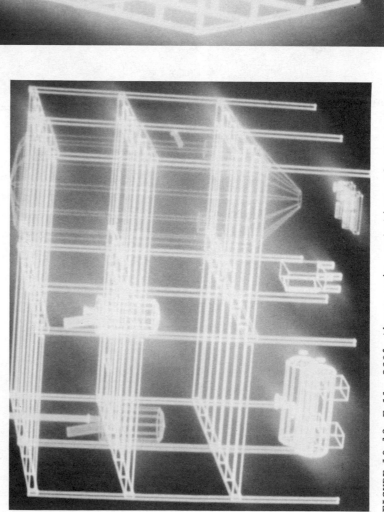

FIGURE 10.10 Full 360°, three-axis rotation of the structure. (Courtesy of Evans and Sutherland, Salt Lake City, Utah.)

Often the section will appear on the same sheet where it is taken. For example, a foundation plan may contain one or more sections through footings, walls, or piers. To control this type of sectioning, a special-purpose program is used. An example would appear as

```
C ************************************************************
C *   THIS PROGRAM CUTTING AN OBJECT TO SHOW THE INTEGRAL MATERIAL  *
C *      THOSE SOLID SECTIONS CAN THEN BE CROSSHATCHED BY CALLING    *
C *      SHADE OR TONE.                                              *
C *   DRAFTING                                                       *
C *   A:  AROHD                                                      *
C *   B:  BAR                                                        *
C *   C:  CIRCL                                                      *
C *   C:  CIRCLE                                                     *
C *   C:  CENTER                                                     *
C *   F:  FIT                                                        *
C *   P:  PLOT                                                       *
C *   P:  POLY                                                       *
C *   S:  SHADE                                                      *
C ************************************************************
C
C   DECLARE:
        DIMENSION X(50),Y(50),SANF(50),EANG(50),DIA(50)


C
C   INPUT/OUTPUT:
        DATA X/1.5,12.,11.,10.25,8.45,2*10.69,2*2.,2*0.5,2*1.5/
        DATA Y/6.853.4*5.5,4.25,6.812,3.5,0.16,3.5,0.16,3.5,0.16/
        DATA SANG/6*0.,45.,-45.,-45.,60.,-60/
        DATA EANG/7*360.,140.,-140.,140.,-140.,120.,-120./
        DATA DIA/1.,5.,3.,1.5,3*0.90,4*0.7,2*2./


C
C   DECLARE:
        DIMENSION X1(50),Y1(50),IPEN(50)


C
C   INPUT/OUTPUT
        DATA X1/0.5,1.5,2*0.,2*2.,2*0.5,2*1.5,7.,2*12.,2*10.25,2*8.75,
       +2*7.,2*8.25,2*10.75/
        DATA Y1/2*5,3.5,0.16,3.5,0.16,3.5,0.16,3.5,0.16,2*0.,2*1.55,
       +2**1.75*1.55,0.,1.55,0.,1.55,0./
        DATA IPEN/3,2,3,2,3,2,3,2,3,2,3,8*2,3,2,3,2/


C
```

```
C  DECLARE:
      DIMENSION XARAY(50),YARAY(50),XXARAY(50),YYARAY(50)
C
C INPUT/OUTPUT
      DATA XARAY/2.5,3.,,4.,,0.,,1./
      DATA YARAY/1.75,2*2.618,0.,1./
      DATA XXARAY/3.,,4.,,4.5,0.,,1./
      DATA YYARAY/2*0.875,1.75,0.,,1./
C
C  DECLARE:
      DIMENSION ARAY(50),ARAY2(50),ARAY3(50),ARAY4(50)
      DIMENSION XLOC(50),YLOCI(50),XEND(50),YEND(50)
C
C  INPUT/OUTPUT
      DATA XLOC/12.5,2*10.56,11.125,9.5,7.879,4.7,4.2,1.,,2.4,1.,,1.6/
      DATA XLOC/5.5,3.75,7.31,1.75,1.95,2*1.75,4.5,8.,,6.853,5.4,4.5/
      DATA XEND/6.5,2*9.935,11.125,9.5,7.875,2.3,2.8,1.,,-0.4,4.5/
      DATA YEND/5.5,4.69,6.3,3*-01,1.75,4.5,5.7,6.853,-0.4,4.5/
C
C  DECLARE:
      DIMENSION ARAYX(50),ARAYY(50),ARAYXX(50),ARAYYY(50)
C
C INPUT/OUTPUT
      DATA ARAYX/8.25,2*8.75,2*10.25,10.75,0.,,1./
      DATA ARAYY/2*1.55,2*1.75,2*1.55,0.,,1./
      DATA ARAYXX/8.25,10.75,0.,,1./
      DATA ARAYYY/2*0.,,0.,,1./
C
C  CONTROL:
      CALL PLOTS
      CALL TITLE(.5)
      CALL PLOT(2.5,2.,-3)
      CALL FIT(0.5,5.,,0.5,4.,,0.,,3.5)
      CALL FIT(1.5,5.,,1.5,4.,,2.,,3.5)
C
C  DO LOOP STATEMENT:
      DO 10 I-1,13
C  CONTROL:
      CALL CIRCLE(X(1),Y(1),SANG(1),EANG(1),DIA(1 /2.,DIA(1)/2.,0.0)
C  CONTROL:
      10 CONTINUE
C
C  CONTROL:
      CALL CIRCL(3.5,4.5,0.5,0.,,30,12.,ARAY1,ARAY2,ARAY3,ARAY4)
      CALL AROHD(6/5.5/5.6/5.6/.0.3,0.1,16)
```

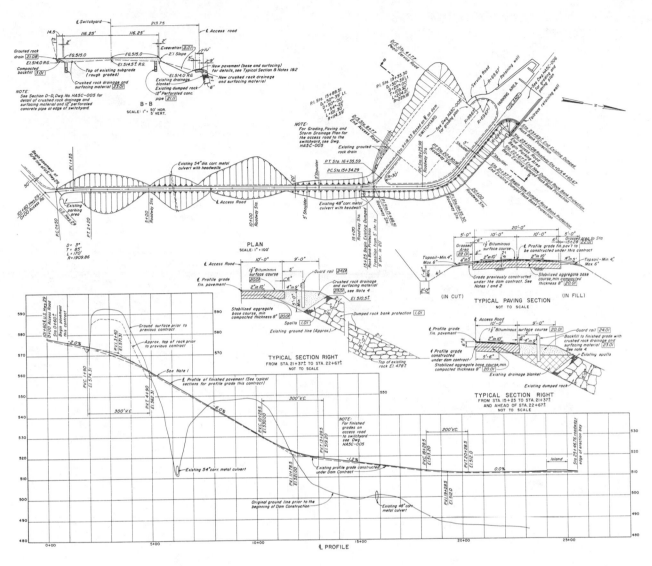

FIGURE 10.11 Typical plan and profile. (Courtesy of the U.S. Corps of Engineers, Vicksburg, Mississippi.)

```
      CALL AROHD(12.5,5.5,12.5,6.,,0.3,0.1,16)
      CALL POLY(0.5,6.,,1.,6.,,0.0)
      CALL POLY(3.0,0.875,1.,6.,,0.0)

C
C  DO LOOP STATEMENTS:
      DO 10 I=1,23
C  CONTROL:
   20 CALL PLOT(X1(1),Y1(1),IPEN(1)
C
C  DO LOOP STATEMENTS:
      DO 97 I=1,12
```

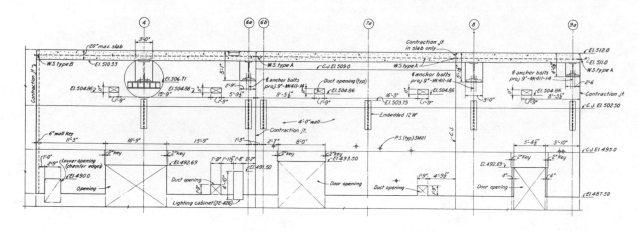

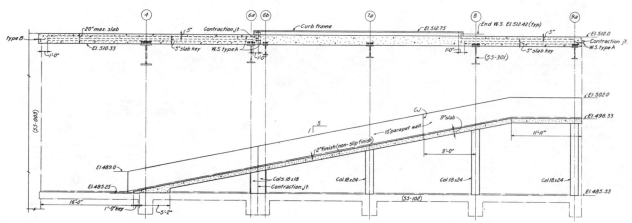

FIGURE 10.12 Basement floorplan. (Courtesy of the U.S. Corps of Engineers, Vicksburg, Mississippi.)

```
C
C  CONTROL:
    97 CALL CENTER(XLOC(1),YLOC(1),XEND(1),YEND(1))
       CALL BAR(7.,0.,0.,1.55,0.5,1.55,2,16)
       CALL SHADE(XZRZY,YZRZY,XXZRZY,YYZRZY,0.07,73.,3,1,3,1)
       CALL SHADE(ARAYX,ARAYY,ARAYXX,ARAYYY,0.07,73.,6,1,2,1)
       CALL SHADE(ARAY1,ARAY2,ARAY3,ARAY4,0.07,73.,15,1,15,1)
       CALL PLOT(18.,1.,999)
C
C  CONTROL:
    STOP
C
    END
```

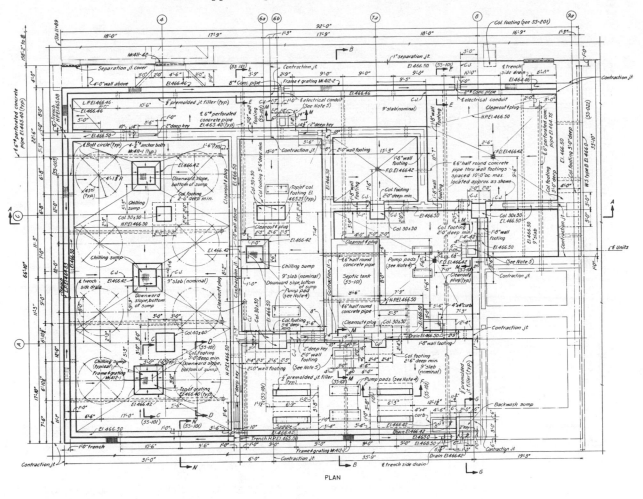

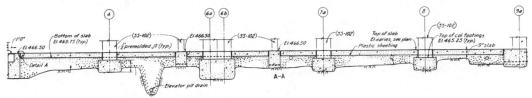

FIGURE 10.13 Footing and foundation plan. (Courtesy of the U.S. Corps of Engineers, Vicksburg, Mississippi.)

Site Example

Figure 10.11 is an example of *plan and profiles* shown on a site and road plan. The profile section shown at the bottom of the plotter drawing indicates the frontal section for the centerline of the roadway shown in the plan view from station points 0+00 through 25+00.

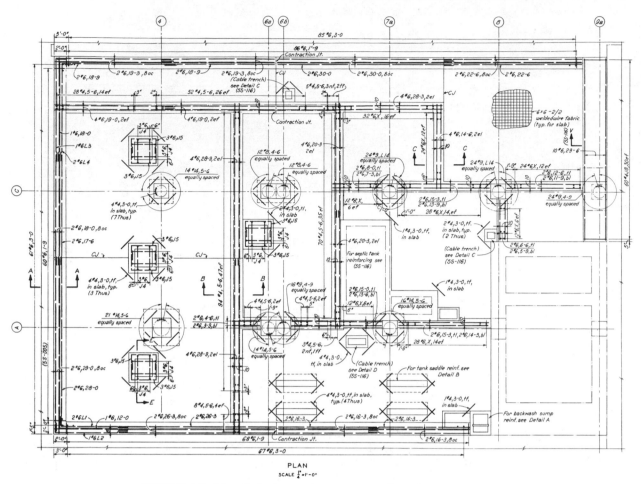

PLAN
SCALE $\frac{1}{4}$"=1'-0"

FIGURE 10.14   Reinforced concrete footing drawing. (Courtesy of the U.S. Corps of Engineers, Vicksburg, Mississippi.)

Floorplan Example

Figure 10.12 is an example of a basement floorplan which contains a section through an existing ramp. In addition a longitudinal section cut is taken and labeled C-C.

Footing and Foundation Plan Example

Figure 10.13 is a footing and foundation plan plus the section generation of the longitudinal section (A-A) taken from the plan. A-A clearly shows footings under walls and a sectional run of the building's foundation. Additional foundation sections are shown in Figure 10.14, which is an example of a reinforced concrete footing drawing. Additional foundation sections are also shown in Figure 10.15: A-A, B-B, C-C, D-D, E-E, F-F, and details A and B.

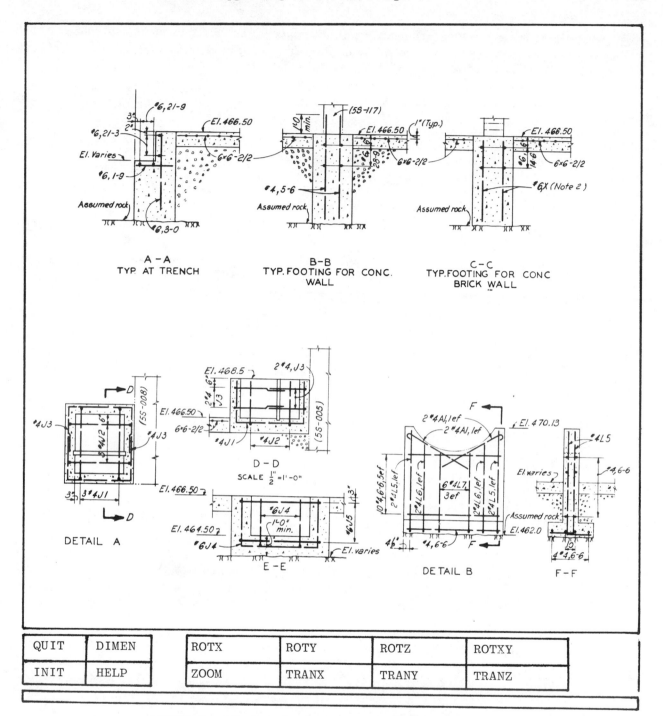

QUIT	DIMEN	ROTX	ROTY	ROTZ	ROTXY
INIT	HELP	ZOOM	TRANX	TRANY	TRANZ

FIGURE 10.15 Foundation details from Figure 10.14.

CHAPTER SUMMARY   This short chapter has introduced the reader to a technique for automatically generating building sections. A series of illustrative figures was used to demonstrate the various techniques and procedures. Special hardware is needed for the successful display of the figures shown in this chapter, and the author is indebted to Mr. Charles Brack of the Gerber Scientific Co. for his expertise and assistance in the production of these illustrations. See the Bibliography for further reading.

EXERCISES   1.   The theory of section generation stems from a graphic structure that is 3D and represents a certain basic architectural structure. Use any of the structures pictured in this chapter and place it directly on the graphics tablet as described in the chapter. Enter it as a wireform data structure as shown in Figure 10.1.

2.   Recall the data from Exercise 1 and display them on the CRT. Rotate the wireform into a plan view by use of the graphics tablet pencil and menu selection available on the CRT screen.

3.   Add interior walls and structural items to the plan view from Exercise 2. See Figure 10.2.

4.   Use the technique shown in Figure 10.3 and create a section taken from Exercise 3.

5.   Recall the data from Exercises 1 and 3. Display them as shown in Figure 10.4.

6.   Rotate the display in Exercise 5 into a horizontal position as shown in Figure 10.5. Now add any special building items to this display frame.

7.   Rotate the display in Exercise 6 into an elevation position as shown in Figure 10.6; continue to move and rotate until the display looks like Figure 10.7. Add any special items or move items displayed in Exercise 6 to another floor location.

8.   Run final clearance checks by rotating the display image as shown in Figure 10.8, 10.9 and 10.10.

9.   Practice site examples by writing a display program for the profile section shown.

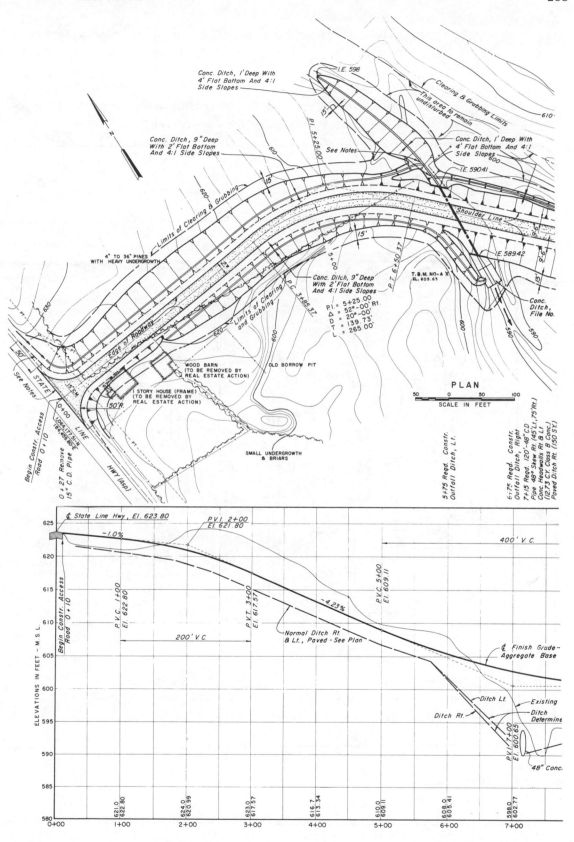

PLAN

SCALE IN FEET

10. Select a floorplan from Chapter 8 or a foundation plan from Chapter 9 and write a display program as outlined in this chapter.

11. Using the data from the building cross-section program, prepare a sectional drawing window as shown.

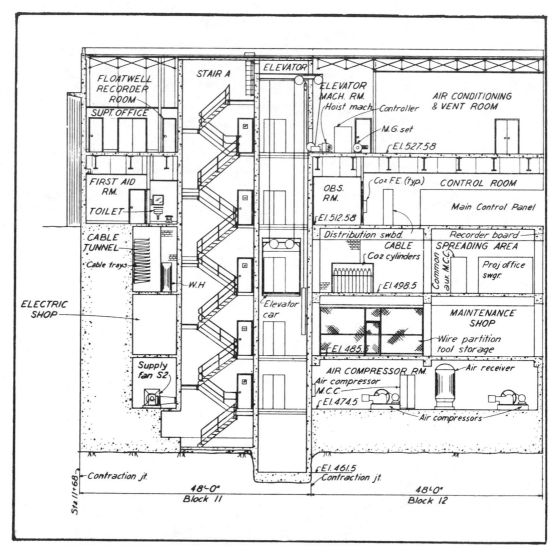

12. Use the display program and the subroutine CUPID to illustrate
     the section shown.

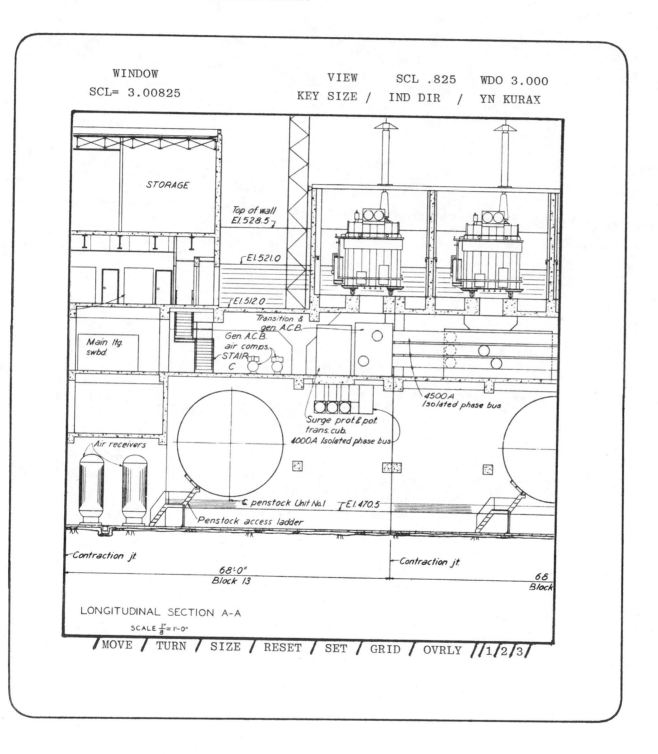

11 Dimensioning and Notation Techniques

This chapter studies the programming techniques needed for dimensioning three-dimensional objects in a two-dimensional space called the display area. The most interesting part of architectural programming is contained in this unit of study. It begins with the description of dimensioning using basic or simple graphic entities such as the display point, line, plan, and wireform. With these simple display entities, objects called primitive elements can be dimensioned and displayed. Primitive elements consist of rectangles, circles, ellipses, polygons, and splines.

The second and third main sections of this chapter contain information on methods of storing related dimensions and using a dimensioning subroutine. Complete subprograms will be presented for orthographic dimensioning of simple and complex architectural objects.

USE OF AUTOMATED DIMENSIONING

Computer-generated two-dimensional annotation represents the combination of a properly written computer program for a graphics output (and input) device as described in Chapter 2. Together they are the medium by which architects use and manipulate visual information. The end result may be the dimensioning of a floorplan, the labeling of a wall section, the notes on a site plan, or the sizing of colors, mass, or forms.

One authority breaks down two-dimensional annotations into the following six general areas of applications[*]:

1. Management information (architectural office related)
2. Scientific graphics (architectural engineering studies)
3. Command and control (architectural user functions)
4. Image processing
5. Real-time image generation
6. Electrical and mechanical diagrams

He points out that each of these application areas can require markedly different programming for hardware and software. The author agrees and refers the reader to the material of earlier chapters.

Another way to look at the programming necessary for two-dimensional annotation is in terms of the visualization functions or architectural services provided by computer graphics devices, which are covered in this chapter:

1. Computer requirements
2. Plan codification
3. Methods of storing related dimensions
4. Dimensioning subroutine

Most two-dimensional applications that have been implemented by programmers use one or more of these functions or services.

Computer Requirements

The replacement of the plastic template and drawing paper as a drafting medium is perhaps one of the most common advantages of a properly programmed graphics system. A software system (collection of these properly programmed approaches) that presents the proper tools at the screen for image creation and dimensioning can make a user much more productive than a draftsperson working at a drawing table with templates. Among the many documented studies of increased productivity, Feder[*] cites productivity time ratios ranging from 1.9 to 17 times improvement where working drawings and/or dimensional objects are the end products. Even though a graphics device such as a simple DVST is used, automatic dimensioning illustrates a properly programmed tool to create architectural images. In this case the images represent graphical structures selected in

---

[*]C. Machover, "Graphic displays," IEEE Spectrum 14, No. 8, 24–32 (Aug. 1977), and 14, No. 22–27 (Oct. 1977).

[*]A. Feder, "Test Results on Computer Graphics Productivity for Design and Fabrication," Paper No. 75-967, presented at the AIAA 1975 meeting, Los Angeles.

an interactive manner; the end product is still a drawing on paper for wide communication of the same information viewed without DVST consoles.

Ryan[†] describes a system of template drawing and dimensioning that normally would be done with paper and pencil. In this text it is shown why the computer-programmed technique is faster than paper and pencil in a working drawing environment. Repetitive structural shapes do not have to be redrawn, but are instantaneously called from computer storage. Any element occurring in the drawing or diagram is immediately displayed on the DVST rather than having to be reprogrammed, and annotations are performed by the main program and do not have to be calculated and sent to a plotter. Also, dimensioning accuracy is often better than can be achieved manually.

All laborious processes involving dimensioning become trivial to the user with an automated system of dimensioning.

Plan Codification

The results of the computations mentioned can be displayed as graphic entities as they occur and before all chain annotations and dimensions are complete. This process is very important because this provides real-time feedback to the designer or to an architect who may be doing a parameter study for a new design. The designer can terminate a particular computation if the partial results show that different parameters are required. Such a dynamic technique is common with DVST-type terminals, but much more immediate, useful information can be provided by the user of a CRT-type device. Users report significant savings in main computer time when computations can be aborted early and when several options can be explored in the time normally required to make one hand drawing.

By using graphic entities large amounts of information can be presented in a short space of time. Many computer programs for graphical display are based on the fact that a graphics console can display a large quantity of information at one time and, for a re-generated CRT, that the console can display changes every display cycle. The reader will recall from Chapter 2 that CRT displays usually cycle at 40 to 60 times/sec to avoid flicker. Chapter 2 also described the resolution of various kinds of display devices. The smallest graphical entity is clearly related to the display POINT. The type of display device determines the size of the point; for example, a color system of 512 by 512 picture elements (pixels) will be quite different from a DVST which contains 1024 display units (dots).

[†]D. Ryan, Computer-Aided Graphics and Design, Marcel Dekker, Inc., New York, 1979.

Most systems provide for a point to be displayed as a LINE. In the case of the DVST, the dots are overlapped to create a very sharp output for the human eye. Highest-resolution CRTs tend to be monochromatic, but 1000 lines are available in color. Plasma panels are also available that have 512 by 512 addressable point resolution, with the PLATO system from Control Data Corp. (CDC) being the most popular of this type. The CDC system offers the advantage of rear-projected color photographs, while monochromatic displays may be programmed with up to 4096 by 4096 addressable points.

Applications that use the POINT and LINE software to create plane surface displays abound. A software system called ECOSITE developed by Mallary and Ferraro[*] made use of the PLANE concept to describe complex views of land sites. Figure 11.1 is an example of the use of PLANE in the construction of simple views for the user to display and manipulate. McCleary[*] has used the PLANE concept in his study of ocean bottom data. Here color aids in the differentiation of data, such as depth and shipping density, as shown in Figure 11.2.

An architectural user can create change or the illusion of change at a graphics console by making use of the POINT, LINE, and PLANE software to build objects called wireforms. Later in this text (Chapter 15) a system will be described that employs multiple planes of information, where each plane can contain a portion of action. An automatic interpolation technique will be used to provide for the illusion of continuous motion. A portion of the book by Ryan[†] points out the problems of automatic interpolation due to the insufficiency of information available to translate a 2D view of a plane into another view without a 3D database.

The use of automatic annotations for presentations where changing information is present includes the status of oil refineries, power distribution systems, and building sites.

Sometimes representation of an unbuilt object can provide insight into potential problems before construction. As an example, a program for designing highways can enable the designer to "drive" down the highway while sitting before the display screen and look for potential hazards such as poor visibility. Another example might be the viewing of an unbuilt building from various viewing

---

[*] R. Mallary and M. Ferraro, "An application of computer-aided design to the composition of landforms for reclamation," Computer Graphics 11, No. 2, 1-7 (Summer 1977).

[*] L. McCleary, "Techniques for the display of ocean data on a raster driven color CRT," Computer Graphics 11, No. 2, 98-101 (Summer 1977).

FIGURE 11.1 Use of the PLANE concept. (Courtesy of Evans and Sutherland, Salt Lake City, Utah.)

FIGURE 11.2   Ocean bottom data displayed on CRT.   (Courtesy of Evans and Sutherland, Salt Lake City, Utah.)

points under changing lighting conditions and architectural modifications.

METHODS OF STORING RELATED DIMENSIONS

Many techniques have been created to support the use of the related dimension entities just described.   These are known as the common primitive elements.   Ryan[†] discusses 35 primitive elements used for the aid of the architect for producing working drawings.   In this chapter only the following elements will be chosen:

    1.   Rectangle: CALL RECT
    2.   Circle: CALL CIRCL
    3.   Ellipse: CALL ELIPS
    4.   Polygon: CALL POLY
    5.   Spline: CALL FIT

The use of just these five primitive dimensional elements will allow

[†]D. Ryan, Computer-Aided Graphics and Design, Marcel Dekker, Inc., New York, 1979.

the architectural programmer to annotate histograms, empirical density functions, pie charts, contour plots, discriminant analysis
diagrams, cluster analyses diagrams, Chernoff *faces* (which are used
for shades and shadows), and Andrews' sine curves. A number of
other cartographic techniques can also be used by the combination of
graphic structures and primitive dimensional elements. Figure 11.3
is the description or listing of the graphics programming for RECT.
It is useful in various forms for maps and working drawings. The
listing shown is typical of rectangle descriptions and has not been
tested on all types of display consoles. It works well on DVST and
plotter-type output devices.

Figure 11.4 is the listing for the primitive element CIRCLE.
With this the user works with a two-dimensional representation of
the primitive (instead of a linear line string). Primitives like
CIRCLE and ELIPS, shown in Figure 11.5, replace alphanumeric human-
machine communication. Many uses of computers before the advent of
interactive graphics employed alphanumeric input and batched plotted
output. In this older graphics technology, for example, the output
for numerically controlled drawing machines would be directed by
input statements created by computer programmers. They would des-

```
      SUBROUTINE RECT(X,Y,H,W,TH,IV,SCAL)
C
C     RECT DRAWS RECTANGLES
C     (X,Y) IS THE LOWER LEFT CORNER
C     H IS THE HEIGHT
C     W IS THE WIDTH
C     TH IS THE ANGLE OF INCLINATION
C     IV IS A CODE
C         IV=2, DRAW A LINE FROM CURRENT PEN POSITION TO (X,Y)
C         IV=3, DON'T DRAW LINE
C     SCAL IS THE SCALE RATIO OF THE OUTRECT
      THETA=TH/57.2958
      XS=SIN(THETA)
      XC=COS(THETA)
      CALL PLOT (X*SCAL,Y*SCAL,IV)
      X1=X-H*XS
      Y1=Y+H*XC
      CALL PLOT(X1*SCAL,Y1*SCAL,2)
      X1=X1+W*XC
      Y1=Y1+W*XS
      CALL PLOT(X1*SCAL,V1*SCAL,2)
      X1=X+W*XC
      Y1=Y+W*XS
      CALL PLOT(X1*SCAL,Y1*SCAL,2)
      CALL PLOT(X*SCAL,Y*SCAL,2)
      CALL DIMEN(X,Y-.2,W,+H,SCAL)
      CALL DIMEN(X+W,Y,H,+H+90,SCAL)
      RETURN
      END
```

FIGURE 11.3 RECT with automatic dimensioning.

```
       SUBROUTINE CIRCLE(T,V,THO,THF,RO,RF,DI,SCAL)
c      CALL CIRCL(T,V,THO,THF,RO,RF,DI)
c      T,V ARE THE COORDINATES OF THE STARTING POINT OF THE ARC
c      THO IS THE ANGLE FOR THE STARTING POINT OF THE ARC, IN DEGREES
c      THF IS THE ANGLE FOR THE END MOF THE ARC, IN DEGREES"
c      RO IS THE RADIUS AT THE START OF THE ARC
c      RF IS THE RADIUS AT THE END OF THE ARC
c      DI IS A CODE USED TO SPECIFY THE TYPE OF LINE
c           0.0 FOR A SOLID ARC
c           0.5 FOR A DASHED ARC
c      SCAL IS THE SCALE RATIO OF THIS OUTPUT
       15=4. 51+DSHI
       12=2
       X=T
       Y=U
       CALL PLOT(X*SCAL,Y*SCAL,3)
       CALL WHERE(DTH,DTH,FCTR)
       KNT=7.0*FCTR
       RORPF=ABS(RO)+ABS(RF)+0.IE-10
       DTH=0.03/(RORPF)/FCTR
       TO=THO/57.2958
       TF=THF/57.2958
       C=X-RO*COS(TO)
       TN=(TF-TO)/DTH
       IF(TF-TO)102,104,104
102    TN=ABS(TN)
       DTH=-DTH
104    B=Y-RO*SIN(TO)
       N=TN
       IF (N) 115,115,105
105    TN=(RF-RD)/TN
       RN=RO-TN
       DO 110 I=1.N
       TO=TO+DTH
       RN=RN+TN
       X=RN*COS(TO)+C
       Y=RN*SIN(TO)+B
       IF(KNT)112,122,111
112    I2=I5-I2
       KNT=T.0*FCTR
111    KNT=KNT-1
       110  CALL PLOT(X*SCAL,Y*SCAL,I2)
115    X=RF*COS(TF)+C
       Y=RF*SIN(TF)+B
       CALL PLOT(X*SCAL,Y*SCAL,I2)
       CALL DIMEN(T-RO*2.,V,RF*2.,0.,SCAL)
       RETURN
       END
```

FIGURE 11.4   CIRCLE with automatic dimensioning.

cribe the geometry of the structure to be produced using special
languages.   Today, the use of primitive elements displayed on
graphics consoles allows the designer to construct the parts pic-
torially, thus eliminating the need for geometric languages.

```
      SUBROUTINE ELIPS(XO,YO,A,B,ALPHA,THETO,THETF,IV,SCAL)
c
c     ELIPS DRAWS AN ELLIPTICAL ARC
c
c     XO,YO ARE THE COORDINATES OF THE STARTING POINT OF THE ARC
c     A IS HALF THE LENGTH OF THE ELLIPSE ALONG THE HORIZONTAL AXIS
c     B IS HALF THE LENGTH OF THE ELLIPSE ALONG THE VERTICAL AXIS
c     ALPHA IS THE ANGLE OF INCLINATION
c     THETO IS THE ANGLE OF THE STARTING POINT FROM THE CENTER
c     THETF IS THE ANGLE OF THE FINAL POINT
c     IV IS A CODE:
c           IV=2.  DRAW A LINE FROM CURRENT PEN POSITION TO THE STARTING
c                  POINT
c           IV=3.  DON'T DRAW A LINE
c     SCAL IS THE SCALE RATIO OF THE OUTPUT
c           IF THE DIMENSIONS ARE ZERO, RETURN
      IF (ABS(A)+ABS(B))4,20,4
    4 ALP=ALPHA/57.2958
      THEO=THETO/57.2958
      THEF=THETF/57.2958
c           D IS THE DISTANCE FROM THE STARTING POINT
c           TO THE CENTER OF THE ELLIPSE
      D=A*B/SQRT((A*SIN(THEO))**2* (B*COS(THEQ))**2)
c           CALCULATE THE COORDINATES OF THE CENTER
      XV=XO-D*COS(THEQ+ALP)
      XC=YO-D*SIN(THEQ+ALP)
c           SET UP VALUES FOR CALCULATING THE POINTS OF THE CURVE
      BSQ=B*B
      ABSQ=A*A-BSQ
      AB=A*B
c           MOVE PEN TO STARTING POINT
      CALL PLOT(XQ*SCAL,YO*SCAL,IV)
c           CALCULATE A DELTA THETA WHICH WILL GIVE A NICE LOOKING CURVE
      CALL WHERE(DTHE,DTHE,FCTR)
      DTHE=0.03/(ABS(A)+ABS(B))/FCTR
c           CALCULATE THE NUMBER OF POINTS TO BE PLOTTED
      N=(THEF-THEQ)/DTHE
c           IF THE CURVE IS SMALLER THAN DELTA THETA, PLOT A STRAIGHT LINE
c           IF THE THEF<THEQ, REVERSE THE NECESSARY PARAMETERS
      IF (N) 6,5,7
    5 N=-1
    6 N=-1
      DTHE=-DTHE
    7 THEN=THEO+DTHE
c           PLOT THE CURVE
      DO !) I=1,N
      ST=SIN(THEN)
c           D IS THE DISTANCE FROM THE CENTER TO THE POINT TO BE PLOTTED
      D=AB/SQRT(ABSQ*ST*ST+BSQ)
      XF=XC+D*COS(THEN+ALP)
      XF=XC+D*SIN(THEN+ALP)
      CALL PLOT(XF*SCAL,YF*SCAL,2)
   10 THEN=THEN+DTHE
c     PLOT FINAL POINT
      ST=SIN(THEF)
      D=AB/SQRT(ABSQ*ST*ST+BSQ)
      XF=SC+D*COS(THEF+ALP)
      XF=YC+D*SIN(THEF+ALP)
      CALL PLOT(XF*SCAL,YF*SCAL,2)
      RETURN
   20 CALL PLOT(XQ,YQ,IV)
      RETURN
      END
```

FIGURE 11.5 ELIPS with automatic dimensioning.

Figure 11.6 is a listing for the graphics subprogram that describes POLY; the end user works entirely with geometric, primitive elements as construction tools at the screen in a manner similar to working at a drafting table. In Figure 11.7 a designer may choose the listing for FIT. With this processes can be simulated and observed for verification before committing real resources.

```
      SUBROUTINE POLY(X,Y,SL,RN,TH,SCAL)
c
c     POLY DRAWS POLYGONS
c
c     (X,Y) IS THE BOTTOM LEFT VERTEX OF THE POLYGON
c           THE BOTTOM EDGE IS HORIZONTAL
c     SL IS THE LENGTH OF A SIDE
c     RN IS THE NUMBER OF BERTICES
c           IF RN>0, POLY DRAWS A REGULAR CONVEX RN-SIDED POLYGON
c           IF RN<0, POLY DRAWS A STAR WITH ABS(RN) POINTS
c           IF RN IS ODD, THE CENTER POINT IS POINTING DOWN
c     TH IS THE ANGLE OF ROTATION
c     SCAL IS THE SCALE RATIO OF THE OUTPUT
      N=RN
      XN=X
      YN=Y
      THO=THO.01745
c           MOVE PEN TO STARTING POINT
      CALL PLOT(X*SCAL,Y*SCAL,3)
      IF (N) 10,100,20
c           RN IS NEGATIVE, DRAW A STAR N
   10 TH1=-6.2832/RN
      N=-N
      DO 11 I=1,N
c           DRAW A LINE TO THE INTERIOR VERTEX
      XN=XN+SL*COS(THO)
      YN=YN+SL*SIN(THO)
      CALL PLOT(XN*SCAL,YN*SCAL,2)
c           DRAW A LINE TO THE NEXT POINT
      THO=THO+TH1
      XN=XN+SL*COS(THO)
      YN=YN+SL*SIN(THO)
      CALL PLOT(XN*SCAL,YN*SCAL,2)
   11 THO=THO+TH2
      CALL DIMEN(X,Y,SL,TH,SCAL)
  100 RETURN
c           RN>0, DRAW A CONVEX POLYGON
   20 TH!=6.2832/RN
      DO 21 I=1,N
      XN=XN+SL*COS(THO)
      YN=YN+SL*SIN(THO)
      CALL PLOT(XN*SCAL,YN*SCAL,2)
   21 THO=THO+TH1
      CALL DIMEN(X,Y,SL,TH,SCAL)
      RETURN
      END
```

FIGURE 11.6 POLY with automatic dimensioning.

```
      SUBROUTINE FIT(XA,YA,XB,YB,XC,YC,SCAL)
C
C      THIS ROUTINE DRAWS A CURVED LIN CONNECTING THREE POINTS
C
C      XA,YA,XB,YB,XC,YC ARE THE COORDINATES OF THE POINT
C
C      THE CURVE IS A HYPERBOLA
C      SCAL IS THE SCALE RATIO OF THE OUTPUT
      DIMENSION SS(8,9),THETA(2)
      M=2
      DY=YC-YA
      DX=XC-XA
      Z3=SORT(DY**2+DX**2)
      IF (Z3) 20,20,21
   21 DO 8 I=1,2
      IF (ABS(DX)-ABS(DY)) 1,2,2
    1 THETA(I)=1. 5708-ATAN(ABS(DX/DY))
      GO TO 3
    2 THETA(I)=ATAN(ABS(DY/DX))
    3    IF (DX) 25,26,26
   25    IF(DY) 5,4,4
   26 IF (DY) 4,5,5
    4 THETA(I)=-THETA(I)
    5    IF (DX) 6,7,7
    6    THETA(I)=THETA(I)+3.1416
    7 DX=XB=XA
    8 DY=YB-YA
      Z2=SORT(DY**2+DX**2)*COS(THETA(2)-THETA(I))
      IF (Z2) 20,20,22
   22 SS91,3)=XA-XC
      SS(2,3)=XA-XB
      KTRA=1
      GO TO 13
   16 A=SS(1,3)
      B=SS(2,3)
      SS(1,3)=YA-YC
      SS(2,3)=YA-YB
      KTRA=2
      GO TO 13
   17 CALL WHERE(X,Y,FCTR)
      DZ=0.01/FCTR
      Z=DZ
      CALL PLOT(XA*SCAL,YA*SCAL,3)
      C=SS(1,3)
      D=SS(2,3)
   18 X=(A*Z+B)*Z+XA
      Y=(C*Z+D)*Z+YA
      CALL PLOT(X*SCAL,Y*SCAL,2)
      Z=Z+DZ
      IF(Z=Z3) 18,19,19
   19    CALL PLOT (XC*SCAL,YC*SCAL,2)
      CALL DIMEN(XA,YA,XA-XC,0.,SCAL)
      RETURN
   13 SS(1,1)=Z3*Z3
      SS(1,2)= Z3
      SS(2,1)=Z2*Z2
      SS(2,2)=Z2
      CALL SOLUT(SS,M)
      IF(M) 20,20,14

      SUBROUTINE FIT(XA,YA,XB,YB,XC,YC)

   14    GO TO (16,17),KTRA
   20    CALL PLOT(XA*SCAL,YA*SCAL,3)
      CALL PLOT(XB*SCAL,YB*SCAL,2)
      GO TO 19
      END
```

FIGURE 11.7 FIT with automatic dimensioning.

DIMENSIONING
SUBROUTINE

The dimensioning subroutine used in each of the related dimensioning entities: RECT, CIRCLE, ELIPS, POLY, and SPLINE (FIT), is a FORTRAN routine which generates a dimension line with short extension lines at the tips of the line's arrowheads. In Figure 11.3 the subroutine RECT not only displays a graphical structure but automatically dimensions its width and height. Likewise the others (CIRCLE, ELIPS, POLY, and SPLINE (FIT)) display patterns that are fully dimensional.

To automate this display procedure a special subroutine CALL DIMEN is used. It is used as

        CALL DIMEN(XO,YO,DS,THETA,SCAL)

where

```
     IF (J) 432, 432, 430
 430 CALL PLOT(X1,Y1,2)
     XD=X1+0.4*XC
     YD=Y1+0.4*XS
     CALL PLOT(XD,YD,2)
 432 RETURN
     END
```

Scale Factors

The actual length of the dimension line displayed is the product of DS (the physical size) and SCAL. If the display size is 1.2 in. or longer, the annotation is placed in the middle of the dimension line. If, however, the dimension line is between 0.8 and 1.2 in. in length, the annotation is displayed to the right side after the line. And if the dimension line is less than 0.8 in. in length, the arrowheads are located outside the extension lines, and the annotation is placed to the right side.

Character Generation

Computer programs for architectural displays frequently contain text and graphics (line drawings, graphs, or images). Some documents consist of 30% character generation. Text generation is most often done on line printers such as the IBM 1403 by using appropriate character sets. The text printing is outstanding; however, the line images are not as good as other types of display hardware. A good blend is the IBM 3800 raster printer, an example of the many printer-plotters on the market. The next choice is to develop a text capability for digital plotters. A technique for text material for output on a digital computer is covered in Chapter 3. The obvious drawback of this approach is the lack of turnaround time from the command string to the display. In other words a plotter is an extremely slow way of producing text materials.

The remaining portion of this chapter will describe a means of producing high-speed text with adequate line quality. The advantages to this approach are the treatment of text and line images together in order to store the entire document digitally and eliminate expense and potential errors.

To understand and use a printer-plotter like the 3800, one must look at those characteristics of the hardware and software that produce the architectural drawings. One of the important items is the ability to load new type fonts (character descriptions) into the writable character generator memory. Characters are defined as a series of dots or print points. Output can be printed at 6, 8, or 12 lines/in. and 10, 12, or 15 characters/in. The resolution is not symmetric; however, at 8 lines/in. and 12 characters/in., the character space or box is 15 print points wide and 18 print points high. The character boxes are contiguous, so both the interline spacing (leading) and intercharacter spacing must be included within the 15 by 18 point box. The output page on a printer-plotter is treated as a mapped entity. This means for a given character box that characters placed only within the uniform array of rows and columns are available.

The upper limit of character codes available on a single page is 255. One font requires 64 positions of character generator memory (12 pitch Gothic). If lowercase and italics or boldface are added, additional character generator storage is required.

If the subprogram listed was modified in order to produce text material on a CRT, a vector by vector character could be built at the higher speeds associated with CRTs. A graphics system that incorporates vector-stroked characters is in effect an all-points-addressable printer. This system will produce camera-ready copy of printer text and graphics of high quality. The high-resolution printer uses a computer-controlled CRT that is capable of projecting an image of 800 dots/in. On a CRT these dots are called *pixels* and not printer points.

The printer projects text characters onto film by referencing appropriate fonts, described earlier. Enhancement to the software allow architects to send their own raster data to the printer either as fonts or vector-stroked special characters.

CHAPTER SUMMARY   This short chapter dealt with the concept of automatic dimensioning of simple geometric objects that appear frequently in architectural drawing. The use of this technique was discussed along with the computer requirements and plan codifications necessary. Methods for storing related dimension were presented in illustrative figures for a few of the many graphical structures possible. It is hoped that the reader will gain insight into how to write or modify his or her own graphical structures for automatic dimensioning.

And finally the dimensioning subroutine was presented in machine-ready format. The software listing can be placed in any FORTRAN compiler and used for automating architectural shapes that require reference dimensions. See the Bibliography for further reading.

EXERCISES   1.   Practice the use of automated dimensioning for the floorplan shown.

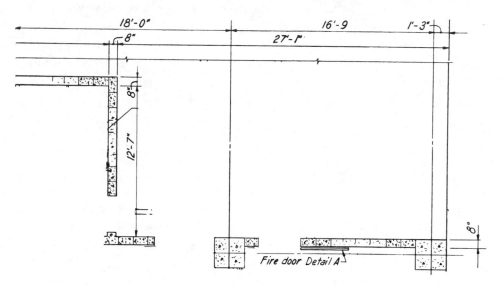

2.   Continue the practice by dimensioning the fire door detail called in Exercise 1 and shown here.

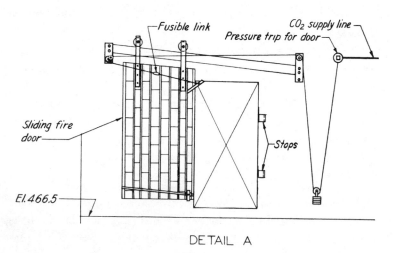

DETAIL A

3. Use the method of storing related dimensions and RECT to
    dimension the object shown.

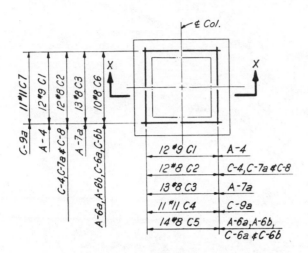

12 #9 C1	A-4
12 #8 C2	C-4, C-7a & C-8
13 #8 C3	A-7a
11 #11 C4	C-9a
14 #8 C5	A-6a, A-6b, C-6a & C-6b

COLUMN FOOTING REINF.

4.   Use the method of storing related dimensions and CIRCL to dimension the object shown.

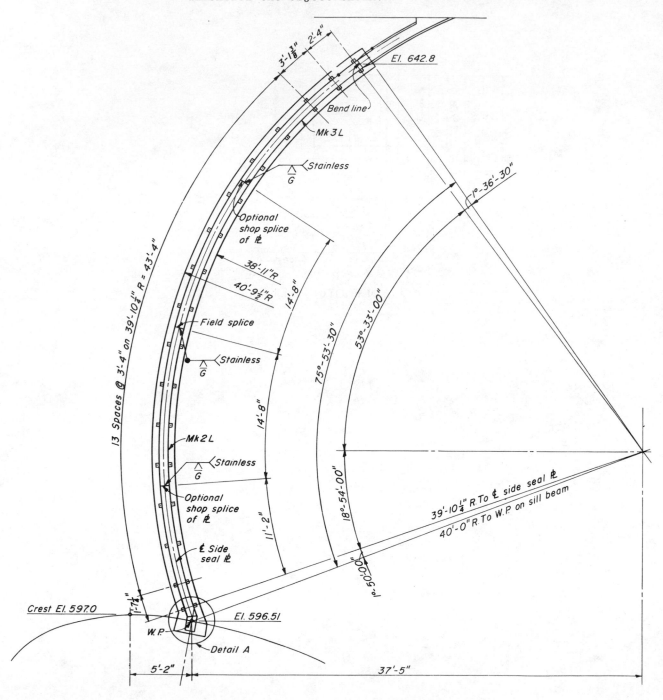

5. Continue to develop the object in Exercise 4 by using POLY to
    dimension the modified object shown.

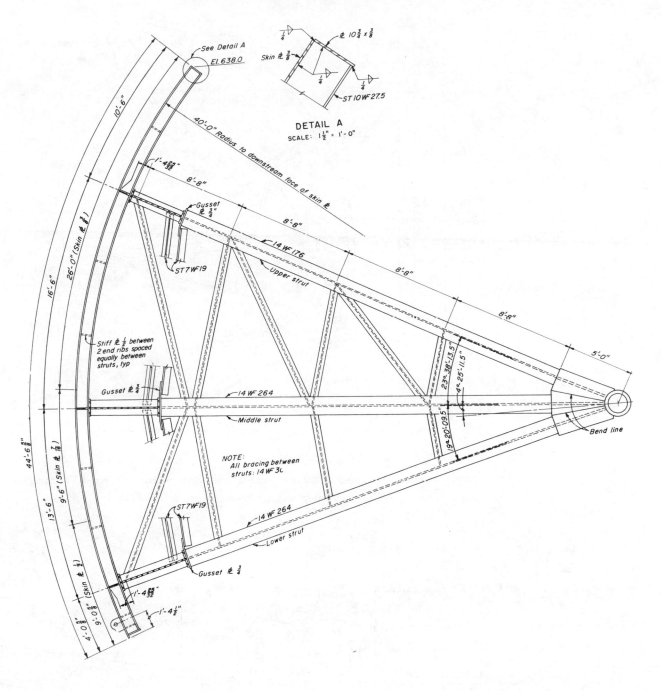

DETAIL A
SCALE: $1\frac{1}{2}$" = 1'-0"

6. Complete the object begun in Exercises 4 and 5 by using ELIPS to finish the object as shown.

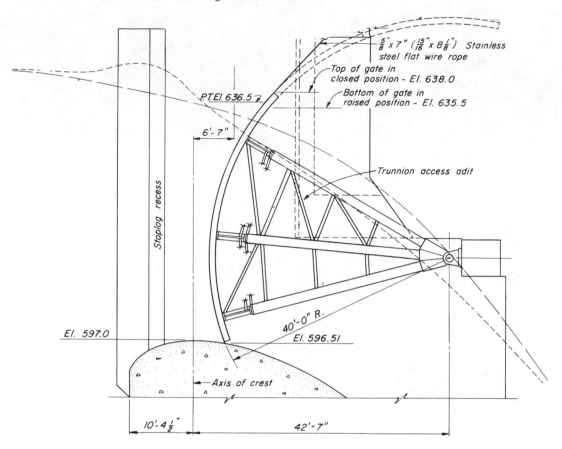

7. Store the detailed drawing shown and dimension it by FIT dimensioning routines, along with the others.

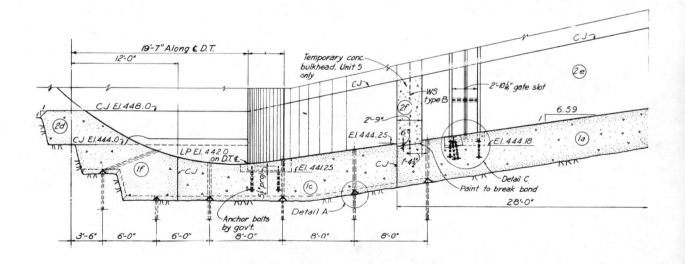

8.   Use the dimensioning subroutine listed in this chapter to size the plan and section views shown.

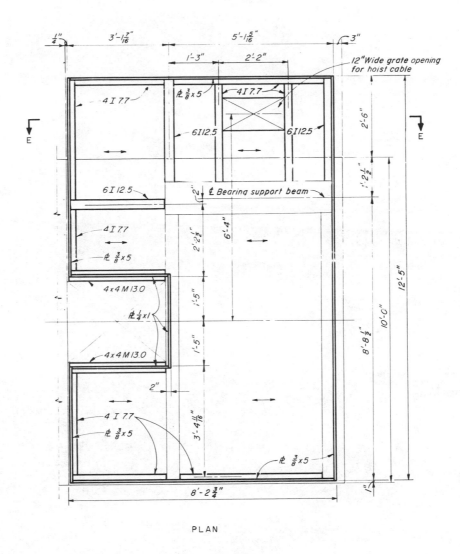

PLAN

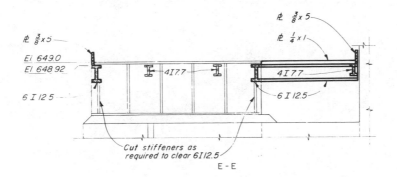

E - E

12 Exterior Elevation Generations

The exterior elevations of buildings are developed along with other information regarding the total project. Once the data are gathered to describe a floorplan, an elevation can also be generated. A floorplan is considered to be a full section view of a building elevation. Therefore the data are three-dimensional. In other words, the height, width, and depth of every point to be displayed must be known. Building geometry is often considered to be large blocks in the early stages of planning. A block has overall height, width, and depth. If all three dimensions are displayed at once, the viewer sees a pictorial object of the structure as shown in Figure 12.1. Building data are composed of the three-dimensional block information times the total number of blocks to describe the final building shape.

To keep the discussion at an elementary level, let us consider that the final building consists of a large single block of data. The block is twice as wide as it is high and half as deep as it is high. If the observer asks the elevation program to display the X and Y data registers, then a frontal elevation is displayed, in this case a rectangle twice as long as it is high. If, however, the user displays the X and Z data registers, a roof plan of the basic block is displayed. It is the same X dimension (length) and one-fourth of X (depth or Z). Other elevations can also be displayed by

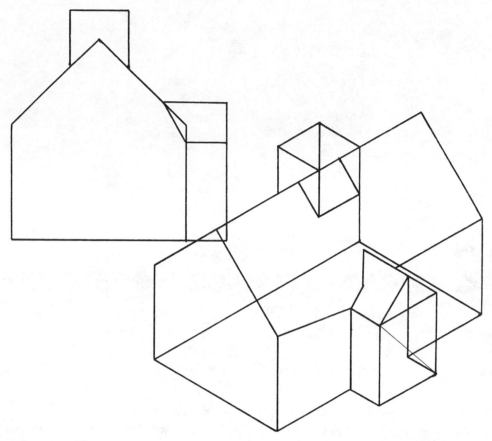

FIGURE 12.1   Block data for elevations.   Top: single elevation;
bottom: multiple elevations.

1.   Using the Z and Y registers for right side elevations
2.   Using the -Z and Y registers for left side elevations
3.   Using the -X and Y registers for rear elevations

Elevations are rarely called front, right side, left side, top, or
bottom.   These terms are used here so that the reader can visualize
how the block data are presented on a CRT screen.   The common labeling is North, South, East, and West.

THEORY OF
ELEVATION
CONSTRUCTION
With this general introduction to the theory of how elevations are
recalled from database storage, it is now possible to advance to the
actual construction of an exterior elevation.   If the operator is
starting from ground zero and wants to display a building elevation,
the database must exist.   The first step then would be the data construction.   A user might input the overall measurements from the
keyboard.   This would not yield a very detailed elevation.   Suppose
a preliminary sketch of a floorplan could be found.   If so, a graphics (data) tablet can be used to enter the basic size of the building in addition to the location of doors, windows, unusual features

such as smokestacks, towers (electrical), communication equipment mounted on the building, and heating and ventilation items located on the exterior of the building.

Remember that a three-dimensional database is to be constructed; therefore, the digitizer (person using the data tablet) must work from two views or input the third location from the keyboard. The database construction portion of the process is the most time consuming, but remember that these data can be used for interior elevations, framing plans, section generation, foundation plans, floorplans, and other working details requiring three-dimensional data. Most first-time users of a computer-aided architectural graphics work station ask, "Why do I need 3D? All my drawings are 2D." If 3D systems are not used, the power and speed of the computer cannot be used to their fullest. Remember that the object that is to be designed is three-dimensional, not two-dimensional.

Orthographic Projection

All elevations are based on orthographic projection. Therefore, all elevation generators are written to handle the database in this manner. A user may write a simple program to use the elevation generator; it would appear as

```
CALL PLOTS
CALL FTELEV(5.5,4.750)
CALL PLOT(0.,0.,999)
STOP
END
```

Where the first statement, CALL PLOTS, will send the output to a CALCOMP digital plotter. If a CRT view were desired, then the statement CALL INITT would be used instead. The second statement, CALL FTELEV(5.5,4.750), will plot the X and Y data registers beginning at 5.5 in. from the plotter origin in the X direction and 4.750 in. in the Y direction. The third statement signals the digital plotter that the job is complete, and the remaining statements stop and end the program. The elevation generator provides the picture by

```
      SUBROUTINE FTELEV(XPAGE,YPAGE)
C     THIS IS A FRONTAL BUILDING ELEVATION GENERATOR THAT WILL PLOT
C     AN ELEVATION ON A CALCOMP DIGITAL PLOTTER.  THE USER PROVIDES
C     THE STARTING POSITION (XPAGE AND YPAGE).
C
      DIMENSION X(10000),Z(10000),IPEN(10000)
C     WHERE X(I) IS THE X REGISTER, Y(I) IS THE Y REGISTER, AND Z(I)
C     IS THE Z REGISTER.  IPEN(I) IS THE PEN CONTROL (UP OR DOWN).
      READ, NPTS
C     WHERE NPTS IS THE NUMBER OF DATA POINTS TO BE PLOTTER FROM DATA
```

```
C     BASE
      DO 10 I=1,NPTS
 10   READ, X(I),Y(I),Z(I),IPEN(I)
C     A DO LOOP IS USED TO INPUT THE DATABASE
      DO 11 J=1,NPTS
 11   CALL PLOT(X(I),Y(I),IPEN(I))
C     THE FRONTAL ELEVATION IS NOW PLOTTER ON THE DIGITAL PLOTTER
      RETURN
      END
```

This example is very simple and could be used to generate a single elevation if needed. A more useful variation of this theory is used in most elevation generators and will be explained in the next section of this chapter.

Three-Dimensional Point Manipulation

A variation of orthographic projection is used to provide a more useful elevation generator. It appears as

```
      SUBROUTINE ELEGEN(XPAG,YPAG,XDATA,YDATA,IPDATA,NPTS,CHOICE)
C     XPAG AND YPAG ARE THE STARTING LOCATION ON THE PLOTTER OR CRT.
C     XDATA IS THE NAME OF THE X REGISTER AS IS YDATA, ZDATA, IPDATA
C     (THE USER MUST PROVIDE A DATA ARRAY IN THE CALLING PROGRAM.)
C     NPTS IS THE TOTAL NUMBER OF DATA ELEMENTS TO BE PLOTTED.
C     CHOICE IS THE NORTH, SOUTH, EAST, OR WEST ELEVATION DESIRED
C     (INPUT 1 FOR NORTH, 2 FOR SOUTH, 3 FOR EAST, AND 4 FOR WEST).
      IF(CHOICE.EQ.1) CALL PLOT(XDATA(I),YDATA(I),IPDATA(I)),I=1,NPTS
      IF(CHOICE.EQ.2) CALL PLOT(-XDATA(I),YDATA(I),IPDATA(I)),I=1,
     +NPTS
      IF(CHOICE.EQ.3) CALL PLOT(ZDATA(I),YDATA(I),IPDATA(I)),I=1,NPTS
      IF(CHOICE.EQ.4) CALL PLOT(-ZDATA(I),YDATA(I),IPDATA(I)),I=1,
     +NPTS
```

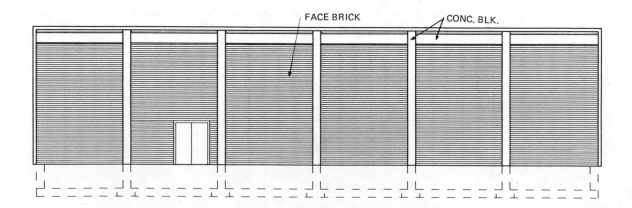

WEST EXT. ELEVATION

FIGURE 12.2   Choice 4.

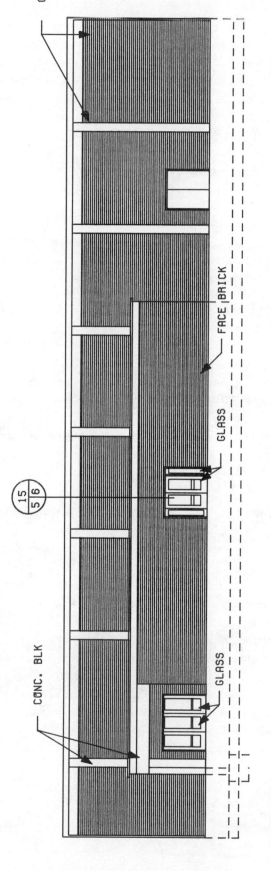

EAST EXT. ELEVATION

FIGURE 12.3   Choice=3 (East exterior).

```
        RETURN
        END
```

In this example a choice of four elevations is given. After each testing (IF) statement a line generator (CALL PLOT) is used in an implied DO LOOP. Some forms of higher-level languages do not permit this type of compact programming. In these cases, the test (IF) is followed by a GO TO statement followed by a number. Example:

```
        IF(CHOICE.EQ.1) GOTO 22
                .
                .
                .
                .
                .
    22  DO 100 I=1,NPTS
    100    CALL PLOT(XDATA(I),YDATA(I),IPDATA(I))
```

will result in the same output. Figure 12.2 is the output if choice 4 is selected. Note in this example that notes have been added for face brick and concrete blocks. At the right-hand side of the elevation data have been displayed. They will be used later for reference dimensions such as EL 512.0, which represents the ground level. Figure 12.3 represents the CHOICE=3 (EAST EXTERIOR). In this example, notes for glass, face brick, concrete blocks, and a door detail elevation are shown. If the elevations are simple, then three-dimensional point manipulation is a convenient method for generation and display of exterior elevations.

DISPLAY BY
DIRECT
PROJECTION

All elevations may be developed for display by direct projection from a plan view, and exterior elevations are no exception. However, this technique is rather common for developing interior elevations and will be explained in detail in Chapter 13. For now, it is important to understand how this method is used by the person developing the architectural display. In Figure 12.4 an exterior elevation of electrical equipment is shown. The plan noted (EL 515.0) sets the ground line at 515.0. Therefore the ground line note can be added to the exterior elevation shown directly below the plan view. In this case the plan information existed as three-dimensional display data (X and Y) by converting the data to (X and -Z), and elevation is displayed below the plan view. If (X and +Z) were used, the elevation would appear above the plan view. This technique of converting data for display is called display by direct

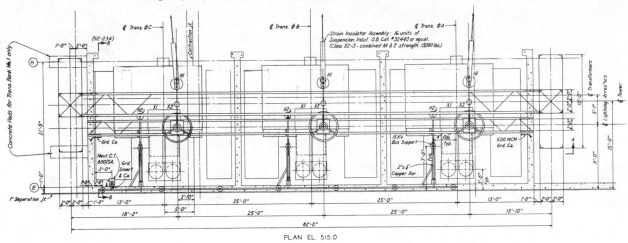

PLAN EL. 515.0

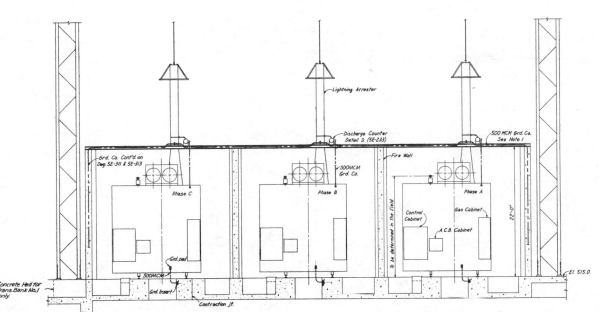

FIGURE 12.4   Exterior elevation of electrical equipment.   (Courtesy of the U.S. Corps of Engineers, Vicksburg, Mississippi.)

projection; in other words, the elevation will appear directly above or below the plan view and nowhere else. If the planner has room on the display device to use this method, it is as easy as any other to generate exterior elevations.

The projection method is very useful for developing parts of an elevation and then blending these parts into a whole. For example, Figure 12.5 contains the exterior elevation data from Figure 12.4 (electrical equipment) along with other building data to form an entire exterior elevation for a plant.

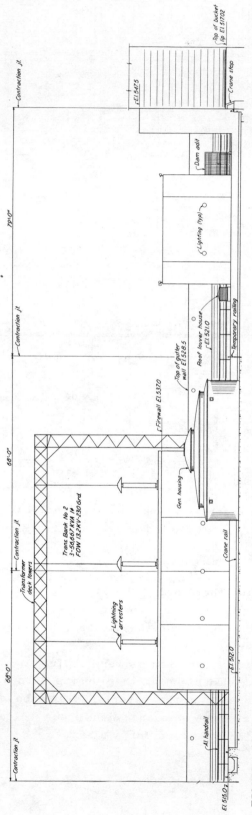

FIGURE 12.5 Exterior elevation data drom Figure 12.4 merged with building data. (Courtesy of the U.S. Corps of Engineers, Vicksburg, Mississippi.)

294

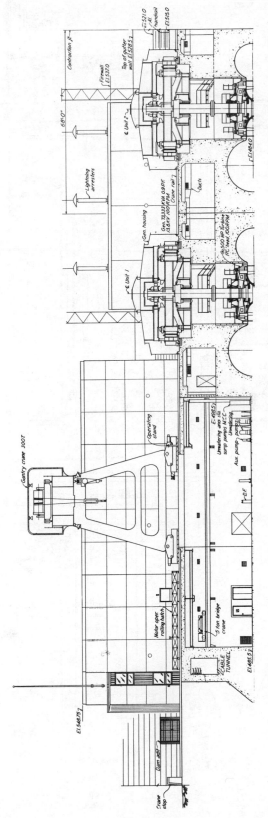

FIGURE 12.6 Combination of exterior elevation and longitudinal section. (Courtesy of the U.S. Corps of Engineers, Vicksburg, Mississippi.)

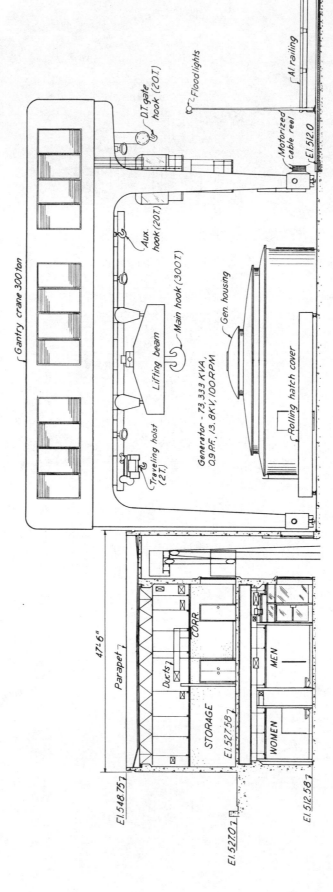

FIGURE 12.7 Orthogonal elevation view from Figure 12.6. (Courtesy of the U.S. Corps of Engineers, Vicksburg, Mississippi.)

PLOTTING
THE EXTERIOR
ELEVATIONS

Now that the three primary methods of generating exterior elevations are known, the planner may use the technique along with others to study the building structure as well as exterior appearance. Figure 12.6 is a combination exterior elevation and longitudinal section. Here the plotting of the exterior elevation along with the necessary section is a valuable aid to the building designer. In Figure 12.5 the interior of the generator housing was not shown. In Figure 12.6 not only the interior of the generator can be studied, but below ground features can be displayed for study and/or modification.

The plotting of the exterior elevation includes exterior equipment such as the gantry crane shown in Figure 12.6. If more information were needed about this 300-ton crane, another exterior elevation could be called for and displayed. Figure 12.7 represents another CHOICE, and the crane is displayed along with the elevation in an adjacent orthogonal relationship (90° rotation from Figure 12.6). A 90° rotation of a longitudinal section is called a transverse section. So in this case an exterior elevation is combined with a transverse section to study the crane and its operation.

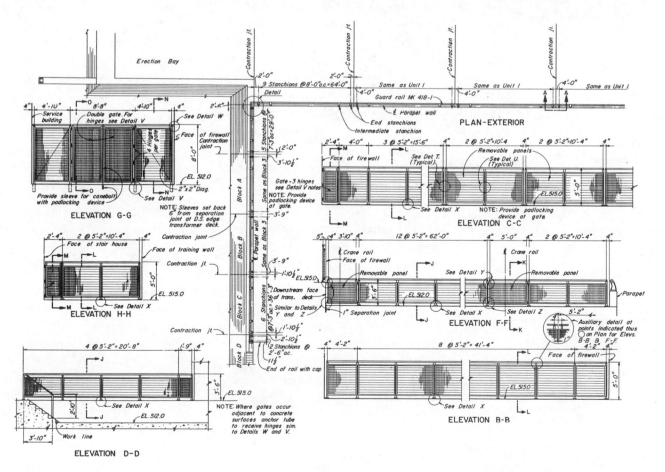

FIGURE 12.8 Use of texture on exterior elevations. (Courtesy of the U.S. Corps of Engineers, Vicksburg, Mississippi.)

USE OF TEXTURE
ON ELEVATIONS
The use of some sort of texture on exterior elevations is an aid in reading them. Both Figures 12.2 and 12.3 contained straight lines at random spaces to represent face brick. The last figure in this chapter, Figure 12.8, also uses texture to better represent exterior elevations. In this case texture is necessary to represent the parapet fences and panel designs for this plant. The most common form of texture is the straight-line patterns, but small gridded sections are used as well as cross-hatching patterns. The use of texture is also quite common in the projection of interior elevations. Additional examples of texture on elevations is shown in Chapter 13.

CHAPTER SUMMARY
Elevations are discussed in at least three other chapters of this book. In this chapter, the discussion was limited to building exteriors only. In architectural graphics the term elevation is used to represent one of the primary orthogonal viewing relationships. It is not unusual to refer to elevation details, objects in elevation (as opposed to PLAN), or datum locations for notes. This leaves the beginning reader at a loss for which is used and for what purpose. Horizontal view relationships are referred to as PLAN relationships in this text, and frontal view relationships are referred to as elevations. The term *exterior elevation* means the fundamental picture for the outside view of the building. It has only four viewing positions called vantage points. They were listed as choices 1, 2, 3, or 4 in one method and NORTH, SOUTH, EAST, and WEST in another.

It is often very easy to generate exterior views if three-dimensional data exist for all exterior portions of the structure. The reader was introduced to three methods:

1. Orthographic projection
2. Three-dimensional point manipulation
3. Display by direct projection

A short discussion of the value for plotting exterior elevations was followed by examples. Examples are often shaded or textured to represent materials used or the depth in the elevation viewed.

There are a number of excellent references available for further study, and the reader is referred to the Bibliography at the end of this book. These references are all current and from leading users in the English-speaking countries.

EXERCISES 1.   From the pictorial object shown, plot a front elevation view.
                 Label this elevation "NORTH."

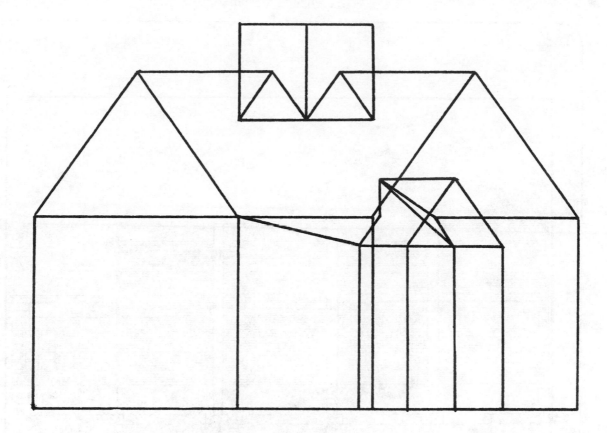

           2.   From the same pictorial, plot a side elevation and label it
                 "EAST."

           3.   Now use the Z and Y registers and plot another side elevation;
                 label it "WEST."

           4.   Continue the elevation plotting by using the -X and Y registers
                 for a rear elevation. Label it "SOUTH."

           5.   Using the data tablet, add windows and doors to the basic block
                 data shown. The block data were entered from the keyboard but
                 are not suited to detailed objects like doors and windows in
                 elevation. Repeat Exercises 1-4 for EAST, WEST, NORTH, and
                 SOUTH elevations.

6.   Develop a North elevation for Figure 12.3 as shown in the win-
     dows pictured.

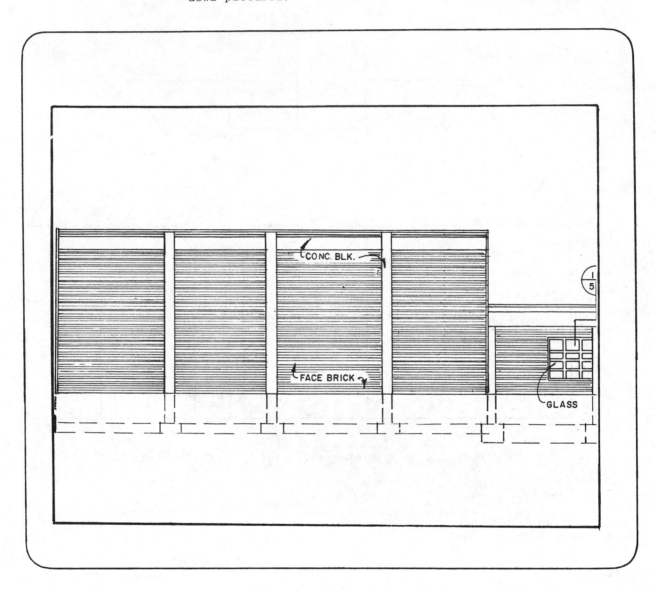

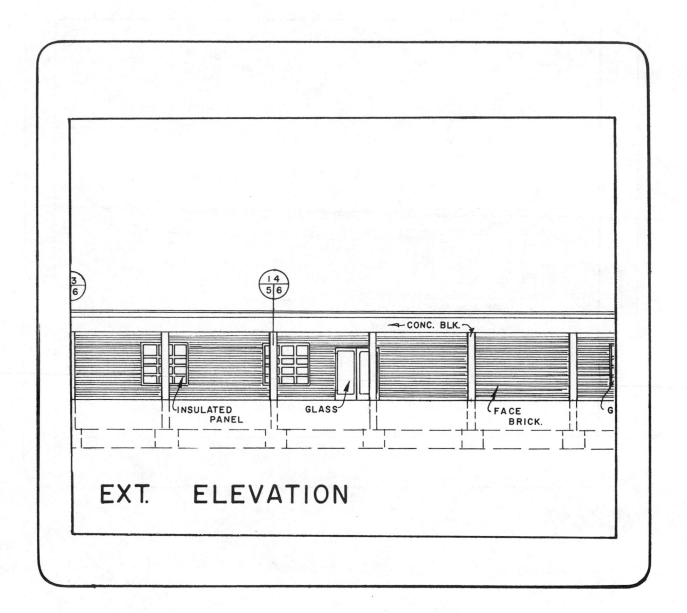

EXT. ELEVATION

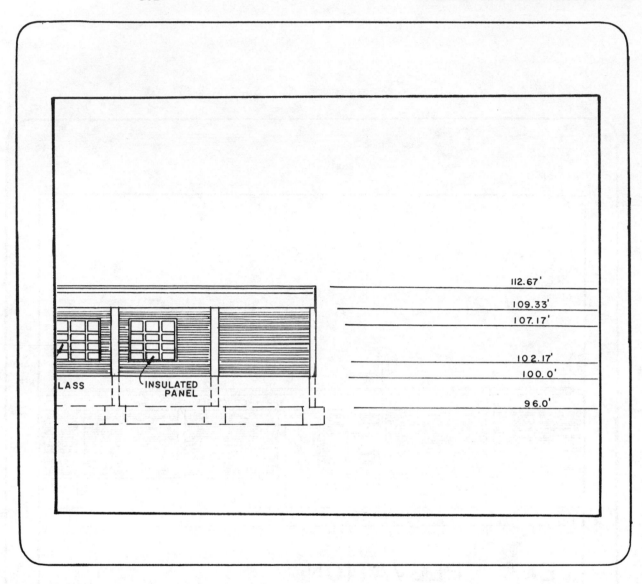

LASS

INSULATED
PANEL

112.67'

109.33'

107.17'

102.17'

100.0'

96.0'

7.   Repeat Exercise 6 with the South elevation using the three windows shown.

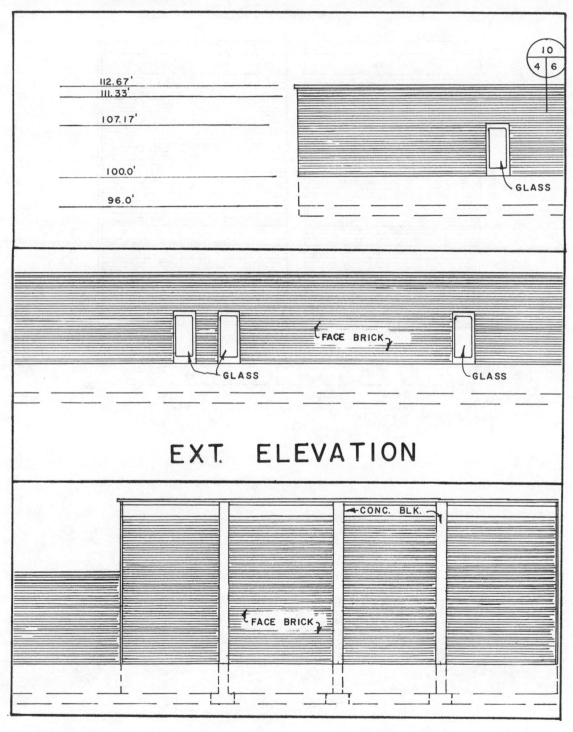

8. Recall Figure 12.2 and add the datum dimension symbols as shown.

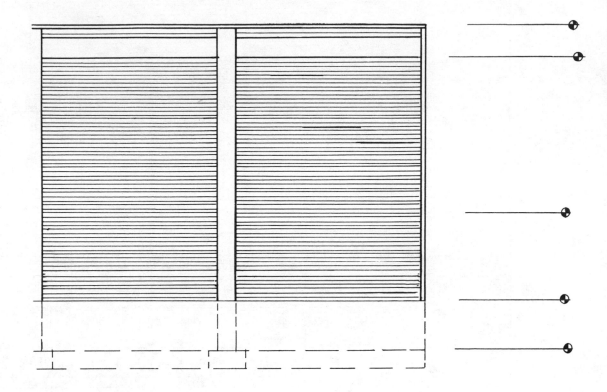

9.   Continue the modification of Figure 12.2 as shown.

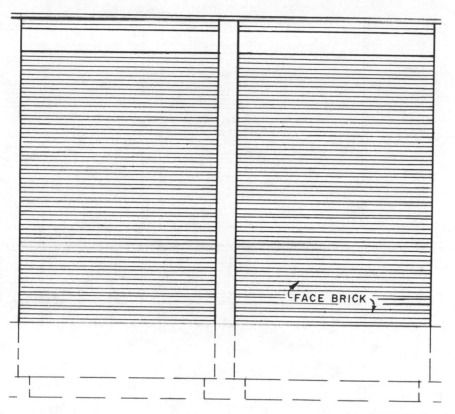

FACE BRICK

WEST EXT. ELEVATION

10.   Complete the modification and recall of Figure 12.2 as shown.

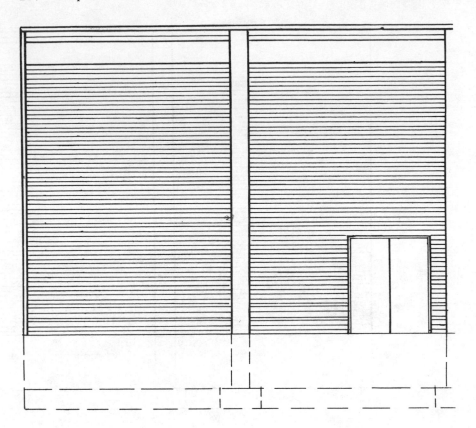

13 Interior Elevations

Elevations have been discussed in Chapter 12 and will appear again in Chapter 15. In Chapter 6 the concept of an elevation window was introduced. Figure 13.1 best illustrates the window and sheet concepts. In this example the window is located in the upper left-hand corner of the sheet. Windows can be recognized by the fact that they have rectangular boxes around them when they appear at the user's work station. Under the box is a menu for easy touch of the light pen. The bar might appear as follows:

/ MOVE / TURN / SIZE / RESET / SET / GRID / OVRLY /

The designer uses the menu bar to assist in the construction of the plan (scale 1/4 in. = 1 ft.) and the corresponding interior elevation labeled A-A. In Figure 13.1 the window area is clearly marked for explanation; it <u>does</u> <u>not</u> appear on a final drawing.

THEORY OF INTERIOR ELEVATION DISPLAY

A careful study of Figure 13.1 also points out that interior elevations B-B, C-C, D-D, E-E, F-F, G-G, and H-H are all taken from the same plan section shown in the display window. These elevations can

307

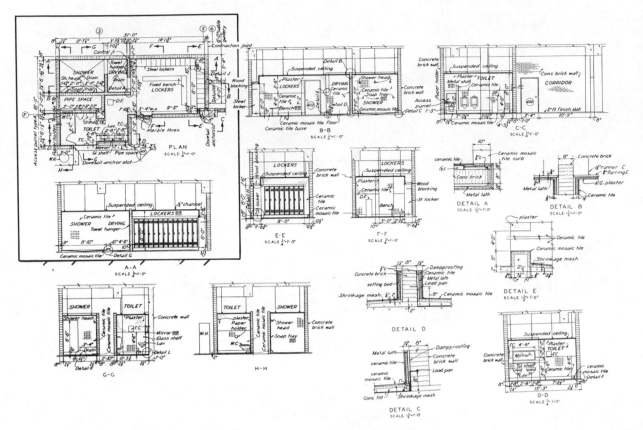

FIGURE 13.1   Interior elevation window.   (Courtesy of U.S. Corps of Engineers, Vicksburg, Mississippi.)

be visualized by placing the viewer in the floorplan facing the arrowed direction. For instance, find the heavy lines and block letters F-F in the floorplan; now place yourself in the direction of the arrows. As a viewer you would be standing in a locker room facing the shower door with steel lockers at your right hand. See interior elevation F-F. Now turn completely around. You are now facing a wall of steel lockers with the exit door at your right hand. See interior elevation E-E. With each of the interior elevations shown in Figure 13.1 you may place yourself inside the floorplan and read (visualize) what the elevation should look like. The example here is a small one, but larger examples are done the same way. Note that construction details are placed on this layer also, because they best represent how to relate the detail to the portion of the structure designed.

Foldout Methods

The technique just described is called a foldout method. To fully understand its importance, a larger floorplan is displayed as shown in Figure 13.2. Here the floorplan is placed across the top half of the sheet space. Only three interior elevations can be placed on the same sheet (A-A, B-B, and C-C). Elevations D-D, E-E, G-G, F-F, H-H, J-J, and K-K are placed on another page as shown in Figure 13.3. Construction details A, B, C, D, J, K, C, M, N, P, R, T, and S are also located on this second sheet.

2D Point Manipulation

A technique often used in interior elevation display is called 2D point manipulation. It is convenient to use this method when eleva-

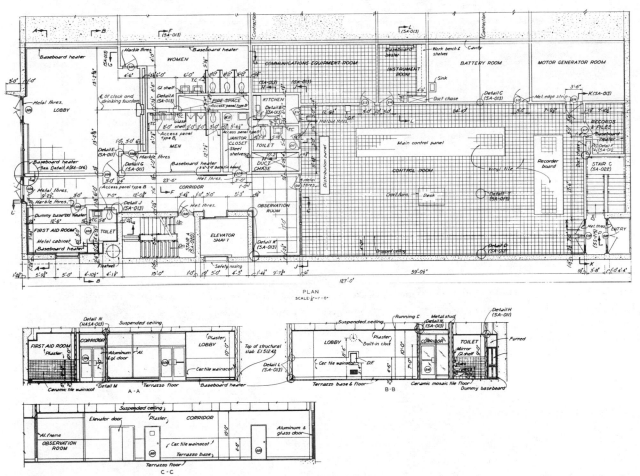

FIGURE 13.2   Large floorplan with foldout elevations. (Courtesy of U.S. Corps of Engineers, Vicksburg, Mississippi.)

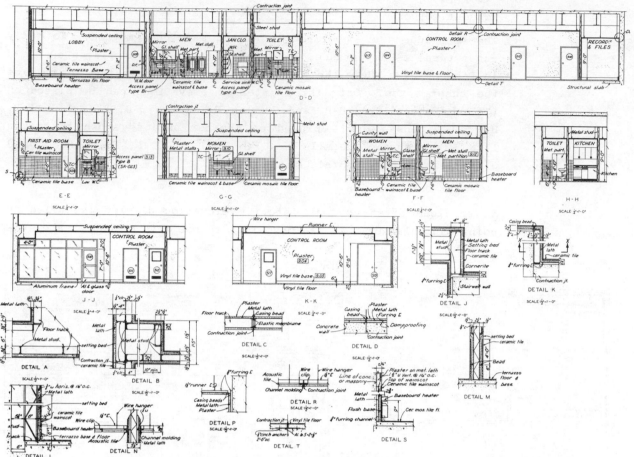

FIGURE 13.3 Sheet of interior elevations taken from Figure 13.2. (Courtesy of U.S. Corps of Engineers, Vicksburg, Mississippi.)

tions must be taken from two-dimensional representations instead of 3D floorplans. Figure 13.4 shows an elevation located in the upper left-hand corner of the sheet. From this elevation, which is two-dimensional, other elevations are to be displayed. In Figure 13.4 secondary elevations A-A, B-B, C-C, and D-D are constructed. These elevations show construction details and fabrication techniques.

Interior elevations constructed in a two-dimensional point manipulation technique are ideally suited for door and window designs.

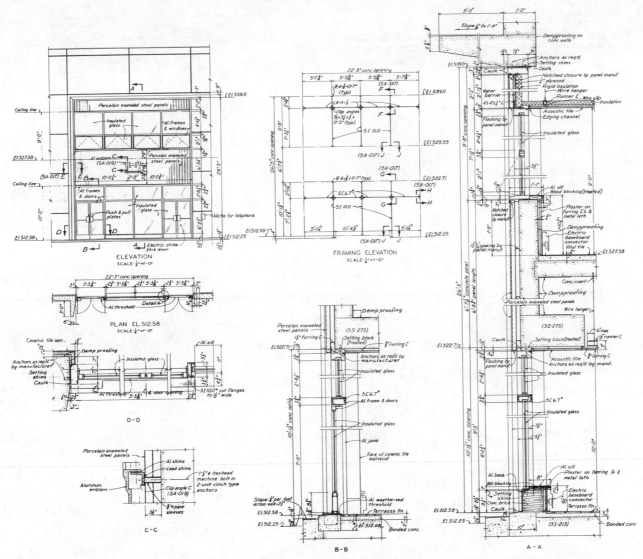

FIGURE 13.4 Two-dimensional point manipulation technique. (Courtesy of U.S. Corps of Engineers, Vicksburg, Mississippi.)

Figure 13.5 shows the elevation in the upper left-hand corner and the 2D elevations L-L, M-M, N-N, and P-P located on the same sheet. Typical window elevations are also placed here along with window details that share the same database (layer) information.

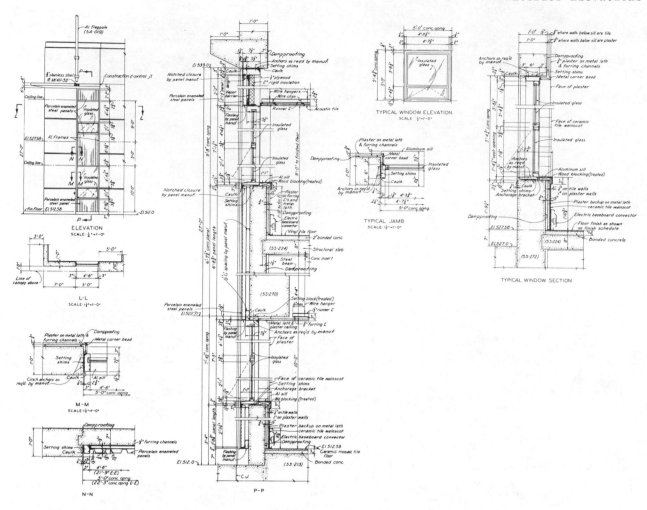

FIGURE 13.5   Interior elevations used for typical window detail. (Courtesy of U.S. Corps of Engineers, Vicksburg, Mississippi.)

DISPLAY BY
DIRECT
PROJECTION

In Figure 13.1, the window display boxed in the upper left-hand corner contained a plan view and directly (orthogonal) below was an interior elevation. In this case a direct projection was used to illustrate elevation A-A. Figure 13.6 also was developed by direct projection. In other words, the elevation is placed in an orthographic relationship to the floorplan and then rotated 90°. Reference lines may be passed from the floorplan anywhere along the A-A cutting plane line and projected directly down to build the elevation shown as A-A.

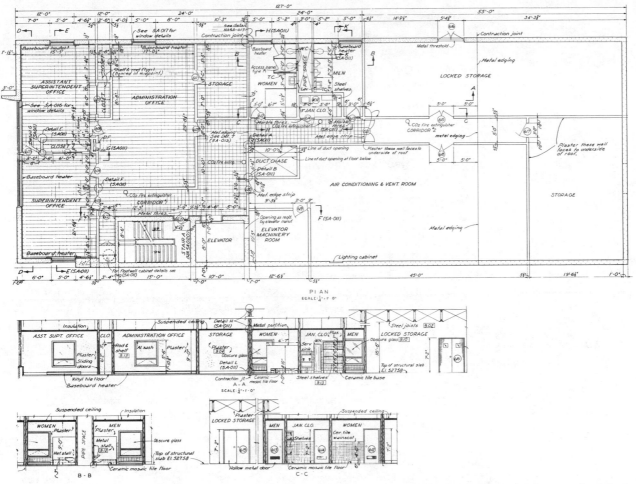

FIGURE 13.6   Interior elevation by direct orthographic projection.
(Courtesy of U.S. Corps of Engineers, Vicksburg, Mississippi.)

PLOTTING THE
INTERIOR
ELEVATIONS
The interior elevations describe the interior walls of each room in
a floorplan.   Each elevation is an orthographic representation based
on

1.   Foldout methods

2.   2D point manipulation between views, or

3.   Direct projection.

Any of these may be used to plot an elevation that is a projection
based on the floorplan of the particular wall and the structural
section at that point.   Examples are clearly shown in Figures 13.1—

13.6 where the display scale was 1/4 in. = 1 ft. In some cases a larger scale was used to plot details.

The plotting procedure used to display interior elevations is practically the same as that used in Chapter 12; the only difference is that the inside rather than the outside walls are projected. Many plotting features are common to the interior walls of any structure, and the following display procedure is used for plotting all interior walls:

1. Project or recall from memory the true width of the wall, and locate all windows, doors, stairs, and other features from the floorplan data.

2. Project, construct, or recall the height of all features of the wall from a section, or get the information from the schedule database.

3. Display in narrower line widths the outlines of all built-ins such as lockers. Whenever items such as lockers return on a wall toward the observer, they should be modified by

    CALL NEWPEN (3)
    which displays a heavy outline. Omit the lines behind built-ins; this makes the elevation easier to read.

4. Display the texture of material such as shown for tile to add to the three-dimensional effect.

5. Display built-in details.

6. Add notes and letters following Chapter 3 guidelines.

Refer to the appropriate sections of this book for specific information on how to add construction details to interior elevations.

USE OF TEXTURE ON ELEVATIONS

A final illustration (Figure 13.7) will be used to demonstrate the use of texture to increase depth for an interior elevation. Note that elevations D-D, E-E, G-G, and F-F do not contain texture shading, whereas elevations H-H and J-J and all the construction details do. The use of textures increases the readability of the elevation or detail. Examples of textures for elevations are the following:

1. Window glass
2. Brick and block
3. Surface tile
4. Concrete
5. Metal studs

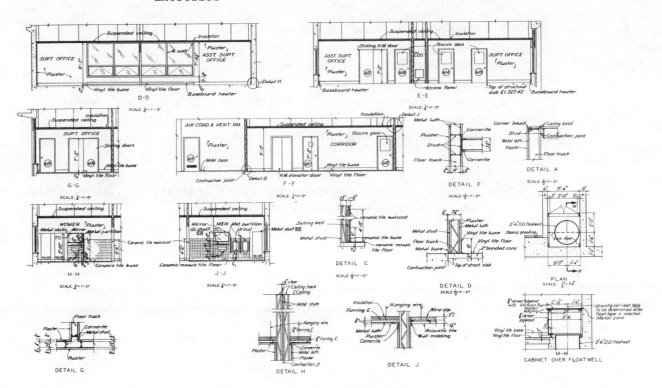

FIGURE 13.7 Use of textures for surface identification. (Courtesy of U.S. Corps of Engineers, Vicksburg, Mississippi.)

CHAPTER SUMMARY This chapter is extremely short in its text approach but quite detailed in its use of graphical displays. The old adage that a picture is worth a thousand words makes this the longest chapter in the book.

A complete sheet format was used for this chapter to illustrate to the reader the building block approach that has been used throughout the early chapters. Computer-aided architectural graphic techniques make such items easier to construct, display, and present in a final form. See the Bibliography for further reading.

EXERCISES 1. The problems at the end of this chapter are a continuation of those in Chapter 12. Begin the display process by considering the North elevation. In this case the observer is inside the building facing the North corridor wall. Develop an interior elevation consisting of three windows as shown here and in Exercises 2 and 3.

2. Continue Exercise 1 as shown.

3. Continue Exercise 2 as shown.

4. Repeat Exercise 1 for the South corridor elevation as shown.

5. Complete the South corridor with the information shown.

6-10. For each of the interior elevations indicated on the floorplan
      shown, develop an interior elevation.

14 Automation of Framing Plans

The automation of computer display of an architectural database to represent framing plans is one of the last general areas that will be discussed before the entire process is merged into layers. Two different types of framing will be presented in this chapter, concrete and steel. While this chapter is not intended to present the design considerations of concrete or steel, it does have rather detailed illustrations. The emphasis is on the display of the data, not on how to create the data. The data are generated during the structure design of a building, not the drafting-display portion. As in Chapter 13, entire sheet displays are used to illustrate various display techniques. These displays should be taken as typical and literal examples of framing plans.

DATABASE FOR
ROOF FRAMING

Framing plans involve such things as floor slabs, walls, and roofs. Figure 14.1 represents a window displayed in the upper left-hand corner of a drawing; it is a typical roof plan for a small structure. The 127 ft. by 47 ft. roof is displayed at the scale 1/8 in. = 1 ft. The plan is divided into three parts called data blocks 11, 12, and 13. A contraction joint is provided between each block. This joint is detailed A-A. Detail B-B is a display of type A framing members and how these members are structurally attached to the building walls. Thirty L 12 open web steel joists are used for the roof framing. See Figure 14.2.

317

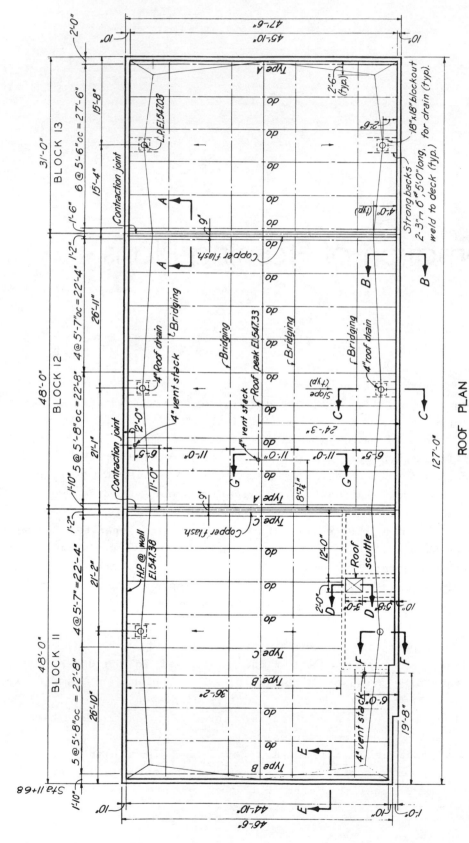

ROOF PLAN

SCALE: $\frac{1}{8}$" = 1'-0"

FIGURE 14.1 Typical roof plan for a small structure. (Courtesy of the U.S. Corps of Engineers, Vicksburg, Mississippi.)

318

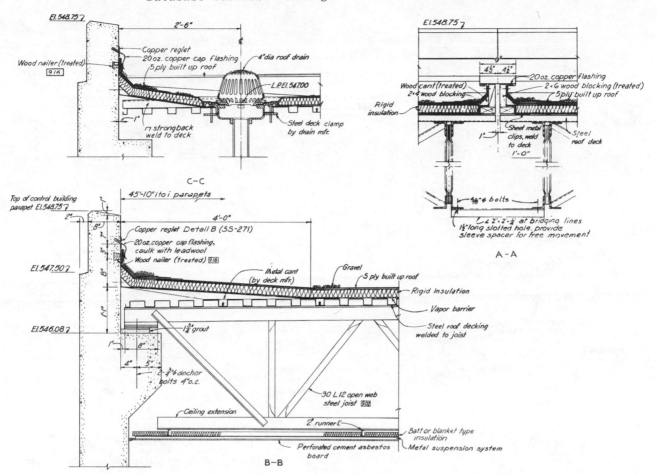

FIGURE 14.2 Windows showing details A-A, B-B, and C-C taken from roof plan. (Courtesy of the U.S. Corps of Engineers, Vicksburg, Mississippi.)

Detail C-C is taken through a roof drain on the roof plan and shown as a construction detail on the left-hand side of a drawing sheet. The roof drain is located with the type A framing members and is omitted here. Two other types of roof framing members are used. They are type B, modified A, and type C, which is also a modified A. The modifications are displayed at the lower right bottom of Figure 14.3. Each framing member is shown in the roof plan by a centerline, labeled type A, B, or C. To save display time the DO which represents ditto is employed.

The roof plan contains other framing members as well. Note that centerlines appear running perpendicular to the open web steel joists. These lines represent bridging, which is Ls welded to the joists. They are clearly detailed in E-E. Roof plans with associated framing details may be shown in steel or concrete.

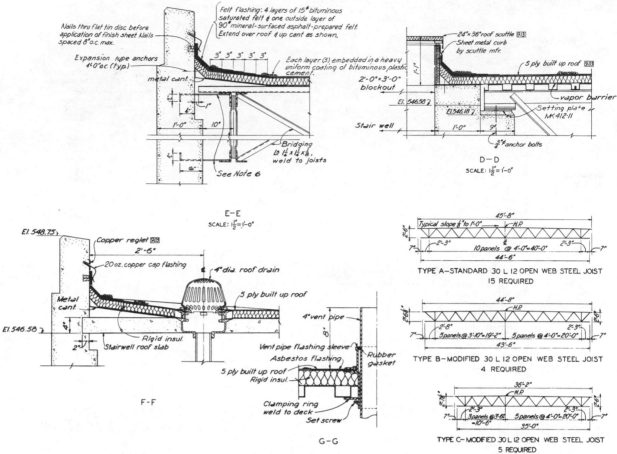

FIGURE 14.3   Details D, E, F, and G with open web steel details.
(Courtesy of the U.S. Corps of Engineers, Vicksburg, Mississippi.)

Roof and Wall Intersections

It is sometimes effective to show the intersection of roof framing
with wall members. This is particularly true around stairways and
open shafts. Figure 14.4 shows the roof framing over blocks 11 and
12. This area contains both an elevator shaft and a stairway. Five
floors join the openings, and the framing for the top four is clearly shown. In this example the reader can see the use of steel and
concrete framing. Note the use of steel supports under the elevator
machine room.

Figure 14.5 represents a section through the stairway to describe the wall framing. Note that in detail A a steel member marked
30 WF is placed on a concrete wall section. In section F-F the wall
framing along with the roof and floor is clearly illustrated. Openings in the roof can be described in these types of computer-generated details; see section J-J of Figure 14.5. In Figure 14.6 a
concrete roof slab is supported by steel framing. To study the

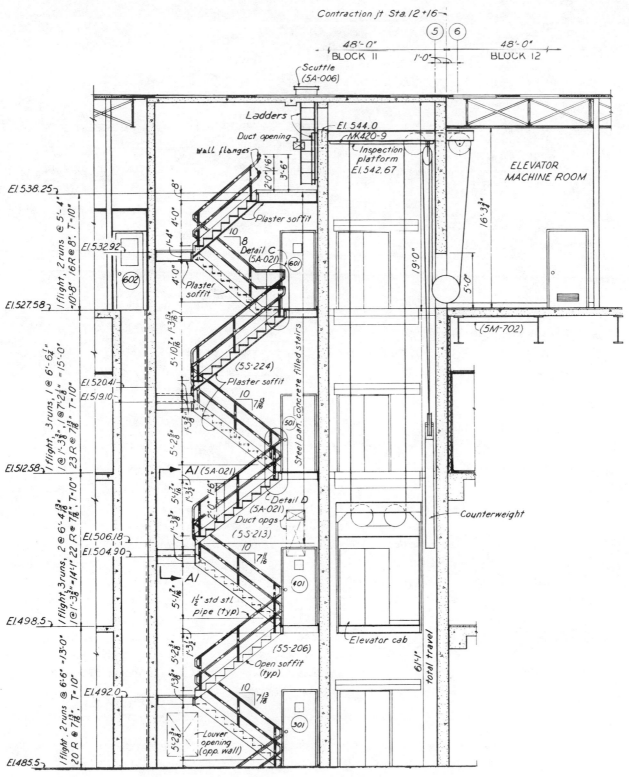

FIGURE 14.4 Roof and wall framing. (Courtesy of the U.S. Corps of Engineers, Vicksburg, Mississippi.)

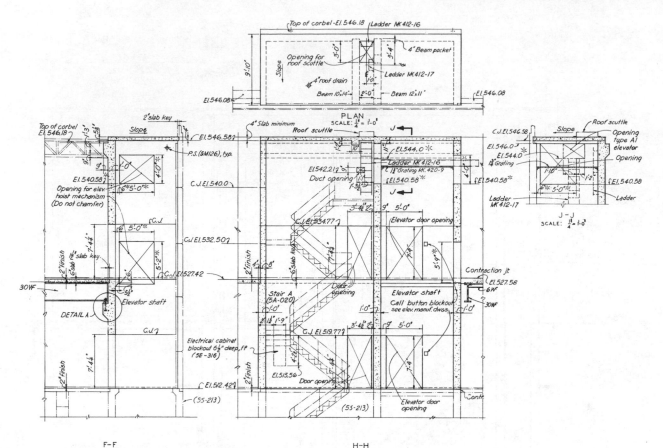

FIGURE 14.5   Section showing wall framing.   (Courtesy of the U.S. Corps of Engineers, Vicksburg, Mississippi.)

framing system more closely and display it separately, the concrete slab is removed from the database.   The display shown in Figure 14.7 is the result.   The careful reader will note that the building section in Figure 14.7 is adjacent to Figure 14.6 and not the same identical portion of the building.   The point to be made here is that it is possible to remove sections of the database to show items such as framing more clearly.   Note that in section B–B of Figure 14.7 the dashed line marked elevation 512.0 is where the top of the concrete roof or floor slab would be.   As shown, framing plans often include such things as fabrication details (shown in Figure 14.8) and design data (bearing capacities).

Structural Details for Roof Framing

At this point in the documentation of the framing plans it is often convenient to stop and prepare structural details of the framing

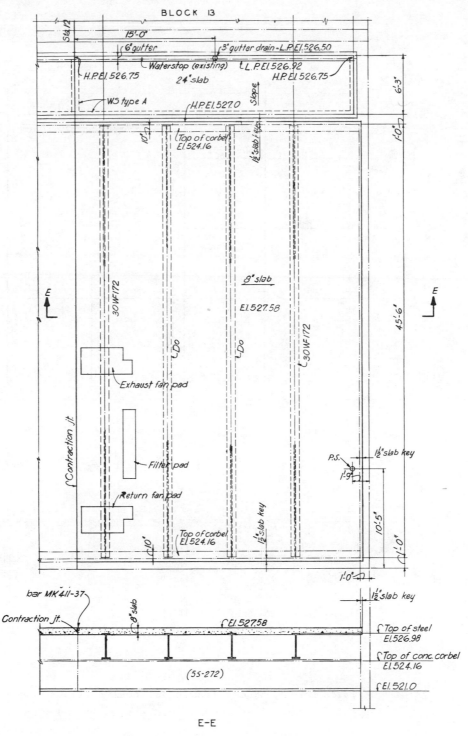

FIGURE 14.6 Concrete roof slab and steel framing. (Courtesy of the U.S. Corps of Engineers, Vicksburg, Mississippi.)

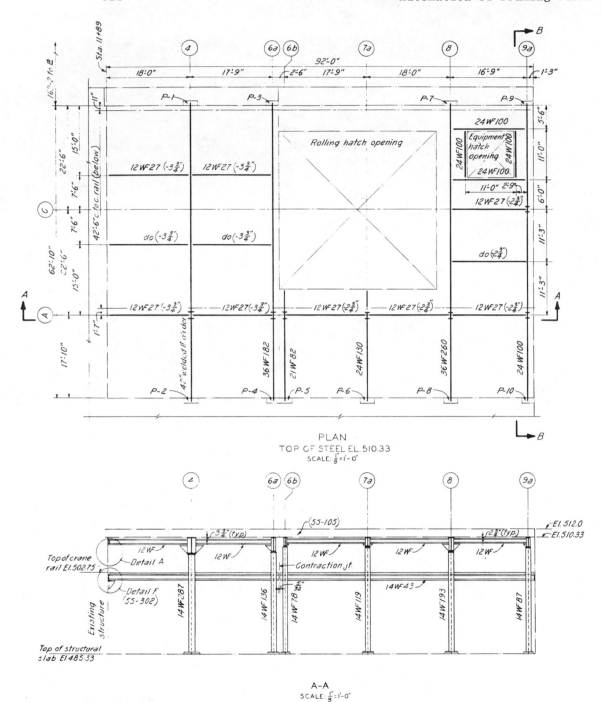

PLAN
TOP OF STEEL EL. 510.33
SCALE: $\frac{1}{8}$"=1'-0"

A-A
SCALE: $\frac{1}{8}$"=1'-0"

FIGURE 14.7 Steel framing without concrete slabs. (Courtesy of the U.S. Corps of Engineers, Vicksburg, Mississippi.)

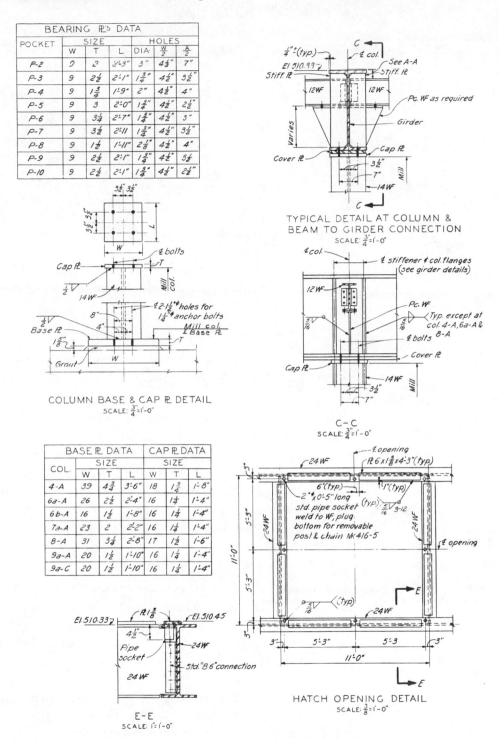

FIGURE 14.8 Fabrication details for framing connections. (Courtesy of the U.S. Corps of Engineers, Vicksburg, Mississippi.)

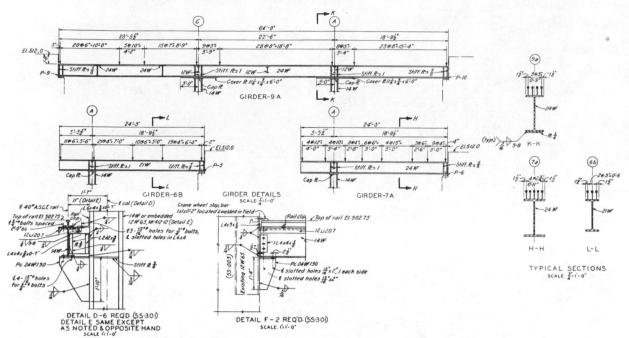

FIGURE 14.9 Steel framing details. (Courtesy of the U.S. Corps of Engineers, Vicksburg, Mississippi.)

members. In the case of the steel framing shown in Figure 14.9, it would be very easy to select the girders from the framing database. For our example we shall select girders 4, 6A, 6B, 7A, 8, and 9A. They are typical. The display is enlarged by changing the scale, and they are plotted as shown in Figure 14.10. At this larger scale it is easier to dimension and prepare structural details of the steel members.

DATABASE FOR FLOOR FRAMING

Building frames are not always structural steel, as can be seen in Figure 14.11. In this example, the same section of a proposed building (4 through 9a) has been designed for concrete framing. The display techniques are the same for steel and concrete, but the display image is different. Compare Figure 14.6 (steel framing) with Figure 14.11 (concrete). The display scale for Figure 14.11 has been increased; otherwise the display technique is similar. The continuation of framing in concrete involves other necessary items, however. Plain poured concrete is not used in floor framing; it must be reinforced with steel bars or other support techniques. In Figure 14.12 a poured slab for building sections 4 through 9a is supported by structural steel members. While this is a common practice in multifloor construction, it is expensive. Figure 14.13

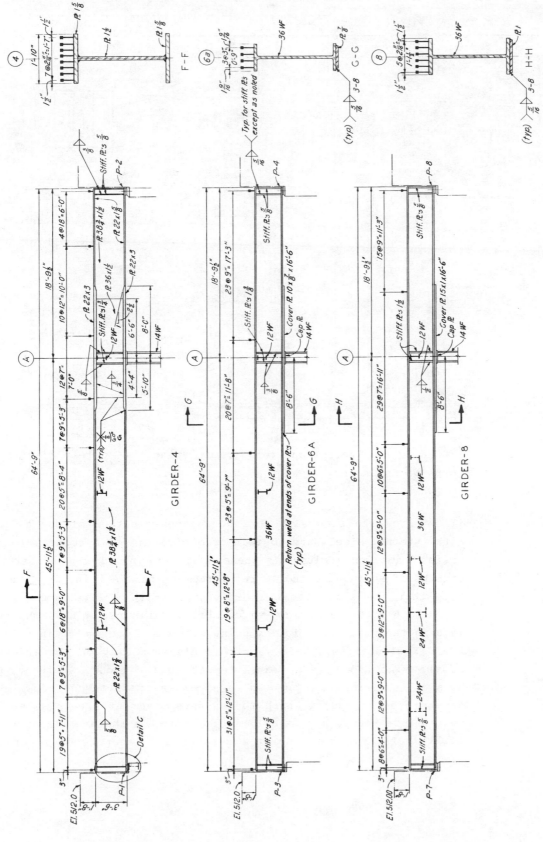

FIGURE 14.10 Continuation of Figure 14.9 (steel framing details). (Courtesy of the U.S. Corps of Engineers, Vicksburg, Mississippi.)

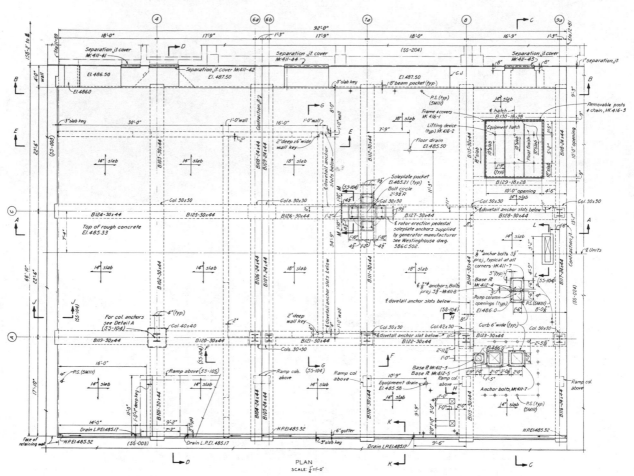

FIGURE 14.11   Typical concrete framing plan.   (Courtesy of the U.S. Corps of Engineers, Vicksburg, Mississippi.)

illustrates the same slab for the adjacent section of the building with internal steel bars to reinforce portions that connect to concrete beams and columns.   These bars are round and numbered in eighths of an inch.   A no. 8 reinforcement bar is 1 in. in diameter. Note that the slab itself is reinforced with a wire mesh.   It is noted as 6 by 6 -2/2 welded wire fabric.   This means that the openings in the grid are 6 in. by 6 in. with no. 2 gage wire in both the X and Y directions.   This fabric is placed midway on the thickness of the slab and to add reinforcement to the floor.   Reinforcement bars called *rebars* can be used in a number of different ways.   They can be used to add strength to concrete slabs at openings, at connections to beams, and at columns, as shown in the details of Figure 14.14.   The computer-generated details and general notes for con-

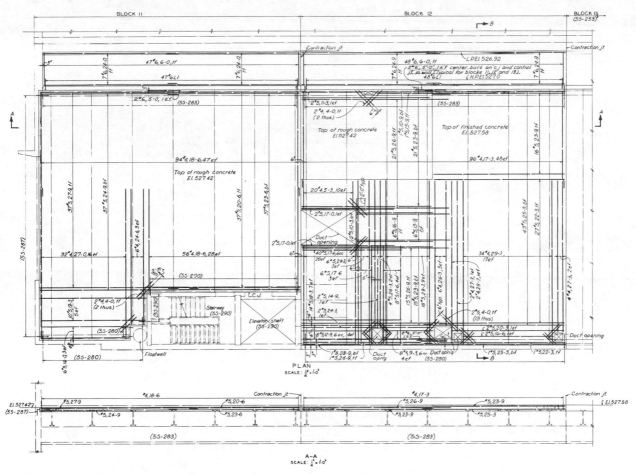

FIGURE 14.12 Typical reinforced concrete framing plan. (Courtesy of the U.S. Corps of Engineers, Vicksburg, Mississippi.)

crete reinforcement along with abbreviations and symbols are easy to display. The techniques from Chapter 3 are used to display items, as shown in Figure 14.15. Many items such as those shown in Figure 14.16 make reinforcement types and bending details easier. Typical reinforcement details as shown in Figure 14.17 can be stored and used in any of the later sheet displays for this chapter. When all the display techniques are used correctly, the reinforced concrete detailing is made straightforward as shown in Figure 14.18. In addition, Figure 14.11, which is a plain concrete slab, can be shown as a reinforced slab as per Figure 14.19. Note that the presentations for Figures 14.11 and 14.19 are related. Figure 14.11 contains several section cuts that must be detailed. Each of these may now be developed using the techniques of Figure 14.18.

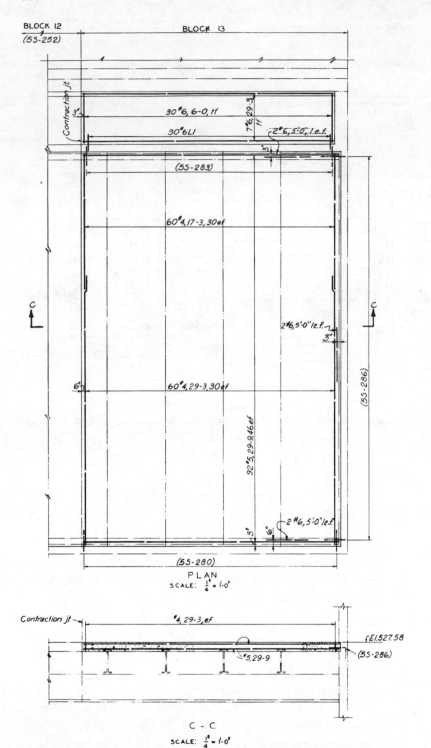

FIGURE 14.13 Details taken from Figure 14.12. (Courtesy of the
U.S. Corps of Engineers, Vicksburg, Mississippi.)

GENERAL NOTES FOR CONCRETE

1. Tool unprotected edges at all contraction joints on surfaces where wood float or steel trowel finish is required.
2. Provide $\frac{3}{4}$" chamfer for all exposed external corners unless otherwise noted.
3. Unless otherwise noted, provide V-groove joints as detailed on this drawing at all contraction joints and at construction joints and control joints where shown on drawings.
4. Interior exposed surface means interior surface subject to view.
5. Waterstops to be continuous.
6. Drawing references shown thus : 5S-120 represents drawing number HA5S-120, etc.
7. Items shown ☐ are payment items.
8. Wire fabric as required by specifications shall be provided in all seperate concrete floor finishes and be paid for under Item ☐4.08☐.

GENERAL NOTES FOR REINFORCEMENT

1. Laps to be 24 bar diameters minimum, except as noted.
2. Main reinforcement to have minimum clear cover as follows : (except as otherwise noted on drawings).
   (a) Bottom of foundation and footings 6"
   (b) Backfilled surfaces, surfaces of water passages 4"
   (c) Exterior faces of all walls and interior faces of walls over 2'-0" thick and exterior slabs 2"
   (d) Interior girders and columns 2"; interior beams $1\frac{1}{2}$".
   (e) Interior faces of walls 2'-0" or less and interior slabs 1"
3. Cover for secondary reinforcement (i.e. stirrups, column ties) may be reduced by the diameter of such bars, except where shown otherwise.
4. Where reinforcement in beams and girders is placed in 2 or more layers, the bars in upper layers shall be placed directly over those in the bottom layer
5. Items shown ☐ are payment items
6. Dimensions locating reinforcing bars from concrete lines or other bars will be to $\cancel{c}$ of bars unless designated as a "clear" distance.

CONCRETE FINISHES:

All formed concrete surfaces shall have finishes as follows:
Class A-A – All exterior surfaces above El. 512.0 .
Class A   – All exterior surfaces between El. 512.0 and El. 472.0 ; walls, columns, and ceiling, including sides and bottom of beams, in turbine room; interior walls, columns, and ceilings, including sides and bottoms of beams in the Control Building above El. 512.0 which are to receive no other finish; and walls of stairwell.
Class B   – Walls, columns, and ceilings, including sides and bottom of beams, in the Service Bay and Erection Bay; walls, columns, and ceilings, including sides and bottom of beams, in Control Building above El. 512.0 to have finishes other than exposed concrete; interior face of walls and ceiling of the cable tunnel; and exposed exterior surfaces below El. 472.0.
Class C   – Surfaces of water passages in draft tube.
Class D   – Surfaces which will not be exposed after completion of construction.

ABBREVIATIONS & SYMBOLS

CJ	Construction joint	Vo	Number
c to c	Center to center	oc	On center
₵	Center line	reinf	Reinforcement
dia	Diameter	R	Radius
dn	Down	std	Standard
dwg	Drawing	Sta	Station
El.	Elevation	sym	Symmetrical
ga	Gage	TW	Tailwater
HP	High point	typ	Typical
HW	Head water	VG	V-groove
LP	Low point	WL	Working line
max	Maximum	WP	Working point
min	Minimum	WS	Waterstop
NTS	Not to scale	NITC	Not in this contract
clr	Clear	₤	Base line
col	Column	conc	Concrete
proj	Projection	jt	Joint
fin	Finish	FD	Floor drain
reqd	Required	PS	Pipe sleeve

FIGURE 14.14 Typical concrete notes. (Courtesy of the U.S. Corps of Engineers, Vicksburg, Mississippi.)

REINFORCEMENT TYPES

TYPE	BENDING DIAGRAM
A	*A* — Std. hook
C	*A* — Std. hooks
D	B A B C
E	B A
F	A B D
H	A D
J	B A
L	A
S	B — Stirrup hooks, A
T	B — Column tie hooks, A

BENDING DETAILS

Std. 180° Hooks (6d for bars #2 to #7; 8d for bars #8 to 11)

Bar#	A
2	4"
3	5"
4	6"
5	7"
6	8"
7	10"
8	1'-1"
9	1'-3"
10	1'-5"
11	1'-7"

Stirrup & Column Tie 135° Hooks

Bar#	H	A
2	2¼"	3½"
3	2½"	4"
4	3"	5"
5	3¾"	6"

90° Bend (not hook) (D=6d for bars #2 to #7; D=8d for bars #8 to #11)

Bar#	D
2	1½"
3	2¼"
4	3"
5	3¾"
6	4½"
7	5¼"
8	8
9	9
10	10¼"
11	11¼"

TYPICAL — Standard size (minimum) pin used for bending

PIN DIA.	USE
6d 8d	Hooks and bends for main reinforcement
5d	Hooks on stirrups, hoops, ties, etc.
2d	Corner bends (other than hooks) in stirrups, hoops, ties, etc.

BAR DESIGNATION STANDARDS

TYPICAL BAR BILLING

STRAIGHT BARS

10 #6,2-0   8 #10,4-6
6oc   12oc,ff

BENT BARS

6 #8F2   12 #8H5
10oc,nf   15oc,6ef

STANDARD ABBREVIATIONS

ml = middle layer
ff = far face
tf = top face
el = each layer
oc = on center
ll = top layer
il = inside layer
nf = near face
bf = bottom face
ef = each face
bl = bottom layer
ol = outside layer
d = bar diameter

NOTES:
1. Feet and inch marks are omitted from length and spacing dimensions.
2. Bar spacings are in inches.
3. Straight bars are designated by size and length, i.e., #9,14-6. Bent bars are designated by size and type, i.e., #9A5. All bar designations will have a prefix corresponding to the reinforcement schedule in which they are listed, i.e., 55-120 #9,14-6 or 55-120 #9A5 are bars listed in reinforcement schedule No.55-120. Reinforcement schedules are given the same number as the drawing for which they list bars.

NOTE
Bar bending diagrams other than the above shall be detailed on the reinforcement schedule on which they are billed. The type marks for such bars shall be K,M,N,P,R,U,V etc. B & G symbols are reserved for beam and girder designations.

FIGURE 14.15 Reinforcement and bending details. (Courtesy of the U.S. Corps of Engineers, Vicksburg, Mississippi.)

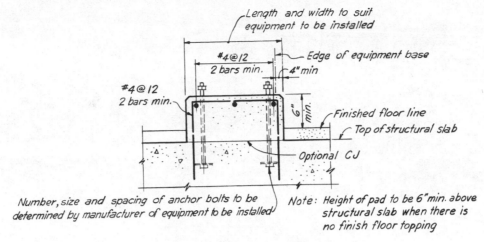

Length and width to suit
equipment to be installed

#4@12
2 bars min.

Edge of equipment base

4" min

#4@12
2 bars min.

6" min.

Finished floor line

Top of structural slab

Optional CJ

Number, size and spacing of anchor bolts to be
determined by manufacturer of equipment to be installed

Note: Height of pad to be 6" min. above
structural slab when there is
no finish floor topping

TYPICAL EQUIPMENT PAD DETAIL
(UNLESS OTHERWISE SHOWN)

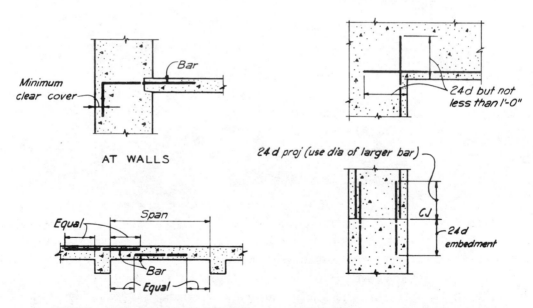

Minimum
clear cover

Bar

AT WALLS

24 d but not
less than 1'-0"

24 d proj (use dia of larger bar)

CJ

24 d
embedment

Equal

Span

Bar

Equal

OVER AND BETWEEN SUPPORTS

EMBEDMENT AND PROJECTION DETAILS

REINFORCEMENT DETAILS
TYPICAL PLACEMENT OF BARS UNLESS
OTHERWISE SHOWN ON DRAWINGS

FIGURE 14.16 Typical reinforcement details. (Courtesy of the U.S.
Corps of Engineers, Vicksburg, Mississippi.)

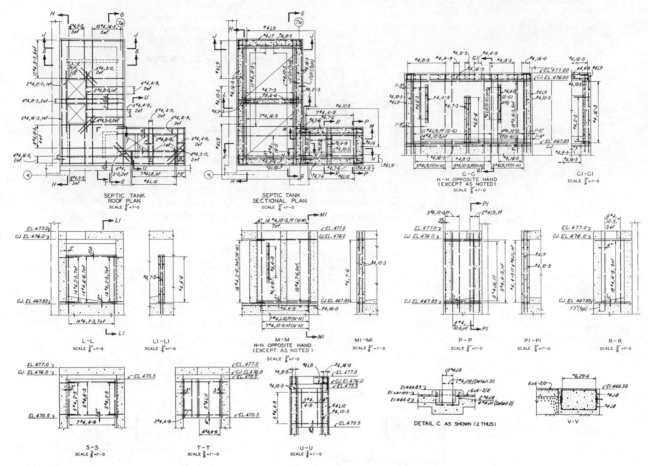

FIGURE 14.17 Complete framing and detailing sheet for reinforced concrete. (Courtesy of the U.S. Corps of Engineers, Vicksburg, Mississippi.)

Floor and Wall Framing

Just as roof and wall intersections were important in framing plans, so are floor and wall framing. This section parallels that of roof and walls but uses concrete framing instead of steel, shown earlier. Figure 14.20 is typical of floor and wall connections and parallels the output shown in Figure 14.7. Study these two figures for similar display techniques. Figure 14.21 is typical of the structural details necessary for reinforced concrete and parallels Figures 14.19 and 14.10 in steel. Both are beam and connection details.

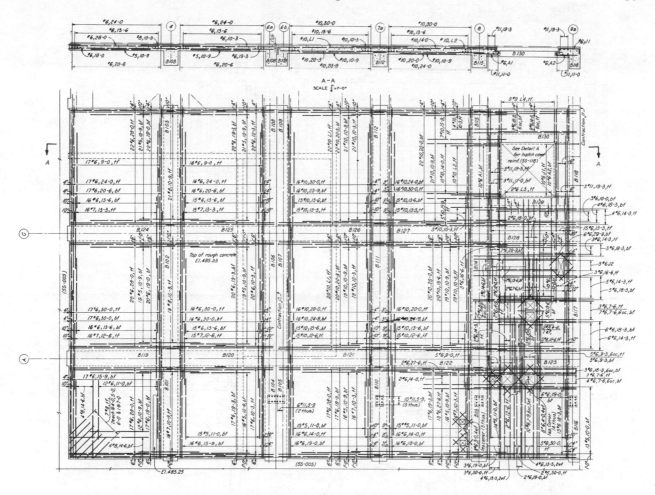

FIGURE 14.18 Reinforced concrete slab. (Courtesy of the U.S. Corps of Engineers, Vicksburg, Mississippi.)

Additional comparisons can also be made. Figure 14.22 is the database from Figure 14.12 with the reinforcing added. Section A-A is taken instead of B-B to represent an orthogonal relationship. Other sections are also taken: B-B, D-D, E-E, and F-F.

Structural Details for Floor and Wall Framing

In building details which describe framing in concrete it is not unusual to have 20 or 30 detail sheets. While this is normal in a complete set of architectural and engineering building drawings, it

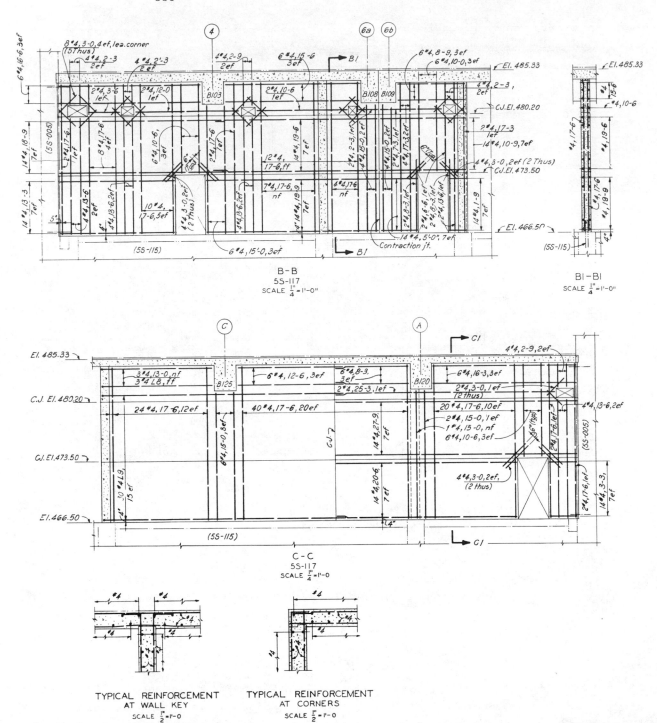

FIGURE 14.19 Typical floor and wann connections. (Courtesy of the U.S. Corps of Engineers, Vicksburg, Mississippi.)

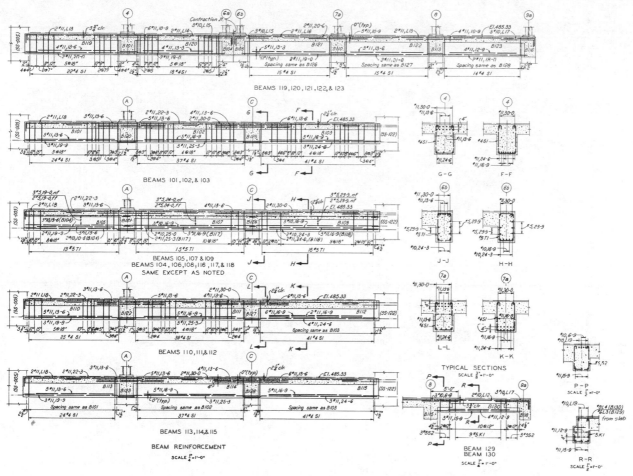

FIGURE 14.20 Structural details necessary for beam reinforcement. (Courtesy of the U.S. Corps of Engineers, Vicksburg, Mississippi.)

would be impossible in a reference text such as this. Therefore, Figure 14.21 will be used to demonstrate all structural details for floor and wall framing. Figure 14.22 represents the reinforcement necessary for girders G320, G321, and G322 of the building we have been discussing throughout the last several chapters. Girders rest on columns. Girders 320, 321, and 322 rest on columns 18 and 19. Columns and girders make up the heavy structural frame, and smaller concrete beams are used to interconnect the frame. Beams 356 through 366 are detailed in Figure 14.23.

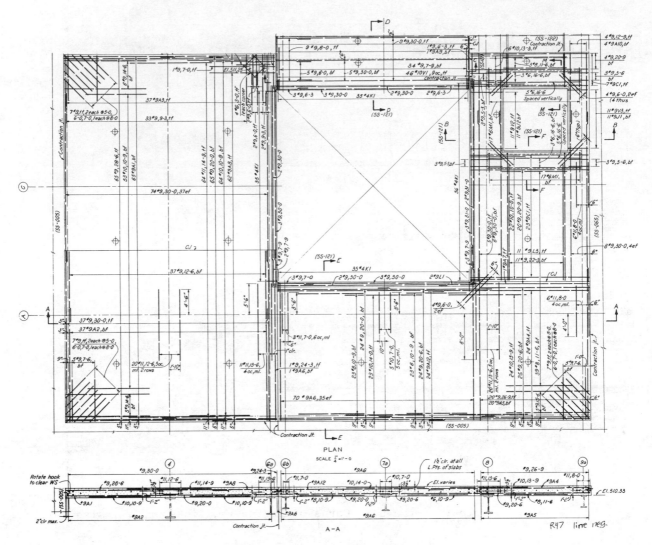

FIGURE 14.21 Database for the reinforcement of a typical concrete slab. (Courtesy of the U.S. Corps of Engineers, Vicksburg, Mississippi.)

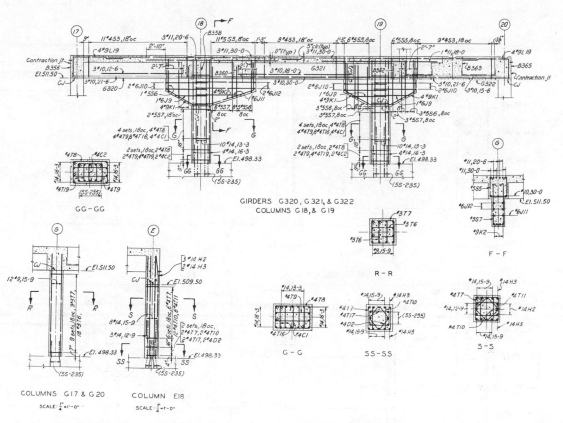

FIGURE 14.22 Reinforcement of girders G320, 21, and 22. (Courtesy of the U.S. Corps of Engineers, Vicksburg, Mississippi.)

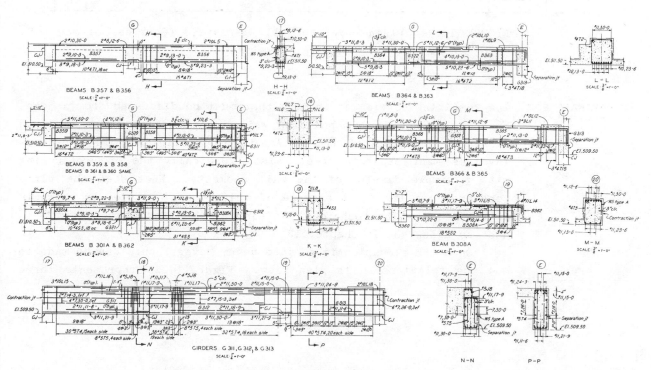

FIGURE 14.23 Beams 356 through 366. (Courtesy of the U.S. Corps of Engineers, Vicksburg, Mississippi.)

339

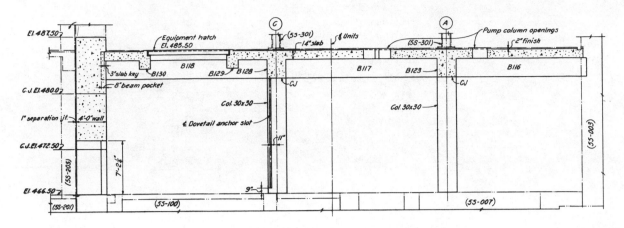

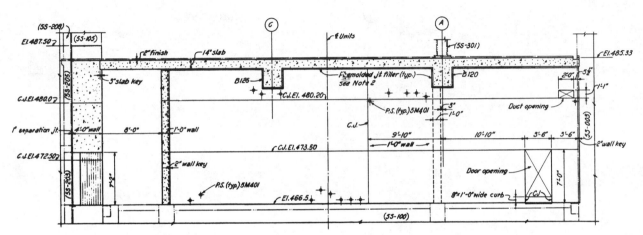

FIGURE 14.24   Plain concrete wall displays.   (Courtesy of the U.S. Corps of Engineers, Vicksburg, Mississippi.)

DATABASE FOR WALL FRAMING

The remaining portion of framing that must be discussed from a database standpoint is the building walls. A database is created and displayed for each of the walls in the building. This process involves many separate sheets also. Basically the process begins with a simple display of the wall geometry. What does the plain concrete look like? An example of this type of display is shown in Figure 14.24. The technique for displaying interior elevations is used as discussed in Chapter 13.

Once the elevation is decided upon, several cuts can be made to see the relationship in plan view. Figure 14.25 represents three

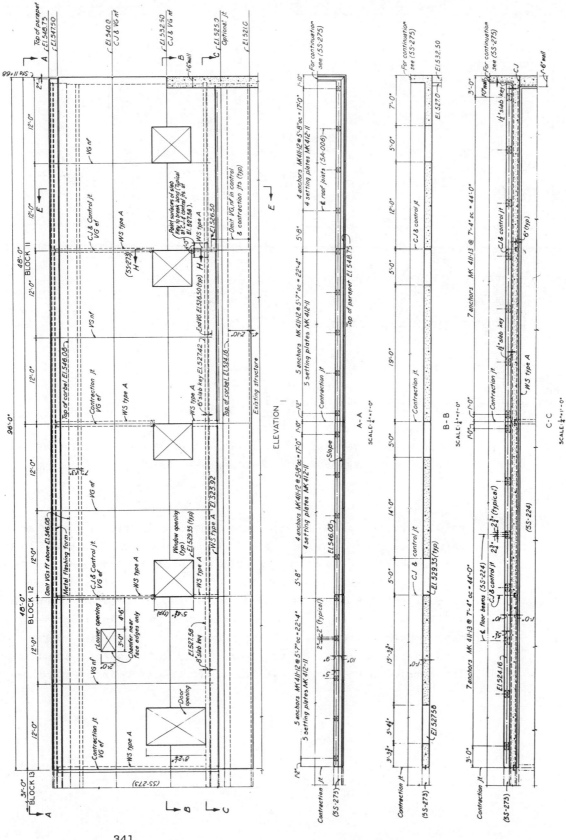

FIGURE 14.25 Trial cuts of a wall in elevation. (Courtesy of the U.S. Corps of Engineers, Vicksburg, Mississippi.)

341

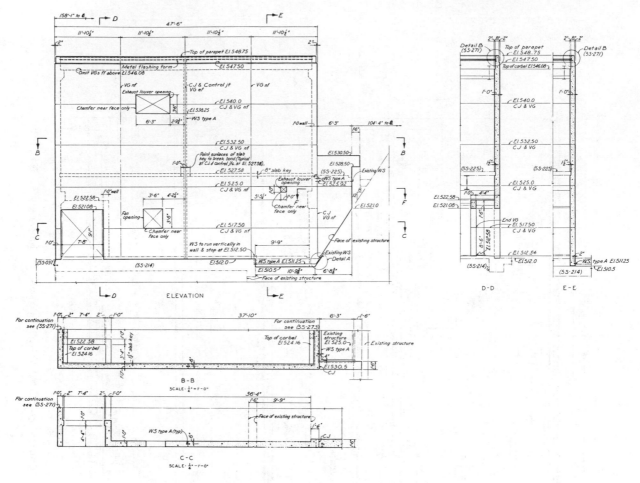

FIGURE 14.26   Vertical reinforcement in walls.   (Courtesy of the
U.S. Corps of Engineers, Vicksburg, Mississippi.)

trial cuts of a wall in elevation.   From this typical wall sections
can be generated.   Figure 14.26 illustrates wall sections D-D and
E-E taken from elevation and plan views of the concrete wall under
consideration.   Just as in the floor slabs, walls must be reinforced.   Figure 14.27 represents this vertical reinforcement in the
walls; this figure is parallel to Figure 14.14 for floor reinforcement.   The complete set of reinforcement is shown in   Figure 14.28
this figure is parallel to Figure 14.19 for floors.   At this point
the working area of the CRT is so crowded that information must be

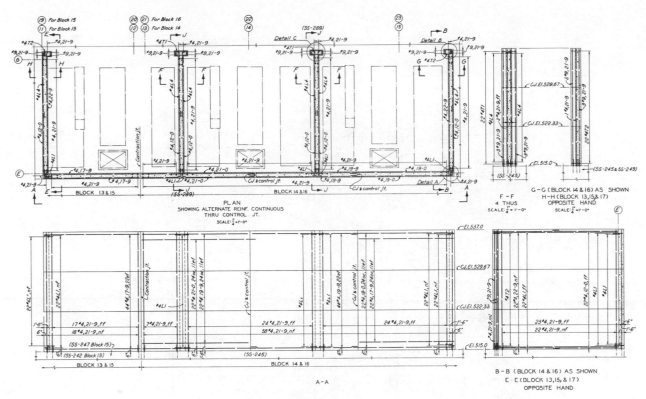

FIGURE 14.27 Wall framing details. (Courtesy of the U.S. Corps of Engineers, Vicksburg, Mississippi.)

assigned to different layers for storage and later recall. The basic techniques of layering are discussed in Chapter 15.

CHAPTER SUMMARY   Twenty-nine sheets of framing information are used to illustrate this chapter. Figures 14.1–14.9 were used to illustrate the database for roof framing plans, sections, elevations, and details. Figures 14.9–14.19 were used to illustrate the database for floor framing techniques. Both structural steel and concrete framing data were used, with frequent comparisons of the two methods.

Figures 14.20–14.28 were used to show wall framing techniques that can be displayed from a common database. While these illustrations are quite involved, they do represent the display power of an automated architectural database. The reader must keep in mind that framing techniques are natural extensions of Chapters 12 and 13. In

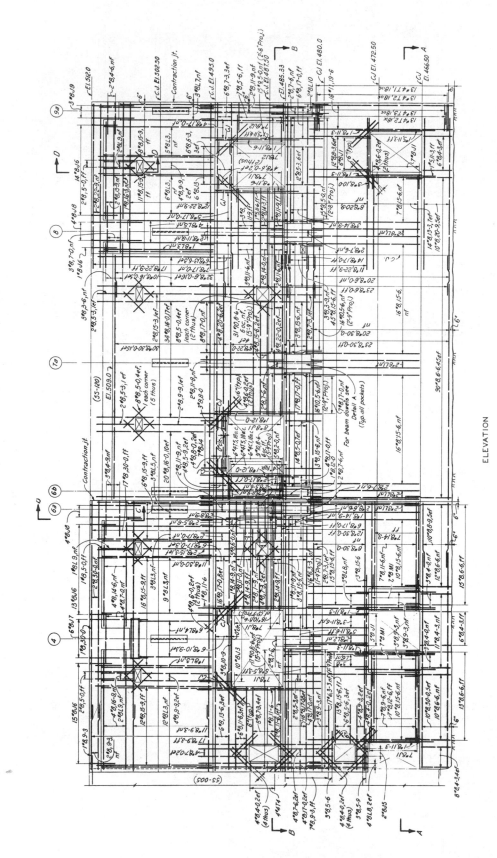

ELEVATION

FIGURE 14.28 Complete set of reinforcement. (Courtesy of the U.S. Corps of Engineers, Vicksburg, Mississippi.)

344

fact no one chapter can be taken from the whole and used to explain computer-aided architectural graphics. Only the first 14 chapters can be used to do this, for they are interrelated and represent how computer-aided architectural graphics can be used in a typical design situation.

EXERCISES 1. Roof plans are shown in Figure 14.1; digitize this plan for storage. Recall it and make modifications to the exterior wall at data block 13 as shown.

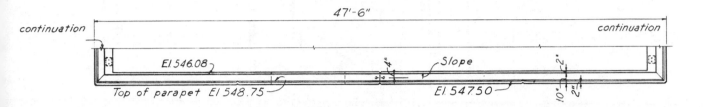

2. Framing details for roof plans often show how structural framing is connected to walls as in Sections E-E and D-D of Figure 14.3. In these cases, open web steel joists are used as roof members. Detail a connection for solid I beam connections as shown.

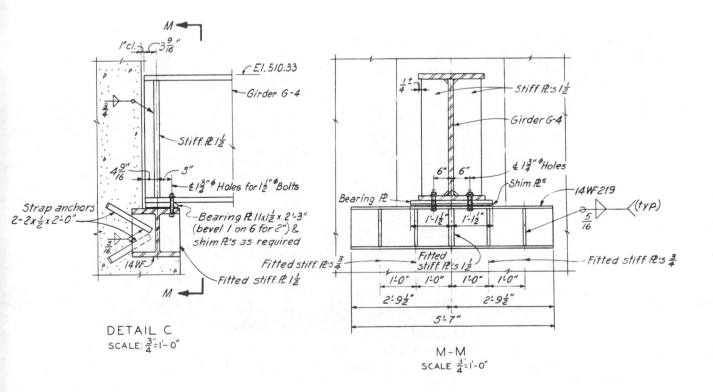

3.   In Figure 14.4 the framing for four floors and the wall connec-
     tions with the roof is clearly shown. For this exercise,
     complete the framing diagram for Figure 14.4 as shown.

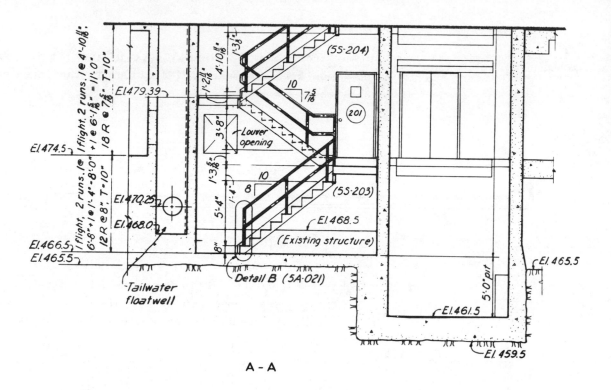

A - A

4.   Enlarge detail A shown in Figure 14.5 to include the items
     shown.

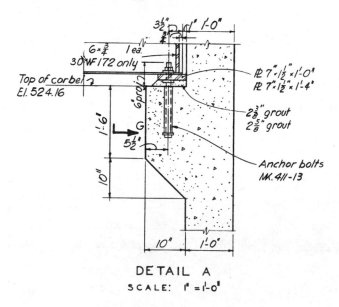

DETAIL A
SCALE: 1" = 1'-0"

5. Provide for section cut B-B from Figure 14.7 to be displayed as shown.

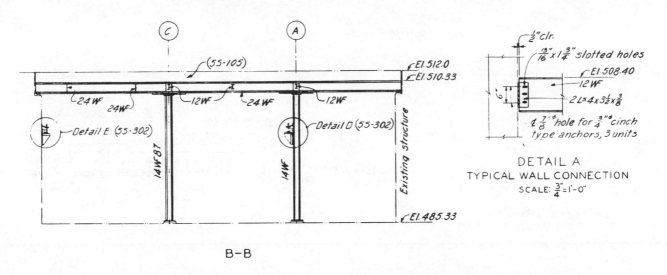

B-B

6. Generate additional fabrication details to accompany Figure 14.8 as shown.

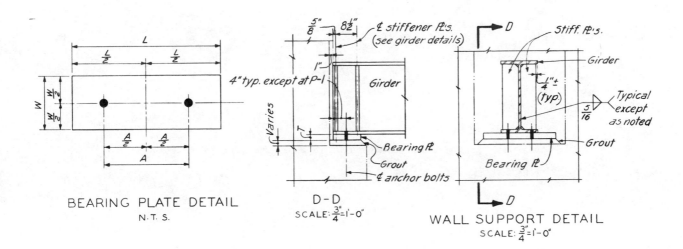

7.   Add the accompanying fabrication detail in Figures 14.9 and
      14.10.

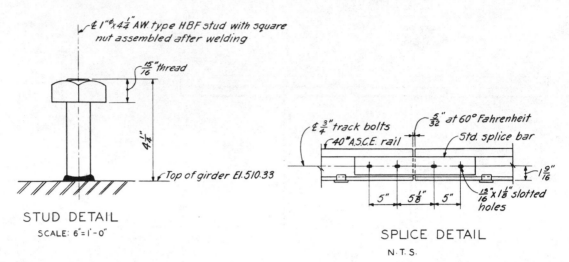

STUD DETAIL

SCALE: 6"=1'-0"

SPLICE DETAIL

N.T.S.

8. Develop a framing elevation for Figure 4.11 at section cut A-A
    as shown.

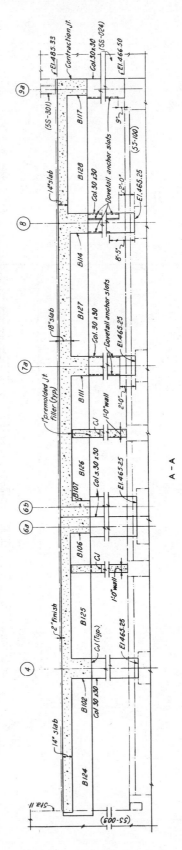

9.   Develop a reinforced framing section as per B-B in Figure 14.13
     and as shown.

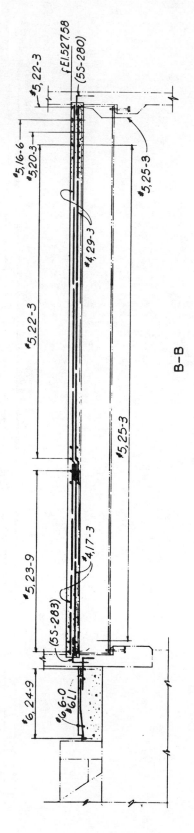

10. Add the accompanying typical reinforcement to those shown in Figure 14.17 and here.

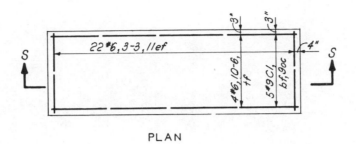

PLAN

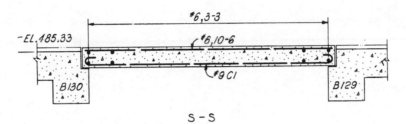

S – S

DETAIL A
HATCH COVER REINFORCEMENT

15 Layering Concepts for Related Diagrams

The basic techniques for layered drawings were introduced in Chapter 6 along with sample programs for gathering data representing each layer. As pointed out in Chapter 6, the purpose for layered drawings is related to the concept of windowing. Different windows are the contributions of the specialists, which include the architect, designer, technician, and detailer. In some cases, one person may often function in more than one capacity and develop ideas for more than one window, particularly in a small design project. On large projects, like those described in Chapters 10-14, the practice is to isolate design functions and activities to a single layer. An example of separate layers for a large project might be as follows:

1. Site description
    a. Property description and neighborhood planning
    b. Topo drawing
    c. Streets, sidewalks, and curbs
    d. Parking and recreation areas
2. Floorplans and sections
    a. Working drawings showing floor patterns
    b. Dimensions and notations
    c. Section generation
3. Foundation plans
    a. Footing notes
    b. Placement details

> 4.   Section and profiles
>   a.   Wall and building sections
>   b.   Construction detail

Each of these layers was described using a windowed drawing approach.

Because of the extensive education and experience with layering methods, the designer or architect acted as a team leader with the advice and representation of the project owner throughout the layering stages. The mechanical group leader was responsible for the planning and layering of the project plumbing, heating, ventilation, and other mechanical systems. The electrical group leader produced the layering for the necessary circuits and fixtures for power, lighting, fire alarm, and clock systems, the intercom, and the telephone system.

The architect, together with the design engineer and approval of the owner, prepared the site data to begin the layers needed. From these data, draftspersons prepared other layers for the entire project. The concept of layering and its speed of production by computer assistance was extremely important throughout Chapters 8-10 and 12-14 and will reduce the costs for the entire building program.

Most building projects involve four layering stages:

> 1.   Preliminary plan sheets
> 2.   Display of single-view drawings
> 3.   Preparation of specifications, dimensions, or descriptions of the single views
> 4.   Scheduling and management of the actual project.

It is not the purpose of this chapter to provide a detailed treatise of construction aspects but simply to present to the student of modern architectural graphics an overview of the main elements of layering and in particular how to generate a single layer.

PRELIMINARY LAYERS

The first layer of any project consists of gathering and analyzing the data for computer input. The data-gathering techniques are called the database formation and will be used in establishing certain premises on which the layering will be based. This is a joint function of the owner, architect, and designers. It includes data-defining space requirements, and then computer passes can be made to determine various factors of the project, such as type of structure, location and orientation of the building, availability of utilities, topography, traffic pattern of surrounding streets, and project costs.

At this layer level budget problems are of primary concern and probably will remain the overriding factor throughout the entire layering operation, since the available funding must be correlated

with space requirements and the current square foot cost for construction. A computer program cost calculation is determined for
the total project area by continually updating material and labor
costs which determine the cost factor. Most often the owner seeks a
building which is more elaborate than the budget can support. It
is, therefore, important that a computerized approach to cost factoring be used so that running costs and future projections are as
accurate as possible so that the owner and project manager can
balance needs and the available budget.

Further economic advantages exist with layering because the
owner will always have expenses other than those of construction
costs, for example, the cost for the use of construction equipment,
site development such as grading and paving, storage of materials,
and the like. To assist the project manager in forecasting these
costs, a computer approach as shown in Figure 15.1 is used. This

```
      CCCCCCCCCCCCCCCCCCCCCCCCCCCCCCCCCCCCCCCCCCCCCCCCCCCCCCCCCCCCCCC
      C  THIS IS A VERSION OF .MY WITH SUB. SYES IN IT..          C
      C                       AND BLOCKED COMMON'S...             C
      CCCCCCCCCCCCCCCCCCCCCCCCCCCCCCCCCCCCCCCCCCCCCCCCCCCCCCCCCCCCCCC
0001          COMMON /FLAGS/NVIEW, FLAG, NWHAT, NONCE
      C..........................................................
0002          COMMON /ANSWER/AA(9)
0003          CALL INITT(120)
0004          CALL PLOTS
      C..........................................................
      C  IF NEW BUILDINGS WERE INPUT   READ OLD SITE DATA.  .
      C..........................................................
0005          CALL SITDAT(1)
0006          CALL SETUP
0007          CALL NEWPAG
0008          CALL ANMODE
0009          CALL DAYDAT
      C..........................................................
      C  DETERMINE WHERE THE USER NEEDS TO GO AT THE START OF THE PROGRAM.
      C..........................................................
0010          DO 1 I=100,500,100
0011          IF(I.EQ.100) WRITE(3,100)
0012          IF(I.EQ.200) WRITE(3,200)
0013          IF(I.EQ.300) WRITE(3,300)
0014          IF(I.EQ.400) WRITE(3,400)
0015          IF(I.EQ.500) WRITE(3,500)
0016          CALL ANBELL
0017          READ(1,10)XX
0018          IF(XX.EQ.AA(1).AND.I.EQ.100) CALL INTRO
0019          IF(XX.EQ.AA(1).AND.I.EQ.200) CALL LISTS
0020          IF(XX.EQ.AA(1).AND.I.EQ.300) CALL POINTS
0021          IF(XX.EQ.AA(2).AND.I.EQ.400) CALL NEWLNS
0022          IF(XX.EQ.AA(2).AND.I.EQ.500) CALL NEWBUI(1)
0023    1     CONTINUE
0024          CALL NEWSCA
      C..........................................................
      C  NOW LET USER PLACE CONSTRUCTION EQUIPMENT ON SITE  .
      C     PLAN THROUGH INTERACTIVE GRAPHICS              .
      C..........................................................
0025          CALL EQUSIT
      C..........................................................
      C  BY NOW THE USER HAS A WELL DEVELOPED SITE PLAN AND  .
      C     CAN NOW ADD OR CHANGE ANY PREVIOUS INPUTS        .
      C..........................................................
0026    2     CONTINUE
0027          CALL CHANGS
      C..........................................................
      C  AFTER CHANGES OR ADDITIONS THE USER MAY REVIEW THOSE.
      C     MODIFICATIONS IF HE CHOOSES.                     .
      C..........................................................
0028          CALL REVIEW
0029          CALL ANMODE
```

FIGURE 15.1   Example computer program for construction equipment.

```
0030                        WRITE(3,1000)
0031                        CALL ANBELL
0032                        READ(1,10)XX
0033                        IF(XX.EQ.AA(1)) FLAG=6.
0034                        IF(XX.EQ.AA(1)) CALL EQUSIT
0035                        WRITE(3,700)
0036                        CALL ANBELL
0037                        READ(1,10)XX
0038                        IF(XX.EQ.AA(1)) GO TO 2
             C.......................................................
             C  AT THIS POINT THE INTERACTIVE SESSION IS COMPLETE   .
             C     THE USER WILL NOW VIEW ALL FIVE VIEWS.            .
             C.......................................................
0039                        WRITE(3,900)
0040                        CALL ANBELL
0041                        READ(1,10)XX
0042                        IF(XX.EQ.AA(2)) GO TO 3
0043                        CALL ALLDON
0044                        CALL ANMODE
0045              3         CONTINUE
0046                        WRITE(3,1010)
0047                        CALL ANBELL
0048                        READ(1,20)NPLOT
             C.............................................
0049                        CALL NEWPAG
0050                        CALL ANMODE
0051                        WRITE(3,600)
             C.............................................
             C  THE PROGRAM IS NOW COMPLETE AND THE INPUTS ARE TO  .
             C     BE STORED IN TEMPORARY DATASETS.                 .
             C.............................................
0052                        CALL SITDAT(2)
             C.............................................
0053                        WRITE(3,800)
0054              100       FORMAT(/T4,'IS THIS YOUR FIRST TIME?  IF SO, YOU"LL NEED AN',
                          +' INTRODUCTION.')
0055              200       FORMAT(/T4,'DO YOU WANT HARD COPIES OF THE BUILDINGS, EQUIPMENT,',
                          +' AND VIEWS',/,T3,' AVIALABLE TO YOU?')
0056              300       FORMAT(/T4,'DO YOU WANT NEW SITE POINTS?')
0057              400       FORMAT(/,T4,'HAVE YOU INPUTED OR DO YOU "NOT" WANT ANY ',
                          +'LINE SEGMENTS?')
0058              500       FORMAT(/,T4,'HAVE YOU INPUT    ANY BUILDINGS AT ALL?')
0059              600       FORMAT(///,70('='),//,T8,
                          +'ALL OF YOUR INPUTS HAVE NOW BEEN STORED IN YOUR PERMANENT',/,
                          +T8,'DATA FILES.  YOU CAN RETURN TO THE PROGRAM AT A LATER DATE',
                          +/,T8,'WITHOUT HAVING TO REINPUT THE DATA.',//,
                          +T8,'THANK YOU FOR YOUR TIME AND PATIENCE.',//,70('='),//////)
0060              700       FORMAT(//,T4,'WOULD YOU LIKE ANY MORE CHANGES, ADDITIONS,',
                          +' OR FILES DISPLAYED?')
0061              800       FORMAT(//////////////.'ENTER "C"')
0062              900       FORMAT(//,T4,'DO YOU WISH TO SEE ALL FIVE VIEWS DISPLAYED?')
0063              1000      FORMAT(//,T4,'WOULD YOU LIKE TO ADD ANY MORE EQUIPMENT?')
0064              1010      FORMAT(//,T4,'ARE THESE TO BE 12"(1) OR 36"(2) PLOTS?')
0065              10        FORMAT(A4)
0066              20        FORMAT(I1)
0067                        CALL PLOT(0.,0.,999)
0068                        CALL FINITT(300,0)
0069                        STOP
0070                        END
0001                        SUBROUTINE SITDAT(NGS)
             CCCCCCCCCCCCCCCCCCCCCCCCCCCCCCCCCCCCCCCCCCCCCCCCCCCCCCCCCCCCCCCCCCCCCCCCCCC
             C                                                                       C
             C   MOST OF THE DATA INPUTED TO THE PROGRAM IS SAVED AND READ           C
             C          FROM THIS SUBROUTINE.   THE VARIABLES :                      C
             C                                                                       C
             C          NRECB  = NUMBER OF RECTANGLES                                C
             C          NCIRB  = NUMBER OF CIRCULAR BUILDINGS                         C
             C          NEQUI  = NUMBER OF PIECES OF EQUIPMENT                        C
             C          NLN    = NUMBER OF LINE SEGMENTS                              C
             C          VARIABLES FOR RECTANGLAR BUILDINGS                           C
             C          VARIABLES FOR CIRCULAR BUILDINGS                             C
             C          VARIABLES FOR LINE SEGMENTS                                  C
             C                                                                       C
             CCCCCCCCCCCCCCCCCCCCCCCCCCCCCCCCCCCCCCCCCCCCCCCCCCCCCCCCCCCCCCCCCCCCCCCCCCC
0002                        COMMON /RECS/XLLC(999),ZLLC(999),HTR(999),THETA(999),
                          +WID(999),NTITLR(3,999),BASER(999),DP(999)
0003                        COMMON /CIRS/XMID(999),ZMID(999),HTC(999),NTITLC(3,999),
                          +BASEC(999),RAD(999)
0004                        COMMON /COUNTS/IRB(999),ICB(999),IBRC(999),IT(999)
0005                        COMMON /MACHIN/NX,NEQ(999),XE(999),ZE(999),W(999)
0006                        COMMON /LINESG/NLINE(99),PLSX(99,9),PLSY(99,9),PLSZ(99,9),
                          +ILIN(99,9)
```

FIGURE 15.1. (Continued)

```
0007                    COMMON /NUMBER/NRECB,NCIRB,NDATA,NLN,NEQUI,NPLOT
0008                    COMMON /CALCOM/THETE,GAMMA,Q,NAME(1,13),WORK(20),DUMMY(1)
0009                    IF(NGS.EQ.1) GO TO 100
0010                    IF(NGS.EQ.2) GO TO 200
0011           100      CONTINUE
0012                    REWIND 21
0013                    REWIND 22
0014                    REWIND 25
0015                    REWIND 23
0016                    REWIND 26
0017                    READ(25,1)NRECB,NCIRB,NEQUI,NLN,Q,THETE,GAMMA,NPLOT
0018                    IF(NRECB.EQ.0) GO TO 10
0019                    DO 10 K=1,NRECB
0020                    READ(21,2)K,(NTITLR(I,K), I=1,3),IRB(K)
0021                    READ(21,3)XLLC(K),ZLLC(K),WID(K),DP(K),HTR(K),THETA(K),BASER(K)
0022           10       CONTINUE
0023                    IF(NCIRB.EQ.0) GO TO 20
0024                    DO 20 J=1,NCIRB
0025                    READ(22,2)J,(NTITLC(II,J), II=1,3),ICB(J)
0026                    READ(22,4)XMID(J),ZMID(J),RAD(J),HTC(J),BASEC(J)
0027           20       CONTINUE
0028                    IF(NLN.EQ.0) GO TO 70
0029                    READ(26,5)NLN
0030                    DO 70 J=1,NLN
0031                    READ(26,6)NLINE(J)
0032                    NLINES=NLINE(J)
0033                    DO 80 K=1,NLINES
0034                    READ(26,7)PLSX(J,K),PLSY(J,K),PLSZ(J,K),ILIN(J,K)
0035           80       CONTINUE
0036           70       CONTINUE
0037                    IF(NEQUI.EQ.0) RETURN
0038                    DO 90 I=1,NEQUI
0039                    READ(23,8)NEQ(I),XE(I),ZE(I),W(I)
0040           90       CONTINUE
0041                    RETURN
0042           200      CONTINUE
0043                    REWIND 21
0044                    REWIND 22
0045                    REWIND 25
0046                    REWIND 26
0047                    REWIND 23
0048                    GAMMA=90.00-GAMMA
0049                    IF(Q.EQ.9999.) Q=5.00
0050                    WRITE(25,1)NRECB,NCIRB,NEQUI,NLN,Q,THETE,GAMMA,NPLOT
0051                    IF(NRECB.EQ.0) GO TO 30
0052                    DO 30 K=1,NRECB
0053                    WRITE(21,2)K,(NTITLR(I,K), I=1,3),IRB(K)
0054                    WRITE(21,3)XLLC(K),ZLLC(K),WID(K),DP(K),HTR(K),THETA(K),BASER(K)
0055           30       CONTINUE
0056                    IF(NCIRB.EQ.0) GO TO 40
0057                    DO 40 J=1,NCIRB
0058                    WRITE(22,2)J,(NTITLC(II,J), II=1,3),ICB(J)
0059                    WRITE(22,4)XMID(J),ZMID(J),RAD(J),HTC(J),BASEC(J)
0060           40       CONTINUE
0061                    IF(NLN.EQ.0) GO TO 50
0062                    WRITE(26,5)NLN
0063                    DO 50 J=1,NLN
0064                    WRITE(26,6)NLINE(J)
0065                    NLINES=NLINE(J)
0066                    DO 60 K=1,NLINES
0067                    WRITE(26,7)PLSX(J,K),PLSY(J,K),PLSZ(J,K),ILIN(J,K)
0068           60       CONTINUE
0069           50       CONTINUE
0070                    IF(NEQUI.EQ.0) GO TO 91
0071                    DO 91 I=1,NEQUI
0072                    WRITE(23,8)NEQ(I),XE(I),ZE(I),W(I)
0073           91       CONTINUE
0074                    RETURN
0075           1        FORMAT(4I10,3F10.3,I2)
0076           2        FORMAT(I3,3A4,I5)
0077           3        FORMAT(7F9.3)
0078           4        FORMAT(5F10.3)
0079           5        FORMAT(I10)
0080           6        FORMAT(I5)
0081           7        FORMAT(3F10.3,I3)
0082           8        FORMAT(I2,3F10.3)
0083                    END
0001                    SUBROUTINE SETUP
0002                    COMMON /CALCOM/THETE,GAMMA,Q,NAME(1,13),WORK(20),DUMMY(1)
0003                    COMMON /PLOTIT/ANG,XP(1100),YP(1100),ZP(1100),IPP(1100)
0004                    ANG=30.00
0005                    THETE=120.0
```

FIGURE 15.1. (Continued)

```
0006                GAMMA=50.0
0007                Q=9999.
0008                RETURN
0009                END
0001                SUBROUTINE INTRO
0002                CALL NEWPAG
0003                CALL ANMODE
0004                WRITE(3,1)
0005          1     FORMAT(/,70('.'),/'.',T70,'.',/'.',T29,
                   +'INTRODUCTION',T70,'.',/,
                   +'.',T70,'.',/,70('.')///)
0006                WRITE(3,2)
0007          2     FORMAT(/,
                   +T8,'THIS IS AN INTERACTIVE PROGRAM TO AID A SITE DEVELOPER IN'/
                   +,T8,'DRAWING BUILDINGS AND PIECES OF CONSTRUCTION EQUIPMENT ON'/
                   +,T8,'A PROPOSED SITE.  THE PLANNER SHOULD HAVE A PREPARED PLAN'/
                   +,T8,'ALREADY SKETCHED OUT AND BUILDINGS LABLED.  THE "OBJECTS"'/
                   +,T8,'AS THEY MIGTH BE CALLED CAN BE MADE BY USING RECTANGLES '/
                   +,T8,'AND CIRCLES IN THREE DIMENSIONS.  THE AXISES ARE "Z" FOR '/
                   +,T8,'DEPTH, "X" FOR WIDTH OR LENGTH, AND "Y" FOR HIEGHT.   ',
                   +'ALL'/,T8,'OF THE DATA DEVELOPED BY THIS PROGRAM IS STORED IN'/
                   +,T8,'YOUR TEMPORARY LIBRARY, AND CAN THEN BE VIEWED AT ANY LATER'/
                   +,T8,'DATE WITH OUT REINPUTING.  ALSO WHEN FIVE BELLS ARE SIG-'/
                   +,T8,'NALED AND A "PAUSE" APEARS YOU SHOULD READ AND OR COPY '/
                   +,T8,'THE INFORMATION AND HIT RETURN.  FIVE BELLS SIGNALS YOU '/
                   +,T8,'THAT NO INPUT IS NECCESSARY.'//
                   +,T8,'NUMBERS ARE PLACED UNDER EITHER --- OR ---.-.  THE FIRST '/
                   +,T8,'BEING FOR INTEGERS AND THE LATER FOR REAL NUMBERS.  SINGLE'/
                   +,T8,'DIGIT NUMBERS SHOULD BE PLACED UNDER THE RIGHT MOST MARK'/
                   +,T8,'FOR INTEGERS.  NO INPUTS MAY BE INPUTED LARGER THAN THE '/
                   +,T8,'GIVEN SPACE.'//
                   +,T8,'>>>>>>>GOOD LUCK AND KEEP YOUR EARS ON<<<<<<<'//)
0008                CALL BELLS(5)
0009                CALL ANMODE
0010                PAUSE
0011                CALL NEWPAG
0012                CALL ANMODE
0013                RETURN
0014                END
0001                SUBROUTINE LISTS
0002                CALL NEWPAG
0003                CALL ANMODE
0004                WRITE(3,1)
0005          1     FORMAT(//,T8,
                   +'THE FOLLOWING IS A LIST OF BUILDING AREAS WHICH CAN BE CAL-',
                   +/,T8,'CULATED FOR YOU.  AN ASTERISK INDICATES A ',
                   +'FINISHED BUILDING.'//)
0006                WRITE(3,2)
0007          2     FORMAT('*1   JOB OFFICE'/'*2   CRAFT CHANGHOUSE-CIVIL'/'*3   CRAFT CH
                   +ANGEHOUSE-MECH.'/'*4   CRAFT CHANGEHOUSE-PIPPING'/'*5   CRAFT CHANGE
                   +HOUSE-ELEC.'/' 6   TIME OFFICE'/' 7   BRASS ALLEY '/' 8   SANITARY FA
                   +CILITIES'/' 9   ELECTRICAL WAREHOUSE'/' 10 MECHANICAL WAREHOUSE'/'
                   +11 INSTRUMENTATION WAREHOUSE'/' 12 WAREHOUSE OFFICE'/' 13 ELECTRIC
                   +AL FABRICATION SHOP'/' 14 MECHANICAL FABRICATION SHOP'/' 15 CARPEN
                   +TRY FABRICATION SHOP'/' 16 STORAGE STAGING AREA'/' 17 ELECTRICAL S
                   +TORAGE FACILITY'/' 18 MECHANICAL STORAGE FACILITY'/' 19 INSTRUMENT
                   +ATION STROAGE FACILITY'/' 20 STRUCTURAL SHORT TERM LAYDOWN AREA')
0008                CALL HDCOPY
0009                CALL NEWPAG
0010                CALL ANMODE
0011                WRITE(3,8)
0012                WRITE(3,3)
0013          3     FORMAT(' 21 CONCRETE PIPE SHORT TERM LAYDOWN AREA'/' 22 LUMBER SHO
                   +RT TERM LAYDOWN AREA'/' 23 STRUCTURAL LONG TERM LAYDOMN AREA'/' 24
                   + CONCRETE PIPE LONG TERM LAYDOWN AREA'/' 25 LUMBER LONG TERM LAYDO
                   +WN AREA'/' 26 CONCRETE TEST SHOP  '/' 27 MATERIALS TEST SHOP'/' 28
                   + TEST SHOP'/' 29 WELD TEST SHOP'/' 30 EQUIPMENT MAINTENANCE SHOP'/
                   +'*31 CRAFT PARKING LOT'/'*32 OFFICE PARKING LOT'/' 33 OWNER PARKIN
                   +G LOT'/' 34 ACCESS ROAD '/' 35 BATCH PLANT'/' 36 RAILROAD SPUR'/'
                   +37 PAINT SHOP'/' 38 SANDBLASTING SHOP/AREA'/' 39 CAMP LIVING FACIL
                   +ITY'/' 40 TRAILOR LIVING FACILITY'/' 41 MEDICAL/FIRST AID FACILITY
                   +'/' 42 REBAR SHOP'/' 43 MAIN GATE GUARD HOUSE'/' 44 PAYROLL OFFICE
                   +'/' 45 WATER TREATMENT PLANT'/' 46 PUMP HOUSE'/' 47 EXPLOSIVE STRO
                   +AGE SHED'/' 48 ICE PLANT')
0014                CALL HDCOPY
0015                CALL NEWPAG
0016                CALL ANMODE
0017                WRITE(3,4)
0018          4     FORMAT(//,T8,
                   +'THIS IS A LIST OF DIGITIZED CONSTRUCTION EQUIPMENT AVAILABLE',
                   +/,T8,'TO YOU.'//)
0019                WRITE(3,5)
```

FIGURE 15.1. (Continued)

```
0020        5    FORMAT(' 1  3-WHEEL ROLLER'/' 2  POWER SHOVEL'/' 3  DRAGLINE'/' 4
                +  CABLE-CONTROLLED BULLDOZER'/' 5  HOE'/' 6  GRADER'/' 7  DUMP TRUC
                +K'/' 8  CLAMSHELL'/' 9  PLATFORM'/'10  TRACTOR AND SCRAPER')
0021             WRITE(3,6)
0022        6    FORMAT(//,T8,
                +'THERE ARE FIVE VIEW TYPES AVAILABLE, THE FIRST FOUR ARE FROM',
                +/,T8,
                +'THE "CLEMSON UNIVERSITY PICTORIAL IMAGE DRAWING-V1" (CUPID1).',
                +/,T8,
                +'THE FIFTH VIEW IS FROM THE "CALCOMP SOFTWARE" PACKAGE.'//)
0023             WRITE(3,7)
0024        7    FORMAT(' 1   TOP'/' 2  FRONT'/' 3  PROFILE'/' 4   PICTORIAL',
                +/' 5  "CALCOMP THREED" PERSPECTIVE VIEW')
0025        8    FORMAT(/////)
0026             CALL HDCOPY
0027             CALL NEWPAG
0028             CALL ANMODE
0029             RETURN
0030             END
0001             SUBROUTINE POINTS
     CCCCCCCCCCCCCCCCCCCCCCCCCCCCCCCCCCCCCCCCCCCCCCCCCCCCCCCCCCCCCCCCCC
     C                                                                C
     C    THIS SUBROUTINE STEPS USER THROUGH THE SITE PERIMETER, AND   C
     C         ASKS FOR NUMBER OF SITE POINTS TO DEFINE THE PERIMETER, C
     C         WHAT THE UNITS ARE, AND THE SITE COORDINATES.           C
     C                                                                C
     CCCCCCCCCCCCCCCCCCCCCCCCCCCCCCCCCCCCCCCCCCCCCCCCCCCCCCCCCCCCCCCCCC
0002             COMMON /BOUNDS/X(999),Z(999),IPOINT,IUNIT
0003             CALL NEWPAG
0004             CALL ANMODE
0005             WRITE(3,4)
0006        4    FORMAT(/,70('.'),/'.',T70,'.',/'.',T27,
                +'NEW SITE POINTS',T70,'.',/,
                +'.',T70,'.',/,70('.')///)
0007             WRITE(3,1)
0008        1    FORMAT(T8,'DEFINE THE BOUNDARY OF THE SITE'//,T8,
                +'INPUT THE NUMBER OF POINTS CONNECTING EACH STRAIGHT LINE'/
                +,T8,'SEGMENT.  FOR EXAMPLE, FOUR DIFFERENT X-Z COORDINATES'/
                +,T8,'SHOULD BE INPUTED FOR A RECTANGULAR SITE.'//,T8,
                +'HOW MANY X-Z COORDINATES ARE THERE?',/'---')
0009             CALL ANBELL
0010             READ(1,50)IPOINT
0011             WRITE(3,2)
0012        2    FORMAT(/,T8,'ARE COORDINATES IN FEET(1) OR METERS(2)?')
0013             CALL ANBELL
0014             READ(1,51)IUNIT
0015             WRITE(3,3)
0016        3    FORMAT(/,T8,'NOW INPUT THE SITE POINTS OF THE X-Z PLANE IN ',
                +'EITHER A'/,T8,'CLOCKWISE OR COUNTER-CLOCKWISE FASHION.',
                +'  THE BELL WILL'/,T8,'PROMT YOU AND HIT RETURN FOR EACH PAIR.'/,
                +'   X          Z    '/'----.-- ----.--')
0017             Y=0.
0018             IPT=IPOINT+1
0019             II=3
0020             WRITE(24,61)IPT,IUNIT
0021             DO 10 I=1,IPOINT
0022               CALL ANBELL
0023               READ(1,52)X(I),Z(I)
0024               WRITE(24,59)X(I),Y,Z(I),II
0025               II=2
0026       10    CONTINUE
0027             WRITE(24,59)X(1),Y,Z(1),II
0028       50    FORMAT(I3)
0029       51    FORMAT(I1)
0030       52    FORMAT(2F7.2)
0031       59    FORMAT(3F10.3,I3)
0032       61    FORMAT(2I5)
0033             CALL NEWPAG
0034             CALL ANMODE
0035             RETURN
0036             END
0001             SUBROUTINE NEWLNS
     CCCCCCCCCCCCCCCCCCCCCCCCCCCCCCCCCCCCCCCCCCCCCCCCCCCCCCCCCCCCCCCCCC
     C                                                                C
     C    LINE SEGMENTS DRAWN ON THE SITE ARE DIGITIZED THROUGH        C
     C         THE USE OF THIS SUBROUTINE.                             C
     C                                                                C
     CCCCCCCCCCCCCCCCCCCCCCCCCCCCCCCCCCCCCCCCCCCCCCCCCCCCCCCCCCCCCCCCCC
0002             COMMON /LINESG/NLINE(99),PLSX(99,9),PLSY(99,9),PLSZ(99,9),
                +ILIN(99,9)
0003             COMMON /NUMBER/NRECB,NCIRB,NDATA,NLN,NEQUI,NPLOT
0004             COMMON /ANSWER/AA(9)
```

FIGURE 15.1. (Continued)

```
0005                    CALL NEWPAG
0006                    CALL ANMODE
0007                    WRITE(3,4)
0008            4       FORMAT(/,70('.'),/'.',T70,'.',/'.',T28,
                       +'LINE SEGMENTS',T70,'.',/,
                       +'.',T70,'.',/,70('.')//)
0009                    WRITE(3,1)
0010            1       FORMAT(//,T8,'HOW MANY LINE SEGMENTS ARE THERE?',/,'--')
0011                    CALL BELLS(1)
0012                    CALL ANMODE
0013                    READ(1,10)NLN
0014                    IF(NLN.LT.1) GO TO 300
0015                    KOUNT=0
0016            2       FORMAT(/,'NOW INPUT NUMBER OF POINTS FOR LINE NO.',
                       +I3,/,'-')
0017                    CALL NEWPAG
0018                    CALL ANMODE
0019                    DO 100 I=1,NLN
0020                    KOUNT=KOUNT+1
0021                    IL=3
0022                    WRITE(3,2)I
0023                    CALL BELLS(1)
0024                    CALL ANMODE
0025                    READ(1,30)NLINE(I)
0026                    NLINES=NLINE(I)
0027                    WRITE(3,3)
0028                    WRITE(3,5)
0029                    DO 200 K=1,NLINES
0030                    ILIN(I,K)=IL
0031                    IL=2
0032            200     CONTINUE
0033                    CALL BELLS(1)
0034                    CALL ANMODE
0035                    READ(1,20)(PLSX(I,K), K=1,NLINES)
0036                    WRITE(3,6)
0037                    CALL BELLS(1)
0038                    CALL ANMODE
0039                    READ(1,20)(PLSZ(I,K), K=1,NLINES)
0040                    WRITE(3,7)
0041                    CALL BELLS(1)
0042                    CALL ANMODE
0043                    READ(1,20)(PLSY(I,K), K=1,NLINES)
0044                    IF(KOUNT.LT.3) GO TO 100
0045                    KOUNT=0
0046                    CALL NEWPAG
0047                    CALL ANMODE
0048            100     CONTINUE
0049            300     CONTINUE
0050            3       FORMAT('PTS',T5,'1',T13,'2',T21,'3',T29,'4',T37,'5',T45,'6',
                       +T53,'7',T61,'8',T69,'9')
0051            5       FORMAT('X',9('----.--  '))
0052            6       FORMAT('Z',9('----.--  '))
0053            7       FORMAT('Y',9('----.--  '))
0054                    CALL NEWPAG
0055                    CALL ANMODE
0056            10      FORMAT(I2)
0057            20      FORMAT(9(F7.2,1X))
0058            30      FORMAT(I1)
0059            40      FORMAT(A4)
0060                    RETURN
0061                    END
0001                    SUBROUTINE NEWBUI(ISEE)
                CCCCCCCCCCCCCCCCCCCCCCCCCCCCCCCCCCCCCCCCCCCCCCCCCCCCCCCCCCCCCCCCCCCC
                C                                                                  C
                C    THIS SUBROUTINE IS USED TO DEVELOPE NEW BUILDINGS.            C
                C                                                                  C
                CCCCCCCCCCCCCCCCCCCCCCCCCCCCCCCCCCCCCCCCCCCCCCCCCCCCCCCCCCCCCCCCCCCC
0002                    COMMON /COUNTS/IRB(999),ICB(999),IBRC(999),IT(999)
0003                    COMMON /NUMBER/NRECB,NCIRB,NDATA,NLN,NEQUI,NPLOT
0004                    COMMON /ANSWER/AA(9)
0005                    GO TO (1111,9001), ISEE
0006            1111    CONTINUE
0007                    NCIRB=0
0008                    NRECB=0
0009                    CALL NEWPAG
0010                    CALL ANMODE
0011                    WRITE(3,1)
0012            1       FORMAT(/,T4,'DO YOU WANT ANY PRE-CALCULATED BUILDINGS?')
0013                    CALL ANBELL
0014                    READ(1,52)XNAN
0015                    IF(XNAN.EQ.AA(1)) CALL SYES
0016                    CALL ANMODE
```

FIGURE 15.1. (Continued)

```
0017                    WRITE(3,90)
0018            90      FORMAT(/,T8,'HOW OTHER BUILDINGS ARE THERE?'/'---')
0019                    CALL BELLS(1)
0020                    CALL ANMODE
0021                    READ(1,50)IBUILD
0022                    IF(IBUILD.EQ.0) RETURN
0023                    DO 9001 J=1,IBUILD
0024                    CALL NEWPAG
0025                    CALL ANMODE
0026                    WRITE(3,100) J
0027           100      FORMAT(/,T8,
                       +'BUILDING NUMBER',I3,/,T8,
                       +'IS THIS A CIRCULAR(1) OR RECTANGULAR(2) BUILDING?')
0028                    CALL BELLS(1)
0029                    CALL ANMODE
0030                    READ(1,51) NCOR
0031                    IF(NCOR.EQ.2)GO TO 5001
0032                    CALL CIRBUI(J)
0033                    IBRC(J)=2
0034                    IT(J)=NCIRB
0035                    GO TO 9001
0036          5001      CALL RECBUI(J)
0037                    IBRC(J)=1
0038                    IT(J)=NRECB
0039          9001      CONTINUE
0040            42      IF(NRECB.EQ.0) GO TO 21
0041                    IF(NRECB.EQ.1) GO TO 22
0042                    NCOUNT=1
0043                    NREC=NRECB-1
0044                    DO 20 IDO=1,NREC
0045                    NCOUNT=NCOUNT+1
0046                    CALL CHEREC(NCOUNT,IDO)
0047            20      CONTINUE
0048            22      IF(NCIRB.EQ.0) GO TO 41
0049                    DO 30 JDO=1,NRECB
0050                    CALL CHRECI(JDO)
0051            30      CONTINUE
0052                    IF(NCIRB.EQ.1) GO TO 41
0053            21      NCOU=1
0054                    NCIR=NCIRB-1
0055                    DO 40 NDO=1,NCIR
0056                    NCOU=NCOU+1
0057                    CALL CHECIR(NCOU,NDO)
0058            40      CONTINUE
0059            41      CALL NEWPAG
0060                    CALL ANMODE
0061            50      FORMAT(I3)
0062            51      FORMAT(I1)
0063            52      FORMAT(A4)
0064                    RETURN
0065                    END
0001                    SUBROUTINE NEWSCA
               CCCCCCCCCCCCCCCCCCCCCCCCCCCCCCCCCCCCCCCCCCCCCCCCCCCCCCCCCCCCCCCCCCCCCC
               C                                                                    C
               C       THE SCALES FOR FITTING THE SITE PLAN TO THE TEKTORNICS SCREEN  C
               C          ARE CALCULATED HERE.                                       C
               C                                                                    C
               C          SCALE = THE SCALE USED IN TOP, FRONT, AND PROFILE VIEWS   C
               C          SCALE2= THE SCALE USED FOR THE PICTORIAL AND "THREED"      C
               C          X     = ARRAY CONTAINING "X" COORDINATES OF SITE          C
               C          Z     = ARRAY CONTAINING "Z" COORDINATES OF SITE          C
               C          NPERM = FILE NUMBER FOR SITE POINTS                        C
               C          IUNIT = 1 FOR FEET OR 2 FOR METERS                         C
               C                                                                    C
               CCCCCCCCCCCCCCCCCCCCCCCCCCCCCCCCCCCCCCCCCCCCCCCCCCCCCCCCCCCCCCCCCCCCCC
0002                    COMMON /RECS/XLLC(999),ZLLC(999),HTR(999),THETA(999),
                       +WID(999),NTITLR(3,999),BASER(999),DP(999)
0003                    COMMON /CIRS/XMID(999),ZMID(999),HTC(999),NTITLC(3,999),
                       +BASEC(999),RAD(999)
0004                    COMMON /BOUNDS/X(999),Z(999),IPOINT,IUNIT
0005                    COMMON /SUBSCA/SCALE,SCALE2,XBIG,ZBIG,YBIG
0006                    REWIND 24
0007                    READ(24,61)IPOINT,IUNIT
0008                    DO 7 K=1,IPOINT
0009                    READ(24,59)X(K),Y,Z(K),I
0010             7      CONTINUE
0011                    XBIG=0.00
0012                    ZBIG=0.00
0013                    DO 2 NA=1,IPOINT
0014                    IF(XBIG.GT.X(NA)) GO TO 1
0015                    XBIG=X(NA)
0016             1      IF(ZBIG.GT.Z(NA)) GO TO 2
```

FIGURE 15.1. (Continued)

```
0017                ZBIG=Z(NA)
0018        2       CONTINUE
0019                XSCALE=1023.00/XBIG
0020                ZSCALE=700.00/ZBIG
0021                IF(XSCALE.LT.ZSCALE)GO TO 3
0022                SCALE=ZSCALE
0023                GO TO 4
0024        3       SCALE=XSCALE
0025        4       CONTINUE
0026                XSCAL2=780.00/XBIG
0027                ZSCAL2=425.00/ZBIG
0028                IF(XSCAL2.LT.ZSCAL2)GO TO 5
0029                SCALE2=ZSCAL2
0030                GO TO 6
0031        5       SCALE2=XSCAL2
0032        6       CONTINUE
0033                YBIG=0.00
0034                IF(NRECB.EQ.0) GO TO 8
0035                DO 8 NA=1,NRECB
0036                IF(YBIG.LT.HTR(NA)) YBIG=HTR(NA)
0037        8       CONTINUE
0038                IF(NCIRB.EQ.0) GO TO 9
0039                DO 9 NA=1,NCIRB
0040                IF(YBIG.LT.HTC(NA)) YBIG=HTC(NA)
0041        9       CONTINUE
0042                YBIG=XBIG/17.
0043                XBIG=XBIG+30.00
0044                ZBIG=ZBIG+50.00
0045        59      FORMAT(3F10.3,I3)
0046        61      FORMAT(2I5)
0047                RETURN
0048                END
0001                SUBROUTINE EQUSIT
            CCCCCCCCCCCCCCCCCCCCCCCCCCCCCCCCCCCCCCCCCCCCCCCCCCCCCCCCCCCCCCCCCCCCCC
            C                                                                    C
            C    THIS IS AN INTERACIVE SUBROUTINE TO PERMIT THE USER TO PLACE     C
            C        CONSTRUCTION EQUIPMENT ON THE SITE PLAN WHERE HE CHOOSES     C
            C        , IF HE IS NOT SATISFIED WITH THE POSITION HE MAY MOVE       C
            C        IT.  ONCE HE IS "HAPPY" THE PIECE AND POSITION WILL BE       C
            C        STORED IN A FILE.                                            C
            C                                                                    C
            CCCCCCCCCCCCCCCCCCCCCCCCCCCCCCCCCCCCCCCCCCCCCCCCCCCCCCCCCCCCCCCCCCCCCC
0002                COMMON /FLAGS/NVIEW,FLAG,NWHAT,NONCE
0003                COMMON /PLOTIT/ANG,XP(1100),YP(1100),ZP(1100),IPP(1100)
0004                COMMON /MACHIN/NX,NEQ(999),XE(999),ZE(999),W(999)
0005                COMMON /NUMBER/NRECB,NCIRB,NDATA,NLN,NEQUI,NPLOT
0006                COMMON /GOTIT/A(90),B(90),C(90),IN(90),WHERE,XSITE,
            +ZSITE
0007                COMMON /ANSWER/AA(9)
0008                CALL ANMODE
0009                WRITE(3,11)
0010        11      FORMAT(/T4,'HAVE YOU INPUTED ANY EQUIPMENT?')
0011                CALL ANBELL
0012                READ(1,55)XNEWEQ
0013                IF(XNEWEQ.EQ.AA(2)) NEQUI=0
0014                IF(FLAG.EQ.6.) GO TO 100
0015                WRITE(3,1)
0016        1       FORMAT(/T4,'DO YOU WANT NEW EQUIPMENT?')
0017                CALL ANBELL
0018                READ(1,55)XNEWEQ
0019                IF(XNEWEQ.EQ.AA(2)) RETURN
0020        100     CONTINUE
0021                NEQUI=NEQUI+1
0022                CALL NEWPAG
0023                CALL ANMODE
0024                CALL BELLS(1)
0025                WRITE(3,2)
0026        2       FORMAT(//T8,'SELECT PIECE OF EQUIPMENT YOU WISH TO',
            +' VIEW'/'--')
0027                CALL ANMODE
0028                READ(1,57)NX
0029        200     CONTINUE
            C       IF(XNEWEQ.EQ.AA(2)) GO TO 300
0030                CALL ANMODE
0031                WRITE(3,3)
0032        3       FORMAT(/T8,'WHERE DO YOU WANT TO PLACE THE EQUIPMENT TO?'/
            +/'    X         Z   '/'----.-- ----.--')
```

FIGURE 15.1. (Continued)

```
0033                    CALL ANBELL
0034                    READ(1,52)XE(NEQUI),ZE(NEQUI)
0035                    WRITE(3,4)
0036          4         FORMAT(//T8,'ENTER DIRECTION HEADED WITH ZERO BEING',
                       +' TO THE RIGHT'/'---.')
0037          5         FORMAT(//T8,'ENTER ANGLE FOR PICTORIAL VIEW, NORMALLY 30.',
                       +/'---.')
0038                    CALL ANBELL
0039                    READ(1,49)W(NEQUI)
0040        300         CONTINUE
0041                    CALL NEWPAG
0042                    CALL ANMODE
0043                    WRITE(3,6)
0044          6         FORMAT(//T8,'ENTER VIEW YOU DESIRE.'/'-')
0045                    CALL ANBELL
0046                    READ(1,51)NVIEW
0047                    CALL ANMODE
0048                    IF(NVIEW.NE.4) GO TO 400
0049                    WRITE(3,5)
0050                    CALL ANBELL
0051                    READ(1,49)ANG
0052                    IF((ANG.GE.0.0).AND.(ANG.LE.180.0)) GO TO 400
0053                    WRITE(3,7)
0054          7         FORMAT(///,T8,'ANG WAS GREATER THAN OR LESS THAN PERMITTED',
                       +/,T8,'VALUE, ERGO, ANG HAS BEEN SET TO....30.0'///)
0055                    ANG=30.00
0056                    CALL BELLS(5)
0057                    CALL ANMODE
0058                    PAUSE
0059        400         CONTINUE
0060                    IF(NVIEW.EQ.5) CALL VFIVE
0061                    IF(NVIEW.EQ.5) CALL READ3D
0062                    NONCE=0
        C..........................................................................
        C     NOW VIEW PLACEMENT OF EQUIPMENT ON SITE PLAN                        .
        C..........................................................................
0063                    CALL NEWPAG
        C               IF(NEQUI.GT.0) CALL GETPTS(3)
0064                    CALL GETPTS(4)
0065                    IF (NCIRB.GT.0) CALL GETPTS(2)
0066                    IF(NRECB.GT.0) CALL GETPTS(1)
0067                    IF(NLN.GT.0) CALL GETPTS(5)
        C               IF(XNEWEQ.EQ.AA(2)) GO TO 500
0068                    WHERE=W(NEQUI)
0069                    XSITE=XE(NEQUI)
0070                    ZSITE=ZE(NEQUI)
0071                    CALL EQUIP
0072                    NEQ(NEQUI)=NX
0073                    READ(NX,54) NDATA
0074                    CALL PLAN
        C..........................................................................
0075        500         CONTINUE
0076                    CALL DISPLA
0077                    CALL HOME
0078                    CALL ANMODE
0079                    WRITE(3,8)
0080          8         FORMAT(T4,'WOULD YOU LIKE TO RE-POSITION?')
0081                    CALL ANBELL
0082                    READ(1,55)XNANS
0083                    CALL NEWPAG
0084                    IF(XNANS.EQ.AA(1)) GO TO 200
        C               IF(XNEWEQ.EQ.AA(2)) RETURN
0085                    CALL ANMODE
0086                    WRITE(3,9)
0087          9         FORMAT(/T4,'WOULD YOU LIKE TO SEE ANOTHER PIECE?')
0088                    CALL ANBELL
0089                    READ(1,55)XNANS2
0090                    IF(XNANS2.EQ.AA(1)) GO TO 100
0091         51         FORMAT(I1)
0092         52         FORMAT(2F7.2)
0093         54         FORMAT(I5)
0094         55         FORMAT(A4)
0095         57         FORMAT(I2)
0096         49         FORMAT(F3.0)
0097                    RETURN
0098                    END
```

FIGURE 15.1. (Continued)

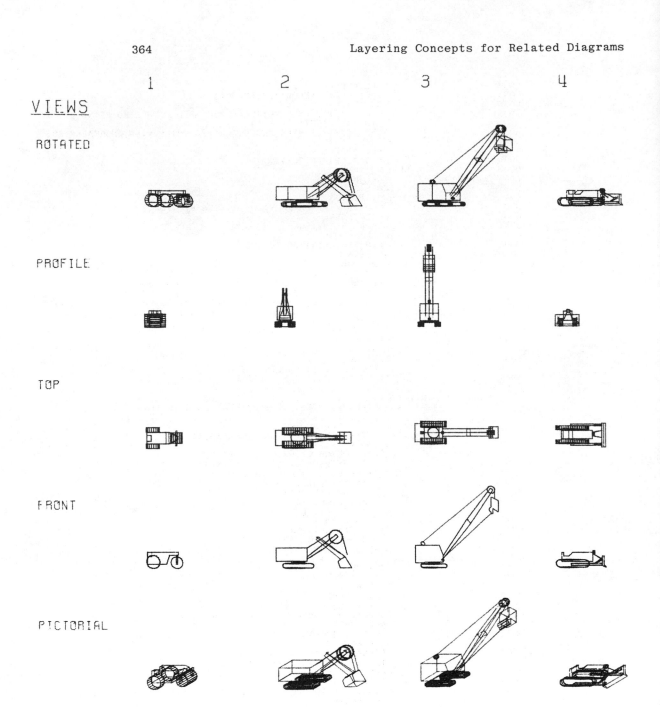

FIGURE 15.1 (Continued)

5   6   7

<u>VIEWS</u>

ROTATED

PROFILE

TOP

FRONT

PICTORIAL

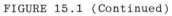

FIGURE 15.1 (Continued)

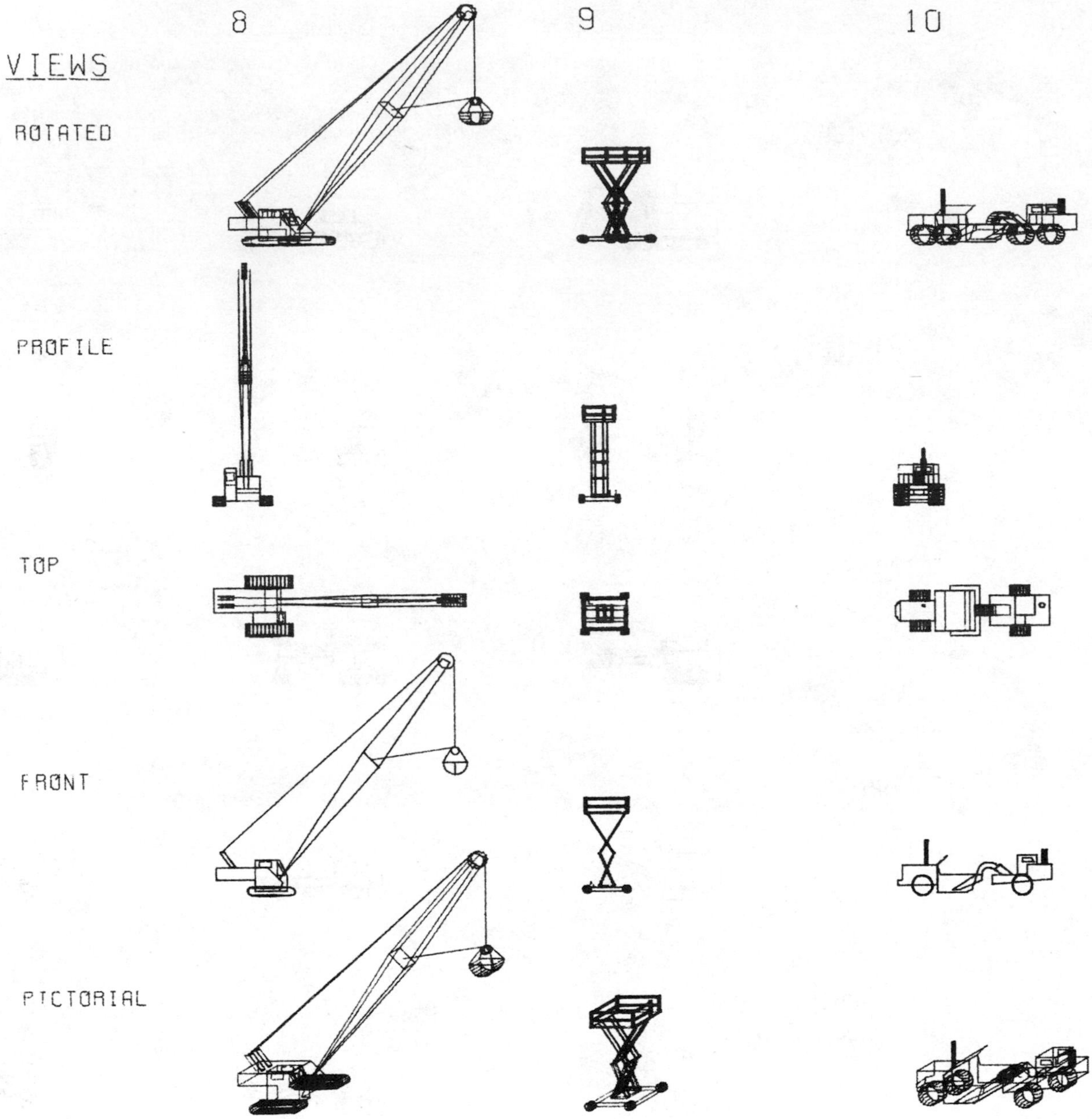

FIGURE 15.1 (Continued)

```
0001              SUBROUTINE CHANGS
        CCCCCCCCCCCCCCCCCCCCCCCCCCCCCCCCCCCCCCCCCCCCCCCCCCCCCCCCCCCCCCCCCCCCCCCC
        C                                                                      C
        C   THIS SUBROUTINE PERMITS THE USER TO CHANGE OR ADD NEW BUILD-       C
        C         INGS IF HE WISHES.                                           C
        C                                                                      C
        CCCCCCCCCCCCCCCCCCCCCCCCCCCCCCCCCCCCCCCCCCCCCCCCCCCCCCCCCCCCCCCCCCCCCCCC
0002              COMMON /NUMBER/NRECB,NCIRB,NDATA,NLN,NEQUI,NPLOT
0003              COMMON /ANSWER/AA(9)
0004              NADDRE=0
0005              NADDCR=0
0006              NADDLN=0
0007              NRE=0
0008              NCR=0
0009              NLS=0
0010              NCHGRE=0
0011              NCHGCR=0
0012              NCHGLN=0
0013         400  CONTINUE
0014              CALL NEWPAG
0015              CALL ANMODE
0016              WRITE(3,8)
0017         8    FORMAT(//,T8,'1= DO YOU WISH TO ENTER "NEW" PRE-CALCULATED ',
                 +'BUILDINGS?',
                 +/,T8,'2= DO YOU WANT TO SEE ANY OF YOUR OVERLAPPINGS?',
                 +/,T8,'3= DO YOU WANT TO SEE ANY OF YOUR INPUT FILES?',
                 +/,T8,'4= NONE OF THE ABOVE, ERGO, CONTINUE.',
                 +/,'ENTER COMMAND DESIRED:')
0018              CALL ANBELL
0019              READ(1,4)NANS
0020              IF(NANS.EQ.1) CALL SYES(J)
0021              IF(NANS.EQ.2) CALL NEWBUI(2)
0022              IF(NANS.EQ.3) CALL DATLOK
0023              IF(NANS.EQ.4) GO TO 500
0024              GO TO 400
0025         500  CONTINUE
0026              WRITE(3,30)
0027              CALL ANBELL
0028              READ(1,6)XNANS
0029              IF(XNANS.EQ.AA(2)) GO TO 40
0030              WRITE(3,20)
0031              CALL ANBELL
0032              READ(1,77)NADDRE,NADDCR
0033              NRECB=NRECB+NADDRE
0034              NCIRB=NCIRB+NADDCR
0035         40   CONTINUE
0036              WRITE(3,10)
0037         10   FORMAT(//,T8,'DO YOU WANT TO CHANGE ANY BUILDINGS?')
0038         30   FORMAT(//,T8,'DO YOU WANT TO INPUT NEW BUILDINGS?')
0039              CALL ANBELL
0040              READ(1,6)XNANS
0041              IF(XNANS.EQ.AA(2)) GO TO 50
0042              WRITE(3,20)
0043         20   FORMAT(T8,'HOW MANY RECTANGLES AND HOW MANY CIRCLES?',/,
                 +2('--- '))
0044              CALL ANBELL
0045              READ(1,77)NRE,NCR
0046         50   CONTINUE
0047              WRITE(3,60)
0048         60   FORMAT(//,T8,'ENTER :',/,T16,'YES = ENTER NEW LINE SEGMENTS',
                 +/,T16,'NO  = DO NOT WANT ANY LINE SEGMENTS',
                 +/,T16,'ADD = MAKE ADDITIONS TO EXISTING LINE SEGMENTS',
                 +/,T16,'CHG = CHANGE ANY EXISTING LINE SEGMENTS')
0049              CALL ANBELL
0050              READ(1,6)XX
0051              IF(XX.EQ.AA(1)) CALL NEWLNS
```

FIGURE 15.1 (Continued)

```
0052                    IF(XX.LE.AA(2)) GO TO 70
0053                    IF(XX.EQ.AA(3)) GO TO 80
0054                    IF(XX.EQ.AA(4)) GO TO 90
0055          80        CONTINUE
0056                    WRITE(3,1)
0057          1         FORMAT(/,T8,'ENTER NUMBER OF ADDITIONS:',/,'--')
0058                    CALL ANBELL
0059                    READ(1,5)NADDLN
0060                    NLN=NLN+NADDLN
0061                    GO TO 70
0062          90        CONTINUE
0063                    WRITE(3,2)
0064          2         FORMAT(/,T8,'ENTER NUMBER OF CHANGES:',/,'--')
0065                    CALL ANBELL
0066                    READ(1,5)NLS
0067                    GO TO 70
0068          70        CONTINUE
0069                    NCHGRE=NRE+NADDRE
0070                    NCHGCR=NCR+NADDCR
0071                    NCHGLN=NLS+NADDLN
0072                    IF(NCHGRE.EQ.0) GO TO 100
0073                    CALL CHGREC(NCHGRE)
0074          100       CONTINUE
0075                    IF(NCHGCR.EQ.0) GO TO 200
0076                    CALL CHGCIR(NCHGCR)
0077          200       CONTINUE
0078                    IF(NCHGLN.EQ.0) GO TO 300
0079                    CALL CHGLIN(NCHGLN)
0080          300       CONTINUE
0081          4         FORMAT(I1)
0082          5         FORMAT(I2)
0083          6         FORMAT(A4)
0084          7         FORMAT(I3)
0085          77        FORMAT(I3,I4)
0086                    RETURN
0087                    END
                        SUBROUTINE REVIEW
            CCCCCCCCCCCCCCCCCCCCCCCCCCCCCCCCCCCCCCCCCCCCCCCCCCCCCCCCCCCCCCCCCCC
            C                                                                 C
            C       THIS SUBROUTINE IS LIKE EQUSIT, EXCEPT THE USER MAY        C
            C          ONLY REVIEW DIFFERENT VIEWS FOR CHANGES OR ADD-         C
            C          ITIONS TO HIS DATA BASE.                                C
            C                                                                 C
            CCCCCCCCCCCCCCCCCCCCCCCCCCCCCCCCCCCCCCCCCCCCCCCCCCCCCCCCCCCCCCCCCCC
0002                    COMMON /RECS/XLLC(999),ZLLC(999),HTR(999),THETA(999),
                       +WID(999),NTITLR(3,999),BASER(999),DP(999)
0003                    COMMON /CIRS/XMID(999),ZMID(999),HTC(999),NTITLC(3,999),
                       +BASEC(999),RAD(999)
0004                    COMMON /FLAGS/NVIEW,FLAG,NWHAT,NONCE
0005                    COMMON /PLOTIT/ANG,XP(1100),YP(1100),ZP(1100),IPP(1100)
0006                    COMMON /SUBSCA/SCALE,SCALE2,XBIG,ZBIG,YBIG
0007                    COMMON /NUMBER/NRECB,NCIRB,NDATA,NLN,NEQUI,NPLOT
0008                    COMMON /ANSWER/AA(9)
0009                    IKEY=49
0010                    CALL NEWPAG
0011                    CALL ANMODE
0012                    WRITE(3,5)
0013                    CALL BELLS(1)
0014                    CALL ANMODE
0015                    READ(1,55)XX
0016          100       CONTINUE
0017                    CALL NEWPAG
0018                    CALL ANMODE
0019                    IF(XX.EQ.AA(2)) RETURN
0020          1         FORMAT(//T8,'ENTER ANGLE FOR PICTORIAL VIEW, NORMALLY 30.',
                       +/'---.')
0021                    IF(IKEY.EQ.49) NVIEW=1
0022                    IF(IKEY.EQ.50) NVIEW=2
0023                    IF(IKEY.EQ.51) NVIEW=3
0024                    IF(IKEY.EQ.52) NVIEW=4
0025                    IF(IKEY.EQ.53) NVIEW=5
0026                    IF(NVIEW.NE.4) GO TO 200
0027                    WRITE(3,1)
0028                    CALL BELLS(1)
0029                    CALL ANMODE
0030                    READ(1,49)ANG
0031                    IF((ANG.GE.0.0).AND.(ANG.LE.180.0)) GO TO 200
0032                    WRITE(3,3)
0033          3         FORMAT(///,T8,'ANG WAS GREATER THAN OR LESS THAN PERMITIED',
                       +/,T8,'VALUE, ERGO, ANG HAS BEEN SET TO....30.0'///)
0034                    ANG=30.00
0035                    CALL BELLS(5)
```

FIGURE 15.1 (Continued)

```
0036                   CALL ANMODE
0037                   PAUSE
0038           200     CONTINUE
0039                   IF(NVIEW.EQ.5) CALL VFIVE
0040                   IF(NVIEW.EQ.5) CALL READ3D
0041                   NONCE=0
0042                     CALL NEWPAG
0043                     CALL GETPTS(3)
0044                     CALL GETPTS(4)
0045                     IF (NCIRB.GT.0) CALL GETPTS(2)
0046                     IF(NRECB.GT.0) CALL GETPTS(1)
0047                     IF(NLN.GT.0) CALL GETPTS(5)
0048                   CALL DISPLA
0049                   CALL HOME
0050                   CALL ANMODE
0051                   WRITE(3,4)
0052           111     CONTINUE
0053                   FG=0.
0054                   IF(NRECB.GE.NCIRB)  NLOOK=NRECB
0055                   IF(NCIRB.GT.NRECB)  NLOOK=NCIRB
0056           115     CONTINUE
0057                   IF(FG.NE.0.) WRITE(3,120)
0058                   CALL ANMODE
0059                   CALL BELLS(1)
0060                   CALL SCURSR(IKEY,IX,IY)
0061                   IF((IKEY.GE.49).AND.(IKEY.LE.53)) GO TO 100
0062                   IF(IKEY.EQ.83) CONTINUE
0063                   IF(IKEY.EQ.78) GO TO 119
0064                   IF(IKEY.EQ.82) GO TO 118
0065                   XLOW=((FLOAT(IX)-30.)/SCALE)-2.
0066                   ZLOW=((FLOAT(IY)-50.)/SCALE)-2.
0067                   XHIH=((FLOAT(IX)-30.)/SCALE)+2.
0068                   ZHIH=((FLOAT(IY)-50.)/SCALE)+2.
0069                   DO 112 K=1,NLOOK
0070                   IF((XLLC(K).LT.XLOW).OR.(XLLC(K).GT.XHIH)) GO TO 116
0071                   IF((ZLLC(K).LT.ZLOW).OR.(ZLLC(K).GT.ZHIH)) GO TO 116
0072                   KSET=K
0073                   FG=1111.
0074                   GO TO 115
0075           116     CONTINUE
0076                   IF(K.GT.NCIRB) GO TO 112
0077                   IF((XMID(K).LT.XLOW).OR.(XMID(K).GT.XHIH)) GO TO 112
0078                   IF((ZMID(K).LT.ZLOW).OR.(ZMID(K).GT.ZHIH)) GO TO 112
0079                   KSET=K
0080                   FG=2222.
0081                   GO TO 115
0082           112     CONTINUE
0083                   IF(FG.EQ.0.) WRITE(3,114)
0084           114     FORMAT('POINTS NOT FOUND...RE-POSITION')
0085           120     FORMAT(/'***POINTS FOUND')
0086                   GO TO 111
0087           119     CONTINUE
0088                   IF(FG.EQ.2222.) GO TO 117
0089                   XLLC(KSET)=(FLOAT(IX)-30.)/SCALE
0090                   ZLLC(KSET)=(FLOAT(IY)-50.)/SCALE
0091                   GO TO 121
0092           117     CONTINUE
0093                   XMID(KSET)=(FLOAT(IX)-30.)/SCALE
0094                   ZMID(KSET)=(FLOAT(IY)-50.)/SCALE
0095           121     CONTINUE
0096                   GO TO 100
0097           118     CONTINUE
0098           4       FORMAT('KEY BOARD INPUTS: R=RETURN,S=SET PTS,N=NEW PTS,',
                       +'1,2,3,4,5=VIEW NO.')
0099                   CALL NEWPAG
0100           5       FORMAT(/,T8,'WOULD YOU LIKE TO EDIT OR REVIEW THE POSITION',
                       +/,T8,'OF YOUR INPUTS?')
0101           49      FORMAT(F3.0)
0102           55      FORMAT(A4)
0103                   RETURN
0104                   END
0001                   SUBROUTINE ALLDON
              CCCCCCCCCCCCCCCCCCCCCCCCCCCCCCCCCCCCCCCCCCCCCCCCCCCCCCCCCCCCCCCCCCCCCCC
              C                                                                     C
              C    WHEN SESSION IS COMPLETED ALL FIVE VIEWS WILL BE DISPLAYED       C
              C       ONE RIGHT AFTER THE OTHER; PAUSING FOR COPIES TO BE           C
              C       MADE IF DESIRED.  IF ANG OR THETE, GAMMA, AND Q ARE           C
              C       SET BY USER THE PROGRAM PRESETS THESE VARIABLES.              C
              C                                                                     C
              CCCCCCCCCCCCCCCCCCCCCCCCCCCCCCCCCCCCCCCCCCCCCCCCCCCCCCCCCCCCCCCCCCCCCCC
0002                   COMMON /FLAGS/NVIEW,FLAG,NWHAT,NONCE
0003                   COMMON /NUMBER/NRECB,NCIRB,NDATA,NLN,NEQUI,NPLOT
```

FIGURE 15.1 (Continued)

```
0004                    DO 1 JJ=1,5
0005                    NVIEW=JJ
0006                    CALL NEWPAG
0007                    IF(NRECB.GT.0) CALL GETPTS(1)
0008                    IF(NLN.GT.0) CALL GETPTS(5)
0009                    IF(NCIRB.GT.0) CALL GETPTS(2)
0010                    CALL GETPTS(3)
0011                    CALL GETPTS(4)
0012                    CALL DISPLA
0013                    CALL HOME
0014                    CALL ANMODE
0015                    CALL HOME
0016                    CALL BELLS(5)
0017                    CALL ANMODE
0018                    PAUSE
0019                    CALL NEWPAG
0020         1          CONTINUE
0021                    RETURN
0022                    END
```

FIGURE 15.1 (Continued)

program includes all possible site preparations, including construction equipment forecasting.

DISPLAY OF
SINGLE-LAYER
DRAWINGS

The preparation of single-layer drawings for display in a project
layer involves two steps. First a rough freehand sketch is made on
a graphics tablet; the procedure for this was described in detail in
Chapter 4, and a typical output is shown in Figure 4.2. Second,
this output is refined into a display drawing.

Display drawings are often preliminary drawings which are
embellished in order to make them more attractive to the client. As
demonstrated in Chapter 4, they are often rendered in a combination
of pencil, ink, and water color. In addition to the use of perspective for main floor and front elevations, as shown in Figure 4.3,
they frequently include imaginary backgrounds such as trees, shrubbery, and other features to achieve a more realistic effect.

Elevations

Elevations as described in Chapters 12 and 13 were either internal
or external views of the upright walls of the structure projected on
a vertical plane. Normally four windows are contained in a single
layer, each having a separate storage area labeled north, east,
west, and south elevations. Each storage location is called a window, and by calling the north window, a view of the north elevation
will appear on the layer. The number of windows saved depends on
the complexity of the structure. Windows are not duplicated if the
elevations are similar in description.

Elevation layers show the exact shape and size of the height
and width of each wall and opening. They can also represent the
finish such as brick or glass by adding standard shading symbols
from computer memory. These memory modules contain special arrangements of building materials that are necessary to construct the
desired display pattern. Invisible lines are rarely used on eleva-

tions except to indicate the outline of the structure below the grade line or possibly a roofline which may be concealed. Likewise very few dimensions are displayed on elevations; they are placed either on the floorplan or section views.

Elevation layers will generally include the diagram for the roof slope. This is displayed just above the roofline. Other lines in elevation displays are sometimes highlighted by a shading technique called tone.

The basic steps in preparing an exterior elevation layer are the following:

1. Locate the footing and foundation layer from computer memory. Make a hard copy of this single view as described in Chapter 12.

2. Locate one wall section layer and scale it to match step 1. This will correspond to the procedures from Chapter 12.

3. Tape the hard copies of the top and side views in their proper positions on the surface of the graphics tablet. Lines now can be projected from both the top and side views for creating the elevation layer.

4. Show the foundation below the grade level with dashed lines. All other lines should be solid. Select material patterns for memory modules for surface finish.

5. Note finished floor and grade elevations. Locate doors, roof drains, and other features to be shown on that layer.

Horizontal, Plan, and Site Descriptions

The foundation plan used to construct the exterior elevations is a horizontal drawing representation. A foundation plan is a top view of the foundation showing the size of footing, various distances from reference and boundary points, locations of columns, and other pertinent details. A typical foundation plan was shown in Chapter 9.

The foundation plan as well as all floorplans are oriented on the layer so that the front of the structure is facing the bottom of the display area. If the structure has a basement, the foundation plan is stored on one layer, and all the necessary units to be installed there will be located on a separate layer. This second layer would also contain partition walls and equipment locations such as heating and cooling units.

The final horizontal layer is the site description. This layer is used to develop site-related drawings such as the plot plan. A plot plan is usually the cover sheet in a set of working drawings and gives the overall picture of the location and orientation of the structure to the site. A typical plot plan was shown in Chapter 10.

If the ground is uneven or hilly or contains unusual features such as a draining ditch, contour lines show the extent of grading changes which the contractor must make. The plot plan also includes provisions for water supply, sewer groundwater drainage, utilities, walls, and drives.

Placing Drawings

From the preliminary database construction and the display drawings, the project team now makes a complete set of placing drawings on separate layer storage locations. These layers must provide enough information so that along with the specifications no design decisions are left to the contractor. See Chapters 10 and 11 for examples.

Placing drawings deal specifically with the preparation of layers for the fabrication of commercial buildings, industrial plants, schools, hospitals, bridges, or large structures. This type of database differs in some respects from the representation introduced in Chapter 6 and used thus far in this chapter. Special techniques are used to present structure form and shape before storing on an information layer in the computer.

The structural engineer determines the design of the structure and the drawing layer information stored. While preparing the layer data, the engineer takes into consideration such factors as code requirements, availability of materials, ease of erection, and site conditions. From this database detailers may build drawing layers for the following:

   1.   Concrete, steel, or other construction
   2.   Special symbols
   3.   Erection plans

Details for Construction Practices in Concrete and Steel. The two most common types of structural details are for reinforced concrete and steel. Few structural applications include heavy timber or wood members. Wood and steel beams are used with masonry and brick construction, however. Chapter 14 presented details involving reinforced concrete, columns, beams, floor slabs, and stairways made of poured concrete with exterior facing of brick or other masonry materials backed up with lightweight concrete blocks.

Steel framing details use standard steel members as the principal framing elements. The elements are joined in several ways. Usually shop connections are welded together. The exterior facing is also of brick or some other masonry material backed up with concrete blocks.

Building Symbols. To ensure that the steel elements in the details are properly fabricated and erected in the correct position, each steel piece is given an ID symbol. This marking is placed on the detail and painted on the steel member.

While no uniform system of building symbols exists, small structures use a capital letter followed by a number. The number designates the drawing layer containing the details of the steel member. The letter indicates the shape of the member, such as B = beam, C = column, G= girder, and L = lintel. Therefore B4 would identify a beam whose detail appears on layer 4.

Building symbols for larger, multistory structures often identify the members with a beam digit followed by an encircled number. This number identifies the story of framing where the member is to be placed during erection. For example, a no. 4 beam which is used for both second and fourth floors would be marked $B4^2$ and $B4^4$.

A similar system is used for concrete building symbols. The various parts of a concrete building are indicated by symbols which assign the floor, the type of concrete member, and the location layer of the member detail. Therefore 3B3 would mean third-floor beam no. 3. The coding for concrete members is B = beams, C = columns, D = dowels, F = footings, G = girders, J = joists, L = lintels, S = slabs, T = ties, V = stirrups, and W = wall portions.
Erection Plans. Erection drawings, which are prepared by the fabricator, are also called placing drawings for foundations, floors, and framing systems. Erection drawings show the location, shape, and size of components in the structure, or the where of the question how (construction details), what (building symbols), and where (erection plans).

The responsibility of the technician in preparing erection drawings is limited to carrying out all instructions on the engineering specifications and where nothing specific is stated in regards to building codes. It is not our intention in this section to discuss all the design factors involved in placing and erecting buildings but we do intend to introduce the student to one of the many uses for layered drawings.

Layered drawings used for erection include all the essential windows from any layer required for the completion of a structure. A complete layering will contain foundation details (already discussed and shown in Chapter 9), room arrangement of floorplans (Chapter 8), elevations (Chapters 12 and 13), and sections (Chapter 10).

Another important function of erection plans is to show the framing system used for the building. A typical framing plan is shown in Chapter 14. A framing system not only presents the layout of the members but also indicates the shape, size, and location of each member.

Design Drawings

Design drawings are made from merging layers of the computer database described and were presented in the figures of Chapters 10-12
and 14. Design drawings must be complete to the extent that every
bit of information contained in these chapter sections is contained
either by a diagram, description, note, or reference to a building
code.

It is not necessary for the designer to make new layers of data
for each structural or architectural member of the project. The
designer merges enough information from various layers to include in
every set of building plans a typical design drawing for such things
as slabs, beams, column design, and the like.

Shop Details. While design drawings show the general layout of
structural members, shop drawings represent how the various parts
are to be fabricated or assembled. All features that are specifically related to the connection of individual structural or architectural members have to be clearly illustrated.

Chapter 7 includes several typical shop drawings taken from a
design drawing. The details of the members shown can be fabricated
off site (in a shop) and transported to the building project. Diagrams for items fabricated on site are called construction diagrams
or field drawings.

Welding and Bolting

The most common practice of fabricating steel structural members in
the field is by welding or bolting with high-strength machine bolts.
The placement of bolts for connecting members is controlled by gage
lines. The location of these lines has been standardized to fit a
text format called a schedule.

Schedules

A schedule is a summary of all the bolt locations, drilled holes, or
welding notes in the structure in the order of their use, complete
with the number of items required. One of the important concepts of
computer-aided design drawings for shop details is the automatic
generation of a schedule or bill of materials. They are often
referred to as a *shop bill,* which lists all the items required for
fabrication and shipment to the site. In some cases shop bills are
output directly alongside the detail of the member or are included
as an 8-1/2 by 11 spec size sheet. With computer database layering,
a list is easy to generate at the same time a plotter or CRT is diagramming the graphic shape of the shop detail.

CHAPTER AND
BOOK SUMMARY

Layered drawings are extremely useful in the industrial marketplace and therefore are subject to the latest technological advancements insofar as how they are produced. This chapter contained the types of layered drawings, how they are formed, and how they are used by the architectural team. One of these team members is the computer-aided graphics programmer. This member operates the many computer-related pieces of hardware explained in Chapter 2. For single-view drawings the operator has three techniques available:

1. Read from a graphics terminal the current database information about each of the layers for a design project.

2. Write by pointing a light pen or using a data tablet to cause input commands to be accepted without computer-language-type programs.

3. Obtain a drawing response for each read or write action. The operator will see immediately, in single-view form, the result of the request in 15 sec. or less, and the operator may make corrections or modify the design immediately.

The three principles of graphic reading, writing, and obtaining drawing response are the basic ingredients of an architectural single-view drawing system. In Chapter 8 an operator processes a floorplan using this system and recalls from memory, library, or files any other information pertaining to the floorplan. By correlation and combination new information is created which can take its place in memory as a document, drawing, memory word, or verbal expression.

EXERCISES

1. Each of the case studies (CS1) presented as exercises for this chapter is given with reference to certain illustrations and programs contained throughout the book. Students may use these case studies as term projects. By using this format, the material presented in Chapters 1-15 is summarized in the following manner:

CS1: Introduction to Computer-Aided Architectural Graphics

Assignment: Read Chapter 1 and work each of the exercises at the end of the chapter. This will require a course notebook which will be used throughout the remainder of the case studies. Directions: You will develop certain preliminary ideas from your reading and class lectures. Organize these materials according to the exercises at the end of Chapter 1.

2.   CS2: Automation of Routine Office Tasks. Assignment: Read
     Chapter 2 and work each of the exercises at the end of the
     chapter. Begin an organized approach to the automation of
     common office tasks as shown in Figure 8.1.

3.   CS3: Computer-Generated Artistic Lettering Styles. Assign-
     ment: Read Chapter 3 and work each of the exercises at the end
     of the chapter. Directions: Each of the items completed and
     turned into the course instructor should provide for architec-
     tural or mechanical lettering styles; while most graphics
     hardware comes with lettering capabilities, architectural
     capability is rarely among them. Make sure that you have
     provided for freestyle lettering input and display capability
     on each of the remaining case studies.

4.   CS4: Computer-Assisted Sketching Techniques. Assignment:
     Read Chapter 4 and work those exercises assigned by your
     instructor. Directions: The shape, size, and arrangement
     inside an architectural structure depends a great deal on what
     the client does for a living and how many people will occupy
     that structure. Of course, building capital makes a big dif-
     ference, but that is not the primary concern here. In this
     case study you are to provide ideas about the inside and out-
     side of the proposed building.

5.   CS5: Geometric and Template Image Processing. Assignment:
     Read Chapter 5 and work those exercises assigned by your
     instructor. Template image processing is a combination of
     sketching and drawing which assists the architect's drafts-
     person in remembering certain things until final drawings can
     be made. Directions: Using the completed exercises as a
     guide, and after examining basic subprogramming techniques,
     made a preliminary plan for the architectural structure chosen
     in CS4.

6.   CS6: Storing Architectural Details. Assignment: Read Chapter
     6 and work the assigned exercises at the end of the chapter.
     The next step in computer-automated building drawing is the
     ability to store the items created in CS5. Directions:
     Details are such trifles. But enough details make an architec-
     tural perfect, and "perfection is not trifle" (Ben Franklin).
     Try to follow Mr. Franklin's quote whenever storing architec-
     tural details; there are never too many. Working drawings are
     composed mainly of details arranged to show the construction of

a building. Provide enough file space so that additional details can be stored at a later date and for other case studies.

7. CS7: Computer Displays for Working Drawings. Assignment: Read Chapter 7 and work each of the exercises at the end of the chapter. Directions: After many of the details have been stored in CS6, they may be recalled in any order desired and displayed at any scale. Recall the details stored in CS6 which were entered by CS5 methods and planned in CS4.

8. CS8: Floorplan Generation. Assignment: Read Chapter 8 and work those exercises assigned by your instructor. Directions: Output a finished floorplan for the structure planned in CS4, created in CS5, stored in CS6, and detailed in CS7.

9. CS9: Foundation Plan Generation. Assignment: Read Chapter 9 and work selected exercises at the end. Directions: Every structure needs a foundation. The function of a foundation plan is to show the design intent to provide level and uniformly distributed support for the structure. Using the exercises as a guide, output the foundation of the case study project.

10. CS10: Section Generation and Profile Drawings. Assignment: Read Chapter 10 and work each of the exercises at the end of the chapter. Directions: Develop a wall section from footing through the roofline for the case study project.

11. CS11: Dimensioning and Notation Techniques. Assignment: Read Chapter 11 and work each of the exercises at the end of the chapter. Directions: Dimension all features in CS10, CS9, CS8, and CS7.

12. CS12: Exterior Elevation Generations. Assignment: Read Chapter 12 and work those exercises assigned by your instructor. Directions: Output an exterior elevation page for each of the sides North, South, East, and West for the case study project.

13. CS13: Interior Elevations. Assignment: Read Chapter 13 and work the exercises at the end of the chapter. Directions: Select at least four interior elevations and display them for the case study project.

14. CS14: Automation of Framing Plans. <u>Assignment</u>: Read Chapter 14 and work those exercises assigned. <u>Directions</u>: New materials and new methods of using conventional materials provide the architect and engineer with much flexibility in framing design. After checking the local building codes, lay out and design the framing system for your case study project begun in CS4.

15. CS15: Layering Concepts for Related Diagrams. <u>Assignment</u>: Read Chapter 15 and work each of the case studies assigned by your instructor. <u>Directions</u>: The related diagrams shown in CS2 are generated from computer files. Reproduce as many of the related diagrams from CS2 as you can from the existing computer files generated for CS1–CS14.

Annotated Bibliography

1. A COMPUTER SYSTEM FOR THE DESIGN OF BUILDINGS WHICH UTILISE
    PREFABRICATED, REINFORCED AND PRESTRESSED CONCRETE COMPONENTS
    West, C. J.
    Genesys Ltd., Loughborough, England
    Cad 80. Proceedings of the 4th International Conference and
    Exhibition on Computers in Design Engineering 493-506 1980
    March 1980 Brighton, England
    Publ: IPC Sci. and Techol. Press. Guildford, England
    XIV + 774 pp.
    Treatment: Practical Applic
    Document Type: Report Section
    (4 Refs)

    This paper describes a computer-aided design system for the
    design and detail for precast concrete floors in buildings.
    The program has been developed for a commercially available
    flooring system and represents the complete computerization of
    the drawing office practice involved in producing final struc-
    tural engineering drawings from architect's general arrange-
    ments. Drawings and schedules are produced for the manufacture
    of the precast slabs as well as their fixing on site.

2. A COMPUTER PROGRAM FOR THREE DIMENSIONAL ANALYSIS OF BUILDINGS
    Humar, J. L.; Khandoker, J. U.
    Dept. of Civil Engng., Carleton Univ., Ottawa, Canada
    Comput. and Struct. (GB) Vol. 11, No. 5 369-87 May 1980

Coden: CMSTCJ
  Treatment: Practical Applic
  Document Type: Journal Paper
  (8 Refs)

A special-purpose computer program for the linear three-dimensional analyses of building structures for gravity, lateral and earthquake loads are presented. The building is idealized as consisting of a series of rigid jointed rectangular frame or frame-shearwall substructures interconnected through a rigid floor diaphragm. Finite joint sizes, shear deformations of columns are considered. Three-dimensional frequencies and mode shapes are evaluated, and a response spectrum approach is used for the dynamic analysis. A front-end processor accepts input data in a conversational mode and in free format. Data input is speeded up by taking advantage of the repetitive nature of frame dimensions, member sizes, and loadings.

3.   A COMPUTERISED GUIDE TO SOME SECTIONS OF THE BUILDING REGULATIONS
      Phillips, R. J.
      Dept. of Architecture, Univ. of Bristol, Bristol, England
      BOCAAD (Bull. Comput. Aided Archit. Des.) (GB) No. 31 31-8
Feb. 1979 Coden: BBCDD8
      Treatment: General, Review
      Document Type: Journal Paper
      (18 Refs)
This is an interim report on research into the construction of a computerized design guide to sections E, F, and G of the current building regulations 1976.

4.   A DRAFTING PROGRAM FOR ISOPARAMETRIC FINITE ELEMENTS
      Hofmeister, L. D.
      Mech. Res. Inc., Los Angeles, CA, USA
      Int. J. Numer. Methods Eng. (GB) Vol. 12, No. 3 505-29 1978
Coden: IJNMBH
      Treatment: Practical Applic: Theoretical
      Document Type: Journal Paper
      (7 Refs)
A new application of the isoparametric finite element concept is introduced which significantly extends its usefulness for many practical structural configurations. In this application, final working or architectural drawings of the structure are made from the same (or similar) finite element model as was utilized in a structural integrity analysis. The hardware

necessary to produce such drawings, a computer-driven plotter or automated drafting machine, is available commercially or through most data centers, and the software concepts required are described herein.

5. A GENERATIVE APPROACH TO COMPOSITION AND STYLE IN ARCHITECTURE
    Stiny, G.
    Centre for Configurational Studies, Open Univ., Milton Keynes, England
    Parc 79. International Conference on the Application of Computers in Architecture, Building Design and Urban Planning 435-46 1979
    7-10 May 1979 Berlin, Germany
    Publ: Online, Uxbridge, England
    XIII + 724 pp.
    Treatment: Applic: General, Review
    Document Type: Report Section
    (12 Refs)
    Composition and style are discussed in terms of the generation, enumeration, and evaluation of architectural forms such as buildings, plans, and elevations. A general approach to these three aspects of composition and style is developed based on shape grammars and parametric shape grammars. Palladian villa plans are used to illustrate the main features of these spatial generating systems.

6. A GRAPHICAL INPUT SYSTEM FOR COMPUTER-AIDED ARCHITECTURAL DESIGN
    Robertz, W.; Greenberg, D. P.
    Cornell Univ., Ithaca, NY, USA
    CAD 80. Proceedings of the 4th International Conference and Exhibition on Computers in Design Engineering 715-23 1980
    March 1980 Brighton, England
    Publ: IPC Sci. and Techol. Press, Guildford, England
    IXV + 774 pp.
    Treatment: Practical Applic
    Document Type: Report Section
    (6 Refs)
    A system for creating geometric volumes for architectural design is presented. Techniques developed conform with procedures currently used in architectural design. Extensive drawing and editing routines for carefully defining two-dimensional polygons are described. Two methods of extrusion are available for three-dimensional generation. Buildings may be composed of

multiple volumes created in reference to each other. Furthermore, volumes created by this program may be used as input into
various other geometric editing and application routines.

7.   A PROPOSAL FOR THE DESIGN AND ORGANISATION OF GRAPHIC INFORMA-
      TION OF A VIEWER BASED ON A RASTER SYSTEM
          Garcao, A. S.; Sarmento, A. M.
          Electricidade (Portugal) Vol. 21, No. 140 325-32 Nov.-Dec.
      1978 Coden: ELDDAB
          Treatment: Applic; Practical Applic
          Document Type: Journal Paper
          Languages: Portuguese (4 Refs)
      The characteristics of a raster system are given and its
      application to architecture is discussed using a viewer of
      240*480 lines. A block diagram is given of the equipment
      needed to feed information to the screen. Architectural draw-
      ing and the use of a graphical processor are dealt with.
      Detailed equipment block diagrams are given. The control of
      points on the screen is described. Supported by simple dia-
      grams. A graphical subprogram is presented.

8.   A RETRIEVAL SYSTEM FOR ENGINEERING DRAWINGS
          Tenopir, C.; Cibbarelli, P.
          Cibbarelli and Associates, Huntingdon Beach, CA, USA
          Spec. Libr. (USA) Vol. 70, No. 2 91-6 Feb. 1979 Coden:
      SPLBAN
          Treatment: General, Review
          Document Type: Journal Paper
          (13 Refs)
      The design and implementation of a complete, computerized
      retrieval system for the engineering and architectural drawings
      of several large southern California land development firms has
      been undertaken by Cibbarelli and Associates, Library Consul-
      tants. The problems encountered and the processes followed in
      developing a specialized cataloging system and format, a cus-
      tomized thesaurus, computer software, and managerial procedures
      for the first system are detailed. The adaptability of this
      system to other engineering and architectural drawing collec-
      tions is discussed.

9.   A SITE MODELLING SYSTEM
          Grayer, J. L.
          Appl. Res. of Cambridge, Ltd., Cambridge, England
          Cad 80. Proceedings of the 4th International Conference and

Exhibition on Computers in Design Engineering, 724-32, 1980
   March 1980 Brighton, England
   Publ: IPC Sci. and Technol. Press, Guildford, England
   XIV + 774 pp.
   Treatment: Practical Applic
   Document Type: Report Section
   (1 Refs)

This system is intended as a design tool for architects,
engineers, and quantity surveyors involved in a building project. The system builds up a site model from randomly scat-
tered data. The basic software of the model is described in
terms of its data structure and how this is used to perform the
tasks required by the system user. Much of the design of this
system, in addition to being able to perform the required
calculations, has been concerned with facilitating the user's
task in preparing and manipulating the necessarily large quantities of data. The user interface and its design are discussed.

10. A THEORETICAL BASIS AND IMPLEMENTATION FOR COMPUTER ASSISTED
ARCHITECTURAL DESIGN EVALUATION
   Bryant, D. A.; Dains, R. B.
   Construction Engng. Res. Lab., US Army Corps of Engrs.,
Champaign, IL, USA
   Sponsor: Nat. Bur. Standards; Nat. Conference of States on
Building Codes and Standards
   Proceedings of the 1st NBS/NCSBCS Joint Conference on
Research and Innovation in Building Regulatory Process 349-68
1977
   21-22 Spet. 1976 Providence, R.I., USA
   Publ: Nat. Bur. Standards, Washington, D.C., USA
   X + 504 pp.
   Treatment: Applic; Theoretical
   Document Type: Report Section
   (14 Refs)

Systematic evaluation and review of criteria for habitability
(search) in an automated architectural criteria maintenance and
design evaluation system. A prototype system is now in the
office of the chief of engineers (COE). Search is used in two
phases of Corps of Engineers design work. First, performance-
type architectural design criteria and selected building code
requirements are checked for consistency, documented as to
information location, and stored for alter use. Second, design
layouts produced by architect/engineers (A/E) are put into

search. The result is full, unbiased evaluation based on the
previously checked and stored criteria. Search is intended to
be used by COE personnel for both criteria maintenance and
design evaluation type of work. An example of criteria maintenance would be in checking and storing criteria of the design
guides now being developed. Design evaluation use will involve
evaluating selected architectural designs submitted by Corps
districts as well as design layouts and relationships in the
design guides.

11. AIM, ARCHITECTURAL INFERENCE-MAKER
    Akin, O.
    School of Architecture, Carnegie-Mellon Univ., Pittsburgh,
PA, USA
    Sponsor: Computer-Aided Design Centre; Dept. Environment; et
al.
    Third International Conference and Exhibition on Computers in
Engineering and Building Design 506-21 1978
    14-16 March, 1978 Brighton, England
    Publ: IPC Sci. and Technology Press Ltd., Guildford, England
    XII + 803 pp. ISBN O 902852 85 X
    Treatment: Theoretical; Experimental
    Document Type: Report Section
    (12 Refs)
Conceptual inference making has been modeled by many computer
systems that deal with complex forms of information processing.
This study examines inference making in the context of architectural drawing, understanding tasks. A three-part knowledge
model (design-symbol representations, transformation rules, and
heuristic rules) is formulated based on the behavior of human
subjects. This model is used to design a computer system
called AIM which can understand architectural drawings based on
the answers it gets from its users. A detailed description of
the architecture of AIM and a hand-simulation of its behavior
are provided.

12. ANALYSIS IN ARCHITECTURAL DESIGN
    Bridges, A. H.
    Univ. of Strathclyde, Glasgow, Scotland
    Parc 79. International Conference on the Application of
Computers in Architecture, Building Design and Urban Planning
175-85 1979
    7-10 May 1979 Berlin, Germany
    Publ: Online, Uxbridge, England
    XIII + 724 pp.

Treatment: Theoretical; Experimental

Document Type: Report Section

(4 Refs)

An interactive graphical output computer program for interior space planning is described. The program, known as magic (multivariate analysis with graphical interaction by computer), is carefully designed to allow the architect to investigate the planning problem. Magic outputs information in diagrammatic form of sufficient generality not to inhibit the designer, while containing a distillation of information such that the final architect-produced design will closely meet the requirements of the organization. Although of use in any layout analysis, the program is illustrated by an example drawn from the design of a large office building.

13. AN APPROACH TO COST ESTIMATING FOR PLANNING AND DESIGN

Schild, W.; Hauber, A.; Logcher, R. D.

IBM Israel Sci. Center, Haifa, Israel

Moneta, J. (Editor)

Information Technology 78 77-92 1978

6-9 Aug. 1978 Jerusalem, Israel

Publ: North-Holland, Amsterdam, Netherlands

XXII + 804 pp. ISBN O 444 85192 5

Treatment: Practical Applic

Document Type: Report Section

This paper describes a computer application developed to enable accurate cost estimation both in the initial phases of design and continuously thereafter. The computer system, COSTMOD, provides a tool for building and operating hierarchically structured models of projects. Models can be developed for classes of projects with project characteristics and required decisions as variables. Determination of hierarchical breakdown and component costs are then based on these variables. Thus small quantities of input are expanded, based on design algorithms, good practice standards, or average usage statistics, into much greater detail and more accurate costs.

14. AN ARCHITECTURAL CRITIQUE ON THE COMPUTER-AIDED GENERATION OF
BUILDING LAYOUTS

Neuckermans, H. C.

Dept. of Architecture, Univ. of Leuven, Leuven, Belgium

Sponsor: Computer-Aided Design Centre; Dept. Environment; et al.

Third International Conference and Exhibition on Computers in Engineering and Building Design 461-9 1978

14-16 March 1978 Brighton, England

Publ: IPC Sci. and Technology Press Ltd., Guildford,
England

XII + 803 pp. ISBN 0 902852 85 X

Treatment: Applic; Theoretical

Document Type: Report Section

(20 Refs)

A computer program called CABLO-2, performing elementary
locations based on architectural criteria, is proposed, showing
the way in which future work should be oriented.

15. AN INTEGRATED AND COMPREHENSIVE DATABASE FOR CAAD APPRAISAL
PACKAGES

Gentles, J. C.; Unsworth, M. A.

Abacus, Dept. of Architecture and Building Sci., Univ. of
Strathclyde, Glasgow, Scotland

Sponsor: Computer-Aided Design Centre; Dept. Environment; et
al.

Third International Conference and Exhibition on Computers in
Engineering and Building Design 578-88 1978

14-16 March 1978 Brighton, England

Publ: IPC Sci. and Technolgoy Press Ltd., Guildford, England

XII + 803 pp. ISBN 0 902852 85 X

Treatment: Applic; General, Review

Document Type: Report Section

(3 Refs)

Describes the concepts behind, and the implementation of, a
central integrated database for use with a CAAD appraisal
package. Full details are given of the construction and use of
the database with special emphasis placed on the roles played
in data manipulation by the building designer, the applications
programmer, and the systems program.

16. AN INTEGRATED CAD SYSTEM FOR ARCHITECTURE

David, B. T.

Lab. Imag, Grenoble, France

Sponsor: IEEE, ACM/SIGDA

Proceedings of the 17th Design Automation Conference 218-25
1980

Publ: IEEE, New York, USA

X + 642 pp.

Treatment: Applic

Document Type: Report Section

(5 Refs)

Discusses the advantages of an integrated approach to computer-aided design and more particularly to computer-aided architectural design (CAAD). The author has studied different ways of organizing integrated systems, and his work has enabled him to define an integrated system for computer-aided architectural design SIGMA-ARCHI which is described. This system is a general support for CAAD, which can, on the one hand, be enriched by new operations of general interest, and on the other hand, be adapted for a specific application by the adjunction of specialized operations. He illustrates these two methods, the first one by showing how he integrates an open industrialized building system, and the second with the example of the subsystem, sigma-housing. Finally he presents the computer aspects of the system to demonstrate that the general systems approach to CAD facilitates the specification and the implementation of the system.

17. APPLICATION OF COMPUTER GRAPHICS FOR VISUALIZATION OF BUILDING OBJECTS

    Gojanovic, D.; Pleska, J.

    Zavod Za Elektroniku, Elektrothehnicki Facultet, Zagreb, Yugoslavia

    Rajkovic, V. (Editor)

    Informatica 78 XIII Yugoslav International Symposium on Information Processing 6-304/1-13 1978

    2-7 Oct. 1978 Bled, Yugoslavia

    Publ: Informatika, Ljubljana, Yugoslavia

    845 pp.

    Treatment: Applic

    Document Type: Report Section

    Languages: CROATIAN

    (5 Refs)

The application of computer graphics for the visualization of building objects helps all people involved in a project to communicate more effectively. This article describes evaluated methods for the visualization of building objects with the help of photogrammetry and computer graphics.

18. APPLICATION OF THE PROLOG LANGUAGE FOR THE DESIGN OF A MULTI-STORY LIVING-HOUSE

    Markusz, Z.

    Inf. Elektron. (Hungary) Vol. 15, No. 5, 256-63 1980 Coden: INFEBF

    Treatment: Applic; Practical Applic

Document Type: Journal Paper

Languages: Hungarian

(7 Refs)

A new architectural application of prolog, the design of a multistory living-house is introduced. The first program generates different versions of ground-plans according to the special needs of the customer. During the design of the house those design versions are selected which meet the functional requirements, the measures, and the environmental data of the building.

19. APPLICATION OF THE SMALL COMPUTER SYSTEM ROBOTRON 4201 FOR CONSTRUCTION PLANNING AND DESIGN WORK

    Thiele, G.

Neue Tech. Buero (Germany) Vol. 23, No. 2, 58-61

March-April 1979 Coden: NTBUB4

    Treatment: Applic; General, Review

    Document Type: Journal Paper

This article shows how a planning and design office of the building industry can operate the small computer system Robotron 4201 to streamline certain jobs. Such small computers can be operated in addition to large EDP installations, e.g. ES 1040 and ES 1055.

20. APPRAISAL OF BUILDING SUB-SYSTEMS

    Parkins, R.; Clarke, J., Laing, L.; Aylward, G.; Turnbull, M.

    Univ. of Strathclyde, Glasgow, Scotland

    Parc 79. International Conference on the Application of Computers in Architecture, Building Design and Urban Planning 205-19 1979

    7-10 May 1979 Berlin, Germany

    Publ: Online, Uxbridge, England

    XIII + 724 pp.

    Treatment: Applic, Theoretical

    Document Type: Report Section

    (11 Refs)

The structure, content, validation, and use of four subsystem appraisal programs are described in this paper: Air-Q, a model of movement within buildings; ESP, a model of energy flow in buildings; BIBLE, a model for generating perspective views of buildings; and VIEW, a model of the visual impact of buildings in rural settings.

21. AUTOMATIC DESIGN OF STRUCTURAL STEELWORK
     Laxon, W. R.; Mountford, D. H.; Malby, K. H.; Shuttleworth, B. T.
     Mountford and Laxon Co. Ltd., Sutton Coldfield, England
     Comput. Aided Des. (GB) Vol. 12, No. 1 35-42 Jan. 1980
Coden: CAIDA5
     Treatment: Applic; Practical Applic
     Document Type: Journal Paper
     (5 Refs)
     A computer system which automatically designs steel pitched-roof portal frame buildings is described. From a minimal amount of input, the computer produces all the design calculations, estimates, drawings, and documents for a contract. Use of the system has reduced lead time and alleviated a shortage of draftspersons. The system runs on an in-house minicomputer.

22. AUTOMATIC DESIGNING AND DRAFTING SYSTEM OF ELEVATORS (MELDAC SYSTEM)
     Mitsuya, C.
     Rep. Stat. Appl. Res. UJSE (Japan) Vol. 24, No. 2 18-27
June 1977 Coden: RARJAT
     Treatment: Applic; Practical Applic
     Document Type: Journal Paper
     With the tendency toward high city buildings in Japan. The demand for elevator equipment has increased rapidly since 1960. Standardized units for small and medium structures and apartment houses have come to form 70% of all demand. Layout drawings of the elevator have been indispensable for arrangements with owners, architects, and general contractors and for applications to the code authorities concerned as well as for installation work. The Elevator Engineering Department of Mitsubishi Electric Corporation started in May 1979 to develop an automatic designing and drawing system using a computer and drafting machine named the "Meldac System" to save manpower in designing and drawing.

23. AUTOMATIC SPACE-PLANNING A POSTMORTEM?
     Henrion, M.
     Inst. for Physical Planning, Carnegie-Mellon Univ., Pittsburgh, PA, USA
     Latombe, J.-C. (Editor)
     Sponsor: IFIP

Artificial Intelligence and Pattern Recognition in Computer Aided Design   175-96 1978

17-19 March 1978   Grenoble, France

Publ: North-Holland, Amsterdam, Netherlands

X + 510 pp.   ISBN 0 444 85229 8

Treatment: Applic; General, Review

Document Type: Report Section

(7 Refs)

Despite initial enthusiasm, automatic space planning has found little practical application in architecture, and there seems to be significant obstacles to achieving this. This paper argues that existing systems are, first, technically inadequate to represent and solve practical space-planning problems, and second, they are methodologically inadequate in that they do not fit happily into the design process. It presents a protocol analysis of the process of problem definition by human space planners to help understand the reasons for the latter difficulty. It concludes that the initial suggestion of systematic design methods that a computer-based system could produce "objective" design without using preconceptions was mistaken and that successful systems will have to incorporate more domain-specific knowledge.

24. BUILDING DESCRIPTION TECHNIQUES FOR RATIONALIZED TRADITIONAL CONSTRUCTION

Rosenthal, D. S. H.

Dept. of Architecture, Univ. of Edinburgh, Edinburgh, Scotland

Parc 79. International Conference on the Application of Computers in Architecture, Building Design and Urban Planning 565-72   1979

7-10 May 1979   Berlin, Germany

Publ: Online, Uxbridge, England

XIII + 724 pp.

Treatment: Applic; General, Review

Document Type: Report Section

(9 Refs)

Techniques for constructing computer-resident descriptions of buildings made from standard components are fairly well understood and have enabled production information to be generated for large and complex buildings. An alternative approach to construction information is to regard the building as composed of "standard details" of in-site construction, the so-called "rationalized traditional" method. Appropriate descriptive techniques for this approach are less well developed, and although they have been successful when applied to housing. Certain problems still impede their wider application. This paper discusses the differences between the techniques, with examples drawn from existing rationalized traditional systems, and identifies the outstanding problems.

25. BUILDING DESCRIPTION TECHNIQUES FOR RATIONALIZED TRADITIONAL CONSTRUCTION

    Rosenthal, D. S. H.

    Dept. of Architecture, Edinburgh Univ., Edinburgh, Scotland

    Comput. Aided Des. (GB) Vol. 11, No. 6, 325-8 Nov. 1979

Coden: CAIDA5

    Treatment: Practical Applic

    Document Type: Journal Paper

    (10 Refs)

Techniques for constructing computer descriptions of buildings viewed as assemblies of "standard details" of in-site construction are described and contrasted with those appropriate for buildings viewed as assemblies of standard components. These techniques have been successfully applied to the "rationalized traditional" method of housing construction, but certain problems impede their wider application.

26. BUILDING DESIGN FOR PASSIVE ENERGY CONSERVATION

    Shaviv, E.

    Faculty of Architecture and Town Planning. Technion-Israel Inst. of Technol., Haifa, Israel

    Parc 79. International Conference on the Application of Computers in Architecture, Building Design and Urban Planning 135-44 1979

    7-10 May 1979 Berlin, Germany

    Publ: Online, Uxbridge, England

    XIII + 724 pp.

    Treatment: Applic; Theoretical

    Document Type: Report Section

    (2 Refs)

A dynamic model for the prediction of the thermal performance of buildings, recently developed by Saviv and Shaviv, is applied to a particular problem of a residential house in Rehovot, Israel. The purpose of this paper is to demonstrate a strategy for the improvement of a given design. The strategy is adapted to widely used commercial computers since it demands no special peripherals or large memory. Moreover, the author strives at economic use of climatological consulting, and consequently, simple, non expensive, widely available equipment is used. The input data nad the output are described. The dynamic model allows the creation of a sequence of improved design alternatives. Conclusions pertinent to the particular design are given. Shows that the use of modest changes can yield 50% saving in the energy requirements of the building.

27.   BUILDING FUZZY CAD SYSTEMS
        Gero, J. S.; Volfneuk, M.
        Dept. of Architectural Sci., Univ. of Sydney, Sydney, New
        South Wales, Australia
        Cad 80. Proceedings of the 4th International Conference and
        Exhibition on Computers in Design Engineering 74-9 1980
        March 1980 Brighton, England
        Publ: IPC Sci. and Technol. Press. Guildford, England
        XIV + 774 pp.
        Treatment: Practical Applic
        Document Type: Report Section
        (8 Refs)
        This paper introduces the need to include subjectivities in
        computer-aided design systems. It commences with the differences between uncertainty. Which has been used to model
        subjectivity, and imprecision. The former provides the basis
        of probability theory while the latter the basis of fuzzy set
        theory. The thesis is that subjectivities introduce imprecision. It shows that subjectivities can be included in the
        description of the interactions between parts of the system.
        After presenting a brief introduction to fuzzy set theory, the
        paper shows how a fuzzy CAD system can be built. An example is
        presented which demonstrates the approach.

28.   CEDAR3 IN PRACTICE, USING A LARGE INTEGRATED COMPUTER-AIDED
        BUILDING DESIGN SYSTEM IN GOVERNMENT DESIGN OFFICES
        Thompson, B. G. J.; Young, J. S.
        Dept. of Environment, Croydon, England
        Comput. Aided Des. (GB) Vol. 12, No. 3 139-48 May 1980
        Coden: CAIDA5
        Treatment: Practical Applic
        Document Type: Journal Paper
        (7 Refs)
        CEDAR3 has been installed in two design offices of the UK
        Department of Environment (property services agency). Architects, service engineers, and quantity surveyors have used the

system for long periods and tested it on real projects of many building types at the outline design stage. Projects ranging from a computer center to a Royal Navy barracks complex are discussed, together with user reactions to CEDAR. Use support, training, documentation, system maintenance, and reliability are other issues examined and future requirements identified.

29. COMPUTER-AIDED DESIGN IN INDUSTRIAL RESIDENTIAL CONSTRUCTION
       Kociolek, A.; Radwanski, A.
       Parc 79. International Conference on the Application of Computers in Architecture, Building Design and Urban Planning 1-11 1979
       7-10 May 1979 Berlin, Germany
       Publ: Online, Uxbridge, England
       XIII + 724 pp.
       Treatment: Applic; General, Review
       Document Type: Report Section
       (1 Refs)
       Describes a CABD (computer-aided building design) system whose aim is to provide facilities to enable designers to utilize the potential of the open industrialization in the context of mass residential construction.

30. COMPUTER AIDED DIMENSIONING OF ARCHITECTURAL PLANS
       Gero, J. S.
       Dept. of Architectural Sci., Univ. of Sydney, Sydney, Australia
       Sponsor: Computer-Aided Design Centre; Dept. Environment; et al.
       Third International Conference and Exhibition on Computers in Engineering and Building Design 482-94 1978
       14-16 March 1978 Brighton, England
       Publ: IPC Sci. and Technology Press Ltd., Guildford, England
       XII + 803 pp. ISBN 0 902852 85 X
       Treatment: Applic; Theoretical
       Document Type: Report Section
       (5 Refs)
       A system for the computer-aided dimensioning of architectural plans is described. It is based on the use of dynamic programming to optimize the room dimensions to minimize the construction cost while satisfying the various planning constraints. The designer works at an interactive graphics terminal and uses a command language to control the system. The results are presented both graphically and numerically. The designer can

examine all feasible solutions as well as the optimal solution.
The results are then used as a database for a drafting program.
With this system the problem of generating the geometry of a
design has been solved.

31. COMPUTER-AIDED PLANT LAYOUT. V. HOW TO MASSAGE THE COMPUTER
     OUTPUT
        Tompkins, J. A.
        Dept. of Industrial Engng., North Carolina State Univ.,
     Raleigh, NC, USA
        Mod. Mater. Handl. (USA) Vol. 33, No. 9, 102-7 Sept. 1978
        Coden: MMHHA2
        Treatment: General, Review; Practical Applic
        Document Type: Journal Paper
        For Pt. IV see Ibid., Vol. 33, No. 8, p. 64-9 (1978). This
     article discusses how the computer layouts can be translated
     and adjusted into practical layout plans.

32. COMPUTER AIDED SKETCH-PLAN DESIGN
        Baxter, A. J.
        Sheffield City Polytech., Sheffield, England
        Heat. and Vent. Eng. (GB) Vol. 53, No. 616, 6-11 March 1979
     Coden: HVENBE
        Treatment: Applic
        Document Type: Journal Paper
        (13 Refs)
        Describes a suite of computer programs "speed" which has been
     produced to assist in the sketch-plan design stage of build-
     ings. Facilities are available with speed to examine the
     thermal and visual environments in a building and the effect on
     building construction. Speed enables a large number of alter-
     native design solutions to be examined very quickly. The
     program is very simple to use, of low complexity, and cheap to
     run.

33. COMPUTER-AIDED STRUCTURAL DESIGN OF BUILDINGS, STATE OF A
     CANADIAN INDUSTRY
        Hartley, G. A.; Carson, D. J.
        Dept. of Civil Engng., Carleton Univ., Ottawa, Ontario,
     Canada
        Adey, R. A. (Editors)
        Engineering Software 443-55 1979
        Sept. 1979 Southampton, England
        Publ: Pentech, London, England

701 pp.   ISBN 0 7273 0501 8
Treatment: General, Review
Document Type: Report Section
(3 Refs)

This paper summarizes the results of a 2-year survey of the computer-aided design of building structures in Canada. The survey was directed toward three key elements of this subject: the consultants, use of computers and programs available commercially and in house; the pool of software commercially available at data centers for computer-aided structural design of buildings; and the data center service provided to engineering consultants engaged in the design of building structures.

34. COMPUTER ASSISTED STRUCTURAL ANALYSIS AND DIMENSIONING OF FLOOR SLABS FOR BUILDING CONSTRUCTION

Engelmann, E.; Beilschmidt, L.; Damrath, R.
Inst. fur Allgemeine Bauingenieurmethoden, Tech. Univ.
Berlin, Berlin, Germany
Parc 79. International Conference on the Application of Computers in Architecture, Building Design and Urban Planning 305-20 1979
7-10 May 1979   Berlin-Germany
Publ: Online, Uxbridge, England
XIII + 724 pp.
Treatment: Applic; Theoretical
Document Type: Report Section
Languages: German (8 Refs)

35. COMPUTERS AND BUILDING REGULATIONS

Phillips, R. J.
Dept. of Architecture, Univ. of Bristol, Bristol, England
Comput. Aided Des. (GB) Vol. 11, No. 5 273-9 Sept. 1979
Coden: CAIDA5
Treatment: Applic; Theoretical
Document Type: Journal Paper
(15 Refs)

Demonstrates the potential of computer-based systems for checking building design proposals against statutory instruments for building and buildings. In the Department of Architecture, University of Bristol, a computer-aided design guide to the thermal insulation of dwellings, Part F of the current English Building Regulations, has been developed. This design guide is explained and is used to demonstrate how design proposals are checked and how guidance is given to the designer.

Some problems encountered in the use of building regulations are indicated, in particular attention is drawn to the problems in building design of increasing essential numeracy, arising as a result of the increasing use of regulations based on performance specification approaches. It is concluded that this guide shows that computer-based techniques could have a useful role to play in helping designers not only with building regulations but with legislation in general.

36. COMPUTER CALCULATIONS OF ULTRAVIOLET RADIATION IN THE INTERIOR OF BUILDINGS UNDER NATURAL ILLUMINATION
      Akilov, Yu. Z.; Turulov, V. A.; Safaev, A.; Khakimov, K. K.
      Tashkent Sci. Res. and Design Inst. for Standard Experimental Design of Domestic and Public Buildings, USSR
      Geliotekhnika (USSR) Vol. 13 No. 3 49-55 1977 Coden: ASOEA6
      Trans In: Appl. Sol. Energy (USA) Vol. 13 No. 3 37-42 1977 Coden: ASOEA6
      Treatment: Applic; General, Review
      Document Type: Journal Paper
      (10 Refs)
      A method has been developed for calculating the ultraviolet radiation in the interior of buildings, which can be used to determine the amount of UV radiation on an insulated surface and the total daily amount of this radiation entering through a window. The quantities considered include the monochromatic flux of direct and scattered radiation on the earth's surface, the relative spectral illumination efficiency, the size and orientation of the windows, the transmission of transparent materials employed, and the structure of the building. Comparison between calculations and observations has shown that the method employed is acceptable.

37. COMPUTER GRAPHICS AND ARCHITECTURE
      Rogers, G.
      School of Architecture, Federal Inst. of Technol., Zurich, Switzerland
      Vandoni, C. E. (Editor)
      Eurographics 80. Proceedings of the International Conference and Exhibition 203-14 1980
      3-5 Sept. 1980 Geneva, Switzerland
      Publ: North-Holland, Amsterdam, Netherlands
      XVI + 347 pp. ISBN 0 444 86107 6
      Treatment: Practical Applic

Document Type: Report Section

(16 Refs)

Because computer-generated architectural drawings derive from common databases, they can be more useful than those drawn manually. Beyond viewing functions, other operations (such as financial, spatial, and thermal analyses) can be applied to the computer-based model. The development of relevant input procedures and a coherent theory and methodology for computer-aided design will make computer graphics more accessible to architects. This paper describes a continuing effort to accomplish such a development.

38. COMPUTER SIMULATION OF FOLIAGE SHADING IN BUILDING ENERGY LOADS
Schiler, M.; Greenberg, D. P.
Program of Computer Graphics, Cornell Univ., Ithaca, NY, USA
Sponsor: ACM; IEEE
16th Design Automation Conference Proceedings 142-8 1979
25-27 June 1979 San Diego, CA, USA
Publ: IEEE, New York, USA
XIII + 567 pp.
Treatment: Applic; Theoretical
Document Type: Report Section
(16 Refs)

The calculation of building thermal loads using the computer has been an accepted practice for several years. A substantial amount of research and theoretical investigation has been thermal behavior. A number of existing simulation packages acceptably model this behavior.

39. CONFIGURATION STUDIES, NETWORK GEOMETRY-AN EXAMPLE
Earl, C. F.; March, L.
Centre for Configurational Studies, Open Univ., Milton Keynes, England
Parc 79. International Conference on the Application of Computers in Architecture, Building Design and Urban Planning 353-63 1979
7-10 May 1979 Berlin, Germany
Publ: Online, Uxbridge, England
XIII + 724 pp.
Treatment: Applic; General, Review
Document Type: Report Section
(13 Refs)

The concept of configurational studies is introduced and a simple example--the geometry of route networks--is used to illustrate some of the leading principles of the approach.

40. COSTMOD, A DESIGNERS TOOL FOR COST ESTIMATING
     Schild, W.; Hauber, A.; Logcher, R. D.
     IBM Israel Sci. Center, Technion City, Haifa, Israel
     Parc 79. International Conference on the Application of
     Computers in Architecture, Building Design and Urban Planning
     255-64 1979
     7-10 May 1979 Berlin, Germany
     Publ: Online, Uxbridge, England
     XIII + 724 pp.
     Treatment: Applic; Theoretical
     Document Type: Report Section
     This paper describes an interactive computer application
     developed to enable cost estimation during the initial phase of
     design and operating hierarchically structured models of
     projects. The system is designed to be operated by designers
     and planners themselves in three independent phases. A model
     building stage provides a convenient format for defining
     models. An "expansion" phase follows in which a model is
     executed with parameters of interest. Finally a reporting
     mechanism is provided for flexible and varied output of
     results.

41. COLOURFUL CAD (IN CONSTRUCTION INDUSTRY)
     Paterson, J.
     Building (GB) Vol. 233, No. 38 99, 101 23 Sept. 1977
     Coden: BULDBE
     Treatment: Applic; Economic Aspects; General, Review
     Document Type: Journal Paper
     Discusses labor-saving microcomputers which can be bought for
     less than the cost of a motor car--and in color.

42. DESCRIPTIVE DATABASES IN SOME DESIGN MANUFACTURING ENVIRONMENTS
     Hoskins, E. M.
     Appl. Res. of Cambridge, Cambridge, England
     Comput. Aided Des. (GB) Vol. 11, No. 3 151-7 May 1979
     Coden: CAIDA5
     Treatment: Practical Applic
     Document Type: Journal Paper
     A comprehensive set of software development tools--BOS
     infrastructure software--is introduced. This system enables
     purpose built data structures to be constructed for a range of
     engineering disciplines. The development of BOS building
     design systems containing three-dimensional assembly data
     structures and comprehensive parts databases and engineering

management systems describing product assemblies are introduced.

43. DESIGNING BUILDINGS FOR MINIMAL ENERGY CONSUMPTION
     Shaviv, E.; Shaviv, G.
     Faculty of Architecture and Town Planning, Israel Inst. of
Technol., Haifa, Israel
     Comput. Aided Des. (GB) Vol. 10, No. 4 239-47 July 1978
Coden: CAIDA5
     Treatment: Practical Applic
     Document Type: Journal Paper
     (8 Refs)
A dynamic model for predicting the thermal behavior and
energy consumption of a full-scale building has been developed.
The model can include most of the design and climatological
factors affecting the building. The time-dependent equation
for the heat flow through the walls is converted into an
implicit scheme and solved numerically. Special effort has
been devoted to producing a model capable of aiding the architect during the various steps of building design, so as to
approach thermal comfort with minimal energy consumption. the
results are presented in graphical form, which allows the
architect to detect easily the crucial factors in the thermal
performance of the building.

44. DESIGN DEVELOPMENT AND DESCRIPTION USING 3D BOX GEOMETRIES
     Hoskins, E. M.
     Appl. Res. of Cambridge, Cambridge, England
     Comput. Aided Des. (GB) Vol. 11, No. 6 329-36 Nov. 1979
Coden: CAIDA5
     Treatment: Practical Applic
     Document Type: Journal Paper
     (1 Ref)
Computer-aided building often relates to complex designed
objects such as hospital buildings. The design image comprises
initially an overall formal description and later a unique
description used here for buildings accommodates both forms of
description simultaneously. The level of description required
for each is, however, not necessarily fully detailed. This
paper outlines the approach taken by ARC (Applied Research of
Cambridge) to modelling large-scale, multiple-element assemblies that make up building designs. These techniques are
employed in the BDS (building design systems) supplied and
supported by ARC.

45. DESIGN OFFICE CONSORTIUM
     Howard, R.
     BOCAAD (Bull. Comput. Aided Archit. Des.) (GB) No. 27-28
     33-7 Feb.-May 1978 Coden: BBCDD8
     Treatment: Applic; General, Review; Practical Applic.
     Document Type: Journal Paper
     DOC was established in 1973 to encourage the sensible use of
     computers in offices concerned with building design and con-
     struction. It was to carry out projects concerned with appli-
     cation rather than research, and it was to act as a focus for
     specification of user requirements. It was established as a
     nonprofit distributing association, supported by government
     departments. The services provided to members include informa-
     tion on sources of programs, presentations of systems in use in
     members' offices, consultancy, and specification of useful
     developments. These are not unique, but DOC provides them in
     return for membership fees which are quite modest and relate to
     the size of the practice. Two unique services which are also
     provided are concerned with the testing of groups of programs
     and the publication of guides to producing programs to work on
     different computers.

46. DEVELOPMENT TACTICS FOR APPLICATIONS OF COMPUTER SCIENCE IN
     BUILDING DESIGNING IN POLAND
     Robakiewicz, M.
     Convention Informatique 1977 (Information Convention 1977)
     214-17 1977
     20-23 Sept. 1977 France
     Publ: Convention Informatique, Paris, France
     283 pp.
     Treatment: Applic; General, Review
     Document Type: Report Section
     The paper focuses on the methods adopted in Poland for pro-
     moting the development of computer science applications in a
     large group of design offices. The author's aim is to show
     organizational methods which have proved useful in practice and
     effective in the development of computer science applications.
     Although these methods are connected with the organization of
     the Polish economy, it is possible to treat them as a general
     proposal for the cooperation within a large group of enter-
     prises specializing in one field.

47. DIGITAL GRAPHICS IN THE BUILDING INDUSTRY
     Haber, W.
     Neue Tech. Buero (Germany) Vol. 23, No. 6 167-9

Nov.-Dec. 1979 Coden: NTBUB4

  Treatment: Practical Applic

  Document Type: Journal Paper

  (5 Refs)

  Discusses the use of computer graphics for architectural cad. Various graphic techniques are described from on-line terminals to computer-controlled drawing machines.

48. DIY CAAD WITH THE ARCHITECTURAL MODELLERS TOOL KIT

  Beacon, G. R.; Boreham, P. G.

  School of Architecture and Landscape, Leeds Polytech., Leeds, England

  Parc 79. International Conference on the Application of Computers in Architecture, Building Design and Urban Planning 593-9 1979

  7-10 May 1979 Berlin, Germany

  Publ: Online, Uxbridge, England

  XIII + 724 pp.

  Treatment: Applic; General, Review

  Document Type: Report Section

  This paper describes a set of programs and subroutine libraries concerned with modeling buildings and their surroundings. It is intended to publish this software in source so that users can implement, modify, and add to the programs to tailor a system to suit their own needs.

49. ECOLE 3, MODELLING AND APPRAISING A 3D BUILD-FORM LAYOUT

  Th'ng, R.

  Holmes and Partners Architects, Glasgow, Scotland

  Comput. Aided Des. (GB) Vol. 10, No. 6 381-5 Nov. 1978 Coden: CAIDA5

  Treatment: Applic; Practical Applic

  Document Type: Journal Paper

  (4 Refs)

  ECOLE 3 is concerned with modeling the building geometry and subdividing this geometry into floors and rooms and is intended to allow the designer to optimize this geometrical form of the building while taking into account factors such as structure, construction, planning, environment, and costs.

50. ECONOMIC EVALUATION OF WINDOWS IN BUILDINGS, METHODOLOGY

  Ruegg, R. T.; Chapman, R. E.

  Issued by: Nat. Bur. Stand., Washington, DC, USA; April 1979

  105 pp.

  Treatment: Applic; Practical Applic

(22 Refs)

Report No.: NBS-BSS-119

Aims at improving the cost effectiveness of window selection and use in buildings. The authors develop and illustrate a life-cycle costing evaluation model and computer program for assessing for alternative window systems the net dollar impact of acquisition, maintenance, and repair, heating and cooling energy gains and losses, and artificial lighting and daylighting trade-offs. The method is applicable to the evaluation of many different window sizes, designs, accessories, and uses, both for new and existing residential and commercial buildings. Two step-by-step examples of evaluating selected window alternatives in a residence and in an office building in Washington, D.C. serve to illustrate the application of the method.

51. ENERGY AND THE ENVIRONMENT, CASE STUDIES OF THE USE OF ESP
     Clarke, J. A.
     Univ. of Glasgow, Strathclyde, Scotland
     Parc 79. International Conference on the Application of Computers in Architecture, Building Design and Urban Planning 153-64 1979
     7-10 May 1979 Berlin, Germany
     Publ: Online, Uxbridge, England
     XIII + 724 pp.
     Treatment: Theoretical; Experimental
     Document Type: Report Section
     (3 Refs)

ESP, a building energy simulation computer program, dynamically models the energy transfers with and within a polyhedral space bounded by any combination of multilayered opaque and transparent surfaces. This paper describes the theoretical basis and operation of the program, its ongoing validation, and, perhaps most importantly, a series of case studies in which the program has been used for both the design of new buildings and the redesign of existing ones.

52. ENERGY EFFICIENT OFFICE BUILDING IS LIVING LAB
     Electr. Comf. Cond. News (USA) Vol. 4, No. 6 14-16 June 1977 Coden: ECCNDA
     Treatment: Economic Aspects; General, Review
     Document Type: Journal Paper

Describes an energy-efficient office building in New Hampshire designed to test out the latest energy conservation technology. Its energy consumption is monitored to provide infor-

mation for similar future designs. A computer program called
national bureau of standards load determination was used to
optimize the design toward the chosen ends. The building is
nearly cubic in shape and should use one-third less energy than
a conventional building. Important features of the design are
the heat recovery and solar energy systems. 750 Sensors measure temperature, humidity, air and water flow, solar radiation, electric power consumption, barometric pressure, and
indoor illumination.

53. ENERGY MODELLING IN BUILDING DESIGN
    Clarke, J. A.
    Dept. of Architecture, Univ. of Strathclyde, Glasgow,
Scotland
    BOCAAD (Bull. Comput. Aided Archit. Des.) (GB) No. 37 23-31
Aug. 1980 Coden: BBCDD8
    Treatment: Applic; Practical Applic
    Document Type: Journal Paper
    (7 Refs)
    Describes thermal simulation appraisal program which has been
developed in the context of the view of the design process as
expounded by Maver. As well as existing in stand-alone mode,
the program can also be considered as one module of an integrated design appraisal package, currently being developed,
which attempts to provide sophisticated information relating to
the spatial, functional, environmental, and economic performance of built form together with a set of perspective views
which simulate visual characteristics. This allows the selection of appropriate design solutions or strategies arrived at
on the basis of "across-the-board" considerations rather than
on the basis of a "narrow" view from within the confines of any
one particular professional discipline.

54. EVALUATION METHODS IN SARA--THE GRAPH MODEL SIMULATOR
    Razouk, R. R.; Vernon, M.; Estrin, G.
    Computer Sci. Dept., Univ. of California, Los Angeles, CA,
USA
    Sponsor: ACM; SIGSIM: Sigmetrics; Nat. Bur. Standards
    Performance Eval. Rev. (USA) Vol. 11, No. 1 189-203 Fall
    1979
    Papers presented at the Conference on Simulation Measurement
and Modeling of Computer Systems, 13-15 Aug., 1979, Boulder,
CO, USA
    Treatment: Practical Applic

Document Type: Report Section
(44 Refs)

The supported methodology evolving in the SARA (system architects' apprentice) system creates a design framework on which
increasingly powerful analytical tools are to be grafted. This
paper describes a fundamental SARA tool, the graph model simulator. During top-down refinement of a design, the simulator
is used to test consistency between the levels of abstraction.
During composition, known building blocks are linked together,
and the composite graph model is tested relative to the lowest
top-down model. Design of test environments is integrated with
the multilevel design process. The SARA methodology is exemplified through design of a higher-level building block to do a
simple FFT.

55.   EVALUATION OF ALTERNATIVE SKETCH DESIGNS USING AN APPRAISAL
      PROGRAM
         Th'ng, R.
         Dept. of Architectural and Related Services, Strathclyde
      Regional Council, Glasgow, Scotland
         Sponsor: Computer-Aided Design Centre; Dept. Environment; et
      al.
         Third International Conference and Exhibition on Computers in
      Engineering and Building Design 629-32 1978
         14-16 March 1978 Brighton, England
         Publ: IPC Sci. and Technology Press Ltd., Guildford, England
         XII + 803 pp. ISBN 0 902852 85 X
         Treatment: Applic; Theoretical
         Document Type: Report Section
         Discusses the application of a computer program spaces 3 used
      in helping to evaluate a series of primary school designs.

56.   EVALUATION OF COMPUTER PROGRAMS IN THE BUILDING INDUSTRY.   A
      EUROPEAN APPROACH
         Bensasson, S.
         Design Office Consortium, Cambridge, England
         Parc 79. International Conference on the Application of
      Computers in Architecture, Building Design and Urban Planning
      677-81 1979
         7-10 May 1979   Berlin, Germany
         Publ: Online, Uxbridge, England
         XIII + 724 pp.
         Treatment: Applic; General, Review
         Document Type: Report Section

Evaluation of computer programs can be useful to computer users who want to select a program that will satisfy a specific need, but it can also contribute to an improvement in the state of the art and the freer flow of software in Europe.

57. EXPERIENCE IN THE USE OF BDS SYSTEM (OXSYS) ON A MAJOR PROJECT IN A MULTIDISCIPLINARY CONSULTANCY
        Collins, E. B.; Prince, M. R.
        Atkins Sheppard Fidler and Associates, Epsom, England
        Cad 80. Proceedings of the 4th International Conference and Exhibition on Computers in Design Engineering 425-34 1980
        March 1980 Brighton, England
        Publ: IPC Sci. and Technol. Press, Guildford, England
        XIV + 774 pp.
        Treatment: Practical Applic
        Document Type: Report Section
        (5 Refs)
        BDS was acquired in order to provide a computer-aided building design system initially for the architectural practice. The system has been used in the design of a major teaching hospital and university at Tlemcen, Algeria and is producing the majority of drawing and schedule output. A major benefit in addition to reduced drafting costs is increased design coordination between all the disciplines involved in the project. It is intended to enhance the system to include associated analysis facilities.

58. FUZZY RELATIONS AND INEXACT DESIGN REQUIREMENTS
        Phillips, R. J.; Richardson, D.; Beaumont, M. J.
        Dept. of Architecture, Univ. of Bristol, Bristol, England
        Parc 79. International Conference on the Application of Computers in Architecture, Building Design and Urban Planning 415-24 1979
        7-10 May 1979 Berlin, Germany
        Publ: Online, Uxbridge, England
        XIII + 724 pp.
        Treatment: Applic; Theoretical
        Document Type: Report Section
        (3 Refs)
        Many of the requirements for a building design are inexact for requirements for some properties of materials such as color and texture. This paper shows how methods based on principles of fuzzy relations may be used to handle such requirements. An abstract mathematical formulation of requirements is followed

by an illustration of how these are represented in the architectural database Aesop developed at Bristol. A simple
example, choosing materials from a set of materials with
various properties so that certain specified requirements are
met, is used to demonstrate the principles of the methods.

59. GUILDFORD CROWN COURTS SKETCH DESIGN APPRAISAL BY CEDAR 3
    Thompson, B. G. J.
    Comput. Aided Des. (GB) Vol. 11, No. 5 305-7 Sept. 1979
    Coden: CAIDA5
    Document Type: Journal Paper
    (2 Refs)

Describes the use of CEDAR 3 and illustrates its application
in one of the projects worked on during trails held between
April and October 1978. An interactive computer-aided building
design system, currently in its third phase, CEDAR 3 is intended to be used at the early stages of building design. The
system is being developed by the property services agency of
the UK Department of the Environment, and enables the designer
to enter and manipulate a description of his or her building
and to analyze and compare alternative configurations for aspects of performance including costs and environmental factors.

60. GRIB 3.1. VERSION 3.1 ONE OF THE FORMULA OF PROBLEM-ORIENTED
    WRITING
    Riepl, C.
    Inst. Fur Bauokonomie, Univ. Stuttgart, Stuttgart, Germany
    Parc 79. International Conference on the Application of
    Computers in Architecture, Building Design and Urban Planning
    49-61 1979
    7-10 May 1979 Berlin, Germany
    Publ: Online, Uxbridge, England
    XIII + 724 pp.
    Treatment: Applic; Theoretical
    Document Type: Report Section
    Languages: Germany (18 Refs)

The paper describes the problem-oriented language GRIB 3.1.
The purpose of GRIB 3.1 is the coding of floorplans. The elements of a floorplan description are building components. Components are mapped onto edges and/or sequences of edges and
junctions onto vertices of a planar floorplan-graph. The
translation of GRIB 3.1 generates a data structure, which
handles the information of the floorplan-graph as well as
attributes associated with edges and vertices. GRIB 3.1 has

been implemented with the aid of the translator-writing-system LANG-PAK.

61. HEATING AND COOLING LOADS COMPUTATION PROGRAM (USING THE THERMAL RESPONSE FACTOR METHOD)

Suenaga, T.

Nippon Telegraph and Telephone Public Corp., Tokyo, Japan

Rev. Electr. Commun. Lab. (Japan) Vol. 25, No. 3-4 271-82 March-April 1977 Coden: RELTAN

Treatment: Applic

Document Type: Journal Paper

(5 Refs)

This program (AIRCON-2) was made as one of the library programs for DEMOS-E (Dnedenkosha Multi-access Online System Extended), NTT. It has been available on a commercial basis since Sept. 1974. The user can calculate annual energy consumptions, room air temperatures and humidities variation, peak room load, etc., at high accuracy for various buildings, and can analyze building thermal performance from several viewpoints, because the input forms have been designed with high flexibility.

62. IMPLICATIONS FOR PRACTICE AND EDUCATION

Maver, T. W.; Smith, M.; Watts, J.; Aish, R.

Univ. of Strathclyde, Glasgow, Scotland

Parc 79. International Conference on the Application of Computers in Architecture, Building Design and Urban Planning 221-32 1979

7-10 May 1979 Berlin, Germany

Publ: Online, Uxbridge, England

XIII + 724 pp.

Treatment: Applic; General, Review

Document Type: Report Section

(17 Refs)

The impact of CAAD techniques may be compared with the impact of the introduction of design drawings 5000 years ago. The new generation of computer-based models--being predictive rather than descriptive, dynamic rather than static, explicit rather than implicit--will have implications for practice, education, and building users. This paper anticipates the impact and projects the development of the models into the future.

63. INTEGRATED APPRAISAL OF BUILDING FORM

Sussock, H.; Gentles, J.; Gardner, W.; Walters, R.

Univ. of Strathclyde, Glasgow, Scotland

Parc 79. International Conference on the Application of Computers in Architecture, Building Design and Urban Planning 187-204 1979

7-10 May 1979 Berlin, Germany

Publ: Online, Uxbridge, England

XIII + 724 pp.

Treatment: Applic, Theoretical

Document Type: Report Section

(8 Refs)

Integrated and comprehensive computer-based design models offer the architect a flexible and neutral design aid by providing an objective information base of predicted cost and performance attributes which guides the search for an optimal solution. The concept of appraisal is developed by reference to the structure, content, and use of three appraisal packages--goal, phase, and bild; together these examples illustrate the range of applicability across the design activity.

64.   INTERACTIVE DRAFTING UTILIZING DATABASE CONCEPTS

Gero, J. S.; Plume, J. D.

Dept. of Architectural Sci., Univ. Sydney, Sydney, Australia

Sponsor: Instn. Engrs. Australia; Australian Computer Soc.; ACADS

Australian Conference on Computer Graphics and Spatial Analysis 167-71 1979

13-15 Aug. 1979 Adelaide, Australia

Publ: Instn. Engrs. Australia, Barton, Australia

182 pp. ISBN 0 85825 117 5

Treatment: Applic; Practical Applic

Document Type: Report Section

(6 Refs)

The requirements of interactive drafting systems are presented. Databases are outlined, and a specific implementation for a drafting system oriented toward the product of drawings for buildings is described. The data in this database can be simply generated from direct input to the drafting system or from the output of a design system. An example is given.

65.   INTERACTIVE STRUCTURAL DESIGN WITH COMPUTER GRAPHICAL OUTPUT

Knapton, J.; Andam, K. A.

Dept. of Civil Engng., Univ. of Newcastle Upon Tyne, Newcastle Upon Tyne, England

Comput. Aided Des. (GB) Vol. 11, No. 4 195-200 July 1979

Coden: CAIDA5

Treatment: General, Review

Document Type: Journal Paper

(10 Refs)

A study has been made of cost patterns of precast concrete portal framed buildings. Studies carried out into fabrication, haulage, foundations, cladding, and erection have been used to develop a cost model computer program. Data describing the structure are input into this cost model, and the resulting overall cost is used to generate cost contour maps for precast concrete portal framed buildings. The cost model program is interfaced with a computer graphical system which enables engineering drawings and bar bending schedules to be output interactively.

66. INTERFACE DESIGN AND THE FUTURE DEVELOPMENT OF INTERACTIVE BUILDING DESIGN SYSTEMS, A STUDY REPORT

Goumain, P.; Mallen, G.

Dept. of Design Res., Royal Coll. of Art, London, England

Sponsor: Computer-Aided Design Centre; Dept. Environment; et al.

Third International Conference and Exhibition on Computers in Engineering and Building Design 44-53 1978

14-16 March 1978 Brighton, England

Publ: IPC Sci. and Technology Press Ltd., Guildford, England

XII + 803 pp. ISBN 0 902852 85 X

Treatment: Applic; General, Review

Document Type: Report Section

(9 Refs)

This program is aimed at clarifying guidelines for the development and implementation of interactive computer aids for the building design process. Its structure tries to integrate technical aspects with social psychological aspects. Also the influence that developments in the theory of design and design methods has had is discussed.

67. MICROCOMPUTERS AND BUILDING ELEVATIONS

Velez-John, G.

Lab. de Tecnicas Avanzadas en Diseno, Facultad de Arquitectura Y Urbanismo, Univ. Central de Venezuela, Caracas, Venezuela

Parc 79. International Conference on the Application of Computers in Architecture, Building Design and Urban Planning 93-103 1979

7-10 May 1979 Berlin, Germany

Publ: Online, Uxbridge, England

XIII + 724 pp.

Treatment: Applic; Practical Applic

Document Type: Report Section

(1 Ref)

This paper presents the initial results of experiences being realized at the Laboratory for Advanced Techniques in Design and at the author's home computing laboratory. Comparative experiences in the representation of building elevations at the early stages of design have been achieved in two different types of microcomputers. In both cases, Boolean graphic representation is utilized as the main technique.

68.   NEW TECHNOLOGIES AND THEIR INCORPORATING PROBLEMS SHOWN AS EXAMPLE OF CAD IN THE BUILDING INDUSTRY

Stelzer, V.

Kernforschungszentrum Karlsruhe GMBH, Karlsruhe, Germany

Parc 79.   International Conference on the Application of Computers in Architecture, Building Design and Urban Planning 233-44 1979

7-10 May 1979 Berlin, Germany

Publ: Online, Uxbridge, England

XIII + 724 pp.

Treatment: General, Review

Document Type: Report Section

Languages: German (19 Refs)

This paper describes the state of the art in CAD in the building industry and the problems of CAD introduction. Also starting points are indicated for promotion by the government in the building industry.

69.   NOTATION AND SYSTEM FOR 3-D CONSTRUCTIONS

Yessios, C. I.

Dept. of Architecture, Ohio State Univ., Columbus, OH, USA

Sponsor: ACM; IEEE

Proceedings of the Fifteenth Annual Design Automation Conference 125-32 1978

19-21 June 1978 Las Vegas, NV, USA

Publ: IEEE, New York, USA

X + 493 pp.

Treatment: Applic; Practical Applic; Theoretical

Document Type: Report Section

(11 Refs)

A linguistic model and its implementation for the description of three-dimensional compositions, primarily as they occur in building construction, are presented. The model, while it also provides for irregular compositions, facilitates the derivation of standard orthogonal arrangements by the use of the junction operator, which does not require the explicit definition of positioning coordinates for each element in the composition.

70.   OBTAINING BUILDINGS' PERSPECTIVE VIEWS COMPLETE OF MATERIALS' TEXTURES
      Nuzzolese, V.
      Istituto di Architettura ed Urbanistica, Univ. di Bari, Bari, Italy
      CAD 80. Proceedings of the 4th International Conference and Exhibition on Computers in Design Engineering 109-17 1980
      March 1980 Brighton, England
      Publ: IPC Sci. and Technol. Press, Guildford, England
      XIV + 774 pp.
      Treatment: Practical Applic
      Document Type: Report Section
      (5 Refs)
      The paper discusses the implementation of computerized techniques to obtain building perspective views complete with material textures and photographic environment background.

71.   ON THE DETERMINATION OF THE OPTIMUM SHADING FACTOR FOR WINDOWS
      Shaviv, E.
      Environmental Design Coll., Univ. of Colorado, Boulder, CO, USA
      CAD 80. Proceedings of the 4th International Conference and Exhibition on Computers in Design Engineering 605-14 1980
      March 1980 Brighton, England
      Publ: IPC Sci. and Technol. Press, Guildford, England
      XIV + 774 pp.
      Treatment: Practical Applic
      Document Type: Report Section
      (9 Refs)
      A method for searching the optimum shading coefficient for a given window was developed. Taking into consideration the energy consumption of the building for heating, cooling, and lighting. A comparison between the performance of different shading devices like dark film, external shading, and internal shading is accomplished. The method is demonstrated on a case study which is compared with other case studies. No rule of thumb can be found for determining a prior the best solution for a given window. Therefore, a computer should be resorted to for solving the optimum shading device for each window.

72. OPTIMIZATION APPLIED TO THE DESIGN OF AN ENERGY-EFFICIENT
    BUILDING
        Jurovics, S. A.
        IBM J. Res. and Dev. (USA) Vol. 22, No. 4 378-85 July 1978
    Coden: IBMJAE
        Treatment: Applic
        Document Type: Journal Paper
        (5 Refs)
    This work reports on an investigation of the imbedding of an
    energy analysis program into an optimization structure. Such
    an arrangement would enable a user to specify a set of archi-
    tectural and construction parameters and the limits within
    which they might vary and from this to determine the parameters
    that yield a local minimum in thermal load and its sensitivity
    to changes in these parameters.

73. OPTIMISATION DESIGN METHODS AND THE BUILDING DESIGN SYSTEM AIM
        Phillips, R. J.; Bastin, C. R. W.
        Dept. of Architecture, Univ. of Bristol, Bristol, England
        BOCAAD (Bull. Comput. Aided Archit. Des.) (GB) No. 31 25-30
    Feb. 1979 Coden: BBCDD8
        For the solution of complex problems involving many vari-
    ables, conditional relations between variables, and external
    constraints on the values of variables, it is often useful to
    divide the solution process into two stages: (1) the achieve-
    ment of a solution which satisfies a subset of the external
    constraints; (2) the achievement of a solution which satisfies
    all external constraints.

74. OPTIMIZATIONS IN ARCHITECTURAL LAYOUT PROCESS
        Moucka, J.
        Inst. Prumysloveho Designu, Praha, Czechoslovakia
        Ekon.-Mat. Obz. (Czechoslovakia) Vol. 16, No. 2 190-210
    1980 Coden: EKMOBF
        Treatment: Applic; Theoretical
        Document Type: Journal Paper
        (5 Refs)
    Three methods for computer-aided architectural layout are
    introduced. The scope of two is limited to single-story build-
    ings, the third being more general in use. The RGR method
    developed by the author (1966) is based on graph theoretical
    background. A simpler RGR-2 algorithm has been developed and
    the program written, thought as a part of a broader computer-
    aided building design system. The architectural phase of the

system gave a considerable role to man-machine interaction. A
nonmetric scaling method based on techniques used by J. B.
Kruskal (1964) has been used as a tool for analysis of large
and intricate layout problems. The first experiences are positive, as the resulting configurations help much to understand
the problem. From the configuration, the architect may derive
a set of good variants, laying the rooms out in multiple buildings, in multiple stories of a building, or in a single story
as well.

75. OXSYS-BDS (BUILDING DESIGN SYSTEMS)
     Richens, P. N.
     Appl. Res. of Cambridge Ltd., Cambridge, England
     BOCAAD (Bull. Comput. Aided Archit. Des.) (GB) No. 25   20-44
     Aug. 1977
        Treatment: Practical Applic
        Document Type: Journal Paper
     OXSYS-BDS is a general-purpose computer-aided building design
     system suitable for buildings which are dimensionally coordi-
     nated on an orthogonal grid. It is suitable for a wide range
     of building types and is independent of the method of construc-
     tion. OXSYS-BDS is capable of enhancement to form a series of
     detail design systems. These relate to particular methods of
     construction, providing facilities beyond the scope of the
     generalized BDS, such as automatic detailing.

76. PARC 79. INTERNATIONAL CONFERENCE ON THE APPLICATION OF
     COMPUTERS IN ARCHITECTURE, BUILDING DESIGN AND URBAN PLANNING
        Parc 79. International Conference on the Application of
     Computers in Architecture, Building Design and Urban Planning
     1979
        7-10 May 1979 Berlin, Germany
        Publ: Online, Uxbridge, England
        Document Type: Dissertation
     The following topics were dealt with: Modeling Visualiza-
     tion, abacus, followed by current development.

77. PREDICTED ENERGY CONSUMPTION FOR AIR CONDITIONING SYSTEMS
     RELATED TO THE BUILDING ENVELOPE AND FORM
        Oughton, D. R
        Build. Serv. Eng. Res. and Technol. (GB) Vol. 1, No. 4
     189-98 1980 Coden: BSETDF
        Treatment: Applic
        Document Type: Journal Paper
        (11 Refs)

Deals with the development of a modular approach to the calculation of energy consumption for air conditioning systems, based on computer prediction techniques. Annual consumption figures are established for perimeter and internal zones of commercial buildings air-conditioned on the variable air volume principle. The sensitivity of annual energy consumption to building shape and orientation is analyzed for buildings conditioned by variable air volume systems. The effectiveness of the current building regulations in respect of limiting energy consumption in air-conditioned buildings is discussed, and proposals are made for their improvement. A comparison is made between the energy consumption of variable air volume systems and induction unit systems related to the heating, cooling, and distribution components of the total energy consumption.

78. PROGRAM FOR FORECASTING THE SOUND PRESSURE LEVEL IN A CLOSED BUILDING

Vo Thanh, T.

Univ. de Liege, Liege, Belgium

Electroacoustique (Belgium) No. 26 3-18 June 1977

Coden: ELACBS

Treatment: Theoretical

Document Type: Journal Paper

Languages: French

A program, written for a Wang 700 minicomputer, is described which allows the sound pressure level at different points of a closed room to be determined. The efficacy of noise abatement measures designed to create a zone of relative calm can also be determined by means of this program.

79. PROGRESS WITH CEDAR 3, A COMPUTER-AIDED BUILDING DESIGN SYSTEM FOR THE SKETCH PLAN STAGE

Thompson, B. G. J.; Webster, G. J.

Professional Computing Branch, Property Services Agency, Doe, Croydon, England

Sponsor: Computer-Aided Design Centre; Dept. Environment; et al.

Third International Conference and Exhibition on Computers in Engineering and Building Design 678-92 1978

14-16 March 1978 Brighton, England

Publ: IPC Sci. and Technology Press Ltd., Guildford, England

XII + 803 pp. ISBN 0 902852 85 X

the art in CABD research and development in computer graphics is presented in a bibliographical sketch. A specific graphics package, as a possible example, is reviewed. And finally, a graphics language, along with the role of government and the private sector in computer-aided design (CAD) is presented.

82. RUCAPS, COST-EFFECTIVE DRAFTING FOR THE BUILDING INDUSTRY
    Davison, J. A.
    GMW Computers Ltd., London, England
    Sponsor: Computer-Aided Design Centre; Dept. Environment; et al.
    Third International Conference and Exhibition on Computers in Engineering and Building Design 654-77 1978
    14-16 March 1978 Brighton, England
    Publ: IPC Sci. and Technology Press Ltd., Guildford, England
    XII + 803 pp. ISBN 0 902852 85 X
    Treatment: Applic; Theoretical
    Document Type: Report Section
    The paper proposes a specification for a computer-aided drafting system to be used in the building industry. It then describes how this specification has been met by the RUCAPS system. It concludes with a detailed case study of the use of RUCAPS on one particular project.

83. SELECTED PROGRAM PACKAGES FOR CONSTRUCTIONAL PLANNING AND DESIGN WORK
    Neue Tech. Buero (Germany) Vol. 23, No. 6 164-6 Nov.-Dec. 1979 Coden: NTBUB4
    Treatment: Practical Applic
    Document Type: Journal Paper
    (1 Ref)
    Lists and describes 22 program packages for architectural CAD.

84. SERVICES CO-ORDINATION AND MODELLING PROGRAMME
    Oliver, B. C.
    Parc 79. International Conference on the Application of Computers in Architecture, Building Design and Urban Planning 245-53 1979
    7-10 May 1979 Berlin, Germany
    Publ: Online, Uxbridge, England
    XIII + 724 pp.
    Treatment: General, Review
    Document Type: Report Section
    The computer program described resolves the problems of physical coordination occurring between building services and

the building envelope and thereby reduces the problem of social
coordination between those involved in both design and construction.

85.   SMOOC, A PRACTICAL APPROACH TO COMPUTER-AIDED DWELLING LAYOUT
        Dinjens, P. J. M.; Amkreutz, J. H. A. E.; Hermens, W. W. A.
        Dept. of Architecture, Building and Planning, Univ. of
      Technol., Eindhoven, Netherlands
        Parc 79. International Conference on the Application of
      Computers in Architecture, Building Design and Urban Planning
      35-48 1979
        7-10 May 1979 Berlin, Germany
        Publ: Online, Uxbridge, England
        XIII + 724 pp.
        Treatment: Applic; Theoretical
        Document Type: Report Section
        (9 Refs)
        SMOOC is a computer-program with the intention to be an
      "assisting tool" in the planning of dwelling layouts. SMOOC is
      based on the well-known SAR methodology. The aim of SMOOC is
      the applicability in the field of education in design and the
      actual design of dwellings.

86.   SPACE PLANNING AND FACILITIES MANAGEMENT
        Potts, J.
        Office of Systems, Social Security Admin., Baltimore, MD, USA
        Computer Graphics, State of the Art Report 209-18 1980
        Publ: INFOTECH, Maidenhead, England
        Treatment: Applic
        Document Type: Conference Paper
        (6 Refs)
        Defines the areas that computer graphics space planning
      covers in addition to furniture and equipment. It also men-
      tions some of the newest space planning applications and the
      use of a service bureau and a dedication turnkey in-house
      system. The hardware and software of a state of the art system
      are described in detail. This system recently prepared space
      planning 1/8 in. scale architectural drawings for 1.2 million
      ft^2 of space in approximately 4 months. This was about 10
      times the normal yearly workload of the draftsperson.

87.   SPACEMAKER, A COMPUTER LANGUAGE FOR MODELLING ARCHITECTURAL
      PHYSICAL FORM
        Gerzso, J. M.
        MIT, Cambridge, MA, USA

Parc 79. International Conference on the Application of Computers in Architecture, Building Design and Urban Planning 573-82 1979

7-10 May 1979 Berlin, Germany

Publ: Online, Uxbridge, England

XIII + 724 pp.

Treatment: Applic; Practical Applic

Document Type: Report Section

(7 Refs)

Spacemaker is a computer language design based on two ideas: the modeling of architectural physical form based on diagrammatic production rules and the coding of such rules in a class-oriented-type system. It is felt that these two ideas are powerful enough for modeling any set of buildings, whether they are industrialized building systems, housing systems, vernacular buildings, etc.

88. SPEED--AN EARLY DESIGN TOOL FOR BUILDING SERVICES

Baxter, A. J.

Dept. of Building, Sheffield City Polytech., Sheffield, England

Comput. Aided Des. (GB) Vol. 10, No. 3 185-91 May 1978

Coden: CAIDA5

Treatment: Applic; Theoretical

Document Type: Journal Paper

(31 Refs)

An interactive program, speed has been produced to assist in the sketch-plan stage of building design. It will allow an architect and building services engineer to examine the interaction between the building envelope and the internal thermal and visual environment. The program is simple to use and follows a design philosophy which will be familiar to users. The amount of data that must be provided by the user is small, and use is made of data files within the program. The program is fast in execution, permitting many different design solutions to be appraised at low cost.

89. STEPS--A PLANNING AND DESIGNING SUPPORT SYSTEM FOR URBAN TRANSIT SYSTEMS

Miyamoto, S.; ILhara, H.; Haruna, K.; Kariya, S.

Systems Dev. Lab., Hitachi Ltd., Tokyo, Japan

Rose, J. (Editor)

Current Topics in Cybernetics and Systems (papers in summary form only received) 278-9 1978

21-25 Aug. 1978 Amsterdam, Netherlands

Publ: Springer-Verlag, Berlin, Germany

409 pp. ISBN 3 540 08977 2

Treatment: Practical Applic

Document Type: Report Section

A computer-assisted planning and designing system, named STEPS, has been developed as a tool for use in the quantitative and rapid planning of urban transit systems. The paper presents the model of planning for urban transit systems, program architecture of STEPS, and the specification of an optimum system as a result of a case study by applying STEPS.

90. SYSTEMATIC PLANNING OF BUILDINGS WITH THE AID OF MATHEMATICAL MODELS OF THE THERMAL ECONOMICS

Wehrli, P.

Landis and Gyr Zug Corp., Zug, Switzerland

Landis and Gyr Rev. (Switzerland) Vol. 26, No. 1 16-21 1979 Coden: LGRVA7

Treatment: Applic

Document Type: Journal Paper

(3 Refs)

Gives an outline of the procedure to get a rough mathematical model of the thermal economics of a room. For judging the quality of the model a result of simulation is compared with the measured curve. Some examples of applications are used to show that it is possible with a mathematical model to find crucial points in the design and energy or cost-saving operating methods by means of a computer. However, in order to exhaust all possibilities for an optimum building and the operation of a building, it is necessary that all the specialists engaged in the construction cooperate in the planning at as early a stage as possible.

91. TEACHING COMPUTER AIDED DESIGN IN A SCHOOL OF ARCHITECTURE

Forwood, B.

Dept. of Architectural Sci., Univ. of Sydney, Sydney, New South Wales, Australia

Comput. and Educ. (GB) Vol. 3, No. 1 1-6 1979 Coden: COMEDR

Treatment: General, Review

Document Type: Journal Paper

(2 Refs)

Architects, in general, have been slower than other building professionals to respond to the challenges offered by the computer. One of the major reasons for this has been the lack of

appropriately educated members of the profession to carry out
the work required to implement CAD systems. To fulfill this
need, the Department of Architectural Science at the University
of Sydney has, since 1967, offered courses in computer programming
and computer applications to undergraduate and post-
graduate architecture students. This paper reviews the aims of
this education program and discusses some of the peculiar
problems encountered when teaching computer methods to architecture students.

92. TECHNICAL COMPUTER APPLICATION FOR THE HOUSEBUILDER
       Brett, S. F.; Walker, B. A.
       Systems (S. Africa) Vol. 9, No. 6 3-4, 6 June 1979
     Coden: SYSMBJ
       Treatment: Applic; Practical Applic
       Document Type: Journal Paper
     The increasing cost and scarcity of technical experts in the
building industry, in conjunction with the decreasing cost of
computer power, are opening a new field of technical applications to the computer industry. This article outlines some of
the characteristics of the building industry in general which
affect the design of technical systems. It then describes, as
an example, an approach to a technical system for housebuilders
currently being developed by the authors as consultants spe-
cializing in technical systems for the construction industry
and allied professions.

93. TEXTURE RENDERING SYSTEM FOR ARCHITECTURAL DESIGN
       Feibush, E.; Greenberg, D. P.
       Program of Computer Graphics, Cornell Univ., Ithaca, NY, USA
       Comput. Aided Des. (GB) Vol. 12, No. 2 67-71 March 1980
     Coden: CAIDA5
       Treatment: Applic; Practical Applic
       Document Type: Journal Paper
       (8 Refs)
     Depicting construction materials in color enhances the
realism of synthetic images and provides the architect with a
powerful design tool. A computer-aided system for creating
textured renderings of architectural designs is presented.
This enables the designer to organize libraries of texture
samples and details extracted from digital images of color
photographs of actual materials. Furthermore, buildings can be
interactively positioned on an optically scanned site background and the textures mapped to simulate any desired view of

the building. The system was designed so that it could be used quickly and easily by architects with little computer experience.

94. THE ACOUSTICAL PERFORMANCE OF SELF-PROTECTING BUILDINGS
       Oldham, D. J.; Mohsen, E. A.
       Dept. of Building Sci., Univ. of Sheffield, Sheffield, England
       J. Sound and Vib. (GB) Vol. 65, No. 4 557-81 22 Aug. 1979
     Coden: JSVIAG
       Treatment: Practical Applic; Experimental
       Document Type: Journal Paper
       (19 Refs)
     Describes the results of an investigation into the performance of self-protecting building configurations (buildings in which part of the structure acts to screen noise from acoustic weak points such as windows). The techniques employed for this study were a combination of computer simulation and measurements on scale models. A method is presented of predicting the performance of self-protecting buildings, in terms of commonly used noise units, from knowledge of their geometry.

95. THE CALCULATION OF TRANSLUCENT AND OPAQUE SHADOW EFFECTS ON BUILDING THERMAL LOADS
       Schiler, M.; Greenberg, D. P.
       Cornell Univ., Ithaca, NY, USA
       CAD 80. Proceedings of the 4th International Conference and Exhibition on Computers in Design Engineering 642-9 1980
       March 1980 Brighton, England
       Publ: IPC Sci. and Technol. Press, Guildford, England
       XIV + 774 pp.
       Treatment: Practical Applic
       Document Type: Report Section
       (8 Refs)
     A multitude of problems is associated with the computer simulation of real shading effects in building thermal load calculations. Two of the most difficult aspects are the mutual shading of translucent objects and the number of objects which must be input. A multiclassed input system is coupled with a scanline clipping algorithm capable of modeling translucency.

96. THE CONSTRUCTION AND EXTENSION OF A GENERAL DECISION MODEL AND ITS APPLICATION TO SPACE-PLANNING PROBLEMS. I
       Berger, S. R.; Briggs, M. P.; Gill, R.; Markovits, N.
       Dept. of Architecture, Univ. of Bristol, Bristol, England

BOCAAD (Bull. Comput. Aided Archit. Des.) (GB) No. 29 15-50
Oct. 1978 Coden: BBCDD8
  Treatment: General, Review
  Document Type: Journal Paper
  This report describes the ideas underlying the construction
and extension of an adaptive general decision model (GDM) and
the difficulties which emerged in attempting to find an
approach to the solution of spatial allocation problems.

97. THE CONSTRUCTION EXTENSION OF A GENERAL DECISION MODEL AND ITS
     APPLICATION TO SPACE-PLANNING PROBLEMS. II
       Berger, S. R.; Briggs, M. P.; Gill, R.; Markovits, N.
       Dept. of Architecture, Univ. of Bristol, Bristol, England
       BOCAAD (Bull. Comput. Aided Archit. Des.) (GB) No. 30 21-54
     Nov. 1978 Coden: BBCDD8
       Treatment: Applic; Practical Applic
       Document Type: Journal Paper
       (9 Refs)
       For Pt. I see Ibid., No. 29, pp. 15-50 (1978). Describes the
     ideas underlying the construction and extension of an adaptive
     general decision model and the difficulties which emerged in
     attempting to find an approach to the solution of spatial allo-
     cation problems.

98. THE DETERMINATION OF THE FORM OF WINDOWS AND SUNSHADES IN A HOT
     CLIMATE
       Shaviv, E.
       Faculty of Architecture and Town Planning, Technion-Israel
     Inst. of Technol., Technion City, Haifa, Israel
       Sponsor: Computer-Aided Design Centre; Dept. Environment; et
     al.
       Third International Conference and Exhibition on Computers in
     Engineering and Building Design 110-19 1978
       14-16 March 1978   Brighton, England
       Publ: IPC Sci. and Technology Press Ltd., Guildford, England
       XII + 803 pp. ISBN 0 902852 85 X
       Treatment: Applic; Theoretical
       Document Type: Report Section
       (20 Refs)
       A method for the design of fixed external sunshades was
     developed, using a computer for calculating the exact geometry
     and a plotter for presentation. The method is applied to the
     design of the elevations of a hospital building under construc-
     tion in Haifa, Israel. The emphasis is on finding the form of

the correct shape of windows and the necessary sunshades so as to avoid penetration of direct sun during the summer.

99. THE EXPERIMENTAL VERIFICATION OF A COMPUTERISED THERMAL MODEL FOR BUILDINGS
    Waters, J. R.
    Industrial Buildings Res. Unit, Lanchester Polytech., Coventry, England
    Build. Serv. Eng. Res. and Technol. (GB) Vol. 1, No. 2 76-82 1980 Coden: BSETDF
    Treatment: Applic; Experimental
    Document Type: Journal Paper
    (17 Refs)

The predictions of a computerized thermal model based on the implicit finite difference technique have been compared with experimental measurements on two buildings. The results show that the model is capable of the accurate prediction of the temperatures and the heat flows in a building for a range of different conditions. It has been found that in certain circumstances the predictions of the model are strongly influenced by the value chosen for the convection coefficient at internal surfaces.

100. THE OXFORD SYSTEM AND ITS APPLICATION
     D'Arcy, R.
     Oxford, Regional Health Authority, Oxford, England
     Parc 79. International Conference on the Application of Computers in Architecture, Building Design and Urban Planning 683-6 1979
     7-10 May 1979 Berlin, Germany
     Publ: Online, Uxbridge, England
     XIII + 724 pp.
     Treatment: Applic, General, Review
     Document Type: Report Section

Use of computer systems to assist in the design of buildings has been subjected to bigoted criticism, governmental inquiry, trades union suspicion, and wholesale misunderstanding. Indeed the high-handed and arrogant attitudes of some CAD proponents have caused unnecessary and counterproductive infighting between the sponsors of similar systems. Despite this, computer-aided design is fluorishing because, as this paper will attempt to describe, CAD is a fundamentally good idea, it works, and it provides significant benefits.

101. THE OXSYS SYSTEM FOR THE DESIGN OF BUILDINGS
     Richens, P.
     Appl. Res. of Cambridge Ltd., Cambridge, England
     Sponsor: Computer-Aided Design Centre; Dept. Environment; et
al.
     Third International Conference and Exhibition on Computers in
Engineering and Building Design 633-53 1978
     14-16 March 1978 Brighton, England
     Publ: IPC Sci. and Technology Press Ltd., Guildford, England
     XII + 803 pp. ISBN 0 902852 85 X
     Treatment: Applic; Theoretical
     Document Type: Report Section
     (5 Refs)
     OXSYS is an integrated CAD system for buildings with ortho-
gonal geometry. At sketch design a building file is built up
containing a hierarchy of zones with functional and spatial
attributes. Measurement, costing, and engineering analyses may
be applied. During detail design components drawn from a
separate database are located in the building. Comprehensive
drawing and scheduling systems give full documentation at all
stages. Enhanced detailing can be provided for specific
methods of construction. The system is implemented on a prime
300 and is currently being used for the design of a district
general hospital, and several other building types.

102. THE PLANNING OF ROOM LIGHTING USING A PROGRAMMABLE POCKET
     CALCULATOR
     Breuer, P.
     Rheinbraun Haustech. GMBH, Koln, Germany
     Elektrotech. Z. Etz (Germany) Vol. 100, No. 4 178-81 Feb.
1979
     Treatment: Applic
     Document Type: Journal Paper
     Languages: German (2 Refs)
     The use of a small programmable calculator (incorporating the
storage of programs on magnetic cards) for making lighting calculations is broadly described, as exemplified by the Tl 59,
made by Texas Instruments. The types of lamp, dimensions of
the room, required intensity of light level, and degree of
reflection must be known. The calculator determines the room
index from which the room efficiency can be found by reference
to manufacturers' data. This figure is entered into the computer and the program is restarted. The printout gives a number

of lamps, connected power of a lamp, total connected power, and
power consumed per unit of superficial area. Calculations on
the economic aspect of the proposed lighting scheme can similarly be carried out. Tabulated examples are given.

103. THE TOPAZ URBAN AND PLANNING ALLOCATION MODEL
     Teicholz, E.; Mation, H.
     Lab. for Computer Graphics and Spatial Analysis, Harvard
     Univ., Cambridge, MA, USA
     Parc. 79. International Conference on the Application of
     Computers in Architecture, Building Design and Urban Planning
     539-50 1979
     7-10 May 1979 Berlin, Germany
     Publ: Online, Uxbridge, England
     XIII + 724 pp.
     Treatment: Applic; Theoretical
     Document Type: Report Section
     (7 Refs)
     This paper describes the authors' recent work in the area of
     planning and allocation models that have been developed for a
     variety of architectural, urban, and regional design problems.
     The work is primarily based on the Topaz (technique for the
     optimum placement of activities into zones) program that was
     originally developed in Australia (Brotchie, 1972; Sharp, 1973)
     and was further developed at Harvard University (by the
     authors) and in Virginia (Dickey, 1974).

104. THE USE OF COMPUTERS AND MICROFILM IN THE CODE ENFORCEMENT
     PROGRAM OF THE CHICAGO DEPARTMENT OF BUILDINGS
     Burke, W. J.; Moran, R. P.
     Dept. of Buildings, Chicago, IL, USA
     Sponsor: Nat. Bur. Standards; Nat. Conference on States on
     Building Codes and Standards
     Proceedings of the 1st NBS/NCSBCS Joint Conference on
     Research and Innovation in Building Regulatory Process 377-82
     1977
     21-22 Sept. 1976 Providence, R.I., USA
     Publ: Nat. Bur. Standards, Washington, D.C., USA
     X + 504 pp.
     Treatment: General, Review; Practical Applic
     Document Type: Report Section
     The Chicago Department of Buildings uses three principal
     types of computer-supported systems. (1) Several systems use
     automated devices to issue documents to the public. Notices of

violation are prepared on minicomputers using stored violation
texts. "Certifications of Inspection" for buildings and elevators are prepared by computer. (2) Computers are used exten-
sively for information retrieval. An on-line system allows
access to selected information on specific buildings via CRT
display and hard copy. Monthly reports summarizing building
permit activity are generated from computer files. (3) Management control reporting is an important computer-based application. Permits, complaints, and follow-up inspection requests
are aged by computer, and items open beyond a control age are
listed on exception reports. A system to report on inspec-
tional performance is currently in development. About 8 years
ago the department was literally forced by the volume of its
paper to convert its files to microfilm. We now have approximately 10 million documents on film and are expanding at a rate
of approximately 1.5 million documents per year.

105. THE USE OF EDP METHODS IN DESIGNING FIREPROOF STRUCTURES
     Kammer, K. K. H.
     Waerme (Germany) Vol. 85, No. 2 46-51 April 1979 Coden:
     WARMAP
        Treatment: Applic
        Document Type: Journal Paper
        Languages: German (2 Refs)
     A data bank containing technical information on 1200
     materials of interest for fireproof construction is referred
     to; this is operated by Karrena Company. The use of computers
     in working out heat flow through various walls is illustrated,
     and optimization of building design with respect to heat losses
     is shown, based on a mathematical model. Sandwich-type walls
     with fireproof layers are illustrated. Multi-dimensional
     problems are also mentioned.

106. THREE DIMENSIONAL GRAPHICS
     King, C.
     Creative Comput. (USA) Vol. 6, No. 6 128-9 June 1980
     Coden: CCOMDB
        Treatment: Applic; Theoretical
        Document Type: Journal Paper
     Describes how to make the necessary three-dimension to two-
     dimension coordinate transformations needed in graphic art,
     games, architectural drawings, and anything else one might wish
     their computer to draw. Basically, this set of routines takes
     a three-dimensional figure (with the X coordinate assumed to be

coming toward you, Y going horizontally to the right, and Z
vertically). Rotates the figure any number of degrees,
elevates it (again, any number of degrees--even below the X-Y
plane) and transforms this to two dimensions. Following this,
the X and Y coordinates of the 2D image are moved toward the
point of view a distance directly proportional to the distance
from the plane of view. Thus making the illusion of perspective or depth. Line blockage is so complex that it has not
been included with these algorithms.

107. THERMAL--A COMPUTER SYSTEM FOR BUILDING SERVICES DESIGN
     Aish, R.
     Ove Arup Partnership, London, England
     CAD 80. Proceedings of the 4th International Conference and
     Exhibition on Computers in Design Engineering 627-40 1980
     March 1980 Brighton, England
     Publ: IPC Sci. and Technol. Press, Guildford, England
     XIV + 774 pp.
     Treatment: Practical Applic
     Document Type: Report Section
     The potential for using computers to evaluate and predict
     building performance and to aid the design of building services
     is widely recognized. This paper sets out to discuss the
     objectives, the context, and the decisions which are involved
     in realizing a comprehensive suite of production programs for
     use by building services engineers.

108. THIRD INTERNATIONAL SYMPOSIUM ON THE USE OF COMPUTERS FOR
     ENVIRONMENTAL ENGINEERING RELATED TO BUILDINGS
     Sponsor: Nat. Res. Council of Canada
     Third International Symposium on the Use of Computers for
     Environmental Engineering Related to Buildings 1978
     10-12 May 1978 Banff, Alberta, Canada
     Publ: Nat. Res. Council of Canada, Ottawa, Canada
     646 pp. ISBN 0 660 50201 1
     Treatment: General, Review
     Document Type: Dissertation
     The following topics were dealt with: Computers in the
     design of air-conditioning systems, computers in the operation
     of air-conditioning systems, computers in the design of solar
     energy systems, computers in building energy systems analysis,
     and computers in the design of lighting systems.

109. TIMBOR, TIMBER FRAME INTEGRATED MODULAR BUILDING OPTIMISATION
ROUTINE
     Davies, M.
     Coll. of Engng., King Abdulaziz Univ., Jeddah, Saudi Arabia
     CAD 80. Proceedings of the 4th International Conference and
Exhibition on Computers in Design Engineering 733-42 1980
     March 1980 Brighton, England
     Publ: IPC Sci. and Technol. Press, Guildford, England
     XIV + 774 pp.
     Treatment: Practical Applic
     Document Type: Report Section
     (4 Refs)
This paper describes an interactive graphic computer system
for use by construction companies and their consultants in the
design, detailing, scheduling, costing, cutting, and assembly
of timber frame shells for houses and other building types.
TIBMOR provides an interface between CAD programs and the
numerically controlled production process by the logical
extension of CAD techniques into the detailed design of timber
frame components. TIMBOR is intended to be the link in a
totally computer-aided design and factory production process.

110. TRANSFORMING A SET OF BUILDING DRAWINGS INTO A CONSISTENT
DATABASE
     Yasky, Y.
     Inst. of Building Sci., Carnegie-Mellon Univ., Pittsburg, PA,
USA
     CAD 80. Proceedings of the 4th International Conference and
Exhibition on Computers in Design Engineering 101-8 1980
     March 1980 Brighton, England
     Publ: IPC Sci. and Technol. Press, Guildford, England
     XIV + 774 pp.
     Treatment: Practical Applic
     Document Type: Report Section
     (13 Refs)
As part of developing an integrated CAD system the author has
implemented a database and a set of operations associated with
it which respond to the following requirements: the generality
of the database, the spatial consistency inherent in its definition, and the capabilities for generating the database incre-
mentally and for modifying it easily. Described in the paper
are both the internal model and the input method, used for

transforming the representation of the geometrical skeleton of a building from drawings to a computer database. Both together offer a tool which has several advantages over the comparable existing ones and which lays a foundation for a general integrated computer-aided building design system.

111. USING A COMPREHENSIVE BUILDING DESIGN SYSTEM
       Collins, E. B.
       Atkins Sheppart-Fidler and Associates, Epsom, England
       Comput. Aided Des. (GB) Vol. 12, No. 5 262-4 Sept. 1980
     Coden: CAIDA5
       Treatment: Applic
       Document Type: Journal Paper
       In July 1978 W. S. Atkins group consultants introduced a CAD system based on a dedicated minicomputer for use in its architectural practice, Atkins Sheppard-Fidler and Associates (ASFA). The system, known as OXSYS, or more correctly BDS, was used to achieve a high standard of design. On completion of preliminary design phases, the system enables all technologies in the multidisciplinary consultancy to assemble components input into a database (Codex) to realize the building for and achieve a high degree of coordination. This system is discussed.

112. USER EVALUATION OF PROGRAMS IN COMPUTER-AIDED BUILDING DESIGN
       Bensasson, S.
       Design Office Consortium, Cambridge, England
       Sponsor: Computer-Aided Design Centre; Dept. Environment; et al.
       Third International Conference and Exhibition on Computers in Engineering and Building Design 75-83 1978
       14-16 March 1978 Brighton, England
       Publ: IPC Sci. and Technology Press Ltd., Guildford, England
       XII + 803 pp. ISBN 0 902852 85 X
       Treatment: Applic; Experimental
       Document Type: Report Section
       (2 Refs)
       If an evaluation of a group of programs is to be useful in selecting a program to meet the individual requirements of a practice, the method of evaluation should be flexible and sensitive to the needs of each application area of computers in the building industry. The evaluation project carried out in the design office consortium in Cambridge leads to the conclusion problems of responsibility in CABD are considerable and

can only be alleviated by better documentation, greater variety, and comparative information.

113. WEIGHTING IN DESIGN (ARCHITECTURAL DESIGN)
     Beran, V.
     BOCAAD, (Bull. Comput. Aided Archit. Des.) (GB) No. 36
     21-30 May 1980 Coden: BBCDD8
     Treatment: Applic
     Document Type: Journal Paper
     (4 Refs)
     The author discusses the relative importance of objectives in design, planning, and decision problems.

114. 3D INPUT FOR CAAD SYSTEMS
     Aish, R.
     Ove Arup Partnership, London, England
     Comput. Aided Des. (GB) Vol. 11, No. 2 66-70 March 1979
     Coden: CAIDA5
     Treatment: General, Review
     Document Type: Journal Paper
     (7 Refs)
     A computerized building block system (BBS) is proposed with which the designer can physically build a model of his/her design as he/she would if using "lego" blocks. Such a physical representation may allow him/her to evaluate many of the visual and spatial qualities of the design in a more direct way than could be achieved using computer graphics. However, because the electronic system can "read" the arrangement of blocks and input this information into a computer, the user's design can be evaluated with the same performance measures that are used in existing CAAD systems.

Index

431